CUSTOMER RELATIONSHIP MANAGEMENT

A DATABASED APPROACH

V. KUMAR

ING Chair Professor of Marketing, and
Executive Director, ING Center for Financial Services
University of Connecticut

WERNER J. REINARTZ

Associate Professor of Marketing, INSEAD

John Wiley & Sons, Inc.

Associate Publisher   *Judith R. Joseph*
Senior Acquisitions Editor   *Jayme Heffler*
Project Editor   *Cindy Rhoads*
Senior Editorial Assistant   *Ame Esterline*
Marketing Manager   *Heather King*
Managing Editor   *Shoshanna Turek*
Designers   *Shoshanna Turek, Benjamin Reece*
Illustration Editor   *Benjamin Reece*
Cover Designer   *Benjamin Reece*
Cover Images   *All images © Royalty-Free/CORBIS*

This book was typeset in 10/12 Minion by Leyh Publishing Services, and printed and bound by RR Donnelley–Willard. The cover was printed by Phoenix Color.

ISBN: 978-0-471-27133-8

Printed in the United States of America

10   9   8   7   6   5   4   3   2

Dedicated with Love

To My Nieces, Amritha and Deepa

To My Wife, Viktoria and My Son, Henry

Brief Contents

Contents

TABLE OF CONTENTS

Chapter 9

EFFECTIVENESS OF LOYALTY PROGRAMS   180

Preface

The past decade saw companies investing millions of dollars in so called CRM systems. However, most firms have not yet realized the benefits of acquiring these expensive systems. Somewhere along the way CRM became more about computers, software, and processes than about business and profitability. This book refocuses on the strategic aspects of customer level management as a key determinant of future firm profitability. It stresses developing an understanding of customer value as the guiding concept for marketing decisions. Firms must adopt new metrics, implement new techniques, and undergo an organizational reorientation to replace current marketing approaches. While harnessing the power of modern day computers, networking, and communications systems is important for CRM to succeed, it is more important to understand the basic approach which sets customer-centric marketing apart from traditional strategies of product marketing. This book reviews traditional CRM practices, but the important contribution this book makes is in terms of strategic insights into the process of CRM. The book illustrates important metrics like past customer value and customer lifetime value. The book analyzes the implementation of CRM strategies in the areas of loyalty programs, marketing campaigns, and channel management. Specifically, the book provides insights into seven customer level marketing strategies that can be implemented by adopting a customer lifetime value approach. They are:

1. Selecting customers
2. Contacting customers by using the right mix of channels and with the right frequency
3. Designing messages appropriate to individual customers and delivering them at the right time
4. Integrating multichannel shopping
5. Dealing with high-cost customers
6. Finding and keeping the right customers
7. Managing loyalty and profitability simultaneously

The goal of this book is to be a useful learning companion to students, teachers, and practitioners of CRM.

To summarize, with this book, you can:

- *Keep up with the latest industry trends.* We emphasize current developments in the field, and illustrate practices with cases and real-world examples.
- *Apply current CRM tools and methodologies.* The text clearly explains procedures for measuring past customer value and customer lifetime value, as well as techniques such as RFM, logistic regression, decision trees, and data mining.

- *Explore the science behind CRM.* We have cited various research studies showing the effectiveness of CRM techniques.
- *Analyze various CRM metrics.* The text walks you through numerical problems, which will help you better understand the relationship between CRM analytics and business performance.
- *Understand the link between CRM and profits.* Throughout, the text emphasizes customer lifetime value as a guiding concept, and uses this concept to link CRM activities to profits.

OBJECTIVES OF THIS TEXT

This book captures the critical elements of managing customer relationships. The objectives in writing this text are as follows:

1. To outline the need for customer-centric marketing strategies.
2. To explain the concepts, metrics, and techniques which form the backbone of CRM activities.
3. To emphasize current developments in the field of CRM.
4. To provide clear examples and illustrations that tie concepts with real world scenarios.
5. To discuss the structure of databases, their uses and benefits from a marketing standpoint, rather than a technical one.
6. To understand the implications of CRM on marketing activities like loyalty programs, channel management, and planning promotional campaigns.
7. To understand the potential for the growth of CRM as the dominant form of marketing strategy.
8. To clearly illustrate the financial benefits of implementing various customer lifetime value based marketing strategies.

HIGHLIGHTS OF THIS BOOK

The book offers a comprehensive treatment of CRM and database marketing. The highlights of the book are as follows:

1. An overview and summary at the beginning and the end of each chapter to help the reader stay focused.
2. Exhaustive cases to help readers appreciate how CRM is being carried out in the age of information.
3. Real world illustrations in various chapters under the title "CRM at Work."
4. Mini cases at the end of various chapters designed to address key managerial issues, stimulate thinking, and encourage a problem solving approach.
5. Illustrations and explanations of key traditional and new marketing metrics in a clear and concise manner.
6. Clear explanations for the need for customer value metrics, such as the traditional past customer value, and the forward-looking customer lifetime value.

7. Procedures to follow when measuring past customer value and customer lifetime value.
8. Explanations of techniques like RFM, logistic regression, decision trees, and data mining in an easy to follow fashion.
9. Presentation of the latest advances in customer value management practices, which include implementation of several CRM related strategies.
10. Adoption of a strategic viewpoint of CRM rather than a technical one.

SUPPLEMENTS TO THE BOOK

1. An online Instructor's Manual with Test Questions **located at www.wiley.com /college/kumar** accompanies this text. This manual provides solutions to end-of-chapter Questions and Problems, and discusses all text cases in greater detail. Exam questions are arranged by chapters and include multiple-choice and true/false questions. An example of a course syllabus is presented, and many suggestions for the organization of the course are provided.
2. Web site support: The Web site will be updated periodically in order to supplement the text with new up-to-date examples. This site includes the cases and Web links cited in the text. Go to **www.wiley.com/college/kumar.**
3. A computerized version of the test bank is available to instructors for customization of their exams.
4. Downloadable PowerPoint presentations are available for all chapters via the text Web site.

ORGANIZATION OF THE TEXT

The book adopts a strategic approach towards CRM and database marketing. It introduces key concepts and metrics needed to understand and implement CRM strategies. It describes the process of successful CRM implementation. It presents techniques to aid in strategic marketing decisions using the concept of customer lifetime value. The book is divided into four parts as follows:

- *Part One* consists of six chapters and introduces the concept of customer value as a key aspect of customer relationship management (CRM). Commonly used CRM terms and techniques such as acquisition rate, retention rate, share of wallet, logistic regression, decision trees, RFM, past customer value, and customer lifetime value are examined and illustrated. Various processes for measuring CRM effectiveness are discussed.

- *Part Two,* consisting of Chapters 7 to 11, describes how to implement database marketing. Types of databases and their uses and benefits are outlined. Loyalty programs that leverage databases are discussed. The data-mining process is outlined. Guidelines to develop and plan marketing campaigns in order to maximize customer value are discussed.

- *Part Three,* consisting of Chapters 12 and 13, focuses on recent advances in CRM applications. New and emerging techniques in customer value based CRM are introduced. Critical marketing issues like optimum resource allocation, purchase sequence, and the link between acquisition, retention, and profitability are examined on the basis of empirical findings.

- ■ *Part Four,* consisting of Chapter 14, discusses the impact of CRM on channels of marketing. Emerging new channels are analyzed. Multichannel consumer behavior is examined on the basis of empirical findings.

ACKNOWLEDGMENTS

V. Kumar would like to thank his wife, Aparna, and daughters, Anita and Prita, for their unrelenting support and encouragement during the writing of this book. We wish to thank Girish Ramani for his countless hours of assistance and contribution in the preparation of this text. We would also like to thank our colleagues at various universities for giving us valuable suggestions in developing this book: Pradeep Gopalakrishna, Pace University; Mike Lewis, University of Florida; Kimball P. Marshall, Loyola University-New Orleans; John A. McCarty, The College of New Jersey; Nancy J. Nentl, Metropolitan State University; and Ruth P. Stevens, Columbia University and New York University. Special thanks are owed to Morris George, Hanqing Ling, Soumitra Banerjee, and Deepa Morris for their assistance in various aspects of the book. We owe additional thanks to Renu for copyediting the book. Thanks also to the Insead R&D department.

PART I

Database Marketing Strategy

CHAPTER 1

CRM, Database Marketing, and Customer Value

Contents

1.1   OVERVIEW

Peter Drucker defined the marketing concept as "the business as seen from the customer's point of view." This definition underwent further refinement when the marketing concept was proposed as a distinct organizational culture, a fundamental shared set of beliefs and values that puts the customer in the center of a firm's thinking about strategy and operations.[1] These definitions of the marketing concept were formulated when the approach to marketing was predominantly by way of addressing the needs of customer segments. In reality, it was difficult to distinguish between individual customers. So, in a traditional mass-marketing approach, the customer population was segmented based on the needs of the consumers in these segments. Standardized products and services were then designed and delivered to meet the general needs of the segments. With mass-marketing, the individual preference of a consumer could not be given the importance that it deserved because of two main reasons. First, individual customer-level data were not available. Second, serving the needs of individual customers was both expensive and, in some cases, impossible for firms. However, with the leap in information technology and the ubiquity of the Internet, and the improvement in flexible manufacturing and outsourcing practices, understanding and meeting individual customer needs has become the important dimension on which firms can forge a competitive advantage. Given this shift, it is important to restate the underlying belief that would drive the success of firms. We should let the marketing concept make way for what should be called the customer concept. The customer concept is *the conduct of all marketing activities with the belief that the individual customer should be the central unit of analysis and action.* This definition of the customer concept emphasizes the analysis and measurement of marketing activities and consequences at an *individual* customer level. When marketing activities are directed at the individual level, interactive relationships are forged by the firm with individual customers. This shift in marketing thought is reflected in the definition of marketing that was updated by the American Marketing Association in 2004 which states that:

> Marketing is an organizational function and a set of processes for creating, communicating, and delivering value to customers and for managing customer relationships in ways that benefit the organization and its stakeholders.

This new definition underscores the importance of understanding concepts unique to a marketing environment that focuses on individual customer relationships. In other words, it is necessary to view marketing as a set of activities that are the result of adopting a belief in the customer concept. In this chapter, we introduce the terms customer value, database marketing, and customer relationship management (CRM). We provide a formal definition of customer value and CRM from a business strategy perspective. Next we discuss the changes taking place with respect to (1) consumers, (2) marketplaces, (3) technology, and (4) marketing functions. We show that the rapid changes, with respect to these forces, are driving firms to be customer centric and market driven. And, there is a visible shift from product-based marketing to customer-based marketing. In other words, firms are updating their processes and practices to be in line with the customer concept and marketing now plays the important role of forging relationships with customers as a means to stay relevant to the customer and accountable to the firm's stakeholders.

1.2 THE LINK BETWEEN CRM AND DATABASE MARKETING, AND THE IMPORTANCE OF CUSTOMER VALUE

Database marketing has traditionally allowed a company to identify and analyze segments of its customer population for valuable information that can be used to increase the impact of its marketing campaigns. The increasing availability of technology over the years has made it possible for companies to gather and analyze large amounts of data on their existing and prospective customers and thereby develop rich customer databases. Customer databases helped identify groups of customers that were similar in identifiable ways. These groups of customers were then treated as segments, and separate marketing campaigns were recommended for these different groups. Direct marketers would send different mailers at varying times and frequencies to these different segments. However, technology now allows firms to not only capture customer data, but also to interact with the customer simultaneously. This provides the opportunity for firms to develop flexible customer-level responses. CRM leverages databases and modern communication technologies to thus act on the basis of customer-level data. *CRM takes the practice of database marketing principles to increasingly disaggregated levels, ultimately individual customers.* Thus, CRM revolves around applying database marketing techniques at the customer level to develop strong, company-to-customer relationships. The use of information technology (IT) is critical to the successful implementation of a good CRM plan. However, the overarching framework of CRM includes much more than just databases and IT systems.

In the past, one of the main goals of marketing campaigns has been to increase customer loyalty to a product or service. The thought was that more loyal customers will do more repeat business and will develop a larger tolerance to price increases and therefore are more profitable to the firm. However, this is not always the case. A very loyal customer may also be an individual who repeatedly calls customer service with questions and is constantly hunting for the best price on a product, taking advantage of every rebate and sale offer. Ultimately, such an individual could actually be costing the company money rather than providing a source of profits. An important part of CRM is identifying the different types of customers and then developing specific strategies for interacting with each customer. Examples of such strategies are developing better relationships with *profitable* customers, locating and enticing new customers who will be profitable, and finding appropriate strategies for unprofitable customers, which could mean eventually terminating the relationship with customers who are causing a company to lose money.

The concept of *customer value* is critical to CRM. We define customer value as the economic value of the customer relationship to the firm—expressed on the basis of contribution margin or net profit. Customer value is a marketing metric that is proving to be an important decision aid in addition to evaluating marketing effectiveness. A firm can both measure and optimize its marketing efforts by incorporating the concept of customer value at the core of its decision-making process.

Adoption of CRM with customer value at the core of its strategy helps us define CRM from a customer value perspective as follows:

> CRM is the practice of analyzing and utilizing marketing databases and leveraging communication technologies to determine corporate practices and methods that will maximize the lifetime value of each individual customer to the firm.

A customer value–based approach to CRM can provide guidelines necessary to answer the following questions:

- When does it pay to go after customer loyalty?
- How do you link loyalty to customer profitability?
- How do you compute the future profitability of a customer?
- How do you measure customer lifetime value?
- How do you optimally allocate marketing resources to maximize customer value?
- How do you maximize the return on marketing investments?

The customer value–based approach can thus be leveraged for superior marketing decisions since *benefits* accrue in the form of the following:

- Decrease in costs
- Maximization of revenues
- Improvement in profits and return on investment (ROI)
- Acquisition and retention of profitable customers
- Reactivation of dormant customers

Since the field of CRM is relatively new, consulting firms and companies have created their own definitions and conceptualizations of CRM. These conceptualizations have evolved over time, but they can still be grouped into three types: functional level, customer-facing front-end level, and strategic level. These types of CRM are explained briefly here and are discussed in more detail in Chapter 2.

1. *Functional level:* The CRM process can be practiced on a very limited functional basis (e.g., it could entail the practice of sales force automation in the sales function or the practice of campaign management within the marketing function). Often, this goes along with a strong technology orientation evolving

out of the need for vendors to position their particular product. For some of the vendors or buyers, functional CRM is nearly synonymous with technology.

2. *Customer-facing front-end level:* This type of CRM evolves from the need for CRM practitioners to describe a new business capability, or a new arrangement of capabilities, that focuses on the total customer experience. The goal is to build a single view of the customer across all contact channels and to distribute customer intelligence to all customer-facing functions. This view stresses the importance of coordinating information across time and across contact channels in order to systematically manage the entire customer relationship. This view also supports the notion of marketing to customers throughout their purchasing lifecycle.

3. *Strategic level:* The primary objective of strategy-centric definitions of CRM is to free the term *CRM* from any technology underpinnings and from specific customer management techniques. These definitions describe CRM as a process to implement customer centricity in the market and build shareholder value. Here, knowledge about customers and their preferences has implications for the entire organization, such as for R&D or for supply chain management.

In this book, CRM will be defined from a business strategy perspective. The aim will be to gain long-term competitive advantage by optimally delivering value and satisfaction to the customer and extracting business value from the exchange. From this standpoint, CRM is the *strategic process* of *selecting* the customers a firm can most profitably serve and of shaping the *interactions* between a company and these *customers*. The goal is to optimize the *current and future value of the customers* for the company.

The key components of this definition include the following:

- *Strategic process:* This means that CRM activities are initiated and managed starting from the very top of the organization. Strategic initiatives, by definition, span multiple, if not all, organizational functions. CRM does not belong to any single department but needs contributions and reinforcements from all corporate functions. There is no place for a *silo mentality* that discourages information sharing and condones that one function "owns the customer." Furthermore, CRM is a continuing *process* that cannot be handled as just another software implementation project. It must be viewed as a continuous effort, with the goal of becoming a more customer-centric company.

- *Selection:* When the economic value of a customer is the basis for resource allocation, it is logical that firms focus on their most profitable or potentially profitable customers first. This is not about denying services to certain customers, but about recognizing a fit between a firm offering and a segment's desires, behaviors, and characteristics.

- *Interactions:* This means that the relationship between the customer and firm takes the form of an interactive dialog. Information and goods are exchanged and, most importantly, the exchange evolves as a function of past exchanges. This is very different from the view that firms sell one-off products and services to the customer.

- *Customers:* The term *customers* is applied broadly here. Depending on the industry and company, a customer can be an individual account, one or several segments within a market, or an entire market. Also, customers include not only end users but also intermediaries such as distributors, retailers, and so on. Generally, it has been observed that firms are moving away from a single all-purpose solution. In other words, firms are starting to satisfy increasingly smaller segments with better-targeted products, services, and communication propositions. Clearly, while segmentation is nothing new to most marketing managers, the degree of fine-tuning is considerably larger in the case of CRM. In fact, we now expect to be able to target *individual* customers with customized product offerings.

■ *Current and future value of the customer:* Optimizing current and future value means that firms are moving away from extracting their profit from single transactions to maximizing profits over a series of transactions. Thus, firms are starting to maximize customer equity—that is, the value of all their customer relationships to them. In this process, traditional measures such as market share are increasingly being replaced with new measures such as share-of-wallet and customer lifetime value.

It is, however, important for managers to recognize the importance of managing fairness in the exchange process. Optimization of the current and future value of customers intrinsically recognizes that unless customers are treated with respect and fairness, it will be impossible to manage and sustain a mutually profitable relationship.

Overall, marketing-driven customer relationship management is the concept of relationship management that is based on established marketing principles and that recognizes the need to carefully balance organizational and customer interests. Marketing-driven CRM is not primarily driven by technological solutions but is supported by them. It is a complex set of activities that, together, form the basis for a sustainable and hard to imitate competitive advantage: the customer-centric organization. CRM also involves automating and enhancing the customer centric business processes of sales, marketing, and service. It not only deals with automating these processes, but also focuses on ensuring that the front office applications improve customer satisfaction, resulting in increased customer loyalty which directly affects the company's bottom line. With CRM, a company would have an environment and a flexible support system to readily deal with the issues of product innovation, increasing levels of customer expectations, acquisitions, globalization, deregulation, convergence of traditional markets, emergence of new technologies, privacy issues, and new customer contact channels.

1.3 WHY IS CRM A BIG ISSUE TODAY?

Today firms face gradual, but—in comparison to two decades ago—seismic changes with respect to four major forces: (1) consumers, (2) marketplaces, (3) technology, and (4) marketing functions. This section looks at the changes to each.

1.3.1 CHANGES WITH RESPECT TO CONSUMERS

Growing Consumer Diversity

A key development in today's consumer markets is the diversity of customers with which vendors are confronted. On the most basic level, this diversity is triggered by a changing demographic composition of the population that can be observed in all industrialized nations, from Western Europe to the United States and Japan. Changing demographics serve as a good indicator of the future marketplace. The marketplace changes the needs and wants when the demographic make-up of the marketplace changes. Three important demographic trends have started to transform the marketplace:

1. *Aging of the population in developed countries.* The birth rate in most developed countries has been falling for more than two decades. This phenomenon has been described as *deyouthing*—a historically unprecedented event. As a result, populations in many developed countries such as Japan are actually shrinking. Between 1990 and 2030 alone, the number of Japanese under the age of 50 will decrease by some 24 million people, a net 26 percent loss of population. The differences in median ages across countries can be quite dramatic. For example, the median age of adults in the United States is now 43 and will reach 50 in less than two decades. This suggests that middle-age values and perspectives will increasingly dominate the national psyche. In particular, older consumers tend to respond more favorably to relationship marketing approaches than younger consumers.

2. *Increasing diversity in ethnicity.* Due to the closer integration of countries in Western Europe, it becomes increasingly easier for people to move and establish an existence abroad. Often, this migration is driven by better economic conditions in highly industrialized countries. Not surprisingly, this migration is causing an increase in cultural and ethnic diversity in those countries (e.g., France, England, Netherlands, and Germany). The United States, of course, has historically been ethnically diverse, and that trend is further on the rise. For example, Hispanics are the fastest growing group, with California and Texas soon becoming white-minority states. As a result of the changing ethnic make-up of American society, several changes are underway. Markets are becoming more segmented. Vendors will have to cater to ethnically diverse needs in housing, clothing, and food. Marketing communications will have to reflect this diversity in the way companies serve their customers.

3. *Increasing individualization.* In a number of Western countries, women who work full time represent approximately 60 percent of all women. This has put tremendous pressure on the traditional family. The old model was that women would stop working when they decided to have kids. The new model is that most women continue working when they have kids. As a result of the loss of its anchor (i.e., a full-time homemaker), the family is evolving as a unit of social and consumption analysis. As single parent or dual-career households proliferate, the need to define a separate existence or space will result in highly individualistic lifestyles and behaviors, even within family units. We will increasingly have to look at the individual behavior as family members spend more time apart. This will increase the need for personalized attention to each household member. Another consequence is a higher degree of perceived loneliness in society. The market place will feel the impact of these developments— more outsourcing of activities due to time constraints, more consumption on demand (24/7), and more consumption on the basis of symbolism and social group values. Customers who are single will seek out products and services that offer them social and emotional value.

As a consequence of these demographic and behavioral shifts, demand is becoming more and more heterogeneous, individualized, and fragmented. A mass-marketing approach focused on pushing similar products is clearly a weak proposition.

Time Scarcity

Today, many households are technologically rich but relatively time poor. When firms impose time or place constraints (e.g., store opening hours from 8 A.M. to 5 P.M. only), their markets react negatively. Time, in particular, is becoming one of the most precious commodities. As activities compete for time, consumers will redesign tasks that consume too much time and embrace time-saving and time-shifting technologies. For example, cooking in the home may become a dying art. The kitchen is increasingly the communication center of the house rather than the food center. Another factor is time spent while going places. The number of vehicles on the road has risen six times faster than the population growth rate. According to Texas Transportation Institute, U.S. drivers in 2002 spent an average of 300 hours on road[2], contributing to the lack of time.

One consequence is that we see consumers increasingly engaging in multitasking activities. For example, it has become normal for many people to use the phone while driving. Consequently, car manufacturers are building GPS, Internet, e-mail, and SMS functionalities as standard features into their cars. The sales of push lawn mowers are up dramatically, not because people cannot afford a gardener, but because they can combine exercise with tending their lawn.

The implication for marketers is clearly to provide products and services on demand and to pay careful attention to time value when interacting with the customer. One reason for the success of Internet banking is that it increases convenience on the part of the customer dramatically by not obeying strict branch hours. Consumer time scarcity provides a window of opportunity for the savvy marketer who can effectively bring relevant, value-added messages, products, and services to time-starved consumers.

Value Consciousness and Intolerance for Low Service Levels

Customers are becoming more demanding. Their expectations for reliable products and responsive services are becoming more extreme. They continuously demand more and are much less tolerant of failures. Customers compare their experiences against best-in-class expectations. As consumers become more educated about the available options in the market, as they try new products and services, and as they develop new needs, their expectation level rises. The customers will raise their bar each time their expectations are met. What used to delight customers a year ago is likely to only satisfy them today.

Figure 1-1 shows that customers are less and less satisfied with the treatment they get from corporate call centers. Few are now willing to hold for more than one minute

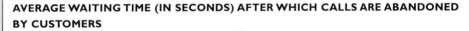

| FIGURE | 1-1 | **AVERAGE WAITING TIME (IN SECONDS) AFTER WHICH CALLS ARE ABANDONED BY CUSTOMERS** |

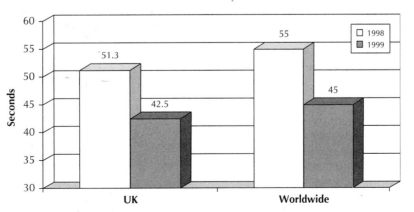

SOURCE: Merchants International Call Center Report.

without being answered. However, it is also clear that consumers have rising expectations as far as service levels are concerned. The average time after which calls are abandoned fell by about 19 percent in just one year. As call centers across companies get better in reducing the time to answer the call, customers adapt their expectations to the new level. It is important to recognize that the phenomenon of increasing expectation levels is not going away. It is a characteristic of doing business and therefore cannot be avoided. It is interesting to note that firms in industrialized economies have recently struggled considerably in satisfying their customers. Across a broad set of industries, customer satisfaction has been flat or declining (see Figure 1-2 for information on the U.S. market). The experience in other countries such as Germany, Sweden, or New Zealand has been similar. One can only speculate about the reasons for this decline, but one ironic reason might be that early technology-focused CRM implementations were actually contributing to the customer malaise. For example, as firms started to use technology to shift from personal customer interaction to Internet or call-center–based interaction, many customers experienced a drop in the quality of the exchange process.

Information Availability and Technological Aptitude

Internet technology has enabled almost all manufacturers and service providers to publish their information and perform transactions with customers online. Powerful online search engines have dramatically decreased customers' searching cost for information. Customers are able to access a tremendous amount of published information by using a digital device connected to the Internet. In 2003, in the United States alone, there were 167.5 million people online and this number is increasing every day (source: nielsennetratings.com).[3] This availability of information has made customers more knowledgeable than they were before when making purchase decisions. Being aware of the options they have and knowing how easy it is to perform comparisons of providers for online transactions have given customers a much more powerful position when dealing with providers. This has both positive and negative impacts on a provider's business. The positive side is that all providers are in an almost equal position when making their information available to customers. The negative side is that this, in turn, makes it much harder for providers to differentiate their products and services from those of their competitors. This makes it harder to grab customers' attention and affect their purchase decisions.

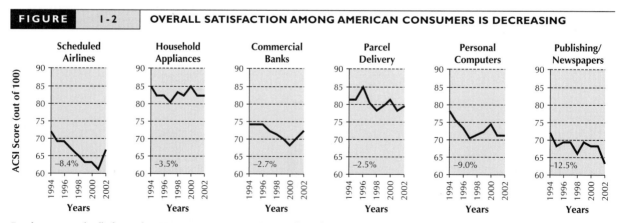

FIGURE 1-2 OVERALL SATISFACTION AMONG AMERICAN CONSUMERS IS DECREASING

Based on an annual poll of more than 50,000 consumers, measuring overall satisfaction (American Customer Satisfaction Index) with products and services.

SOURCE: http://www.theacsi.org, University of Michigan.

Decrease in Loyalty

Consumers are becoming increasingly selective and diversifying their business at unprecedented rates. This happens as institutions implement more intensive cross-selling campaigns. Figure 1-3 answers the question, "How many financial service providers do you currently hold relationships with?" from a survey of bank customers. Although 35.1 percent were loyal to one provider in 1993, this figure decreased to 30.2 percent in 1996. So, one in seven monopolized customers became "promiscuous" during the three years between the polling. Even more striking is the fact that the number of households with four or more relationships doubled in the same three years. As more and more options have become available for consumers to diversify their holdings across providers, consumers have taken advantage of these options.

Consequence

The changes in markets and consumer lifestyle are having a powerful impact on customer behavior. New trends in customer behavior are already emerging because of this. The overarching result is that consumers are putting greater demands on firms in terms of high value products and services provided at the right place at the right time. Marketers must be extremely wary of placing heavy time demands on consumers. Generally speaking, customers will have more power vis-à-vis the vendor due to technological aptitude and greater product knowledge. Diversification and time scarcity will enhance the pursuit for more personalized products and services. In a nutshell, there are increasing forces that make consumers hunt for the best deal. This trend is corroborated by the increasing inefficiency of traditional mass-marketing approaches (to be discussed later). Paradoxically, consumers' time scarcity and need for consumption-on-demand make them good targets for *well-crafted* relationship strategies. Consequently, firms that are able and willing to satisfy this demand will thrive in this new environment.

The reality of the changing customer environment is underscored by the results of an international top management survey by PriceWaterhouseCoopers. A key question asked was, "What are the critical challenges that confront senior management today?" By far, the highest rated responses in this survey were "meeting consumer demands" (67.5 percent)

| FIGURE | 1-3 | **NUMBER OF DIFFERENT FINANCIAL SERVICE PROVIDERS WITH WHICH RESPONDENTS ARE ASSOCIATED** |

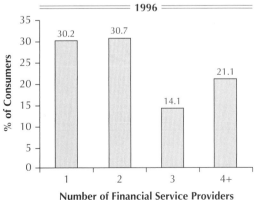

SOURCE: Unidex Report, Atlanta, 1996.

and "technological change and integration" (67.3 percent). Cost reduction (21.3 percent), once the major challenge facing most companies, is no longer ranked as high.

1.3.2 CHANGES WITH RESPECT TO THE MARKETPLACE

Until the past few decades, the business of the global economy was essentially manufacturing. This focus on goods rather than services led to a mass-market, product-focused marketing strategy in which businesses tried to sell the same product to as many people as possible. This product-focused, mass-marketing strategy led to a high cost of acquiring new customers and a low cost for customers switching to other brands. Due to the globalization of the marketplace, the growth in the services economies and technology advances market has shown the following changes.

- *Competition for customers is becoming more intense.* As trade barriers are removed and geographic boundaries are redefined both by established and emergent trading blocs, location advantage is being eroded for most companies. As access to markets is becoming less localized, demands on logistics management and distribution partnering are becoming more significant.

- *Markets are becoming more fragmented.* In a developed market where supply exceeds demand, customers have differentiated needs. To address customers' particular needs, the market has to be initially broken down into multiple segments, which would later facilitate individualized marketing.

- *Differentiation is becoming more difficult.* The quality of objective product attributes has risen substantially in the recent past and is no longer a source of competitive advantage for many companies. Brand loyalty founded on product differentials is just a relative, not absolute, matter. As products' quality differentials are diminishing, companies have to seek competitive advantage in closer, service-focused relationships. Case in point is an example from the U.S. grocery industry, illustrated in Figure 1-4.

Figure 1-4 shows the market share evolution of private label products in U.S. supermarkets, and for the same time period, the unemployment rate. Until the early 1990s, the

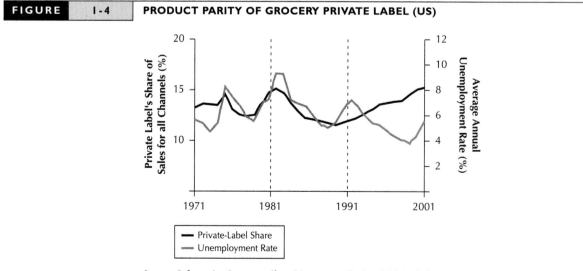

FIGURE 1-4 PRODUCT PARITY OF GROCERY PRIVATE LABEL (US)

SOURCE: Information Resources, Sloan Management Review, BCG Analysis.

two curves moved in sync. That is, as consumers' disposable income decreases (through higher unemployment) more switching to private-label products occurs, since private-label products are priced 20 to 40 percent below national brands. As the economy picks up and unemployment decreases, consumers switch back to national brands, probably due to reasons of better quality. Today, this link is broken. Although unemployment is at a low since 2000, the private-label share reaches record highs. This is simply because the objective quality features of private-label products have become in many cases entirely comparable to national brands. Consumers have come to realize this, and they see fewer reasons to pay a premium for the national brands' equity.

Consequence

Having a good product is not sufficient any longer to compete in a world of, generally speaking, very high product standards. As products and services improve and become very similar in objective performance, companies have to question the traditional way of marketing. As a result, companies start to shift away from a transaction model, and focus more on enduring commercial relationships. The benefit of this is that it allows firms to learn about new and latent customer preferences by observing their purchase and behavioral histories. Given the developments in mass-customization, firms can now add genuine value to customers by offering customized product and service propositions.

As these changes drive the marketplace to become relationship-based, the only way to maintain market share is to realign the companies' business strategy and become customer centric. Thus, customer relationship management has become strategically important in positioning a company in today's market.

1.3.3 CHANGES WITH RESPECT TO DATA STORAGE TECHNOLOGY

Both the supply and demand of data storage technology has changed dramatically. On the supply side, technology is getting better and storage is getting radically cheaper on a cost-per-bit basis. The units of storage are getting radically larger. Looking back at the mid-1990s, the whole of the Western economy had around one petabyte (1,024 terabytes, where 1 terabyte equals 1 trillion bytes) of data storage available. Today, half of that is used to develop a single oil field. In the late 1990s, one gigabyte (GB) of hard disk memory would make PC users swoon. In 2004, most computers come with at least 100GB of hard drive storage. Storage prices have dropped an average of 40 percent annually over the past few years, and there is no foreseeable reason that such a trend will not continue as storage densities increase from year to year.

On the demand side, since we discovered the Internet and the World Wide Web and electronic business, the amount of data available to be stored has grown geometrically. It's not just in industry verticals like energy exploration where better technology, better instrumentation, and better mathematics have increased the demand for data to be stored and to be analyzed. Now, with roughly 600 million people on the Web worldwide, every business needs to keep track of the people who shop on its Web site.[4] Web log files have grown. Many other factors are also driving the demand for storage, including packaged applications (CRM, sales-force automation, and data-marts), growth in data-warehousing applications, storage service providers, and storage-intensive consumer applications. Today, many companies are faced with the need to double their storage capacity every six to twelve months. As Adam Couture, an analyst at Gartner[5] in Stamford, Connecticut, predicts, worldwide storage capacity will swell from 283,000 terabytes in 2000 to more than 5 million terabytes by 2005. IDC[6] estimated that world-wide revenues in the data storage industry will grow to $53.3 billion in 2004, up from $28.4 billion in 1999 (showing a compound annual growth rate of 12 percent).

In addition, data warehouses have become more and more popular since the early 1990s. According to a recent survey by Winter Corporation, the number of corporate data-bases containing more than one terabyte of data doubled between 1998 and 2000. Furthermore, Gartner[7] Group estimated that the average enterprise will have approxi-mately 2.7 million terabytes of stored information in 2004, representing a compound annual growth rate of 72 percent from 1999 to 2004. Wal-Mart's data warehouse had a size of 460 terabytes in November 2004.[8]

Consequence

Firms have never been in a potentially better situation to inform themselves about cus-tomer behavior and attitudes. If firms do it correctly, they can develop unprecedented insight and information on a customer's buying behavior. At the same time, having too much data can be challenging as well. Misapplied and wrong-footed analyses are often the consequences of being overwhelmed with too much data.

1.3.4   CHANGES WITH RESPECT TO THE MARKETING FUNCTION

Media Dilution and Multiplication of Channels

The nature of marketing communications is undergoing significant shifts. Brand man-agers, service providers, and product manufacturers used mass communication vehicles (print, TV, radio) as their prime carrier. The message often focused on product and price with little regard to heterogeneity in customer's needs and wants. Communication based on mass advertising is now only a model of the past. Customers needs and wants have sim-ply become too diverse for marketers to satisfy them with a single, all-purpose approach. For example, Figure 1-5 shows that after many years of growth, coupon distribution for packaged goods is clearly on its way down. This means of creating short-term and deal-focused consumer response is neither appropriate for today's customers nor for manufac-turers. It creates a lot of switching and supply-chain spikes, both very undesirable for packaged goods manufacturers.

Given the availability of new data collection and communication tools, such as loyalty programs, there is less need to employ techniques that indiscriminately focus on price only. Driven by technological advancements, the concept of commercial communication has been completely restructured. For example, the ubiquity of TV has increased, and the num-ber of options in most media categories except dailies has greatly increased in the past fif-teen years.

Communication Medium	1997–2002 % Change[9]
Houses with cable TV	+14.0%
Television stations	+9.6%
Commercial radio stations	+6.4%
Periodicals	+62.0%
Daily newspapers	−3.4%

Combined with the Internet, the amount of communications media focused on the customer is staggering. It is particularly the direct-to-consumer channels (mail, e-mail,

PHYSICAL GROCERY COUPON DISTRIBUTION IN THE U.S.

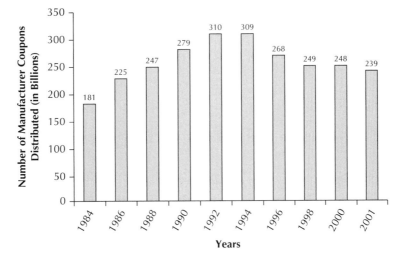

SOURCE: NCH Promotional Services, Lincolnshire, IL.

telephone) and the interactive media (Internet, interactive TV) that outpace the traditional media in spending.[10] Technology is the key here: small-batch catalog production, catalog customization, cable-TV proliferation, and pay-per-use are some examples. Clearly, firms start to take advantage of this modified media landscape because they find that direct-to-consumer communication fits perfectly with the objective of building two-way conversations with longstanding customers.

Decreasing Marketing Efficiency and Effectiveness

The pressure has been growing on corporate marketers to revamp their departments in order to demonstrate marketing investments that can be linked to the company's bottom line profits. The famous saying by John Wanemaker (1838–1922), "I know that half of the money I spend on advertising is wasted, I just don't know which half," has probably never been as true as it is today. Consider the following malaise in the U.S. car industry. Between 1996 and 2000, the marketing costs per vehicle for the big three automakers increased by 87 percent to $2,900 per vehicle (55 percent of the marketing budget is composed of rebates and incentives). During that same time period, their combined market share decreased by 4 percent.[11] One can rightfully understand shareholders and CFOs who demand better accountability and documentation of value added from the marketing function.

The problem stems in part from our past marketing practices that focused on acquisition and not so much on retention, that focused on price and not so much on added value, and that focused on short-term transactions and not so much on development of lasting profitable relationships. The proliferation of new contact channels undoubtedly contributes to a decreasing efficiency and effectiveness. Combined with more sophisticated and knowledgeable customers, this has led to a situation where the cost of contact has remained flat or increased, but the resulting consumer response has decreased. Consequently, the impact of advertising in any medium has lost some of its value. Figure 1-6 presents how the response rate of marketing offers for the credit card industry has decreased in the past decade.

The phenomenon of media proliferation is paralleled by the difficulty of communicating with customers meaningfully. As more and more media channels become available, the

FIGURE **1-6** **INCREASING ACQUISITION COSTS IN BANKING**

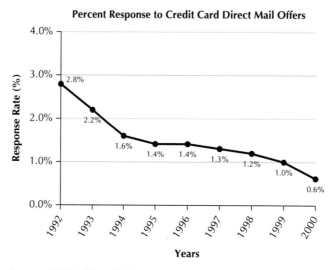

Percent Response to Credit Card Direct Mail Offers

SOURCE: BAI Global, Inc., U.S. Census Bureau, Accenture.com.

challenge of channel coordination is increasing. As firms offer more channels, they need to coordinate messages across these channels. As the numbers of channels increase, managing their complexity increases exponentially.

Consequence

The pressure on the marketing function is on. Marketers must become better at showing their impact on the bottom line. Otherwise, marketing will take a back seat and effectively be restricted to advertising and media planning.

1.3.5 IMPLICATIONS

Given all these changes in the environment, we are looking at a marketing scenario that places much greater demands on learning about customer preferences, or value provision, and product and service customization. Product-centric strategies are no longer capable of dealing with these advanced requirements. As a consequence, customer-centric strategies are emerging as a response. It is exactly this environment, where CRM, if executed correctly, represents a formidable competitive means of satisfying these new demands.

Our conclusion is that we need a management approach that is able to satisfy the increasing customer heterogeneity, to address concerns of marketing accountability, to put the available data to use, and to use customer profitability as the key objective function. We term this approach *data-based customer value management*.

1.3.6 THE BENEFITS OF THE DATA-BASED CUSTOMER VALUE MANAGEMENT APPROACH

A successful data-based CRM system, with customer value as its driving metric, will empower the company to do ten things.

1. Integrate and consolidate customer information. With the relevant customer information and client history, the treatment toward a customer will be consistent across contact and service channels.

2. Provide consolidated information across all channels throughout the company to assist in timely and relevant communication with the customers, matching their needs with the most appropriate product.

3. Manage customer cases. This provides the right person with management control in a planned and transparent manner, ensuring that appropriate action is taken at the proper time.

4. Personalize if possible the service and products offered to each customer to satisfy his or her special expectation.

5. Automatically and manually generate new sales opportunities by measuring the customer profile against the predefined business rules or contact between a customer and an employee.

6. Generate and manage campaigns by providing flexibility to adapt to changes in the customer information or behavior.

7. Yield faster and more accurate follow-up on sales leads, referrals, and customer inquiries.

8. Manage all business processes by introducing a central point of control, ensuring that all business processes are executed in accordance with correct and effective business rules.

9. Give top managers a detailed and accurate picture of all sales and marketing activities.

10. Instantly react to a changing market environment.

1.4 SUMMARY

The increasing availability of technology allows firms to collect and analyze customer-level data and interact with customers simultaneously. CRM uses this information to identify profitable customers and develop specific strategies for interacting with each customer. Assessing the value of a customer is critical to CRM. Customer value is defined as the economic value of the customer relationship to the firm—expressed on the basis of contribution margin or net profit. From a customer-value perspective, CRM is defined as the practice of analyzing and utilizing marketing databases and leveraging communication technologies to determine corporate practices and methods that will maximize the lifetime value of each individual customer to the firm. The conceptualizations of CRM can be grouped into three types: functional level, customer facing front-end level, and strategic level. In this book, we view CRM from a strategic perspective. CRM is the strategic process of selecting the customers a firm can most profitably serve, and of shaping the interactions between a company and these customers. The goal is to optimize the current and future value of the customers for the company.

Rapid changes are taking place in the environment in which firms operate. These changes are with respect to (1) consumers, (2) marketplaces, (3) technology, and (4) marketing functions. On the consumer front, there is a growing diversity triggered by changing demographic composition of the population. Consumers are also becoming more value conscious, less loyal and intolerant to low service levels, increasingly time poor, and more technology savvy. The marketplace is characterized by more intense competition, greater fragmentation, and increasing difficulty to differentiate. These changes have driven the marketplace to become relationship-based and customer-centric. Data storage technology has become cheaper, so we see an exponential growth in storage capacity. This has created a favorable situation for firms to collect and analyze information about consumers and their needs and preferences, and has set the stage for CRM implementation.

1.5 EXERCISE QUESTIONS

1. How do you define CRM?
2. How are CRM activities similar/different from marketing activities? Please discuss.
3. What makes CRM the preferred approach to marketing in the Information Age?
4. What is the distinction between traditional database marketing and a customer-value–based approach toward database marketing?
5. Illustrate situations where you think companies are following CRM practices. Point out where they are going wrong.
6. Companies want relationships with customers, but do customers want relationships with companies? Please discuss.
7. What are the key changes in the business environment? Why are these changes driving the shift from product-based marketing to customer-based marketing?
8. Do call centers in general improve customer satisfaction? Are customers increasingly accepting the use of call centers and the Internet as the only available interfaces with the firm? Can the success of companies like Dell be attributed to this?

ENDNOTES

1. Rohit Deshpande and Frederick E. Webster, Jr., "Organizational Culture and Marketing: Defining the Research," *Journal of Marketing* 53, no. 1 (1989): 3–15.

2. Debbie Howlett, "Americans driving to distraction," *USA Today*, www.USAtoday.com (March 3, 2004), accessed on January 13, 2005.

3. http://www.imagequestdesign.com/downloads/learn_net_impact.pdf (January 14, 2005).

4. CIA World Fact book. http://www.odci.gov/cia/publications/factbook/rankorder/2153rank .html (January 14, 2005).

5. Gartner Inc., CRM Project Volume 2 (June 15, 2001).

6. "Growth of the CRM industry", IDC (June 2000).

7. Wendy S. Close, "The Need for a Multi-vendor Strategy in Achieving Outstanding CRM," Gartner Inc., CRM Project Volume 2 (June 2001).

8. *New York Times* (November 14, 2004).

9. "Statistical Abstract of the United States" 2004–05 edition, www.census.gov/prod/2004pubs /04statab/infocomm.pdf (January 13, 2005): 717–719.

10. "The DMA 2003 Economic Impact: US Direct Marketing Today."

11. McKinsey Report, 2001.

CHAPTER

2

CRM Industry Landscape

Contents

2.1 OVERVIEW

As companies started moving from transaction-based marketing to customer-based marketing, there was increasing need for collecting, storing, and analyzing customer-level information. This led to the evolution of the term *customer relationship management (CRM)* in the mid-1990s. In the initial years, the collection and storage of customer information was limited to the sales and service functions, and the prospect and customer databases were independently used by different functional groups in the firms. As a result, sales force automation (SFA) and customer service support (CSS) existed as two independent systems. The integration of a number of different independent subsystems into one package posed the biggest challenge for CRM. Once this was overcome, CRM underwent a significant evolution. The timeline of CRM evolution and the growth stages are discussed in this chapter. We look at the misconception that CRM is an information technology project. We understand that technology is only the backbone in the successful implementation of CRM. The rapid growth and increasing awareness and adoption of CRM are illustrated. We examine the need for CRM technology in light of the various factors driving CRM industry. We describe ways in which a company can develop and implement a CRM solution. We provide an overall picture of how different industries have implemented and integrated CRM solutions, with specific examples from the telecom and pharmaceutical industries.

2.2 EVOLUTION AND GROWTH OF CRM

This section describes the stages of development of CRM from the 1990s until today. CRM has moved from being a tactical marketing tool to a strategic element in all marketing decisions. The growth of the Internet has positively affected the adoption rate of CRM in many industries.

2.2.1 THE TIMELINE OF CRM EVOLUTION

Since the concept of customer relationship management came into vogue in the mid-1990s, CRM has undergone a substantial evolution. To provide a historical perspective, in Figure 2-1 we present a timeline of the evolution. This section describes the phases outlined in that timeline.

First Generation (Functional CRM Approach)

The collection of activities, which later obtained the umbrella acronym CRM, originally developed as two independent product offerings:

1. *Sales force automation (SFA).* These products addressed such presales functions as maintaining prospect and customer data, telemarketing, generating leads, creating sales quotations, and placing sales orders.
2. *Customer service and support (CSS).* This addressed mainly after-sales activities such as help desks, contact and call centers, and field service support. CSS databases often worked with specific customer information, completely isolated from other systems.

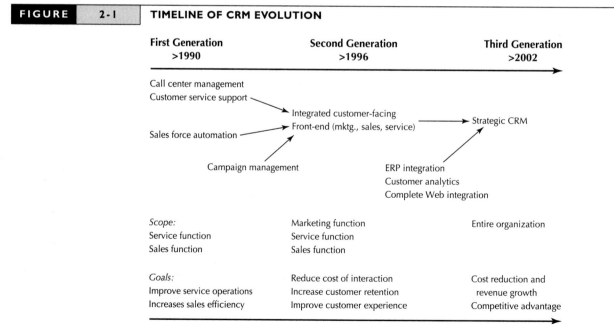

| FIGURE | 2-1 | TIMELINE OF CRM EVOLUTION |

Note: ERP = Enterprise Resource Planning.

Though fragmented and poorly integrated with the back office, the early SFA/CSS applications delivered the promise of sales and service improvement. The combined SFA/CSS market niche remained small, however. At the same time, the market for enterprise resource planning—a tool designed to integrate all company departments and functions across a company onto a single computer system serving every department's needs—was growing.

Second Generation (Customer-Facing Front-End Approach)

In a way, the CRM innovation during the 1990s was similar to that of ERP—the integration of a number of different independent subsystems into one package. CRM technology was expected to fill the gaps left in ERP functionality and address the business needs of the company's customer-facing front end.

The pursued goal was to create a single view of all interactions with customers, independent of the purpose of the contact (pre-sales, sales transaction, or post-sales service) or the means of contact (phone, e-mail, Internet, or any other channel). For the most part, this goal was not achieved during the 1990s. In fact, from 1999 on, more and more disillusionment with CRM technology and CRM implementations began to surface. Customer expectations in this period far exceeded the realized benefits of CRM technology. The industry began talking about the demise of CRM.[1] The Internet fuelled new expectations from this technology, but it became very clear that revenue increases through technology were difficult to implement, realize, and measure, unless a more strategic understanding of the process was undertaken.

Third Generation (Strategic Approach)

By the end of 2002, the CRM market had started to pick up and the gap between customers' perceived value and the value realized was closing fast. Organizations learned from their experience in implementing the not-so-successful earlier versions of CRM practices. The best organizations now focused on integrating the customer-facing front-end systems with back-end systems, as well as with partners and suppliers (see Figure 2-2).

FIGURE 2-2 **INTEGRATION OF FRONT-END CUSTOMERS WITH BACK-END SYSTEMS**

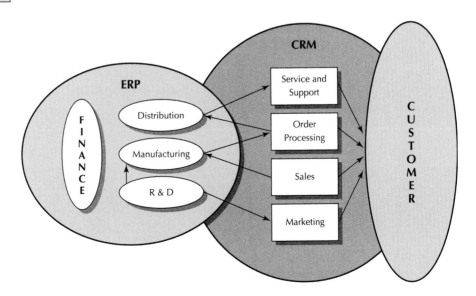

The integration of Internet technology helped give a boost to CRM. Many organizations came to the realization they could benefit by adopting a strategic CRM approach rather than by blindly implementing technology-based solutions. Companies realized that the eventual goal of CRM is to grow the revenue line and not just control the cost line.

2.2.2 CRM AND THE IT REVOLUTION—THE VIEW FROM THE INDUSTRY

In my discussions with senior executives around the world about the power of IT systems and networked computing, I consistently make the point that the real revolution isn't about the technology itself. The real revolution here has to do with institutional change—the fundamental transformation of time-honored ways of doing things.

—Lou Gerstner, CEO IBM[2]

The following is a comment by a CRM consultant:

One of the reasons, I prefer to deal with SMEs (small- and medium-sized enterprises) in implementing CRM is that I always have direct access to the CEO of the business to ensure they understand what CRM is about. We always put the strategies together first, then find a technology solution that makes carrying out those strategies easier. I strongly believe the much-touted 70 percent failure rate of CRM projects has resulted from a too-heavy reliance on technology …
There is still a major issue in CRM of people not understanding what it is all about—which is listening to the customer and communicating with them in a manner most likely to increase their satisfaction and win repeat and referral business. Unfortunately, I believe this reliance on technology has been driven by the big CRM IT players. CEOs of major companies see it as something that they simply must do, without understanding what it is all about.

The industry's view of CRM has gone through a substantial adjustment period between 1999 and 2003. Some managers became disillusioned with the process and results of implementing CRM solutions and systems. They felt that they reaped only very limited benefits from new IT systems, that they faced resentment among employees when implementing these new systems, and that the new IT systems did not add any value to what was already being offered to the customer.

This negative reaction to CRM as it was practiced was based on an IT view of the world. Too often, the introduction of CRM was viewed as a technological project and a temporary activity. Many managers believed that CRM equaled software or technology. However, nothing could be further from the truth. Given these misconceptions, it is no surprise that many CRM efforts never met the expectations of the companies implementing them. For example, Deloitte Consulting—CSO Forum 1999—found that 28 percent of respondents thought their CRM investments yielded significant improvements, while the remaining 72 percent said they received little or no benefits from their CRM initiatives.[3]

A META Group/IMT Study found that most CRM plans are highly fragmented and lack customer focus, that 64 percent of respondents lack techniques for measuring the business value of CRM, and that respondents provide multiple, conflicting, and incomplete definitions of CRM.[4]

In order for CRM to be implemented successfully, the top management must support integrating all of the corporate functions to focus on customer value. Growth of CRM must not be equated with the growth of what has been called the CRM industry, consisting mainly of IT vendors. Darrell Rigby from Bain & Co. has been researching the use of management tools over the years. He finds that both CRM tool usage and satisfaction with CRM have been increasing, in the past few years (see Figure 2-3).

Of late, as companies view CRM as a strategic marketing element; they are realizing there is untapped potential in it. The future is bright for CRM, and with the aid of appropriate IT systems, CRM will become the preferred marketing approach for many firms in the years to come.

2.2.3 GROWTH OF THE CRM INDUSTRY

Today, the CRM industry has become a fast-growing industry where billions of dollars are being spent on CRM applications, consulting, and training every year. If one wants to track past CRM spending and predict future spending, one runs into the difficulty of creating an understanding of exactly what and what *not* to include. Many statistics on the size of the CRM market exist, and most studies differ with respect to geography covered, technologies included, and type/size of firms included. Figure 2-4 derives the expenditures on CRM from a set of different estimates from different market research firms.

Overall, the expectation is that the CRM technology market is reemerging after the drop in growth rates during the recession of 2001 to 2002.

2.2.4 THE FACTORS DRIVING THE CRM INDUSTRY FORWARD

As we discussed, the emergence and development of CRM have been driven by the shift from transactional to relationship-based markets. In addition to this factor, five other factors are driving the CRM industry:

1. *Growing proof about the profitable impact of the right customer relationships.* Continued investment in the CRM practice has confirmed the belief that value lies in targeted customer relationships.

2. *Improved marketing communication effectiveness.* Integrated marketing agencies have made great progress in improving the effectiveness of their communications

---

| FIGURE | 2-3 | **USAGE AND SATISFACTION WITH CUSTOMER RELATIONSHIP MANAGEMENT AS A MANAGEMENT TOOL** |

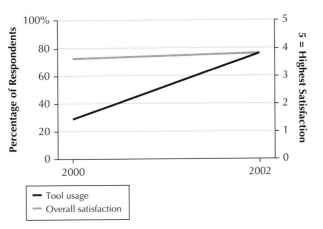

SOURCE: Bain & Co., author: Darrell Rigby.

FIGURE 2-4 **APPROXIMATE WORLDWIDE CRM INVESTMENTS**

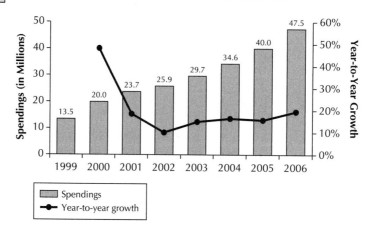

Notes: Mean estimates as of 2002 and 2003 across various providers. CRM outsourcing services not included.

SOURCE: IDC, Aberdeen, Gartner, Forrester.

activity, with superior database technology, analysis tools, targeted communication activity, and performance measurement techniques.

3. *IT vendors and associated change management consultancies.* To IT vendors and associated change management consultancies concerned with the technology and process side of customer relationships, CRM represents a vast arena of untapped IT potential. The initial demand for stand-alone products—such as sales force automation, marketing campaign management, or call center management tools—has given way to increasingly integrated strategic CRM solutions.

4. *The continually reducing costs of data capture and storage.* The economies of CRM improve with drop in data capture and storage costs. CRM solutions therefore are increasingly becoming attractive investments.

5. *Customer value measurement.* Firms are now aware that CRM investments need to be based on accurate metrics that take into account expected returns. The developments in the area of customer value measurement and utilization have provided the needed assurance that CRM efforts will bear fruit.

2.3 STRATEGIC CRM VERSUS FUNCTIONAL CRM

Very often, a CRM project is associated with an IT project or with a particular vendor solution. However, there are two components that make up a CRM project—*strategic CRM* and *functional CRM.* Implementing a CRM project is about adopting a corporate strategy that should be designed to optimize both profitability and customer satisfaction. To realize CRM, organizations must foster behaviors and implement processes and technologies which support coordinated customer interactions throughout all customer channels. In order to achieve this, organizations must develop the strategic and functional components of the CRM project: define the company strategies and tactics, develop new skills, redefine new processes, and implement new technologies. Generally, to obtain an integrated view of their own customers, companies need to integrate the various databases and applications existing in the enterprise. As discussed, this usually involves the integration of back-office with front-office applications, or the integration of legacy systems with new IT platforms. In the past few decades, it was a common procedure for companies to buy a system from a particular vendor, and each time the company needed to change or develop the system, the vendor would be asked (and paid) to perform the requested changes. This is defined as a proprietary system. The company has no inside knowledge or skills to perform changes on its own, and is also contractually restricted to do it. When the company envisages a CRM project, most of these proprietary systems present problems at the integration level. Some new companies have opted for nonproprietary systems. They buy systems that can be developed by internal IT teams and create the internal skills to develop and adapt it to new needs.

Either way, CRM should allow companies to address two key issues:

1. Companies should be able to analyze and understand the customer data through sophisticated but easy-to-use reporting tools.
2. Once they understand and analyze the data, they should act on that knowledge to customize services and products through all channels of communication (Web, sales, call center, etc.) and to anticipate and fulfill the customer needs.

2.4 CRM Implementation Options

Companies can opt for any one or a combination of three different ways to implement a CRM solution: developing software in house, buying licensed software, or outsourcing creation of software.

2.4.1 DEVELOPING SOFTWARE IN HOUSE

Building and managing a CRM solution in-house requires the company to define all its requirements, pay for software development, and bear all the R&D costs internally. Companies choosing this route must invest heavily in storage, application software, and hardware. The initial hardware and software expenses constitute only a small portion of the total cost, which is largely shaped by maintenance demands, especially those arising from changing requirements inside the organization. This can be done with or without external consulting help, although it is useful to have external help because collecting data, managing related systems, and driving value from data is not a core competence of most businesses.

Advantages

Companies develop a tailor-made solution adapted to their needs and structure. They develop internal resources and skills that allow them to develop the system each time the company requirements change. By doing do, they can avoid dependence on CRM software vendors and on new software releases or developments.

Disadvantages

This is usually the most expensive option because the company has to maintain, operate, and improve the system on its own. Usually, it is very difficult to attract and retain the skills to solve and develop data warehousing challenges. The typical time commitment is one to two years, which might be long when compared to other out-of-the box solutions in the market.

2.4.2 BUYING LICENSED CRM SOFTWARE

Companies that choose to buy licensed CRM software will also need extensive IT resources. Even with a licensed CRM software solution, companies still need to develop the IT infrastructure and integrate the new software with existing applications. This solution can be sold as a block (it may be composed of different modules adapted to each front-office application) or it can be sold as independent modules (e.g., the company just buys the sales automation module or the contact management module).

Although the CRM vendor should provide knowledge and training for the new system, considerable effort still needs to be invested in order to develop internal expertise and skills to effectively run the new CRM solution. Also, each time the CRM vendor releases a new or an upgraded version of the software, the company needs to go through the process of upgrading the systems, buying additional modules, and resolving other associated problems.

Advantages

Many of these software packages have a proven record of success, and the company can feel reassured that this solution has worked for other companies. The IT concept and developments will be implemented with the help of the CRM vendor and the company will only need to adapt its IT structure to integrate the new solution.

Disadvantages

This is also an expensive option. The initial fees and the licensing costs are usually high. Companies are often charged to renew the license each year. Maintenance costs are required over the life of the software, and each time a new version comes out, companies have to pay for it. If the company chooses to customize the solution to its needs, it will have to pay for consulting services, which are generally very expensive. Integrating the new software with existing applications is usually a tough and expensive job, usually taking one to three years to implement.

2.4.3   OUTSOURCING A MANAGED SERVICE

Companies can outsource the CRM solution from a third-party company. The outsourcing company provides the hardware, software, and human resources in exchange for a monthly fee. Implementation takes less time because applications are already built and operational and the outsourcing company has an incentive to get the system running so that it can initiate service and fees.

Advantages

The upfront costs are lower than in the other two approaches. Companies do not need to pay for software licenses and hardware systems. The firm doesn't need to recruit or develop internal IT skills to manage the new CRM solution. The company can adopt a *pay-as-you-go* approach, meaning that it can start the process of paying as the CRM results are visible, instead of paying upfront costs and licensing and maintenance costs.

Disadvantages

Each time the company needs to adapt the solution to new requirements it has to contact the outsourcing company and pay for the developments. The firm does not possess the necessary skills and knowledge to manage the CRM solution, and it risks losing the CRM solution investments if the outsourcing company goes out of business.

The Decision Process for Implementation

When deciding about implementing the CRM project, the organization follows a structured hierarchical process (Figure 2-5). In the particular case that the company opts to buy

FIGURE   2-5   IMPLEMENTING CRM: THE DECISION PROCESS

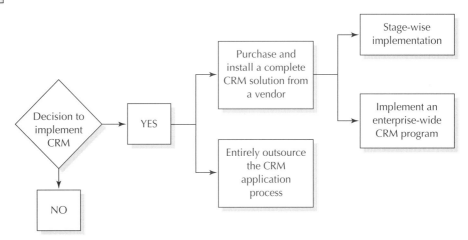

a CRM solution, integration middleware suppliers and consulting services at the management, technical, and information systems levels are often employed, even though they are not always required. Depending on the type of application, these services may be included in the original contract.

2.5   CRM SOFTWARE AND APPLICATIONS

In this section we will focus on the option where the company chooses to buy licensed CRM software or to outsource the CRM solution.

2.5.1   STAGE-WISE IMPLEMENTATION VERSUS AN ENTERPRISE WIDE CRM SOLUTION

The CRM industry offers different types of solutions based on the company needs and processes. CRM software solutions can be looked at in two different ways:

1. CRM software is offered in different, independent modules, which are adapted to a specific department's needs (e.g., the company buys the sales automation software and the contact management module from different providers). This approach is also called *best-of-breed.*

2. The enterprisewide CRM solution is composed of different modules from the same provider. These modules may be adapted to each department's needs, yet they are implemented as a whole by connecting the different modules and the existing databases. Individual components may be weaker than best-of-breed products; however, the organization knows the different components are fully compatible.

Sometimes the enterprise wide CRM solutions are not customized to specific needs. This could lead to further consulting costs in the future. Current market conditions and competition have resulted in CRM vendors now customizing individual modules to company needs.

Ideally, all CRM software solutions should integrate information and databases from marketing, sales, customer service, e-business, call-center, and other sources. The total CRM solution comprises a series of many different hardware devices and software components. These components may or may not come from different suppliers and may run on different platforms.[5] It is the company's decision, based on the precedent requirements, to choose between a stage-wise implementation of CRM modules or an enterprise wide CRM solution.

2.5.2 RELATIONSHIPS AND FLOWS BETWEEN CRM MODULES

As stated earlier, CRM modules can be implemented independently in phases or together in a global solution. In both cases, the important thing is to integrate the modules so the company can have an integrated view of the customer. All the information obtained from the customer is stored in a data warehouse which will be used to perform analysis, modeling, and data mining. Consequently the analysis information will be used in different ways by each department to interface with the customer in the future, via the available channels of communication. When applied to the context of a specific industry, the information flow is adapted to the environment. To illustrate this adaptation, we provide two examples from two different industry types. Figure 2-6 shows an example of an integrated CRM solution in the telecom industry. Figure 2-7 depicts the prototypical situation in the pharmaceutical industry.

A new trend emerging in the CRM industry is that of strategic supplier partnerships. These consist of a partnership between the company that implements CRM and the supplier of the software and services. The goal is not only to customize the CRM offer to the company's needs, but also to ensure that the supplying company takes part in the implementation processes. This is in response to buyers increasingly demanding a risk-sharing proposition from the supplier. This means that the seller of the tool has an interest in delivering the impact that was promised at the time of sale.

2.6 CRM: WHERE DOES THE FUTURE LIE?

2.6.1 WORLDWIDE CRM COSTS

Many IT market research firms supply information on market tendencies in the CRM market. For example, in early 2001, Gartner predicted that worldwide spending on CRM would reach about $76 billion (U.S.) in 2005, which would represent an increase of more than double the effective expending in 2000 ($23 billion).[6] In terms of spending at the enterprise level, Forrester Research estimated that a typical Global 3,500 firm will spend on average $15 to $30 million (U.S.) per year on CRM software and systems.[7] Looking at the user level, a study from Reuters and Mason[8] points out that price per seat (CRM license costs/number of users) is about U.S. $250 to U.S. $2,500.[9]

2.6.2 NEXT GENERATION CRM

As companies increasingly understand the value of forming profitable long-term relationships with their customers, the CRM industry in general is poised for growth. The traditional CRM solutions have focused on building competitive advantage for companies in terms of products, services, pricing, and distribution, but the new and evolving view focuses on building sustainable competitive advantage that cannot be easily imitated by the competitors. Specifically, we can expect further developments in the following areas:

- Firms increasingly recognize that it is imperative to integrate the human resource (HR) function into their strategic CRM efforts. First and foremost is the need to adjust employee incentive schemes to make them compatible with the goals of their CRM strategy.

FIGURE **2-6** **CRM CONFIGURATION IN THE TELECOM INDUSTRY**

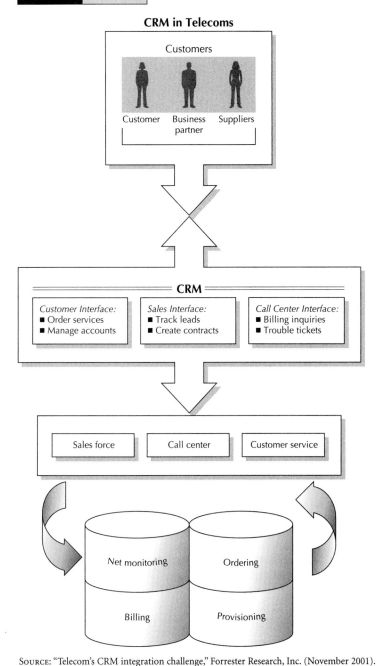

The telecom industry defines CRM as a strategy and a technology which will help them increase retention rates while cutting costs and delivering better and cheaper service.

Their primary investment objective in CRM is to solve ordering, billing, and service challenges as:

- Customers inability to order services online. Most of the product configurators are still embedded in the sales force automation and don't allow this information to pass to the Web site.
- A customer who subscribes to multiple services receives a billing for each service, instead of receiving an integrated bill.
- Product types separate customer service. When a call goes beyond basics like voicemail set up, the caller has to be transferred to the respective product agent.

To succeed, carriers need to build an integrated access control to manage user access to the system; to create custom interfaces for each user group; to create immediate IT support to multi-channel users. Carriers should integrate information with other partners via Web services (like checking available stock of the partner) and improve customer service via the call-center and Web-channel.

Source: "Telecom's CRM integration challenge," Forrester Research, Inc. (November 2001).

- Another common trend is to create a truly single view of the customer. Synchronizing customer information across all channels and touchpoints is not easy, but best-practice firms are attempting just this.
- A third trend is to continuously fine-tune and micro-segment the customer database. True one-to-one marketing is rare, yet most firms seek to create more customized products and service for increasingly smaller segments. The driver behind this development is the growing ability to handle deep customer analytics.

FIGURE	2-7	CRM CONFIGURATION IN THE PHARMACEUTICAL INDUSTRY

Analytical CRM in the Pharmaceutical Industry

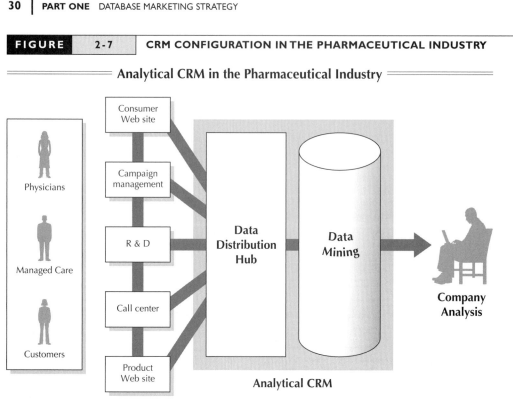

Pharmaceutical firms believe CRM will help them build a unified and connected view of prescribers, patients, and payers across all organization factions; this will help them improve customer service and sales. However, they still have some challenges to solve:

- Each department within the pharma industry manages external relationships, interacts with customers, and presents opportunities to streamline internal payoffs. However, the departments don't interact with each other to provide a unified view of the customer.
- Many of the key product teams of pharma firms target the same customers, but they don't share insight between them. This way they miss opportunities to leverage investment in one product to support another.
- Doctors, patients, and payers are related, but firms have them separated. An aggregation of this information would give marketers a more complete view into a doctor's drug decision process.

Analytical CRM will transform tactical connections into a strategic value. It will help firms to rationalize the M&A activity by integrating information. R&D will benefit from the uncovering of connections between doctors, patients, and diseases. CRM will position the firm as the go-to channel for biotech since it allows them—with a good marketing engine—to take the biotech new partner's product to the market fast.

Source: "Pharma CRM analytical cure," Forrester Research, Inc. (April 2002).

2.7   SUMMARY

During the last decade, CRM has evolved from the first-generation functional CRM, consisting mainly of sales force automation (SFA) and customer service support systems (CSS) in the mid-1990s to strategic CRM. This transformation was mainly done by integrating the customer-facing front-end with back-end systems, as well as with partners and suppliers. The integration of Internet technology and rapid improvement in information technology facilitated the growth of CRM. Now, most global companies have either implemented or are in the process of implementing CRM strategies. The worldwide spending on CRM is rapidly increasing, and new trends are emerging, such as integrating HR functions with strategic CRM, micro segmenting the customer databases, and synchronizing customer information across all channels.

Currently, CRM solution providers are evolving their sales processes and changing their selling propositions. End users inside the firms are now demanding comprehensive solutions for specific business problems, causing some vendors to make two major changes in the types of products they offer. First is the development of industry-focused solutions. Vendors are realizing that the one-size-fits-all concept does not necessarily work anymore, and a number of CRM companies are developing specialized solutions for vertical industries. The second change is the development of specialized tools for specific process problems. Some vendors are developing tools that address just a single process or subprocess of the overall CRM challenge, optimizing only this component or module.

In order to control CRM costs, maximize flexibility, and minimize risks, firms are renewing their efforts to standardize their application programs servers and the platform components. The heavy customization required by CRM application programs places a premium on development resources. The increasing pressure to reduce CRM costs is leading firms to shift from high-cost proprietary development systems to new systems that can be further developed and upgraded internally (e.g., Java).

Due to the increasing pressures to reduce costs, companies are buying cheaper options that use business intelligence software to glue CRM applications together at the front end. At the same time, companies are taking a step-by-step approach in their CRM projects. Instead of doing a three-year CRM project, without controlling the results, they may opt to undertake three-month integration projects. Doing short-term projects and implementing the CRM software at different stages is actually a low-risk approach to this investment. Business processes are not interrupted, and companies can reap the benefits quickly.

2.8 EXERCISE QUESTIONS

1. Practicing CRM without technology is not possible. Do you agree with this statement?
2. What are the various ways to deploy CRM? What are their advantages and disadvantages?
3. Describe some of the key CRM software applications and their functions.
4. Describe the evolution of CRM practices over time.
5. What was behind the disillusionment with CRM practices in the late 1990s?

ENDNOTES

1. J. Thomas Gormley, III et al., "The Demise of CRM", *Forrester Research Inc.* (June 1999).
2. Lou Gerstner, CEO IBM, *Think Leadership* 3, no. 2.
3. *Ibid.* "A Guide to Marketing, Sales and Service Transformation," Deloitte Consulting—CSO Forum (1999).
4. Sarah Fraser, "Most CRM Initiatives at Risk of Failure" Database Advisor Portal Doc # 05654 26 October 1999, http://crm-advisor.com/doc/05654 (January 13, 2005).
5. A platform is any base of technologies on which other technologies or processes are built. It is also an underlying computer system on which application programs can run. On personal computers, Windows 2000 and the Mac OS X are examples of two different platforms. Source: http://www.opensolutionsinc.com/resq_architecture.htm (January 13, 2005).
6. Wendy S. Close, "The Need for a Multi-vendor Strategy in Achieving Outstanding CRM," *Gartner Inc., CRM Project Volume 2* (June 2001).
7. Bob Chatham et al., "CRM: At What Cost?" *Forrester Research, Inc.* (March 2001).
8. Vivian Acharya, Mike Olive, The Mason Group, "Customer Relationship Management: Practical Strategies for Successful Implementation", *Business Insights Reuters* (January 2002).
9. Price per seat represents the total cost of a software license, or the CRM cost divided by the total number of seats. In a networked computer system, a seat is a workstation that can be operated by one user at a time.

CHAPTER 3

Strategic CRM

Contents

3.1   OVERVIEW

Many companies think CRM is only about technology, and they look for a software quick fix without examining the key elements of successful CRM. This is why you notice so many failures in the field of CRM today. Too many projects have been abandoned and investments have been written off. Just as building a house first requires an architectural plan, successfully implementing CRM must be preceded by a sound CRM strategy. In this chapter we present CRM as a business strategy and company-level philosophy where the knowledge about customers and their preferences have implications for the entire organization. In this customer-centric business philosophy, the customer is treated as an asset, and the focus is shifted away from the product to the customer as the source of wealth generation. Hence, the goal of strategic CRM is to actively deepen the knowledge about customers and use this knowledge to shape the interactions between a company and its customers in order to maximize the lifetime value of customers for the company.

We present four key components of a successful CRM strategy. Each component is explained using real-life case studies. We then deal with the aspects of defining and developing a CRM strategy, keeping in mind the key components of CRM strategy. We stress the importance of the integration of various functions and an enterprise wide commitment in the success of a CRM solution.

3.2. THE COMPONENTS OF STRATEGIC CRM

3.2.1 A STRATEGIC PERSPECTIVE OF CRM

CRM can be viewed from three different perspectives: the functional level, the customer-facing level, and the companywide level (See Figure 3-1). If viewed from a functional perspective, CRM can be seen as the set of processes that need to be in place to execute marketing functions such as sales force automation or online campaign management. CRM could also be viewed from the customer-facing perspective. In this case, CRM is the set of activities that provides a single view of the customer across all contact channels. This implies that obtained customer intelligence is available uniformly to all customer-facing functions. This view stresses the importance of coordinating information across time and contact channels in order to systematically manage the entire customer relationship. For example, a bank customer might have a loan product and a savings product, the person might interact with the bank through various channels for various reasons (transaction, information request, complaint), and the nature of these interactions might change over time. Finally, the CRM process can be viewed as a company-level philosophy where knowledge about customers and their preferences has implications for the entire organization with regard to such things as R&D or supply chain management. When CRM is adopted by a firm at the companywide level, it can be termed *strategic CRM.*

Strategic CRM stems from sound marketing principles. As mentioned earlier, it recognizes the need to carefully balance organizational interests and customer interests. The goal of strategic CRM is to shape the interactions between a company and its customers in a way that allows maximizing the lifetime value of customers for the company. This also reflects the philosophy that not all customers are created equal. Firms recognize that customers differ in their economic value to the firm and in their expectations toward the firm (e.g., in terms of willingness to engage in a long-term relationship). Shaping the customer-firm interaction via attraction and retention of the target customer groups is woven into the strategic and operational fabric of successful CRM adopters. As a result, successful strategic CRM will be a complex set of activities that together form the basis for a sustainable and hard-to-imitate competitive advantage.

A CRM strategy requires the following four components (see Figure 3-2):

1. A customer-management orientation
2. Integration and alignment of organizational processes
3. Information capture and alignment of technology
4. CRM strategy implementation

FIGURE   3-1   CRM PERSPECTIVES

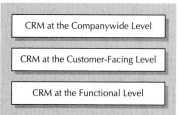

CRM at the Companywide Level

CRM at the Customer-Facing Level

CRM at the Functional Level

FIGURE **3-2** **THE COMPONENTS OF CRM STRATEGY**

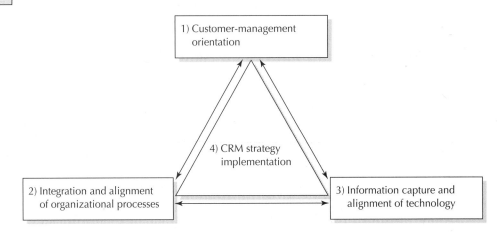

A Customer-Management Orientation

Customer-management orientation is defined as the set of organizational values, beliefs, and strategic actions that enable the implementation of customer management principles.

A customer-management orientation is characterized by a top management belief and commitment that the customer is at the center of activity (meaning the focus is not on the product, geography, etc). A successful CRM strategy starts from the top of the organization (see CRM at Work 3.1). This might sound obvious, but the main reason many CRM efforts have failed is due to a lack of commitment from the top management. If the top management does not initiate the appropriate structural design and reward system, the result of CRM efforts could be insignificant, or even negative. Customer-management orientation recognizes that customers are heterogeneous in needs and value to the firm and that a customer orientation reflects a readiness to treat different customers differently. It is also characterized by the recognition that no single function can be equated with CRM, but that all corporate functions have to be implemented, integrated, and aligned to this strategy. Also, a longer-term view of revenues from customers needs to be taken.

The following questions should be asked to find out if a company has a customer-management-oriented strategy:

1. Does the top management subscribe to a customer-centric philosophy, and does it show?
2. Does the entire organization engage in the implementation of this philosophy?
3. Does the company attempt to establish a win-win relationship with the customer?
4. Does the company recognize that customers differ in their needs and in their value to the firm? Is that reflected in its interaction with customers?

Integration and Alignment of Organizational Processes

In the context of strategic CRM, the integration and alignment of organizational processes comprises the organization wide creation and synchronization of processes, systems, and reward systems which enable the implementation of customer management principles.

The notion that CRM affects only activities and processes in sales and customer service often prevails to this day. However, what a customer experiences when interacting with

CRM AT WORK 3.1

CAPITAL ONE—CRM BUSINESS MODEL

To appreciate the key role of the top management in a customer-oriented strategy, consider the example of Capital One in Falls Church, Virginia. Capital One, one of the fastest-growing financial corporations in the United States, was founded in 1988 and had witnessed phenomenal growth. From its IPO in 1994 to 2000, the stock price of Capital One increased by 1,000 percent, and the company grew at an average annual rate of 40 percent, excluding mergers and acquisitions. In 2001, the company handled more than $24.2 billion loans and 36 million customers worldwide, serviced by more than 20,000 employees. How was such phenomenal growth possible?

Richard Fairbanks, CEO, comments that the business model of Capital One is founded on the simple, yet crucial premise that every customer carries a specific and unique credit risk and potential revenue profile, which determines the customer's risk-return profile from the company's point of view. The better the company can understand and assess a customer's specific risk, the better it can manage it. At the same time, the better the company understands individual customers, the more it can tailor its products to their needs. Thus, low risk and high returns for the company, on the one hand, and high satisfaction for the customer, on the other hand, can ideally go hand in hand.

Capital One was successful in not only subscribing to a customer-management–based business model, which recognizes the heterogeneous needs of different customers, but to integrate and align the structure and functioning of the organization with this strategy. This means, for example, that the goal is to use information to acquire the type of customers Capital One can most profitably serve. Or it means that management and employee evaluation is, among other things, tied to customer retention and customer profitability measures. Overall, Capital One is a remarkable example of a company which has thoroughly implanted customer management principles in the minds of its members.

a company's sales or service staff is arguably affected by internal activities such as product development, IT support, and human resource management. In fact, most, if not all departments and functions must be involved in a strategic CRM initiative. The notion that sales, marketing, or IT does CRM is false. Thus, it is not surprising that strategic CRM works best for organizations organized around cross-functional processes rather than functional silos (see CRM at Work 3.2).

Why are processes so important? Processes are a way to firmly incorporate the needs of the customer and the goals of the firm into product and service delivery. The process view forces managers to think more deeply about the purpose of activities and their expected outcomes, not about the names of the activities or their individual, functionally oriented goals. It is therefore important for processes to cut through the internal barriers hampering efforts to build customer relationships effectively.

Integration and alignment of organizational processes is characterized by understanding the value provided to the target customers should be what drives all processes. These outcomes should be used to define and design the organization's processes. Individual processes work in sync with the common goal of attracting and retaining target customers. It has incentive-based schemes which reflect and reinforce the relationship approach and customer-management processes and outcomes. Stated differently, customer-management–compatible incentives drive employee and organizational goals simultaneously. Processes are designed in such a manner to automate a feedback. Learning from customer management outcomes helps improve functioning and refinement of the process.

CRM AT WORK 3.2

CAPITAL ONE—INTERFUNCTIONAL MANAGEMENT

Capital One entered the U.K market in 1996 and emerged as a major issuer of credit cards in this market. It is a good example of a company with a strong alignment of organizational process and customer-focused strategy. It is exactly this alignment of its customer-focused organizational processes that forms the backbone of its CRM success. Having built the company around CRM, Capital One has close cooperation between back-office and front-office department and activities, both of which are oriented toward customer service. Back-end activities such as account management, strategy, and product testing—which the customer never sees!—contribute to the performance of front-end activities and incorporate, in turn, the front-end agents' feedback.

Take, for example, the cooperation between front-end service operations and the marketing and analysis department (M&A), which is responsible for new product development. Operations cooperate closely with M&A in the new product introduction process, where M&A designs the new products, develops marketing material, and follows up on customers' responses, while operations collects the feedback from customers and makes improvement suggestions. Information from operations is used to improve the Net Present Value (NPV) models which serve as decision-making aids and make these models more sophisticated. M&A work closely with operations to see how products are working—for example, by listening to comments on online application and by identifying which questions in the application are not understood as intended.

Much of the information on customers used to craft strategy is obtained from the front-end people. There is a partnership between operations and M&A to review the risk perspective of today as well as the strategy for tomorrow. Furthermore, numerous permanent or ad hoc cross-functional teams exist. For example, a credit policy team, composed of members from operations and M&A, defines the credit policy for a new product.

The following questions help assess the extent of integration and alignment of a company's organizational processes.

1. Does the company have a clear understanding of the desired value of the target customers? Do its processes produce this value?

2. Are its various processes in the value chain synchronized to maximize value to the customer?

3. Are the processes configured such that the learning from outcomes is applied to make process improvements?

Information Capture and Alignment of Technology

In the context of strategic CRM, the capture of information and alignment of technology comprises all the necessary technology and processes to collect, store, and process relevant and timely customer information, which enables the implementation of customer management principles (see CRM at Work 3.3).

Information technology has made processes more efficient, transformed processes and services, and has enabled entirely new processes, especially in terms of online activities.

Information capture and alignment of technology is characterized by the capability of leveraging data into actionable information (sounds generic but is very hard to properly execute). Firms able to generate intelligence and act on it will derive competitive advantage. The recognition that technology is built around strategy, processes, and people, not the other way around, is very important. Information capture and alignment of technology can be used to make customer management processes not only more efficient, but also more effective, and to create entirely new processes and channels based on online and wireless applications.

CRM AT WORK 3.3

CUSTOMER PROFILING AT A GERMAN TELEPHONE COMPANY

At a German phone company, the following question was raised:

> How do we leverage the enormous amount of data we collect to provide a unique and valuable customer experience?

The answer was a combination of predictive behavior analysis and proactive proposal generation. This operator uses the combination of call detail data and demographic data to score each customer along key dimensions of their relationship. Profitability and behavior are cataloged to create a unique customer profile. These profiles become the basis for proactively tailored, one-to-one marketing campaigns, delivered directly to their handset. As a result, this operator has been able to reduce customer turnover significantly and increase the average profitability of mobile customers.

The following three questions help assess where a company stands with respect to information capture and alignment of technology:

1. Does your organization harness the enabling capabilities of IT systems in terms of customer management?
2. How timely and relevant is the available customer information?
3. Are you able to leverage data about customers into information that can be acted on?

CRM Implementation

The implementation of CRM pertains to the processes and activities required for a successful CRM strategy. These processes and activities are captured in the *CRM Implementation Matrix*. This implementation matrix spans the scope of potential activities and is structured along two key dimensions:[1]

1. A *customer dimension*, i.e., the influence of the changing phases of a customer-firm relationship (customer acquisition, growth, retention, and exit phase)
2. A *management dimension*, i.e., the activities and processes that constitute analytical CRM (to obtain a good understanding of customer needs, behaviors, and expectations) and operational CRM (to meet the functional and technical requirements).

The implementation matrix allows the mapping of a set of managerial activities and processes onto the various phases of a customer–firm relationship. Each cell in the matrix corresponds to a specific implementation activity or process.

CRM Implementation Matrix: Specific CRM Activities and Processes (in Each Cell)

		Customer Dimension		
		Acquisition Stage	*Growth and Retention Stage*	*Decline and Exit Stage*
Management Dimension	*Analytical CRM*			
	Operational CRM			

Marketing-driven CRM implementation is characterized by the following:

- Activities and processes that constitute analytical CRM and operational CRM. These could include, for example, customer data collection, building satisfaction and loyalty metrics, customer-needs analysis, relationship economics, and segmentation.

- Activities and processes that constitute operational CRM. These could include, for example, value proposition management, campaign management, channel management, referral management, and loyalty management.

- A firm's ability to understand the value of the customer to the firm and the variety of needs of different customers (refer to CRM at work 3.4).

- An acquisition and retention process which continuously aligns the offering with customer needs and values.

- An ability to continuously improve the company's offerings by learning about its customers.

The following three questions help assess where a company stands with respect to CRM implementation:

1. Do you have systematic testing in place to rationalize product development and marketing spending?

2. Do processes continually align customer needs and customer value with the offer proposition?

3. Does your CRM system provide feedback and improve upon the learning from past interactions?

CRM AT WORK 3.4

CAPITAL ONE—TESTING NEW PRODUCTS

Capital One employs a unique process for constantly improving the company's offerings by learning about its customers. In the credit card business, individual customer risk is the key determinant of profits. In order to adjust its product offering to the customer's risk, it uses an approach dubbed *poking the bear*. Poking a bear will make it move, just as incentives will make customers react and reveal their characteristics and preferences. Many tests administered by the company seek to determine what type of customer behavior can be associated with a certain level of credit risk. For example, offering a higher credit line might make customers with a higher default risk respond more favorably (since they need the money), thereby revealing their higher risk. This method therefore provides a way to learn which customer characteristics might be a predictor of their risk profile.

In practical terms, hypotheses on customer characteristics are developed and used to run experiments to test which characteristics best correlate with utilization and risk profiles. For example, mailings with different texts, different designs, and different credit conditions are sent out to a limited group of customers. Their response rates are carefully monitored, as is their behavior during the first months of using the card. Capital One can then use this data to determine the value of each mailing sent out.

Depending on the test type, results may be available after just a few weeks of solicitation or may take as long as several years. As soon as the test results are clear, the viability of new products is assessed and the potentially successful ones are rolled out. As product development is based on customer data and feedback, final products are truly mass customized. Test results are integrated into the databases and can be used to again initiate the process of idea development and product design. This strategy has led to an innovative product portfolio of more than 600 credit card products, all of which are very well aligned with diverse customer needs.

All four components taken together in an integrative form constitute the complete CRM strategy. They interact and reinforce each other. Each component plays an essential role—with none being sufficient in and of itself. In order to be competitively ahead, the firm should be at least on par with competition across all components, with positive interaction between these components. In fact, the effects of these positive interactions make CRM champions truly excel.

3.3 DEVELOPING A CRM STRATEGY

3.3.1 THE STEPS IN DEVELOPING A CRM STRATEGY

Developing a CRM strategy consists of four steps:

1. Gain enterprisewide commitment.
2. Build a CRM project team.
3. Analyze business requirements.
4. Define the CRM strategy.

Step One: Gain Enterprise wide Commitment

As we have discussed in Chapter 1, strategic CRM involves multiple areas within a company. Therefore, it is important to get support from all departments involved (e.g., sales, marketing, finance, manufacturing, distribution, etc.) and utilize their valuable input when developing the company's CRM strategy. The involvement of these departments will promote both cooperation and the vital acceptance of the new system by all segments of the company.

Generally, enterprise wide commitment includes these attributes:

- Top-down management commitment
- Bottom-up buy-in from system users
- Dedicated full-time project team
- Budget allocation for the total solution

To get support from all the departments concerned, the CRM strategy developers should keep the departments informed of every progress in the development and implementation and emphasize the positive end results of the CRM strategy.

Step Two: Build a CRM Project Team

Once the enterprise wide commitment has been secured from all the departments, the next step in the development of a CRM strategy should be selecting the CRM project team whose members will take the responsibility of making key decisions and recommendations and communicating the details and benefits of the CRM strategy to the entire company.

The most effective CRM project team should contain active representatives from the following work groups to ensure the groups' specific desires will be addressed by the CRM strategy:

- Management
- Information services/technical personnel
- Sales, marketing, and service groups

- Financial staff
- External CRM expert

Management Management should provide leadership, motivation, and *supervision* at every step of the CRM strategy development, especially when the development and implementation of a CRM strategy involves significant change to business processes, organizational structures, or roles and responsibilities. Managers typically evaluate a CRM strategy based on basic criteria.

- Will the CRM strategy provide information required to make key decisions?
- Will the CRM strategy significantly impact and improve existing processes?
- Will it significantly reduce costs?
- Can the ROI justify the investment?

Information Services/Technical Personnel The development of a CRM strategy must be based on a comprehensive analysis of the company's information. Information services should be deeply involved. The technical group must also be actively involved because it can provide a valuable input with respect to what CRM processes can be automated. Furthermore, they should ensure the CRM system is compatible with existing software applications.

Sales, Marketing, and Services Groups Sales, marketing, and services groups are among the final users of the CRM system, after the CRM strategy is developed and implemented. A CRM strategy is successful only if the users are satisfied and comfortable with the final CRM system. Involving sales and marketing groups in the development of the CRM strategy will help in the evaluation of the potential CRM system's usability, based on three criteria:

1. *Effectiveness.* Users have to be able to complete the tasks they wish to perform. Having an effective system is paramount because it determines the quality of the outcome.
2. *Efficiency.* Efficiency measures the required input for completing any given task. In view of the large number of users of a final CRM system, minor improvements in efficiency can also have a significant effect on the overall productivity of the company.
3. *Satisfaction.* If the final CRM system is not user friendly, there is a possibility that it will not be fully used by the users. Consequently, the benefits of the investment in the CRM strategy will not be justified. This problem is particularly prevalent in the CRM market, where many CRM systems have failed because of the user's resistance to adopting new practices.

Financial Staff A CRM strategy must also be evaluated from the financial point of view. Financial members of the CRM project team will provide critical analysis of the proposed CRM strategy with respect to (1) assessment of increased sales productivity, (2) evaluation of operating costs, and (3) estimated cost of system expansion and ROI projections.

External CRM Expert In many cases, external CRM experts (business consultants or CRM system vendors) will be very helpful for the development of a CRM strategy, if the company does not have sufficient CRM expertise, experience, or technology. A consultant's experience can provide a valuable source of objective information and feedback. He can help analyze the company's real business needs, assist with the formation of the CRM project team, and work with the team to review, amend, and approve the functional specifications of a CRM system. Selection of this external expert and the decision as to when and how to integrate this source in the internal CRM team may be a critical element in the success or failure of the CRM project.

In addition to these work groups, the CRM project team may also contain members from other internal or external parties (e.g., personnel who are responsible for managing relationships with suppliers, strategic partners, and investors), if necessary, to ensure the relationships with all the important related parties will be addressed by the CRM strategy.

Step Three: Analyze Business Requirements

An effective CRM strategy must be developed based on the business requirements of a company. An analysis of business requirements—where the objective is to gather information on a companywide scope—assesses the current business state and identifies problem areas. This process is an absolutely critical factor in developing a good CRM strategy. In this step, a series of sessions and surveys should be held to canvass top sales, marketing, and customer service managers to gather their expectations of a CRM strategy, and a consensus should be formed as the final result. Companywide goals should be defined and objectives established for each department and work group. Special care should be taken to acknowledge and evaluate all ideas so all participants feel they are a part of this important process. Ideas which seem unnecessary or unrealistic may be eliminated at a later stage of the CRM strategy development.

At this juncture, information on specific problem areas must be gathered uniformly throughout the company, identifying particular goals and defining objectives must be done. After gathering information, the company should be able to take the following ten steps:

1. Identify the services and products being supported.
2. Map current workflows, interfaces, and inter-dependencies.
3. Review existing technologies, features, and capabilities.
4. Discuss the vision for the business and the operational plan.
5. Define business requirements.
6. Develop enhanced business workflows and processes.
7. Identify gaps in technology functionality.
8. Map functionality to business processes.
9. Develop a new technology and functionality framework.
10. Develop a conceptual design and prototype plan.

The following are some sample CRM survey questions designed to gather crucial information from different departments for developing a CRM strategy:

- What functions do you perform?
- What types of data do you use?
- How do you interact with customers?
- What data can be made available to you to help you better understand customers?
- How can you improve your communication with customers and management?
- How can you reduce administrative and scheduling requirements which detract from time for building relationships?
- How involved are you in outreach activities such as telemarketing and direct mail?

- What are your reporting needs and requirements?
- How are you involved in lead tracking, lead follow-up, data transfer, and other daily actions, and how can they be improved?

When the survey is performed, input from the end-users of the CRM system, such as the sales force, customer service representatives, marketing personnel, order fulfillment and account management staff, and so on—those who actually deal with customers on a daily basis—must be gathered. These people know what changes are needed to develop and improve customer relationships. Based on the result of an analysis of business needs, the functions which need to be automated will be identified, and the basis for determining which technological features are required for the CRM system will be provided.

Step Four: Define the CRM Strategy

Once the business needs analysis is completed (which means sufficient information has been gathered for the CRM strategy development), it is time to define the CRM strategy that can be implemented in the future.

A good CRM strategy should address the following five areas, although they are not necessarily treated as five separate areas in the subsequent implementation.

A Defined CRM Strategy → *addresses*
- Value proposition
- Business case
- Customer strategy
- Enterprise transformation plan
- Other stakeholders

The Value Proposition The goal of a CRM strategy is to retain strategically important customers, and the objective of customer retention is to develop, communicate, and deliver value propositions which meet or exceed customer expectations.

The value proposition is the multifaceted package of product, service, process, price, communication, and interaction, which customers experience in their relationships with a company. It is the soul of the company's business because it differentiates the company from others. If the value proposition is not affected by an investment in CRM, then the company is either as customer-centric as it needs to be or lacks a basic understanding of what its customers value. The value proposition must address the following three areas:

1. What the customers value
2. What the company says it offers the customers
3. What the company actually offers the customers

The company should strive to offer what the customers value. However, if all three elements of value proposition are not aligned, the company is not likely to become customer-centric because the company is not delivering what the customers value.

Business Case The business case for CRM must be addressed because it determines whether the company will meet its specific and measurable expectations from the investment. An effective business case should directly link the delivery of customer value with the creation of shareholder value, show good ROI, and take into account these three areas:

1. *The planned increase in the economic value of the customers over the duration of their connection with the company.* Obviously, the lifetime value, the risk

involved in unlocking that value, and the growth potential by customer segment should be considered.

2. *Reference and referral effects.* Reference and referral effects must be taken into account because the above calculations alone will hardly be sufficient to justify ROI. If the company is investing more in satisfying the needs of the customers in a better manner, there should be a significant impact on increased customer acquisition through referral. So, a value must be placed on new customers acquired as a result of the investment.

3. *The impact of learning and innovation.* The enhanced learning and innovation resulting from CRM add more value by reducing the cost incurred by the company through higher marketing effectiveness and through improved products and services delivered to customers.

Customer Strategy   A customer strategy defines how the company will build and manage a portfolio of customers. A portfolio is likely to consist of customer segments differentiated by actual or perceived characteristics of the customers within each segment. An effective customer strategy will cover at least these four areas:

1. *Customer understanding.* To develop, communicate, and deliver a customer-satisfactory value proposition, a company has to understand its customers' expectations. There are six distinct levels of customer expectations—*delight, excellent, should, will, minimally tolerable, and intolerable.* These levels form a hierarchy from the highest to the lowest. *Will* expectations are those the customers anticipate based on previous experience. *Should* expectations are based on promises made or inferred by the company. *Delight* is not always desirable from a company's perspective (it is costly and shifts customer expectations considerably). Customers benchmark their expectations against past experience and best-in-class standards. In most cases, even the best companies habitually fail to meet customers' *excellent* expectations. Therefore, meeting their expectations becomes the realistic goal of most companies' CRM strategies. To understand customers' expectations, a company should have effective customer segmentation and try to obtain as much customer data as possible regarding their needs of products and services (both active and passive needs), and then extract information from the data by using specific analytical tools.

2. *Customer competitive context.* The company should be aware of how its competitors are servicing their customers and how it should retain and increase its share of customers in the competitive marketplace.

3. *Customer affiliation.* Customer affiliation is critical because it is a primary factor affecting a company's ability to both retain and extract greater value from the customer through cross-sell and up-sell. Comparative assessment of the strength of customer affiliation will affect strategies for customer retention.

4. *Customer management competencies.* The company must have a defined standard process about who should and how to manage customers. To keep the customer management competency, the company also needs to benchmark its customer management with that of the competitors and improve it continuously. Apparently, the best way to meet customers' expectation is to provide them with customized offers instead of generic ones. The customized offers should include not only customized products but also customized services, processes, distributions, communication, and even prices.

Enterprise Transformation Plan   The transformation required by a CRM strategy must cover these six areas:

1. *Business process.* All primary business processes should be assessed from the perspective of the customer strategy to determine whether the distinct needs of the customer are met and how this can be done.

2. *Organization.* Most customer strategies will result in organizational changes, which include cultural changes.

3. *Location and facilities.* Since particular locations customers visit will have a profound impact on their perception of the company, the physical assets of the company will also need to be adjusted based on a customer-centric strategy.

4. *Data flows.* CRM strategy should also lay out a data strategy, which requires collecting more data, creating and deriving additional data from this data, and distributing the data to different data users (both staff and customers).

5. *Application architecture.* To implement a CRM strategy, the application architecture should be changed accordingly to develop the new application software—or at least to integrate the existing software in new ways.

6. *Technology infrastructure.* A CRM strategy definitely requires a change of technology infrastructure, including new hardware, new operating software, and operations personnel.

A change strategy that manages the change process in well-paced steps can relieve much pain. It needs to ensure there is buy-in from employees. They need to be prepared for the new paradigm through adequate and effective training.

Relationship Management of Other Stakeholders   As already pointed out, strategic CRM is a comprehensive practice involving all facets of an organization, as shown in Figure 3-3.

Stakeholders of a company include *management, customers, suppliers, employees,* and *partners.* In addition, *owners/investors* are important stakeholders. Management is the initiator of CRM, and it is management's responsibility to ensure that, when developing a comprehensive CRM strategy, the relationships with all the stakeholders of the company should be effectively managed. The key point is that the CRM strategy must manage and coordinate all stakeholders to ensure that preferred value propositions are created, communicated, and delivered to the selected customers (see Figure 3-4).

It is worth mentioning that there are exceptions where the customer may not be the most important constituency. For example, in industries where customers derive satisfaction mostly by interacting with employees, such as in the airline and hotel industry, the most important constituency may be the internal customer—the employee. For a company just entering a new market, the most important constituency may be distribution partners, because building a reliable distribution network is the company's initial focus.

Despite these exceptions, any company that fails to deliver customer-satisfactory value proposition to its external customers will definitely fail, because relationships with all four constituencies generate cost, and only the relationship with external customers can generate revenues.

Suppliers   Suppliers are all those who contribute to a company's value chain, including suppliers of raw material, components, technologies, money (loaners and creditors), people (recruitment agencies), and knowledge (consultants).

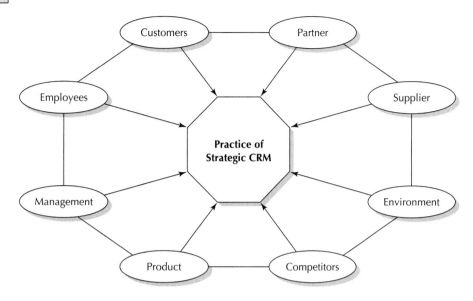

Customer
- Customers are the major focus of the CRM Strategy.

Employees
- Employees are involved in the execution of the CRM strategy.

Management
- Strategic CRM is a top-down approach.
- CRM will be successful only if management is committed to the CRM strategy.

Products
- A product is the link between the organization and the customer.
- Products are goods/services provided by the company.
- Customers often evaluate the company based on the value of the goods/services provided.

Competitors
- Competitors play a major role in a firm's CRM strategy.
- A firm is always compared to the other competitors in the market.
- The key is to always provide better value than the competitors.
- Competitors help the firm to benchmark the strategy and definition of success.

Environment
- The external factors always play a critical role in devising any strategy.
- We do not have any control over the external factors.
- Before devising the CRM strategy, a firm has to perform its own SWOT analysis (strength-weakness-opportunity-threats), and be ready to exploit the opportunities and face the threats based on its own strengths and weaknesses.

Suppliers
- Often, the quality of the product depends to a large degree on the suppliers.

Partners
- Partners can be the sister concerns, distributors, consultants, and so on.
- Every partner, in one way or another, is connected with the products and/or customers.
- Thus, partners also play a critical role in CRM.

Like customer management, supply chain management is shifting toward a more relationship-oriented operation. Traditionally, companies have focused on negotiating for low prices, and they played many suppliers against each other. Driven by the development of total quality management, companies now have a tendency to build strategic, long-term, and more interactive relationships with fewer suppliers. This new relationship with suppliers has the following important benefits:

FIGURE **3-4** **KEY STAKEHOLDERS OF STRATEGIC CRM**

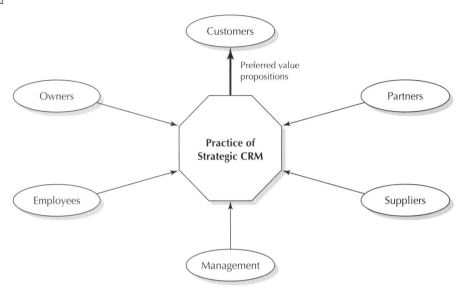

First, improved communication, quicker problem resolution, and closer cooperation enable the suppliers to be more responsive to the purchasing companies' special needs, which are often derived from the customers' expectations.

Second, purchase costs are reduced in two ways:

1. The cost incurred by searching for 'cheaper' suppliers is eliminated.
2. The cost per transaction decreases because of the aligned information management system and simplified transaction process with strategic and long-term suppliers.

Third, the long-term relationship and joint investment drive both parties to cooperate more in sharing information and developing new products, so that both can be more innovative in producing value for customers.

Owners/Investors   A successful CRM strategy should create value not only for customers but also for the company's owners/investors. If the value proposition offered to customers cannot ultimately reap benefits for the investors, the CRM strategy will lose its support from them. From this point of view, creating more value to customers goes hand-in-hand with the owners' benefits. However, conflicts do occur. A CRM strategy focused on delivering higher value to the owners in the long term sometimes requires sacrificing short-term benefits. This strategy may not please those owners who seek short-term benefits from their investments. Unfortunately, the reality in many large companies is that the carrousel of CEO replacement is accelerating. From 1997 to 2000, 65 percent of Fortune 500 companies replaced their CEO.[2]

Therefore, to develop a successful CRM strategy, a company needs more owners with a long-term orientation. For most public companies, where short-term profit-seeking is common among the investors, there are four principal ways of increasing long-term-oriented investors: (1) educate current investors, (2) shift the investor mix toward institutions that avoid investment churn, (3) attract the right kind of core owner, and (4) take the company into private ownership.

When shifting the investor mix toward low-churn institutions, the target should be an institution or individual who will acquire a controlling interest in the company. Investors who focus only on the long-term returns would free the companies from the counterproductive pressures of short-term returns. This type of investor is more likely to become an enthusiastic CRM strategy advocate.

Although going private is also an option, it should be noted that there is considerable risk in doing so. Share buy-backs from the public, whether leveraged or not, may bring the company into considerable debt, which may even intensify the company's financial pressure and motivate the company to seek a short-term profit.

Employees An employee's behavior can either enhance or damage value for the selected customers. It is believed that only those employees who are satisfied at work can deliver excellent service. In other words, employee satisfaction is likely to drive customer satisfaction, especially for businesses in the service industry. Therefore, in those situations, a company's CRM strategy must effectively address employee satisfaction in order to increase customer satisfaction.

An effective way of improving employee satisfaction is the process of internal marketing (IM). IM is the philosophy of treating employees as if they were customers. The practice of creating jobs and the ideal work environment will promote job satisfaction and positive behaviors. Employees should be viewed as part-time marketers who can create value for customers when the customer, employee, process, and system converge. Internal marketing may involve a number of activities and processes at both strategic and tactical levels, including improving management style, improving recruitment practices, integrating all employees into the planning cycle, refocusing training on interactive and service skills, opening communication lines, and empowering front-line staff.

Partners Partnerships, strategic alliances, and joint ventures enable partnership participants to share technological expertise and customer data with each other, develop new products more rapidly, and share costs. As a result, the participants will have lower costs, accelerated learning, expansion of their customer base, reduction of risk for new product development, and enhanced customer satisfaction, by delivering additional value to customers.

As part of the CRM strategy, the company must have a partnership strategy to identify the strategic area where partnership is necessary, determine the partner profile, search for appropriate partners, enter a strategic alliance agreement with the partner, and manage ongoing partnership-relationship.

3.4 CASE STUDY: CRM IMPLEMENTATION AT IBM[3]

IBM is the world's largest information technology company, with revenues in 2003 of $89.14 billion. Its portfolio of capabilities ranges from services including business transformation consulting to software, hardware, fundamental research, financing, and the component technologies used to build larger systems.

In 1990s, the landscape of the IT industry changed significantly. A narrow set of incumbents, particularly IBM, Hewlett Packard, and Compaq, faced fierce competition from domestic and foreign invaders, combined with highly exchangeable, hard-to-differentiate products. This led to the creation of an environment with tight margins and shrinking market share. In order to survive, companies had to minimize inefficiencies in their operations and develop an ability to deliver the highest-quality customer service. To increase customer satisfaction and loyalty—and to reduce the cost of serving customers—IT companies had to implement CRM programs, which allowed them to create more transparency between customers and partners.

Part of the implementation of the CRM program was to streamline all client offerings and strengthen the brand image across all lines of business. The main target was to offer full-scale solutions for the client, instead of multiple products. This meant going from sale of boxes to real solutions for the client. The CRM implementation started with the need to manage the increasing complexity of today's Web-based, multichannel business environment. Most companies in the same market were faced with frustration, while trying to combine consistent, high quality customer experience with improving cost structures. For IBM, CRM was an opportunity to streamline and integrate their customer facing operations, primarily represented by sales, marketing, and customer service. In 2004, IBM implemented the world's largest CRM application with 60,000 users linked with Siebel. In 2005, it is expected that more than 80,000 employees, thousands of business partners, and ultimately millions of IBM customers will use the system.

3.4.1 CRM IMPLEMENTATION PROCESS OBJECTIVES

The company's overall goal in its CRM implementation initiative was to ensure each and every customer interaction is handled with the same degree of excellence using the same tools and data across all IBM geographies and sales channels. This will improve customer satisfaction, and encourage collaboration among its employees and business units. Moreover, the CRM implementation will enable the company to reduce the internally supported IT systems from about 800 in 1997 to less than 200 by 2006 through rigorous integration.

Through the implementation of CRM, IBM sought to create a disciplined framework that enables its organization to do the following:

- Share information and collaborate easily internally and across the entire value chain.
- Focus on core capabilities while shedding less profitable or nonstrategic business activities.
- Build a fully integrated IT infrastructure to support the business vision and reduce the total cost of operations.

3.4.2 CRM IMPLEMENTATION PROCESS STAGES

IBM developed a six-step process for CRM implementations:

1. *Establish a common CRM vision and strategy across the enterprise.* This strategy should include the following key objectives: decreasing operating costs, driving incremental revenue, creating market advantage, and reducing risk. At this stage, it is crucial to obtain senior management support and ensure necessary trade-offs will be possible to achieve enterprisewide efficiency. One of the key factors at this stage is also to foresee how these stated values will be implemented top-down within the organization. This can be achieved through carefully adjusted incentive systems linked to the balanced scorecard measures.

2. *Identify the required capabilities to execute the vision.* Here, the company needs to assess the current situation within the major blocks: organization (structure and corporate culture), business processes, and IT; then the company needs to identify the gaps in the desired state.

3. *Develop a roadmap of prioritized initiatives.* This stage foresees the detailed design of the to-be architecture, together with the master plan on how to close the gaps. Specific initiatives would be prioritized based on their impact, constraints, risks, and dependencies, with the goal of creating customer value at the end.

4. *Manage the end-to-end change process.* This stage requires skillful change management implementation. The program must foresee the end-user support,

across all phases of implementation. User involvement and training are crucial at this stage.

5. *Implement in phases, with a broad initial deployment of each CRM application.* A phased approach will decrease the time for deployment, as well as decrease resistance and frustration within the organization. It will also allow for plan and scope revisions down the road.

6. *Adopt a comprehensive, end-to end deployment methodology.* This framework will ensure coordination of different project teams toward the common goal.

3.4.3 CRM IMPLEMENTATION

Initial Stages—Opportunity Management (1993–2000)

The CRM initiative at IBM started with the development of an in-house application. The initial feature on this early stage, implemented before 1995, was the opportunity management piece of the CRM implementation. Opportunity management is primarily designed for use by the sales organization in the customer acquisition phase of a sales cycle. IBM selected this area as the starting point in the implementation, since the company was looking for the biggest possible initial return on the investment, as well as for the quickest way to prove the positive impacts of the initiative to senior management. This initiative had cross-organizational effect, and touched a large group of people in the organization. Since there was no application ready on the market for this purpose, the company developed the *Virtual Machine,* which is a host-driven IBM application.

This initiative was first designed to work for the customer acquisition process within a particular geography. This initial phase was then followed by system implementation, rolled out across all offices. The customer acquisition processes were reengineered to be consistent across all the products and geographies. Moreover, the opportunity management program included additional supporting processes for customer acquisition, which involved tools to help create solution design and delivery plans. In addition to these tools, the solution could be tested, checkpoints could be identified, and quality assurance could be performed across all the involved individual products and services through the application. A team was created to pursue each opportunity. The system allowed identification of opportunities, as well as tracking methods and storing information on winning conditions. If a particular opportunity could not be pursued, information about the customer requirements or needs that could not be fulfilled was provided.

The system allowed storage of certain pieces of data, such as pricing, inventory, and customer master record (i.e., name of the company, address, key contacts, client financing options like leasing etc.). The marketing department provided this data.

Customer segmentation in the system was performed based on two criteria. The first criteria involved two levels. In the first level, all customers were put into two major segments according to the size of the company: large and small/mid-market. In the second level, larger companies were segmented by industry. The second criteria allowed segmentation based on customers' needs and their geography.

The collected information was used to drive marketing campaigns. Opportunity teams tracked customer behavior and past revenues from the client, as well as identified growth rate for that business. The prospective clients were added to marketing campaigns or forwarded for telesales contact. Each client was assigned with a code linked to planned revenues.

The implementation of these processes and systems continued until 2000.

Motivation of Employees (1993–2000)

As indicated earlier, a CRM implementation strategy can be successfully achieved only with the full support, participation, and commitment of employees to the program. As such, there were substantial efforts to streamline organization according to the lines of business. Selected employees were identified as *change champions* to drive others through the change process. Even though there was no direct link in the incentive program with the CRM initiative, people most adept at adapting to new requirements got appreciation. An example of such a rewarding mechanism would be employees' receiving better laptops as a result of their significant contributions to the CRM implementation.

Encouragement was provided to the IBM CRM project members each time a module was implemented successfully. Employees were enrolled in required training programs, which typically lasted for two to three days, and they received further support, as needed, during the implementations. All these measures prepared the necessary organizational background and made it possible to start, in 2000, the full-scale CRM implementation across the entire IBM organization.

Siebel Implementation (2000–Today)

Siebel Systems, which is "the world's leading provider of customer relationship management (CRM) solutions and a leading provider of applications for business intelligence and standards-based integration,"[4] was chosen as the base for the CRM implementation at IBM. Through its extensive partnership with Siebel Systems, IBM has been implementing various modules of Siebel internally. The company then uses its extensive technical and business process expertise in implementing the software for executions at its customers.

The modules of Siebel CRM software that IBM has and will implement are Sales, Call Center, Marketing, Field Service, Service, e-Channel, e-Marketing, e-Service, and General e-Business.[5] Figure 3-5 illustrates several steps of the Siebel project at IBM, in terms of the scope of each of the different phases within the implementation.

As illustrated in Figure 3-5, Siebel was first implemented through the launching of *"ibm.com Call Center,"* which was a channel for contacting all the business partners, particularly the dealers and the solution vendors. The initial rollout of Siebel's call center package started with twenty six ibm.com call centers. As of October 2003, the system has been deployed in forty seven ibm.com call centers in thirty two countries.

This system enables information flow, mainly from IBM to the dealers. When a particular opportunity to acquire a new customer or to initiate a new sales cycle appears, IBM informs dealers about this identified opportunity. After this notification, dealers are

| **FIGURE** | **3-5** | **THE SCOPE AND TIMING OF SIEBEL IMPLEMENTATION AT IBM** |

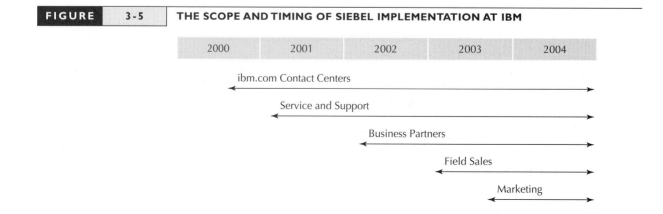

expected to respond within forty eight hours, specifying whether they would like to pursue this opportunity. If the opportunity is rejected, the rejection message returns to IBM. IBM then seeks other dealers suitable and interested in going after this opportunity.

Even though the dealers are the main source and owners of customer data, they do not act as a reliable source of customer information to IBM. Due to confidentiality agreements with their multiple customers, their customer records remain confidential. Although the dealers fill out some customer data, this information is not reliable. Since both IBM and the dealers are aware of the benefits they will receive through more seamlessly integrated and two-way data flows, both parties joined efforts in marketing campaigns towards the end of 2003.

Call Center implementation included telesales and telemarketing, as well. This sub module of the Call Center initiative is used mainly for managing the simple product campaigns.

In 2001, the implementations for the Service and Support initiative started. Within this functionality, *Service* refers to back-office operations. More specifically, this functionality supports exchanges with other applications like pricing and configuration. *Configuration* refers to the arrangement, customization, and preparation of a customer order based on the variation of product features within this order. Configuration of orders, both for hardware and software solutions, is currently available only for internal and partners' use; the functionality is not available for customer use. However, IBM foresees customer access to this functionality in the future, although it is not clear whether the customers would be sufficiently technically literate to perform configuration on their own. Moreover, the initiative would bring in challenges in terms of performing change management at each of the business customers. The implementation of the *Support* part for the "Service and Support" initiative is under progress.

Please note that the involvement of business partners within the *ibm.com Call Centers* and *Service and Support* were briefly explained. As Figure 3-5 portrays, the inclusion of business partners within these initiatives started in 2002.

IBM is now tackling the field sales initiative within the Siebel implementation. Field sales operations mainly refer to activity management processes, which enable efficient task allocation to sales personnel. This assignment is based on a specific sales opportunity available, customer sales history data and requirements, the order specifications, and so on.

In 2004, IBM implemented the marketing block, which is an effective tool to facilitate IBM's interactions with its business partners, and enhanced the existing "one-way" communication processes to bidirectional communication.

These initiatives have contributed to the fact that IBM increasingly responds to customer requests in real-time (or *On-Demand,* as IBM calls it). The company promises to provide products, services, and information for its customers as they demand individual modules or components. This system also allows customization for particular customer orders and requests. These On-demand capabilities are really appreciated by customers in the rapidly changing high-tech area. For example, on-demand services are related to insourcing capabilities, such as providing customers the access to CRM applications, without having to implement the entire solution.

3.4.4 CASE SUMMARY

At a more specific level, the following points illustrate the key strengths of the IBM CRM initiative, which allows the company to generate competitive advantages against its competitors:

- One of the competitive advantages created by the IBM CRM strategy is the *On-Demand Operating Environment*—the ability to provide customized solutions which are available on an immediate and, if desired, piecemeal basis.

- Although some of the competitors have been implementing Siebel solutions, none has full-scale CRM implementation covering as many people and functions as IBM's system.

- Integrated process management through CRM allows instant updates about inventory levels, customer complaints, latest recommendations, and so on. This, in return, enables sales and production strategies to be updated quickly and efficiently.

- The pricing and revenue data are integrated in Siebel. This provides opportunities to IBM in revenue analysis. Each customer gets a code in Siebel, which describes each customer's revenue-generation potential. When IBM seeks to sell a particular hardware or software solution, these codes provide potential customers for sales in the next cycle.

The above competitive advantages allowed IBM to achieve the following benefits:

- Improved sales productivity, effectiveness, and channel integration
- Increased visibility to market dynamics and the elimination of many integrated legacy applications
- Higher customer satisfaction through better responsiveness and ease of doing business
- Improved sales management effectiveness, reflected in tighter management controls and in proactive sales coaching
- Better forecast accuracy and reporting
- Enhanced partnership management
- Putting IBM back to number one, according to a recent survey by *Forbes* magazine, in the IT area
- Decreased time to complete the sales cycle, as well as to serve a customer (These numbers are lower than the competitors, enabling IBM to serve its customers faster.)
- Transformed contract management process to a more efficient and simpler procedure

As of today, IBM estimates its internal CRM implementation has delivered benefits of $2 billion in cost reductions,[6] 22 percent productivity improvement, significant IT cost avoidance, reduced sales staff requirements, as well as improved management reporting.[7]

Key Lessons: Insights from IBM

IBM summarizes the lessons for the implementation of large-scale CRM initiatives via the following points:

- *Genuine top-level support within the organization is essential.* The lack of such support during the initial phases of the implementation caused significant bottlenecks and delays at IBM.

- *To deliver a truly enterprisewide CRM solution, chief information officers must stand firm.* They must have the willingness, as well as the power, to say no to any request for separate CRM solutions which are not fully integrated with other supporting IT systems within the organization.

- *CRM is not just an exercise for IT; without the cooperation of each business unit, an enterprisewide implementation like CRM is not possible.* Data integration plays an essential role.

- *Data are typically in much worse condition that one would think.* To acquire the full benefit of an investment in CRM, data cleansing at the initial stages of an implementation is crucial.

- *Frontline people cannot simply be pulled off their posts and expected to be in training for several weeks at a time.* Business units within the enterprise cannot afford to lose the man-hours. Hence, the CRM training time should be planned well in advance and managed carefully.

- *CRM implementations come with extensive business process reengineering and change management initiatives.* The potential difficulties, bottlenecks, and delays that might result from these initiatives could cause much more severe impacts than initially foreseen. Moreover, for an effective CRM implementation, an organization's structure and philosophy might radically change, such as alterations in customer service values, incentive systems within the company, and critical success factors.

Conclusion

IBM, the leader in implementing CRM solutions both internally within the business units and externally for its customers, provides one of the best examples of how a CRM initiative affects the entire organization. Implementing CRM goes far beyond implementing software. Achieving complete success requires the commitment of the entire organization, from the bottom to the top level. Planning such an initiative brings in a wide range of business process reengineering and change management issues. Designing efficient processes, creating appropriate milestones, engaging the business partners and customers at the right time, and effectively managing data are some of the key points to achieving success in CRM implementations. It is vital that commitment and patience be embedded within CRM initiatives at all organizations.

3.5 SUMMARY

In this chapter, we looked at CRM from a strategic perspective. When CRM is viewed as a company-level philosophy where knowledge about customers has implications for the entire organization, it is termed as *strategic CRM*. The goal of strategic CRM is to shape the interactions between the firm and its customers in a way that facilitates maximizing the lifetime value of the customer to the firm. The four main components of CRM strategy are (1) customer-management orientation, (2) integration and alignment of organizational processes, (3) information capture and alignment of technology, and (4) CRM strategy implementation. Customer-management orientation is the set of organizational values, beliefs, and strategic actions which enable the implementation of customer management principles, and is driven by a top-management belief that the customer is at the center of activity. The integration and alignment of organizational processes consists of creation and synchronization of processes and systems which enable the organization to implement customer-management principles. An understanding of the value provided to the target customers drives these processes. These processes work in line with the goal of attracting and retaining target customers. The processes and activities required for a successful CRM strategy are structured around two key-dimensions in a CRM implementation matrix. Customer dimension captures the influence of the changing phase of a customer-firm relationship, and the management dimension constitutes the analytical CRM and operational CRM.

Developing a CRM strategy consists of (1) gaining enterprise-wide commitment, (2) building CRM project team, (3) analyzing business requirements, and (4) defining the CRM strategy. A defined CRM strategy addresses (a) value proposition, (b) business case, (c) customer strategy, (d) enterprise transformation plan, and (e) other stakeholders. Value proposition is the multifaceted package of product, service, process, price, communication, and interaction that customers experience in their relationship with the company. It differentiates the company from others. Business case for CRM determines whether an investment in CRM meets its expectations by linking the delivery of customer value with the creation of shareholder value, or ROI. It should take into account not only the economic value of customer, but also the increased customer acquisition through referrals and the impact of learning and innovation. Customer strategy is for building and maintaining a portfolio of customers by understanding their expectations, competitor context, and customer affiliation, and providing them with customized offers. CRM strategy calls for a transformation in business process, organization, location and facilities, data flows, application architecture, and technology infrastructure. Finally, strategic CRM is a comprehensive practice which covers all facets of an organization—such as customers, management, products, competitors, environment, employees, suppliers, and investors. In the next chapter, we will discuss how to carry out investment and operational decisions to implement the various elements of a firm's CRM strategy.

The implementation of CRM in an industry is illustrated with the help of the IBM case study. When IBM implemented CRM, the main objective was to offer full-scale solutions for the client, instead of multiple products. The first step in implementing CRM was establishing a common CRM vision and strategy across the enterprise, or the enterprise wide commitment. IBM also developed in-house application for opportunity management, primarily designed for use by the sales organization, in the customer acquisition phase of a sales cycle. This initiative had cross-organizational impact, and touched a large group of people in the organization. Since there was no application ready on the market for this purpose, the firm developed the Virtual Machine, a host-driven IBM application. It also recognized the importance of employee motivation. IBM selected a group of employees identified as *change champions* to drive others through the change process. Encouragement was provided to the IBM CRM project members each time a module was implemented successfully. IBM also organized training programs for employees and extended further support for the employees during the implementations. All these measures prepared the necessary organizational background for successful implementation of CRM.

Once the stage was set for CRM implementation, IBM installed the Siebel CRM modules in a phased manner. It started with *ibm.com Call Center,* a channel for contacting all the business partners, particularly the dealers and the solution vendors. This system enabled a one-way communication process between the dealers and IBM, thus involving the business partners early on in the implementation stage. This was followed by implementation of the Service and Support module, which supported the back-office operations. IBM continued to implement other modules in phases. This project yielded significant results for IBM. The estimated benefits were to the tune of $2 billion in cost reductions, 22 percent productivity improvement, significant IT cost avoidance, reduced sales staff requirements, and improved management reporting.

3.6 EXERCISE QUESTIONS

1. Do you think traditional marketing principles are valid in the age of CRM? What are the fundamental differences between transaction-based marketing approaches and relationship-based marketing approaches?

2. What structural changes must an organization undertake to switch from a product-oriented company to a customer-oriented company? Should companies start investing in such structural changes?

3. Will a heavily operations-oriented company such as Wal-Mart benefit by practicing CRM?

4. Have you heard about stories where a company had difficulties implementing CRM? What was the nature of the problem, and how can it be solved?

5. What are the key steps in implementing CRM?

ENDNOTES

1. Reinartz, Werner, Manfred Krafft, and Wayne Hoyer, "The Customer Relationship Management Process: Its Measurement and Impact on Performance," *Journal of Marketing Research* 41, no. 3 (2004): 293.

2. Anthony Bianco and Louis Lavelle, "The CEO Trap," *BusinessWeek* (December 11, 2000).

3. Based on the research of the INSEAD MBA students Alper Aras, Natalia Boksha, Tatiana Kachalova, and Eyal Katzenstein.

4. http://www.siebel.com, accessed January 13, 2005.

5. *Implementing Siebel e-Business Applications in IBM,* Internal Paper, Copyright © IBM Corporation, 2003.

6. A component of savings comes from gaining efficiencies in the sales process through CRM. These savings are measured through the hours saved resulting from the usage of the CRM system by each sales personnel. These saved hours are multiplied by the cost per hour to employ that sales person, leading to the total savings figure coming from sales efficiency improvements (Source: *Ibid*).

7. "CRM: Transformation for an On-Demand World: The Road to Successful Customer Relationship Management," *IBM CRM Executive Brief,* Copyright © IBM Corporation, 2003.

CHAPTER 4

Implementing the CRM Strategy

Contents

4.1 OVERVIEW

Firms recognize that customers have a large degree of control over the firm–customer relationship. However, it is the firm that must make investments in creating and managing the various points of interactions with a customer. From the customer's standpoint, CRM is about courteous service. Over a period of time, customers develop expectations from their interactions based on information gained from their experience with various touch points such as the salespersons, e-mail and mail messages, telephone, and so on. Every touch point is therefore critical in improving the firm–customer relationship. Touch-point efficiencies are maximized when integrated with the sales, marketing, and service functions of the organization. From the firm's perspective, managing customer expectation and maintaining ongoing relationship with customers has a cost. There are the costs of gathering and analyzing information about customers, providing customer support, and implementing customized strategies for customers. Companies need to balance these costs with the benefits to be profitable. In other words, they have to calculate the long-term return on investment (ROI) from CRM implementation before they invest in the customer interface elements and applications of CRM.

This chapter provides guidelines to identify the costs and benefits involved in implementing CRM. We not only look at the economic costs and benefits but also at the people costs and indirect benefits. A three-step process of arriving at ROI for a strategic CRM implementation is explained. It is easy to overcome challenges and resistance from employees when CRM implementation is broken down into a series of small projects.

4.2   ELEMENTS OF A CRM SYSTEM

Before implementing a CRM system, we need to understand the various elements involved in it. One way to do this is by separating the CRM activities into front- and back-office activities (as done by many practitioners and software vendors). Figure 4-1 depicts the various elements in a composite CRM system.

Customer interface and application components include:

■ *Customer interface/touch points.* Customers interact with the company through a variety of touch points. The CRM system should be able to offer a consistent view of all customers regardless of the touch point being used by the customers. For example, a salesperson should have knowledge of the products that the customer browsed for recently on the Internet, before suggesting an appropriate upgrade in a face-to-face meeting.

■ *CRM applications.* CRM is implemented by a wide set of applications which enable the firm to deliver offers, generate orders, and respond to customer enquiries and feedback. These applications span the sales, marketing, and customer service functions in an organization:

  □ *Sales and sales management function.* Contact and quote management, account management (activities, order entry, proposal generation, etc.), pipeline analysis (forecasting, sales cycle analysis, win/loss analysis, territory alignment and assignment, roll-up, and drill-down reporting) are important sales functions that a CRM system needs to integrate. The sales process must be managed across many domains including other

FIGURE   4-1   CUSTOMER INTERFACE AND APPLICATION COMPONENTS OF CRM

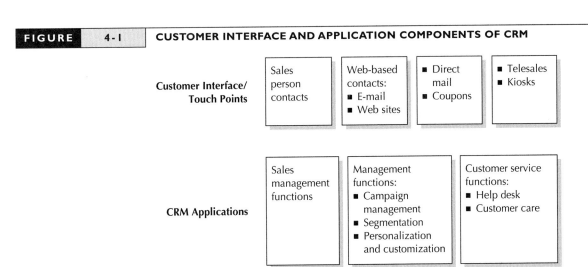

business units. Sales personnel are an essential source of information for the company and must have the tools to both access up-to-date field information and provide this information to various domains of the business. The interaction of the sales force with the prospect, turning the prospect into a customer, and then maintaining a mutually profitable relationship, are key aspects of the business.

☐ *Marketing function.* Multichannel campaign management, opportunity management, Web-based encyclopedia, market segmentation, and lead generations/enhancement/tracking are critical marketing functions that the CRM system should integrate. Today, initial mass-marketing activities are often used for the first contact, and are then followed up by more focused campaigns with specific target audiences in mind. Personalization, where customers' preferences and buying habits are taken into account, is quickly becoming the expected norm of interactions. Content management and one-on-one marketing are now key aspects of conducting business.

☐ *Customer service function.* This includes incident assignment, escalation, field personnel tracking, reporting, problem management, resolution, order management, and warranty/contract management. The customer service function is the key to a company's ability to maintain proactive relations with customers and hence retain satisfied loyal customers. CRM systems can assist in managing the help desk and providing customer care across all types of customer queries, including product concerns, information needs, order requests, and quality field service.

4.3   ROI (Return on Investment) of CRM

Once a firm decides which elements are required for its implementation of a CRM system, it must ask one important question: Is the investment in CRM elements worth it? The practice of developing and implementing a CRM system should always measure the expected monetary benefits to see if the investment is likely to pay off. The estimation of ROI of CRM determines many critical decisions, such as whether a CRM strategy is needed, what CRM strategy should be developed, and how it should be implemented.

The formula for ROI is well known:

Profits/Investment $\times$ 100% = ROI (%)

The formula is simple, but some complicated questions are involved when it is applied in the context of CRM.

- What should be counted as an investment in CRM?
- What should be counted as a return on that investment?
- What is the time period over which ROI should be measured?

4.3.1   WHAT SHOULD BE COUNTED AS AN INVESTMENT IN CRM?

Due to the cross-functional nature of strategic CRM, costs are also incurred in many areas. Generally, the cost level is determined by the following factors:

- How much will consulting for the project cost (business case, strategy, IT engineering, implementation, training)?

- To what degree is business process redesign necessary?
- What new software and hardware must be purchased to accommodate the new system?
- Does the system need to be customized, or will it work out of the box? How much customization is required, and at what cost?
- Can the system be easily configured and maintained by internal information technology (IT) staff, or is continuous external assistance required?
- What is the cost of training the company's staff to use the CRM system?
- What is the timeframe for implementation, and what will happen to the current system processes during that time?
- What are the recurrent costs?

Costs generally fall into three categories: IT costs, people costs, and process costs.

Information Technology (IT) Costs

Information technology costs include investments in IT infrastructure, database development, and software. For the typical CRM project, IT costs usually account for one-fifth to one-third of the total cost. This might remain an accurate prediction for future years too, because the savings associated with the falling costs of hardware and software are offset by the rising cost of hiring IT professionals.

Software can be purchased or licensed. Several software components may be required for a large-scale CRM investment:

- *Sales force automation:* contact management, account management, order processing, proposal generation
- *Sales management automation:* pipeline analysis, territory design, sales reporting
- *Call-center automation:* auto-dialing, scripting, Automated Voice Recognition (AVR), Computer Telephony Integration (CTI)
- *Customer-service automation:* incident analysis and escalation, problem resolution, warranty management
- *Marketing automation:* campaign management, opportunity management, market segmentation, lead generation, reporting event management
- *Operations management:* customization, production control, quality assurance
- *E-commerce functions:* extranets, Electronic Data Interchange (EDI), procurement
- *Knowledge management:* customer service, resolving complaints

The customer database is at the heart of an IT-enabled CRM system. Creating a single database by combining internal data from several channels and divisions, with relevant external data, is a huge challenge faced by many companies, particularly those who have grown through mergers and acquisitions.

People Costs

People costs include recruitment, redeployment, and training costs. The talents required for developing and implementing a CRM system may include statisticians and operations researchers. The analytical side of CRM may require expertise in segmentation analysis, migration modeling, lifetime value estimations, customer acquisition planning, and customer churn analysis. Recruitment of CRM talent in direct marketing, campaign management, and many other areas may also be required. Other employees may need to be reskilled.

Process Costs

Process costs may also be significant. Current working practice and workflow may have to be reengineered. For some companies, the market segmentation process may have to be overhauled to accommodate notions of customer value. The selling process and campaign management process may need reinvention. All these cost time and money.

Typically, these investments will be incurred over a number of years as the CRM strategy is developed and implemented, often as a series of small projects. The investments in CRM could be quite high. Even small-scale implementations in which only a single activity is automated could require a six-figure investment.

4.3.2 WHAT SHOULD BE CONSIDERED TO DETERMINE THE RETURN ON A CRM INVESTMENT?

People usually want to know how much additional profit CRM investments will yield. However, for a complex, long-term, multiphase CRM project, this is an impossible question to answer during the development stage of the CRM strategy. There are three reasons for this:

1. *To compute the gain associated with a CRM initiative requires that all other variables impacting the profit equation are held constant.* Generally, it takes two to five years to develop, implement, and accomplish large-scale CRM systems. During this period, the competitive environment might have changed dramatically, with new competitors emerging, mergers and acquisitions, new products on the market, and customer expectations going up.

2. *Some CRM investments are necessary costs which enable the functionality of CRM.* The development and implementation of every large-scale CRM system consists of a number of small projects: database development, market segmentation, customer portfolio analysis, campaign management, Web site upgrade, customer contact center integration, and so on. Each of these small projects will have cost profiles and time scales. However, not all of them generate revenue streams (e.g., investments in database development and market segmentation typically represent necessary costs without which it would be impossible to run CRM-driven campaigns and events). This definitely increases the complexity of computing financial ROI on CRM investments.

3. *Although measuring the return on CRM investment becomes easier with small-scale projects, without appropriate controls in place, the management cannot be sure that the cause of the change is the CRM investment.* For example, when a single function is automated, it is possible to establish clear performance targets such as the number of proposals written before and after the automation.

Because it is hard to compute concrete CRM profits, companies are also likely to count indirect future returns on CRM investment. Some of these indirect returns reflect CRM's direct impact on costs and revenues, including lower customer acquisition costs, lower costs-to-serve, higher average transaction margin, higher average customer value, and so on. Some other indirect returns reflect neither cost nor revenue, but the drivers of either or both. Among these are improvements in customer satisfaction, customer retention, customers acquired, customer attrition rates, cross-sell rates, up-sell rates, products owned per customer, inventory turns, average number of transactions, share of wallet, customer complaint rates, process costs, rework, employee satisfaction, and employee retention.

Companies in different industries face different CRM problems and emphasize different returns on CRM. For example, the biggest customer problem for companies in the telecom industry is *customer churn rate*, which can be up to 40 percent a year.[1] Therefore, their most valued CRM return should be the retention of the most valuable customers and the opportunities of cross selling to them data and other communication services so as to build a multiproduct bond that is hard to break. In the financial services industry, the companies' major CRM concern could be to reduce transaction costs by shifting customers from branches to the phone or to the Web, and to cross-sell and up-sell to customers based on their past behavior and propensity to buy, thus earning a greater share of customer wallet.

Profits are what remain after costs are subtracted from revenues. As we can see from the previous examples, CRM investments can lead to reduced costs and improved revenue for a company. Thus, the ultimate return on CRM investments is the improved long-term customer profitability. Since this return is long-term and indirect, recognizing it during the stage of developing the CRM strategy is critical, because it provides the decision makers correct judgment of whether a CRM strategy is really worth the cost.

4.3.3 WHAT IS THE TIME FRAME WITHIN WHICH ROI SHOULD BE MEASURED?

For many companies, CRM is a long-term investment which is expected to pay off over periods of up to ten years. Companies will often seek to maximize short-term profits because of market pressures. They can avoid investing in CRM because they are unable to emphasize the long-term benefits of such an investment. As we concluded in the previous chapter, CRM is basically a business strategy rather than a single technique or technology, so companies should be thinking strategically when investing in CRM. Measuring the overall strategic ROI on CRM should involve looking at the entire cycle of developing, implementing, and continuously improving the CRM strategy—a process that is long and complex.

CRM projects are normally composed of smaller CRM projects with clear-cut objectives and timeframes. For some operational or analytical projects with immediate impacts on costs and revenues, the time period of ROI measurement could be a matter of weeks or months after the completion of the projects. However, for those projects where significant assets are created (e.g., development of a customer database), the time period of ROI measurement should be much longer, maybe up to two to three years after the projects are completed.

4.3.4 THE PROCESS OF ARRIVING AT ROI ESTIMATES

As we can see, the ROI estimates vary according to the assumptions made by the firm's management. It is important, therefore, to get a defendable picture of the expected return from a CRM project. How do you ensure the figures are accepted by the business? This is about ownership as well as accuracy. Management must create a shared view of how the returns on a CRM project are to be computed, and this results in a degree of shared belief in the numbers. These estimates are usually arrived at through a three-stage process, as shown in Table 4-1.

Before a consensus can be reached, there are likely to be iterations between stage 1 and stage 2. Estimating ROI for strategic CRM is by no means easy. Yet, if approached objectively, our discussion shows that a satisfactory measure of the ROI is not elusive.

4.4 CRM IMPLEMENTATION

As mentioned earlier, the implementation of a CRM strategy is a process of developing and executing a series of small CRM projects. These projects are all aimed at the business needs

TABLE 4-1	STAGES OF ROI ESTIMATION	
Stage	**Content**	**Questions to Raise**
1. Setting the target	Determine ROI goal of CRM project based on benchmarking, similar projects, external and internal knowledge.	▪ Is the goal sufficient? ▪ Is this goal achievable?
2. Reaching the target	Generate ideas of how to reach target through internal bottom-up participation, external views, consultants, benchmarks, etc.	▪ What factors have to change and by how much to achieve the goal? ▪ Does it work from a technical perspective? ▪ Are the proposed benefits clear/unclear? ▪ Will customers and/or staff accept these measures?
3. Building consensus and commitment	Have executives and line staff agree on proposed ROI goals and ensure commitment on both sides.	▪ Are we collectively prepared to sign them off?

and value propositions identified when the strategy is defined, and they normally fall into three categories:

1. Operational CRM projects that enable the company to meet the technical and functional requirements of the CRM strategy
2. Analytical projects, whose objective is to obtain a good understanding of the customers' needs, expectations, and behaviors
3. Implementation projects that deploy the operational and analytical outputs to improve marketing decision and customer relationships

---

CRM AT WORK 4.1

DELL, SOUTH AFRICA—BENEFITS OF ADOPTING CRM

Dell South Africa's CRM system has allowed Dell to strategically align with customer needs. It also provided Dell with a single integrated view of its customers. Dell had been utilizing a Data Warehouse (called Dell Data Warehouse) in Ireland before realizing the need for a more focused system. By obtaining detailed information pertaining to their customers (like demographics, volume of past transactions, and medium of preference), Dell was not only able to service the customers better, but also affected a positive change in the processes of various other departments. For example, it changed the functioning of the salespeople by taking away the need to maintain customer information in any other format such as spreadsheets and outlook. The Marketing team extracted value by tracking customer activity, utilizing readily available segmentation data and tools aiding the development of marketing campaigns. The new system's focus on the local market resulted in better sales forecasts. There was an overall improvement in Dell's performance in South Africa as a direct consequence of adopting a CRM system tailored to its needs.

SOURCE: Adapted from a case study that appeared in http://www.microsoft.com/southafrica/casestudies/it_expand.mspx.

4.4.1 OPERATIONAL PROJECTS

The objective of these projects is to construct an infrastructure that meets the technical and functional requirements of CRM. Examples of these projects include automation of functions such as a call center or an order-processing system, developing an online transaction Web site, changing the process of data collection and data management, selecting and installing appropriate hardware and software, upgrading or reconfiguring the IT infrastructure, setting up a customer database and/or a data warehouse, and so on. On the surface, most of these projects do not create revenues directly, but, if successfully developed and completed, they provide the company the necessary resources to perform value-added CRM projects.

From a technical perspective, a typical CRM infrastructure should have the components listed in Table 4-2.

In addition to the components listed in Table 4-2, many companies may want to develop a comprehensive data warehouse to store real-time data to facilitate marketing data intelligence analysis. The operational projects should, of course, have been conceived with the objective to maximize profitability, reduce support costs, and increase sales and customer loyalty.

4.4.2 ANALYTICAL PROJECTS

Delivering desirable value propositions to customers requires understanding customers' needs and expectations. Analytical projects are implemented to help the company understand its customers by using data analysis tools that burrow into the company's databases. This area of CRM is also called *data analytics*. Data analytics is the process of combining data-driven marketing and technology to increase the company's knowledge and understanding of customers, products, and transactional data to improve strategic decision making and tactical market activity. Analytical projects draw from the investments in the operational projects by leveraging the resources that the latter has created, and add value by enabling the firm to understand its customers. These projects create the ability for a firm

TABLE　4-2	**COMPONENTS OF CRM INFRASTRUCTURE**
Component	**Description**
1. Information delivery/ online catalogs	Capability to display and list the company's products and services online
2. Customer database	Capability to capture, organize, present, and analyze customer-specific data, in order to identify sales opportunities and address product development and delivery requirements
3. Personalization and content management	■ Utilizing results of data analysis to create an individualized experience for the customers ■ Enhance/modify service delivery vehicles to match the specific needs of customers (based on their user profiles)
4. Sales force automation	The deployment and use of tools and services designed to automate the sales and marketing life cycle
5. Partner channel automation	The deployment and use of tools and services designed to integrate a company's service vehicles with those of its provider and third-party partners
6. Customer services	The deployment and use of technology and business processes designed to successfully support a company's products and services

to establish and manage profitable relationship with its customers. Also, the results of these analyses provide critical information for determining a company's customer strategy and help develop an on-going CRM strategy.

Data analytics projects include two major types of activities: customer data transformation and customer knowledge discovery.

Customer Data Transformation

This involves extracting and transforming raw data from a wide source of internal and external databases, marts, or warehouses, and then pooling the total data value and information into a place where it can be accessed and explored. To perform customer data transformation, the company needs to first build a data warehouse. Data warehousing involves getting all organizational data together under one roof and making it accessible to the people who need it. Although the proportion of companies having implemented a data warehouse application is limited, most of them plan to deploy one as part of their CRM projects. However, even where the data warehouse is up and running, accessing and analyzing the data is not as easy, fast, or as accessible as it should or could be. Unless the data are available in a useful format, in a timely fashion, and enable the train of thought analysis that marketers rely on, the data are of no value at all.

Second, a firm must enhance the data on a customer by integrating information from various sources. If the picture of the customers is incomplete, the company should enhance the data with externally available information. For example, geographic, lifestyle, and psychographic data can help in developing a complete image of a customer. All this information can be pulled together to a single source, and a historical perspective can be developed over time.

Customer Knowledge Discovery

Providing marketers with the tools and processes to discover customer data, converting information into usable customer knowledge, and deploying it to enhance marketing decision making requires two activities—analyzing the data using statistical tools to better understand customers, and predicting the future based on analytical results obtained from existing data.

Successful analytical CRM should cover the following major areas.

Capturing All Relevant Customer Information

An effective customer data analysis must be based on as complete a customer database as possible. Building a complete customer database requires capturing all relevant customer information, and this can be a significant challenge to many companies. However, it is a necessity for accurate and proper analysis that a complete database be constructed.

First, before the CRM strategy is implemented, customer information may have been distributed across the entire company in different formats, and different departments may have different data sources. In order to ensure data integration, which is very important for analytical purposes, all the information should be standardized from both the business and technical point of view.

Second, customers can interact with the company in a number of new ways over time, and this will generate a new range of data sources. Therefore, the analytical solution should also be able to flexibly and consistently integrate all the data across all the channels and touch points at which the company interacts with customers to make sure the customer information is updated in real time and that no important information is left out.

Third, external sources of information should also be incorporated to keep the company aware of the competitive situation.

The following are examples of external sources:

- Competitors' data dealing with the company's customers
- Published survey results to supplement the customer information with details about customer satisfaction and customer preferences
- Data from communities or clubs with a common interest

Finally, the customer-related back office data related to billing and shipment should be evaluated from a financial perspective and should be consolidated into a coherent picture of financial success and customer profitability.

Successful data intelligence solutions integrate customer data and ensure that useful analytical results are delivered.

Customer Demographic Analysis and Customer Behavior Modeling

With customer demographic analysis, the company will be able to know who its customers are: their name, gender, address, age, education, number of people in the household, and so on. By observing and modeling customers' behavior, the company can know how customers have behaved and then predict how they will behave. Therefore, the company should be able to define customer segments and use them as the basis for making differential decisions in marketing, sales, and customer services to different customer segments. For example, by analyzing customers' transaction history, the company can know the customers' recency, frequency, and monetary value of their purchases. Analyzing customer service records can also indicate customers' attitudes and their feedbacks. Based on this information, the company should be able to model a behavior pattern for specific customers and predict whether they will buy again, what they will probably buy, when they will buy, how much they will spend, and what additional services they may need.

Customer Value Assessment

Customer valuation is central to analytical CRM projects. It helps the company focus its limited resources most efficiently on the best and most valuable customer relationships. Subsequent chapters in this book deal extensively with the measurement and analysis of customer value and customer profiling and scoring processes that are based on these measures of customer value.

4.4.3 DEPLOYING OPERATIONAL AND ANALYTICAL OUTPUTS (TO IMPROVE MARKETING DECISIONS AND CUSTOMER RELATIONSHIPS)

Although an operational CRM project can put the CRM architecture into place, and an analytical CRM project can extract helpful information on customers' needs and expectations, no value will be created until this system and the information are utilized to improve the company's marketing decision making and the company's relationships with its customers.

Generally, the goal of these projects is to increase revenue and profit by improving relationships with customers. For example, automation of a call center will service customers more promptly and effectively, and on-line transaction processes will enable customers to transact through self-service. Using the analytical result of customer value assessment and customer profiling, marketing campaigns will target the customers or prospects most likely to respond. Also, customer calls would be directed to the appropriate contact person in the call center depending on customer rating and customer value, to ensure that the most profitable customers get the greatest satisfaction. Products or service should be customized, or even personalized, based on customer behavior modeling and customer segmentation, to meet their unique expectations. The planning and forecasting of sales, marketing, and customer service will be improved based on customer life-cycle patterns (engage, transaction, fulfill, and service) to make the sales and marketing efforts more focused and efficient. All these will help the company acquire and retain more ideal customers and improve profitability of existing customers.

None of these projects is technical or analytical, but they are as important as the operational and analytical projects, because they cover the last few miles to the destination—the successful value delivery to both the company and the customers. They are even harder to define and execute because they deal with people, where the most important and difficult change occurs.

Defining and executing these projects requires dealing with what is going on inside of people (the ones who use the system and information), their perceptions, feelings, and ability to adapt and accept external changes. No value can be realized from CRM without understanding and managing its impact on the people who live with it and make it work on a daily basis. The key to successfully dealing with the people aspects of change is to accept change and to deal with issues as and when they arise. If the management ignores the uncomfortable aspects of change, the entire CRM strategy will fail. It must be willing to prioritize human issues in order to ensure that the CRM strategy succeeds.

Three major issues must be addressed here:

1. Resistance from employees
2. Motivation and training
3. Availability of information

Resistance from Employees

The first issue these projects have to address is resistance. People resist change, but there are two ways to positively work with resistance.

First, think of resistance as energy. If employees are resistant, then this shows that they do indeed care, and this is much better than total apathy. When the management recognizes resistance as energy and passion, its goal will be to channel that energy into positive commitment and behavior.

Second, resistance is information that tells management what is and is not working in the change process. By paying attention to resistance and even encouraging it, management harnesses the energy of change and learns about the next steps it must take to make the change succeed.

There are some guidelines that companies can follow to overcome resistance and help people utilize the CRM system as well as the information:

- Think through the impact of changes on people, individually and collectively; build a case for change by focusing attention on reasons for change, including consequences for not changing and benefits of changing.
- Hold regular communication meetings.
- Manage the stages of confusion by providing lots of information and clarity about what is happening and when and how it will impact people.
- Listen and encourage people to talk about what is happening.
- Allow people to make the change and to "grieve."
- Support managers who become champions of the change.
- Understand that there are no quick fixes for this cultural and psychological challenge.

Motivation and Training

To help handle resistance, the company should not only motivate employees to utilize the new system and analytical information, but also train them on how to use the new system and information. Internal marketing campaigns should be performed to motivate the information users, such as sales reps, customer service reps, marketing analysts, and even decision-making executives, to use the analytical information to achieve obtain their objectives, improve their productivity, and affect the company's bottom line so that they can show their importance and their impact to the company.

Implementing CRM requires employees to change their work habits. The most effective way to do this is training. Users need to be trained on how to utilize the information. This process may include demonstrating to users how to access and utilize needed information, providing users with frequently updated and understandable user documentation, offering online tutorials that can be customized for each user, providing a telephone help line to stand-by users, and training the "trainers" to ensure that new users can quickly be up and running the system.

Availability of Information

Another important issue here is the availability of information. The company should have an information system that makes the results of the analysis available to all relevant employees in marketing, sales, and customer service to support their decisions in real time. This will necessitate that a person or department take up the responsibility for overseeing this information system. Information sheets should be developed for the individual tasks involved and they must contain results of the analysis that is consistent throughout the company and across all customer touch-points. Furthermore, the processes must be supported so that the relevant information is readily accessible for transactions in operational CRM activities.

Figure 4-2 shows how investing in CRM by overcoming challenges ultimately results in the reduction of time and money resources.

4.5 CASE STUDY
CUSTOMER RELATIONSHIP MANAGEMENT AT CAPITAL ONE (UNITED KINGDOM)[2]

SOURCE: Copyright © 2003 INSEAD, Fontainebleau, France.

Ian: "Customer Relationship Management is another buzzword to me, but what does it actually mean? It just seems like a nice concept. We don't talk about it internally—we have many buzzwords, but not this one."

Phil: "We've internalized it so much—that's why we don't talk about it."

Ian: "You're right, we don't do Customer Relationship Management—we just get on and manage Customer Relationships!"

—conversation between Phil Marsland, director of Marketing and Analysis, and Ian Cornelius, account manager, Capital One, June 2002.

INTRODUCTION

Capital One's leaders, Richard Fairbank and Nigel Morris, had a vision of creating an information-based company rather than a financial services company when they worked

FIGURE **4-2** **IMPROVING PROFITABILITY BY INVESTING IN CRM**

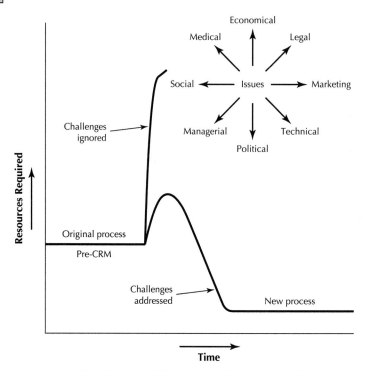

SOURCE: Adapted from *Essentials of CRM: A Guide to Customer Relationship Management,* Bryan Bergeron, 2002, John Wiley & Sons, Inc., New York.

in the consulting business in the late 1980s. They envisioned that the strategy for credit card providers should be to deliver "the right product to the right customer at the right time, at the right price." While sounding obvious, their statement marked a revolution that would trigger huge changes in the credit card business. However, this revolution did not happen overnight.

As consultants, Fairbank and Morris could see the potential for improving the credit card business for both customers and shareholders alike through the application of their nascent strategy ideas. The U.S. credit card market during the 1980s was characterized by financial institutions offering very similar products across the whole spectrum of their customer bases, charging a standard 19.8 percent interest rate and a $20 annual fee. The market lacked a customization of offers, and one-to-one marketing was practically inexistent. The prevailing story was very much "one size fits all."

The journey began in late 1988, when Signet Bank, in Virginia, not only bought Fairbank and Morris' concept but also engaged them to execute the plan from within. In contrast to the prevailing attitude of the major players, Signet put a different understanding at the heart of its new strategy. According to Morris and Fairbank:

> Credit cards are not banking, they are information. It's all about collecting information on millions of people that you've never met, and, on the basis of that information, making a series of critical decisions about lending money to them and hoping they pay you back.

Therefore, Signet Bank rebuilt its credit card operations around information technology and sophisticated analytical techniques. This new strategy, named *information-based strategy (IBS),* was to compile what was ultimately to become the world's largest

Oracle database, allowing the company to understand its customers and to develop mass-customized products, which would ideally suit their needs and risk profile.

By early 1994, Signet made the decision to float the credit card business separately, and hence *Capital One Financial Corporation* was born in November 1994, with Richard Fairbank as chairman and chief executive officer, and Nigel Morris as president and chief operating officer.

Since its IPO in 1994 to 2000, the stock price of the company has increased by 1,000 percent and the company has grown at an average annual rate of about 40 percent, excluding mergers and acquisitions. In December 2001, the company handled more than $45 billion in loans and 43.8 million customers worldwide, serviced by more than 20,000 employees (see Figure 4-3 for awards given to the company).

Encouraged by its U.S. success, Capital One decided to launch its first overseas operations in the United Kingdom. In July 1998, Capital One opened its operations center in Nottingham. On day one, 250 associates were employed. By 2001, this number had grown to more than 2,000, and Capital One associates in Nottingham now deal with application processing, customer service, product design and marketing, card issuing, collections, business development, and database management. In 2002, the company reached profitability and is now one of the United Kingdom's top six credit card issuers.

Capital One's percentage of outstanding bad debt, a key performance measure in a risk-driven business, was significantly lower than that of key competitors. This is especially significant, given that the company, unlike most of its competitors, lends to customers across the whole credit risk spectrum. At year end, 2001, Capital One posted its eighteenth consecutive quarter of record earnings: annual earnings grew by more than 20 percent and delivered a yearly return on equity of more than 20 percent. Reaching this goal seven times in a row put Capital One in a league with only seven other publicly held U.S. companies. (See Figure 4-4 for the growth history of Capital One's revenues.)

In early 2001, Fairbank and Morris could not help wondering about its success: while all their competitors were also embracing CRM (Customer Relationship Management), and most seemed to pursue the concept with significant investments in software and reorganization, Capital One's customer base was developing at a compound annual growth rate of 40 percent. It seemed as if Capital One could indeed be seen as creating industry best practice in developing valuable customer relationships and managing risk based on an intimate understanding of the customer. But what exactly was it that made Capital One's approach to CRM so unique? Was the company's success based on luck, or was it based on

---

| **FIGURE** | **4-3** | **CAPITAL ONE: SELECTION OF AWARDS AND ACCOLADES** |

2001 Capital One is named the 3rd "Best Place to Work in the UK" by *The Sunday Times*.
 Capital One named in *Forbes* 400 list—Best Big Companies in America.

2000 Capital One is named in the *Information Week 500* for innovation in IT.
 Capital One receives *CIO 100 award* for Customer Excellence (the second consecutive year of recognition from CIO).

1999 *Business Week* names Capital One Number 15 in its list of top 50 performers in the S&P 500.
 Computer World ranks Capital One Number 13 in its list of the "100 Best Places to Work in IT."

1998 Rich Fairbank is named Executive of the Year by *Credit Card Management* magazine.
 Future Banker names Rich Fairbank and Nigel Morris "Future Bankers of the Year."
 Capital One is named in the *Information Week 500* for innovation with information technology.

1997 *Forbes* names Capital One as one of the fastest-growing companies in its list of top 25 "Champs."
 Beyond Computing presents Capital One with its Gold Award for successful integration of IT and business strategies.

1996 Capital One wins the *Gartner Group* "Excellence in Technology" Award.

1995 *Credit Card Management* magazine names Capital One "Issuer of the Year."

FIGURE 4-4

CAPITAL ONE: GROWTH OF CAPITAL ONE'S REVENUES (WORLDWIDE OPERATIONS)

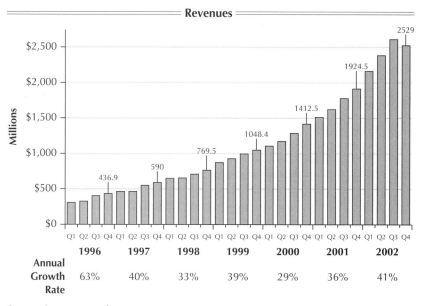

SOURCE: Company annual reports.

a real competitive advantage—and, if so, would this be a sustainable advantage, in the light of competitors' efforts on CRM?

INDUSTRY BACKGROUND

An Overview of the UK Credit Card Market

In the early 1990s, the major British banks dominated the market (such as Barclays, Lloyds, The Midland, NatWest, and The Royal Bank of Scotland) These banks would typically charge all customers interest rates of about 22 percent, as well as an annual fee of £12. Products were barely differentiated and customers had little real choice. In the mid-1990s, the market was shaken up by the entrance of competitive U.S. banks such as Capital One, Morgan Stanley Dean Witter, and MBNA, which targeted the UK market to expand their own business. The Internet wave also prompted the emergence of new competitors such as the online banks Egg, Cahoot, and IF.

The introductory offer of the new entrants revealed an aggressive pricing strategy. By offering lower interest rates and lower fees, they built sizable customer bases. Working on the basis that around three quarters of the sums owed on credit cards are attracting interest, providers have begun to offer extremely low-cost balance transfer deals (see Figure 4-5 for balance transfer rates). As a consequence, the credit card market today is highly competitive, and the market share of the major UK banks (two thirds of credit cards in issue) is eroding (see Figure 4-6 for market shares). It is clear that the days of the 22.9 percent standard interest rate are truly over.

Credit Card Revenues

Credit card issuers have many sources of income from the use of credit cards as a payment device or as a form of credit. The most frequent are interest charges paid by customers taking

FIGURE	4-5	CAPITAL ONE: COMPARISONS OF SELECTED CREDIT CARD RATES AND BALANCE TRANSFER OFFERS, JUNE 2002

	Standard Rate (%)	Balance Transfer Rate (%)
High Street Banks:		
Abbey National*	14.9	1.9
Bank of Scotland	17.9	0.0
Barclaycard	14.9	6.9
HSBC	18.9	4.9
Lloyds TSB	17.9	1.9
NatWest	17.4	5.9
Royal Bank of Scotland	16.9	2.9
Selected other providers:		
American Express	19.5	4.9
Capital One	12.9	6.9
Egg	13.9	0.0
Goldfish	17.9	4.9
MBNA	15.9	0.9
Tesco	14.9	1.5

*Cards issued by MBNA.

Source: Moneyfacts.co.uk. June 2, 2002.

FIGURE	4-6	CAPITAL ONE: CREDIT CARD BRAND SHARES IN THE UK

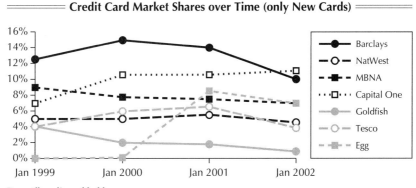

Base: All credit card holders.

Source: MORI Financial Services, June 2002.

extended credit, annual card fees, interchange (a service commission from the merchants accepting the card), and other fees, such as late or over-limit fees.

Another valuable source of income for credit card issuers is the revenue originated by cross-selling other financial products related to the cards, such as insurance against fraud, or personal loans and mortgages. However, the main source of profit for a card company is the annual percentage rate (APR) on an outstanding balance—that is, the use of the credit card requires that the customer pays a specific minimum proportion of their balance each month, and, in addition, an interest rate on the outstanding balance. The more outstanding balances customers have, the greater the company's revenues are, and the higher the APR, the higher the interest charges incurred.

Consumers

As mentioned, credit cards may be both a payment device and a form of revolving credit. Credit card customers can be divided into two main segments:

1. *Transactors:* clients who regularly repay their entire balance
2. *Revolvers:* clients who pay less than their entire balance and usually benefit from an interest-free grace period, which may be up to fifty four days

Revolvers are the customers who provide the biggest source of revenue, since they are always revolving their credit and therefore always providing revenue as they pay their interests. Relatively buoyant consumer confidence and low interest rates have combined to create an environment in which consumers are happy to take on extra debt. An example of this confident environment is the comparative strength of both credit and debit card markets, with charge cards in issue trailing far behind (see Figure 4-7 for the evolution of card issues). The growth in the number of credit cards in issue is, in part, a result of the increased market competition but also a consequence of the changing attitude of the British towards credit. The amount of total consumer credit increased by 96.7 percent from 1995 to 2001 (£89.1 billion to £175.3 billion). Credit cards represented 53.5 percent of this total credit in 1995, rising to 59.6 percent in 2001 (source: Mintel). For many, consumer credit is simply another financial tool to be taken advantage of, in the same way as a current account or mortgage.

Also, consumers are increasingly happy to play credit card providers off against one another, switching from card to card in order to take advantage of introductory deals. Although APR is clearly a key factor in customers' preferences for specific cards, there are other factors that influence their choices. These include, for example, the availability of a reward point system, the acceptance rate at stores, the size of the credit line, the card design, or the affiliation with a charitable organization.

CAPITAL ONE COMPANY BACKGROUND

Business Model

The business model of Capital One is founded on the simple, yet crucial, premise that each customer requires a different product and service from its credit card provider. The company believes in the assertion that customers, if offered what they want and need, as opposed to what banks want to offer them, will choose the provider that gives them choice and individuality.

Each customer carries a specific and unique credit risk and potential revenue profile, based mainly on their previous credit history (or lack thereof). The better the company can understand and assess a customer's specific risk, the better it can manage it. And the better

---

FIGURE	4-7	CAPITAL ONE: NUMBER OF PAYMENT CARDS IN ISSUE: 1992–2001

	Number of Credit Cards	Number of Debit Cards	Number of Charge Cards
1992	28.28	22.60	2.35
1995	28.27	28.44	2.51
1999	41.42	46.08	3.45
2001	51.70	54.31	4.43
% change 1992–2001	+96.8	+140.3	+88.1

SOURCE: APACS Report, *Plastic cards in the UK 2002.* (http://apacs.org.uk).

it understands the customer, the more it can tailor its products to his or her needs. Risk is a crucial factor in the credit card business. "We're in a risk-driven business where one bad debtor can easily wipe out the benefits from 20 average customers or 4 to 5 good ones—thus, it's vital to manage them carefully," explains Ian Cornelius. "It is one of our competitive advantages to understand and manage these different levels of risk."

Information-Based Strategy (IBS)

Capital One's goal is to use information to acquire the types of customers it can most profitably serve. In order to understand them, the company uses information technology to accumulate and manage large amounts of data on its customers. Alongside publicly available data on credit risk, the company supplements this with data on customer demographics and behavior collected internally during the application and account management process, where every transaction is carefully registered. None of this could be achieved without the entire company being completely aligned behind the whole process.

With the data accumulated, the company executes its proprietary "Test & Learn" strategy. Test & Learn is a scientific, hypothesis-driven approach to test any customer-related activity in a controlled condition on a sample of customers before rolling it out on a large scale. Using this scientific process, Capital One's Marketing and Analysis teams develop ideas, design products, and select target customers. Real products are empirically tested with genuine customers: the number of tests run is impressive—36,000 in 1999 and 45,000 in 2000. (Figure 4-8 summarizes the principle behind the Test & Learn strategy.) For example, mailings with different copy and/or letter design are sent out to potential customers. Their response rates are monitored, as is their behavior as new customers, so that Capital One can understand the relative value of different offers. All test results are then analyzed and integrated into databases that can be referenced later to initiate further ideas on development and product design. Similarly, by analyzing customer behavior, the view of risk can be refined, and the credit offer can be improved accordingly. Balance-building programs can be targeted at the low-risk customer, thereby reducing the average loss rate of the portfolio.

| FIGURE | 4-8 | **CAPITAL ONE: TEST AND LEARN STRATEGY** |

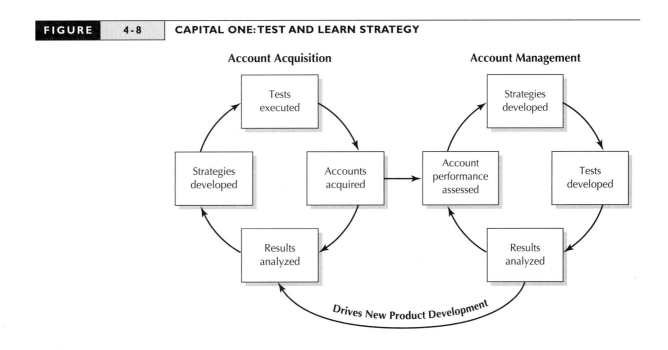

As a result, the company continues to improve its portfolio of products and services, and it now offers more than 6,000 products, most of them variations of credit cards. Here are some key products:

- Credit cards with different conditions (APR, credit limit, fees) and designs
- Products directly related to the credit card such as card protection plans and payment protection insurance (cross-selling)
- Other financial services such as travel insurance

CUSTOMER RELATIONSHIP MANAGEMENT PRACTICES AT CAPITAL ONE (UK)

Managing its relationships with customers is at the heart of Capital One's strategy. CRM is not seen as a tactical or functional approach but as a key strategic process. This strategic CRM orientation expresses itself; for example, in the way the various corporate functions are interlinked. It is not only the way in which departments are structured but also the way they interact with one another. As Capital One managers usually say: "All departments work in an integrated fashion, and there are no silos within the company." Internally, the company is grouped into four key divisions:

1. *Marketing and Analysis (M&A).* Responsible for Capital One marketing strategy, product development, credit and risk management, pricing strategy, and monitoring market trends and competition.
2. *Operations.* In charge of all front- and back-office operations and for all customer inter-processes (e.g., cross-selling, customer acquisition and retention, etc.).
3. *Information Technology (IT).* In charge of the development and maintenance of the systems infrastructure.
4. *Human Resources (HR).* Responsible for employee recruitment, training, and development, the internal satisfaction survey, and for nurturing the company's culture.

Marketing and Analysis (M&A)

Capital One's M&A department has, as its main functions, segmentation, testing, and analyzing customer data in order to elaborate the company's marketing strategy, and developing new products and services. To segment customers, Capital One uses analytical techniques and tests to identify groups of customers and to cluster them into segments according their risk profile and behavior.

Segmentation Strategy

Capital One's segmentation strategy focuses on a full spectrum approach (i.e., it targets all types of risk profiles, offering them different products and prices accordingly). The company's database has many types of customers, such as *transactors,* with a low risk profile, and *revolvers.* Capital One was able to further distinguish two sub segments in the latter group: *high-risk revolvers,* with a high level of credit line utilization and high probability of default, and *low-risk revolvers,* who use their credit line extensively but pay back their balances. In order to identify this profitable low-risk revolvers segment, Capital One carried out some tests which revealed that these customers could be targeted by making them a better interest rate offer. In fact, offering them a lower APR to encourage them to transfer their balances from other banks to Capital One proves to be an attractive offer, since these customers intend to repay the balance they have already created. Many other tests were conducted to fine-tune the solicitation of these customers in terms of contact channels, credit offers, and mailing preferences.

The company's other large customer segment is composed of customers for whom the Capital One card is very often the first card. This segment also includes people who have had problems obtaining or handling credit in the past, people with limited or nonexistent credit records, and young people. Since this segment carries a relatively higher risk, these customers are usually not well served by products offered by the main high street banks. Capital One's strategy in this case is to offer these customers an initial higher APR with an annual fee and a lower credit line. Although this is clearly higher than other Capital One offers, it usually compares very favorably with alternative credit offers on the market, and represents good value to these customers.

Account Manager Cavendish Elithorn explains why the offer is an attractive one for this segment: "Given their credit history, the Capital One card is still a better deal than other sources of credit—store cards where interest rates are 30 percent, brokers who charge 40 to 50 percent, or door-to-door lenders with 100 percent rates." The potential volume of this segment is significant, which is why Capital One has the potential to grow this customer base alongside the low-risk segment. The challenges to identify this segment are the same as those of low-risk customers: Identify the customers, their risk assessment, and managing attrition. To evaluate the customer risk profile on application, the company rates them based on their credit scoring, information taken from the application forms, and credit bureau data.

Retention Strategy

To attract low-risk revolvers with balances in other banks, Capital One may offer them a card with an introductory low rate that expires after a few months, and no annual fee. However, when the introductory rate expires, Capital One may witness increasing attrition from these clients, as many price-sensitive customers tend to reduce their debt or leave Capital One without notifying the company or closing their account. "This is a dangerous development, as it's the best customers—those that are low risk—that tend to leave to get better credit deals elsewhere," explains an account manager. "Consequently, we have active strategies to keep these customers, and their balances."

Many of the account management activities seek to keep these customers from being *dormant* or becoming permanently inactive. These retention activities are designed to help retain customers when their introductory rate expires or when other accounts risk dormancy. "If a customer's account is dormant for a while, there is an increasing risk of losing that customer," explains Ian Cornelius. "That's why we have a number of activities in place to guard against this—by making a range of offers to reactivate their account."

Capital One's retention strategy with this type of low-risk segment is basically to grow the low credit line they received at the beginning of their relationship. Furthermore, they may also receive increased benefits, different card designs, and other incentives to stay with Capital One. The key strategy with these customers is to treat them as well as any other customer segment. Just because Capital One was the best available offer on the market when they joined, it does not mean it will always be the case. Consequently, Capital One works hard to retain these customers.

At various points in time in the customer lifecycle, Capital One analyses its customer database to fine-tune its offers and retain customers. The behavioral and performance data allows the company to make proactive rate or credit limit offers, whenever appropriate. IBS testing is also used to help identify low- and high-risk customer profiles. By making different offers to customers, the company learns more about customer behavior and therefore improves its targeting and retention.

Operations

In order to offer a wide variety of cards and services, Capital One aligns its Operations department with customer requirements. This strategy has proven to give Capital One a competitive advantage over other banks in the market. Rather than taking the assembly-line approach, the company attempts to handle its customers in a personalized and flexible way.

Operations handles front-end customer relationships. There are more than 1,000 people working in Capital One's call-center, handling more than 10,000 incoming calls per day. Most call-center type operations are aligned managerially and operationally in order to achieve specific targets which often compete with one another: (1) low cost efficiency, (2) high-quality customer service, (3) flexibility, and (4) associate satisfaction. In fact, these four measures are the cornerstones of a model known as the *Big Yellow Square (BYS)*. Each quarter, the management team rate themselves on these four corners to take a qualitative assessment of how "big" and "square" the BYS is at any time. This is a simple model, and is easy to buy into emotionally. The BYS indicates that Capital One's view on operating a call center differs from most other organizations, particularly in the way it weights *associate satisfaction,* which is equally important as *service quality* and *cost efficiency.*

As mentioned, *flexibility* is one of the BYS corners. Because the company tests so many products in the marketplace on a regular basis, flexibility in the approach and attitude of the Operations staff is a key part of the business' success. Flexibility is also present in the way that Capital One deals with operational overloads. Many associates, even those who normally do not work with Operations, are trained in one or more disciplines. Also, when volumes exceed expectations in a particular area, managers take the decision to ask associates to temporarily move jobs to cope with the peaks. Eventually, this action is more likely to be taken when there is an unexpected surge in high-value customer contacts, such as applications for new products.

Another important aspect of Capital One's strategy is the way it uses customer profitability analysis. Profitability is calculated on an individual basis to improve the product offer to each customer. However, the company does not normally differentiate customer service levels according to a customer's profitability. As Mitch Beres, Vice President of UK Operations, explains:

> We would not be comfortable matching up high-value customers with high-level service—every customer has a choice of whether to use us or go elsewhere, and our quality of service can be a reason for them to stay. We aim to offer high-quality service to all our customers, regardless of their profitability.

However, Phil Marsland reflects on the subject of differentiating customer service: "It is a real question to me whether the lower-risk customers should cross-subsidize those with higher risk, or whether everyone should get the deal they deserve." Although Capital One does not currently follow this line of thinking, Marsland's comment indicates that Capital One's management is constantly contemplating new ways of managing its business, and may even consider changing this current strategy.

Another element that differentiates Capital One's Operations department from others is its IT infrastructure. IT is used to route calls and provide associates with the necessary information to best handle specific calls. The systems are updated directly by call-center associates. Therefore, as soon as each call is completed, associates enter information about the interaction in an encoded form into the system, which will then be available for the next contact with the customer. In some ways, this ensures a modern version of so-called *old-fashioned* personal service.

More specifically, the Operations department is divided in four main areas:

1. Operations processing
2. Customer relations

3. Sales
4. Collections

Operations Processing

Operations processing handles all back-office operations. Some examples of its key functions are: keying in credit card applications, scanning all incoming correspondence into a document management system, managing vendors such as card embossers and statement printers, and handling payments from customers.

Customer Relations

Customer relations handles incoming calls. Although it is primarily devoted to providing particular service requirements and receiving customer complaints, it also attempts to cross-sell when appropriate. In customer relations, 400 customer service associates receive about 8,000 to 10,000 calls a day. These associates use the sales system (called SALSA—also used in the Sales department) when attempting to cross-sell. This allows them to identify suitable products to the customer who is calling and to avoid offering the same product twice.

Customer service associates, as well as sales associates, work to an incentive scheme that encourages sales and quality service. This incentive scheme is characterized by the following criteria:

- *Average handling time of the call.* (as measured by the number of calls routed per day and the average call length in seconds)
- *Sales points per contact.* A sale is encouraged by awarding points per product sold in order to reflect product profitability.
- *Quality.* This is measured by using a system that records ten random calls a month, per associate, to which managers listen and give feedback.

Associates receive a review of their performance weekly; it shows how they rank against overall department targets and against their own past performance. The call listening program, introduced two years ago by senior management, is very rigorous. As one customer relations manager explains: "This feedback from senior management has served not only as an extra quality screen, but also as a visible signal to our front-line associates that they are important." Competition between individual associates and call-center teams is also encouraged. On the call-center walls, colorful charts track the performance of different teams. Awards are given to the best performing teams or individuals, and their pictures are displayed on internal notice boards or appear in in-house publications.

Sales

The sales department is divided into the following units:

- *Inbound.* Customers call to activate their cards or to respond to a marketing offer.
- *Outbound.* Capital One associates call the customers to sell them a product or to provide a proactive service (e.g., customers who received a card but did not take out the payment protection insurance).
- *Retention.* Associates try to retain customers who intend to close their accounts.
- *New Business.* Sales are attempted with new customers.

Within all units, teams of twelve to fourteen associates plus a supervisor and a manager are formed. Although some specialization is encouraged, there is also cross-staffing and rotation to familiarize sales people with other tasks and teams, and to allow for flexibility in meeting peak demand.

Offering new products to customers is one of the key tasks of the sales department. Given the variety of new products offered every month, computer-based training modules are developed to familiarize sales personnel with the new offers. When cross selling, Capital One's cross-selling system determines the likelihood of customers to buy certain products based on the projected NPV of a product to a customer, and suggests different products to different customers, or even no selling attempt at all (see Figure 4-9 for the model).

The SALSA sales system (see Figure 4-10 for screenshot) enables targeting cross-sell offers to specific customers likely to be interested in particular products. To avoid inundating the customer with offers, SALSA prevents Capital One associates from offering the

---

FIGURE **4-9** **CAPITAL ONE: NPV-BASED CROSS-SELLING PROCESS**

1. Customer 4324 1223 7874 3335 calls in.
2. System checks whether any sale is permissible in this channel (e.g., have we tried a CSM approach recently).
3. Product priority is sourced from the NPV table:

	CPP	PPI	Loan	BT	Shopping
4324 1223 7874 3333	10	30	40	21	1
4324 1223 7874 3334	43	22	9	45	24
4324 1223 7874 3335	12	59	8	43	3
4324 1223 7874 3336	0	1	5	12	33

It's PPI, BT, CPP, Loan, Shopping.

4. System checks whether approaches are allowable on these products (e.g., excludes product if customer already holds it or where the product has been attempted recently).
5. The list of products we are "happy to offer" is shown to the associate, with the primary product at the top of the list.

FIGURE **4-10** **CAPITAL ONE: SCREENSHOT FROM CUSTOMER-SERVICE COMPUTER SCREEN (SALSA SYSTEM)**

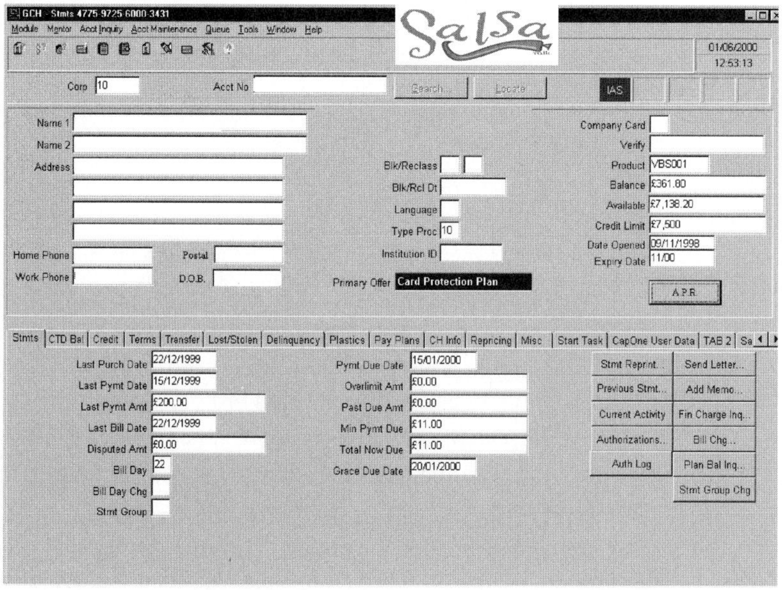

SOURCE: Capital One (UK).

same product twice within a short period of time. Associates are not encouraged to sell more than one product during a single call, even if SALSA suggests more than one product offer. As one sales associate explains: "the target time for a call is challenging—this means you really need your sales pitch honed and ready!" This minimizes the chances of wasting the time of both customers and associates.

The SALSA system also uses accumulated data on customers to suggest how to react to specific customer requests. For example, if a customer asks for a credit line increase, a reduced APR, or a cash advance, data on past behavior and risk assessment are used to decide whether to grant the request.

Collections

The collections department deals with customers who have fallen behind with their payments or with accounts affected by fraud. The department is split into three main areas: payment assistance, recoveries, and fraud.

In *payment assistance,* Capital One associates work with customers who are behind with their payments to try and help them recover their account. For example, if the customer cannot pay his bill because he is unemployed, payment assistance may put him in contact with a recruiting agency. If the customer is ill, payments may be temporarily suspended. In other circumstances, customers who are behind with their payments may be offered revised terms, enabling them to make smaller, and regular payments. The overriding goal is to keep customers until they can pay and help them not to default. Elithorn explains:

> We believe we are better than most working with all customers to come to satisfactory solutions. For example, other card issuers might ask customers what they intend to do, in order to get out of debt, or give them few workable options. We might say that for a specific customer, based on our data, the best solution would be to lower its interest rate. We are still a long way away from individual solutions, but closer to it than most others in this field.

In *recoveries,* Capital One looks after those customers whose debt has been charged off and whose accounts are no longer open. The objective is to work with the customer to recover as much of the debt as possible.

Finally, the *fraud* team has two fundamental tasks: to help customers who have been victims of fraud and to prevent fraud itself. In the case of fraudulent activity, the team closes the old account, writes off any fraudulent charges, and transfers genuine transactions into a new account. Customers affected by fraud usually need a higher level of support, and the fraud team is trained to treat each case with sensitivity. A wide range of systems is in place to help prevent fraud, including real-time transaction models and account behavior pattern systems. Very often, the fraud customer service team calls customers to let them know that they might have been victims of fraud, even before the customer realizes it. This is yet another strong selling point for Capital One from the customer relationship management perspective.

Cooperation between M&A and Operations

Given the large number of tests carried out and new products developed within Capital One each year, there clearly has to be a great deal of cooperation between these two major departments. For example, when introducing a new product, M&A and Operations work very closely together. While M&A designs the product, develops marketing material, and follows up customer responses, Operations collects regular feedback from customers and make improvement suggestions. The information from Operations is also used to improve the NPV models that serve as decision-making mechanisms.

Much of the information on customers used to craft strategy is obtained from front-end associates, who are, of course, closest to the customer. There is a partnership between Operations and M&A to review the risk perspective of present as well as future strategies. Of course, such a tight link between Operations and M&A would not function without the enablement through IT. Furthermore, numerous permanent or *ad hoc* cross-functional teams, composed of members from Operations and M&A, exist to define, for example, the credit policies for new and existing products.

Information Technology (IT)

IT sits at Capital One's head table and reports directly to the board in its own right—it is highly valued as the enabler of business strategy. The IT division performs a broad function, ranging from pure business issues and decisions on how the company should deploy its resources and finances, through applications and software engineering, to detailed technical issues of hardware, operating systems, and networking. After Operations, IT is the company's second-largest division.

Against common practice in the financial industry, Capital One chose to *in-source* the majority of its IT capability, relying on the speed, management acumen, and expertise of its in-house provision. Much of the IT intellectual property of the business is implemented internally, which proves that IT has become a core competence. This department offers a full-service capability to the business (Operations and M&A), covering the spectrum of products and processes through their genesis and complete life cycle. It houses the data, performs guardianship of the information, excels in data warehousing, and ensures the information can be readily accessed. All the terabytes of customer behavior data are kept indefinitely in-house for online or near-online access. Through query tools, batch updates, and transactional data, IT provides the tools that enable IBS to work successfully.

IT interacts with the company in the following domains:

- Prospect pool and solicitation management
- Account acquisition and management
- Account servicing and call-center technologies
- Core systems

Prospect Pool and Solicitation Management

Capital One differentiates itself from the competition because of its internal prospect pool management and solicitation process. Rather than outsourcing the data on a prospect's behavior and lifestyle, Capital One runs an in-house database with this information, which targets and selects customer audiences and matches products according to the prospects' profiles. The information gathered over the years on Capital One customers has proved to be very useful in this perspective to tailor products to individuals.

Traditionally, Capital One has been using direct-mail campaigns to target new customers. This approach has proved to be very beneficial because it allows the company to predict gross and net response rates to various offers, according to the product, customer type, and creative process chosen. This allows an accurate prediction of its marketing effectiveness. Once the campaign results are received, data are introduced back into the prospect and solicitation management system to provide further data that will improve future acquisition programs.

Account Acquisition and Management

When a prospect becomes a customer, Capital One creates an account on the account management system, where all interactions with customers, from account detail changes to transactions and payments, are recorded. This information will create the customer profile, which allows the company to differentiate offers according to customer preferences. In fact, front-end customer acquisition processes rely on sophisticated sets of credit models and automated decision algorithms to process the high volume of applications via the various channels (telephone, Internet, mail). Hardcopy applications are scanned and retained on optical disk. This information is subsequently communicated to credit bureau and external fraud prevention agencies that provide Capital One with up-to-date information about applicants. All the raw data are recycled to management information systems (MIS) on a daily basis. This consolidates the core of the IBS account management programs through which Capital One can develop reward schemes, change fees and products, or make special offers to customers. In order to protect existing accounts against potential fraudulent card activities, expert real-time neural network solutions are deployed to trigger the alarm at the earliest possible instant.

Account Servicing and Call-Center Technologies

The call-center is supported by automated call dialers, power dialers, voice response units (VRU), and local systems integrated with voice solutions. Many of the special systems for customer contact (cross-sales, balance transfer, retention, and correspondence activities) are specifically designed to support the IBS approach. The system also stores information on customers' telephone numbers, which allows it to identify the origin of the call and route it to the most suitable associate. The sophisticated form of Computer Telephony Integration (CTI) ensures efficient customer handling and provides high-quality service. (See Figure 4-11 for systems infrastructure description.) When customers call in, they can choose to talk to an associate or to use the VRU system. The VRU, which currently handles about 7,500 calls every day, is used mainly for tasks such as balance enquiries.

Core Systems

In addition to the development of solutions to the Operations and M&A, IT also develops and maintains solutions in other divisions of the company, such as Finance or Human Resources. IT also develops the *Internet* system that allows customers to apply online, get real-time information, and manage their accounts. It also maintains the *Intranet* system, which provides accurate and accessible information to the company and functionality to all associates.

Human Resources (HR)

The Human Resources function is critical to Capital One's CRM strategy. Finding and keeping top quality associates is key to the company's success. HR is responsible for two main activities: managing associate selection and supporting and developing the company culture.

Associate Selection

Capital One considers the hiring process crucial and wants the selection process to be as science-driven as the overall customer strategy.

Hiring & Training All associates are hired and evaluated based on the same criteria, which the company believes helps to prevent the formation of cliques. During the recruitment interviews, they test analytical and conceptual skills. The company also performs "behavior interviews" in order to access candidates' competency by asking them to provide examples of situations where they supported change, managed several tasks, or made difficult decisions. According to one recruiter:

> We do not hire for specific experience, but for competencies. We try to find the best fit between a person and a role, and then train them. For example, we have a systems testing manager who used to test racing car engines before

FIGURE 4-11 **CAPITAL ONE: SYSTEMS INFRASTRUCTURE**

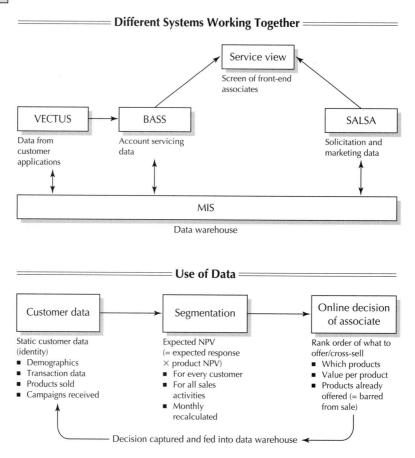

joining us—he had no direct experience, but certainly possessed all the competencies we were looking for.

Specific training, including some cultural induction, is offered for new hires. Managers at all levels are offered a range of performance and skill enhancement classes that are carried out by either in-house trainers or external organizations. There is also a learning center with books, videos, and simulations, which are grouped around the core competencies that the company seeks to build. Career development is another important aspect. Capital One has a highly structured people-management process that include 360-degree appraisals twice a year, personal *development action plans (DAPs)* to help employees prepare for their next job, and a weekly one-to-one ten-minute meeting between each associate and his or her manager to discuss key issues. In fact, the company won a *Training* magazine award in 2001 in the United States and was featured as the "3rd Best Place to Work in the UK" in 2001 by *The Sunday Times* newspaper.[3]

Evaluation   All associates are evaluated every six months. Half of the evaluation is based on targeted achievements and the other half based on Capital One's defined core competencies. Several categories are used to evaluate the competencies of call-center associates and team supervisors. Among the key elements are communication, support of others, integrative decision making, responsiveness to feedback and coaching, taking ownership, and job-specific knowledge. Evaluation is taken very seriously, and if metrics turn negative, managers spend time attempting to understand what went wrong. Says Mitch Beres:

> We see ourselves as coaches, rather than controllers or discipliners, nurturing talent and providing freedom. Even if our associates get it wrong, good coaching should help them improve—and we avoid getting the atrophy that often exists in other organizations.

Compensation   Incentives are an important part of the compensation package for all Capital One associates. For example, front-line associates can achieve a bonus of up to fourteen percent, based on their results and competencies. Senior managers are awarded share options as well as cash bonuses. On several occasions, since the company floated in 1994, options have been awarded to junior associates on a one-off basis to share the feeling of ownership throughout the company. Also, a subsidized share purchase scheme allows all associates to purchase stock at a substantial discount on the market price. Take up is currently running at about 20 percent, and ownership behavior is very visible. According to one operations manager:

> People really watch the stock price—there is a refreshing clarity on the fact that what we do affects the share price, and, since we have share options, it makes a real difference to us.

Company Culture

As Capital One searched for suitable premises to house its operations center in Nottingham, England, its main goal was to bring most activities inhouse and under one roof, as well as to create a springboard for new products and businesses and a center for recruitment. Combining all operations in one main location would also have the advantage that new employees could be more easily integrated.

Housing   A place with the potential to meet these goals was found in a huge, 1950s building that matched not only Capital One's accommodation needs but also its culture of openness. Capital One kept the two huge floor areas of 10,000 m^2 and a smaller second floor of 2,800 m^2. Call-center and professional areas are not differentiated, allowing flexibility in use and reinforcing the company's open business culture. The open-plan spaces in which most associates work are arranged in team configurations, while a few glass-fronted offices and meeting rooms are separated from the main areas. The building also has a convenience shop with refreshments, relaxation rooms, training rooms, a library, and locker rooms with showers. Also, a large staff restaurant, with relaxed design elements, provides the feel of a trendy restaurant or bar.

The atmosphere of the huge floors of the Capital One building is busy and professional, yet relaxed and colorful. The associates' cubicles are personally decorated with photographs and nametags, cuddly toys sit on almost every computer, inflatable palm trees stand in the corridor and remote-control air balloons fly through the room. On the computers, 'Golden Nugget' stickers signify each sale of a priority product made by that associate. There are flipcharts showing how the different teams rank against one another. On the Wall of Greatness, associates who have received special company awards are shown alongside great people from American history, like Henry Ford, Thomas Edison, and Muhammad Ali. As Scott Woolveridge, operations processing manager, sees it:

> What you see reflected in our decoration is that we try to avoid being a manufacturing shop. Our raw material is our people—so let them be themselves and have an environment to suit! If people are having fun, they do a better job—that's why

we give them all these cuddly toys and stress balls. We want to make people feel they belong to something. And they do.

Culture of Involvement   Developing this strong culture of employee involvement was a conscious decision and part of the business plan. "If you do not treat the people who deal with customers as well as you want them to treat those customers, then you are in trouble," continues Woolveridge. "People on the front line need to be empowered—they *are* the company as far as customers are concerned. We try to take care of individual needs, so it is a natural step for this to be translated into customer treatment."

In line with its focus on associates, Capital One aims to create a culture of involvement and buy-in for all objectives. "We spend a lot of time explaining our objectives and ensuring that they are meaningful for everyone—where we are going and why—which is what creates a sense of excitement, of ownership, of understanding why we are making certain trade-offs," explains Paul Hawker, collections manager. Trips, simulations, and training programs are some of the other tools that Capital One uses with its managers to ensure that objectives are aligned, and to create a common language and methodology. Managers estimate that they spend about 10 percent of their time on creative activities. They comment that it greatly helps them in decision making, as they tend to "assume positive intent on the other side of any discussion and know that we are all trying to do the right thing."

The company conducts an associate survey twice a year, containing more than 100 questions to "help the company remold itself for the future" as one manager puts it. The survey completion rate is well over 90 percent, and the managers carefully analyze the data obtained. Although some questions evaluate overall work satisfaction, others request more specific detail, such as quality of management communications and stress levels. Using regression analysis, Capital One identifies the key drivers of employee satisfaction and devises action plans to improve weaknesses and exploit the opportunities identified.

Capital One's employee satisfaction was extremely high in 2001: 97 percent of staff regard the company as a friendly place; 96 percent report that people are willing to give that bit extra to get the job done; and 66 percent (20 percent above the market average) believe that they are getting a fair share of company profits. Associate turnover is extremely low— the attrition rate at Capital One's call center is around two thirds of the average figure of 35 percent at a standard call center. In Capital One's non–call-center functions, turnover is even lower, and there has been virtually no senior management turnover.

Continuous Improvement   Improvement suggestions from front-line associates are highly encouraged. An example of an improvement suggestion made by call-center associates is the APR indicator. Call-center staff noticed that customers often wanted to discuss their APR, so IT and M&A built in a quick-access function that enabled them to view a customer's effective yearly APR without needing lengthy calculations. There are high levels of motivation and cooperation for these initiatives. Those employees who contribute with particularly valuable ideas are given awards and are highlighted on posters around the building.

There is also a high degree of cooperation among the various departments in the improvement process. As one operations manager explains:

> Our business is all about IBS, change and innovation—that is true for every department involved, and it is very liberating that there is no "who's in charge" debate. There is an overall acceptance that we will change, and that we will launch new products—some will succeed, others will fail. We don't have conflicts of issues as regarding "Marketing wanting to do this, but Operations not wanting to."

FUTURE CHALLENGES

Building a Deeper Understanding of Customer Needs

While acknowledging the success of their approach, Capital One's Operations management is concerned with taking its understanding of customers and their behavior further. Today, Capital One knows which product a given customer holds, which financial transactions they have made, and what interactions with the company have taken place. However, the company still knows relatively little about the customer as an individual, which would enable a deeper understanding of their behavior and needs. Mitch Beres envisions the following:

> If we could identify why customers call, we could segment them according to their needs—for example, if customer X calls mainly to check his balance, then he could immediately hear the message "Mr. X, your balance is... if you have more questions, please press one."

Increasingly, the company realizes that profitability is not necessarily driven by product ownership, but by customer characteristics (e.g., if they are working or studying, married or single, with or without children) and by product usage. Consequently, Capital One needs to ensure that it is able to address real customer needs at an individual level.

Managing Costs

In terms of cost structure (e.g., cost-per-customer account), Capital One's costs are currently higher than those of most of its competitors. The company views its heavy investment in IT and people as justified, but also seeks to keep costs within limits. David Farlow, Director of operations strategy, comments:

> We don't need to be more costly than our competitors. In fact, as IBS helps us to know our customers and their needs better, we should be well positioned to decide where to spend our resources. However, we are not yet at the part of the curve where increased spending on IBS does not add incremental value.

There is general agreement that associates are an expensive resource, and that they should be allocated to the highest-value activities while lower-value activities might be treated as a commodity, be outsourced, or, at the limit, not serviced. It is debatable to what extent VRUs and the Internet can decrease operational costs.

Coordinating Channels

Capital One clearly sees a challenge in coordinating its customer interaction through all its different channels, which are currently coordinated, yet not fully aligned. "As every contact with the customer is precious, our next step will be to integrate our systems further so as to view customers through the same lens and align customer communications fully," explains Mark Sanders, sales manager. Sanders also believes that the company has to work to avoid giving conflicting messages to customers. "There is a clear degradation of responses when customers receive too many mailings, and we have to avoid an uncoordinated situation where account management contacts a customer to raise their credit line and then sales contacts offer them a new product."

The fact that additional communication channels such as Web sites and e-mail now exist, and others might be established in the future, creates future challenges. As Sanders continues: "Whenever we add a new channel, we witness an increase in demand also in the older channels because of the need for explanation. For example, customers telephone to make sure their Internet payment was processed okay." Furthermore, when information comes from new sources or when it is more frequently published, enquiries increase. For example, there are more customer enquiries now that balances are produced continuously on the Internet than when the traditional paper version was mailed once a month. Of course, this can be viewed either as a cost or an opportunity.

4.6 SUMMARY

The key elements of CRM are touch points and the CRM applications that span the sales, marketing, and service functions. Touch points are means of interaction between the company and the customer. Once the elements of CRM are identified, it is important to calculate the ROI of CRM to see whether the investment is worthwhile. In calculating the ROI, care should be taken to identify the costs, gain or profit from CRM and the time period for assessing ROI. Three main categories of CRM costs are IT costs, people costs, and process costs. The investments in IT infrastructure, database development, and software are the main components of IT costs, and this may be usually one-fifth to one-third of total costs. The costs involved in recruitment of CRM talent and in redeployment and training of both the existing and new employees constitute the people costs. Process costs include investments in redesigning and reengineering of existing work practices. It is very difficult to compute concrete CRM profits because (1) the implementation takes two to five years to complete, during which the competitive environment might have been changed, (2) some CRM costs are necessary but do not generate revenue, and (3) the change or performance improvement cannot always be attributed to CRM investment. However indirect benefits of CRM in terms of lower customer acquisition costs, lower cost to serve, higher customer satisfaction and retention, and higher average customer value should be considered in arriving at the benefits of CRM.

The timeframe of ROI measurement varies, depending on the size of the project. The implementation of a CRM strategy is a process of developing and executing a series of small projects aimed at the business needs and value proposition of customers. These projects can be categorized as operational projects, analytical projects, and implementation projects. Operational projects construct infrastructure to enable companies to meet the technical and functional requirements of CRM. These include automation of functions, setting up a customer database, information delivery, and changing the process of data collection. Analytical projects, by contrast, are implemented to help a company understand its customers using data analysis tools. This is also called *data analytics,* and it combines data-driven marketing and technology to better understand customers. Data analytics projects include customer data transformation and customer knowledge discovery. Customer data transformation consists of pooling data from a number of sources to a data warehouse and enhancing the data with externally available information. Customer knowledge discovery is the stage when the data are analyzed using statistical tools and the future is predicted based on analytical results in order to enhance marketing decision making. Building a complete customer database incorporating all the relevant customer information from different departments and external sources is crucial for a successful analytical CRM project. This database is the basis for the customer demographic analysis, customer behavior modeling, and customer value assessment. The implementation projects deploy operational and analytical outputs to increase revenue and profits by improving marketing decisions and customer relationships. This is difficult to execute because this requires dealing with the perceptions and feelings of people and their ability to adapt to changes. Only a company that effectively handles the resistance from its employees and trains and motivates them can expect to see positive results from a CRM project.

The Capital One case study illustrates how the company successfully implemented a CRM strategy. Its business model was founded on the crucial premise that each customer requires a different product and service from a credit card provider. Following this business model, Capital One adopted an information-based strategy (IBS), which collects information about the customers. *Test & Learn* tests customer-related activity in a controlled condition before it is introduced in the market. This helps to develop ideas, design products, and select target customers. CRM is viewed as a key strategic process in Capital One, and different departments work in an integrated fashion toward understanding and satisfying customers and their needs. For example, there is a partnership between Marketing and Analysis (M&A) and Operations to review the risk perspective of present as well as future strategies. We can see that in Capital One all the departments implement the operational projects, analytical projects, and implementation projects in a coordinated way. This strategic approach to CRM has helped Capital One to be seen as creating industry-best practices in developing valuable customer relationships and managing risk based on an intimate understanding of the customer.

4.7 EXERCISE QUESTIONS

1. What factors will you consider when measuring the ROI of CRM investments?
2. What are the advantages and disadvantages when implementing CRM on an organizational basis versus on a limited functional basis (e.g., sales force only)?
3. What are the various components of the CRM architecture from an operational perspective?
4. What analysis is involved in assessing the value of a customer?
5. What customer backlashes can be expected when a company introduces CRM practices? What cautionary steps would you advise companies to take to avoid these?

MINI CASE 4.1

IMPLEMENTING CRM IN THE FAST-MOVING CONSUMER-GOODS INDUSTRY

Henkel is a globally operating group of companies, offering a wide range of consumer goods extending from detergents, household cleaners, cosmetics, toiletries, to adhesives. In Europe, Henkel has held a leading position for decades in the detergents and household cleaners market with brands such as Persil, Dixan, Vernel, and Weißer Riese. In the United States it is represented by the Dial brand. In the hypercompetitive European retail markets, many of the large manufacturers such as Henkel, P&G, and Unilever have focused on improving and managing supply chain efficiency.

Part of this ongoing activity is the concept of category management, where manufacturers and retailers collaborate to improve the profitability of the category at the store level. However, as an increasing number of firms are mastering the category management process, manufacturers such as Henkel are looking at how they can differentiate themselves further. This is where many of them have started to experiment with customer relationship management practices. The environment in which these companies operate is characterized by branded products, low absolute margins on a per-product basis, and lack of direct consumer contact. In line with the general CRM idea, the goal of a CRM approach would be to identify and target high-value customers and to then devise a retention or growth strategy for them. In practice, this means to allocate disproportionate resources to these customers. Whereas CRM is strongly established in direct to consumer environments such as banking or telecommunications, the exact nature of CRM in the fast-moving consumer-goods (FMCG) environment is less clear. Therefore, the challenge that lies in front of firms such as Henkel is to define, conceptualize, and implement a suitable CRM approach.

Questions:

1. How would you define and measure customer value to Henkel? Should it define value on the individual level or on the segment level?
2. What is the look and feel of CRM in the FMCG environment?
3. Is there a necessity for manufacturers to partner up with retailers in order to implement an effective CRM strategy?

MINI CASE 4.2

B-TO-B CRM IMPLEMENTATION AT DEUTSCHE POST WORLD NET

Deutsche Post World Net (DPWN) is a fast-growing international logistics service provider. Its portfolio of companies includes its European business-to-business (B-to-B) parcel service Euro Express, its express delivery service across the globe DHL, and its global logistics provider (air, sea, and road transportation) DANZAS. Revenues for the three divisions in 2001 were approximately 15.5 billion, with an increasing portion (45 percent) coming from outside its home market of Germany. The central problem of DPWN was that the three companies often served the same customers without knowing this. Each company has its own sales force and was calling simultaneously on many identical clients—for example, virtually all of the large companies in Europe. As one would expect, the organizational structures and systems support (IT) was quite different for the three companies. DPWN felt that the group of individual companies could achieve much better results by coordinating their sales efforts, specifically, by being able to systematically cross-sell its various products and services to the many existing clients. Therefore, the company set out to leverage the entire customer base across the three companies and to build an integrated customer management approach. Specifically, DPWN wanted to first create a key account management system that allows the three companies to coordinate their offerings and sales communication to the most important business clients. Given that the three individual companies offered complementary services, the objective was to present one face to the customer, with the idea of providing complete logistics solutions for these clients regardless of the type of desired service. The challenges ahead of DPWN were to (1) create transparency across customer relationships and customer potentials, (2) design cooperation processes across the three companies, and (3) develop sales support tools.

Questions:

1. How would one define and measure the potential for cross selling in this context?
2. If DPWN creates an integrated key account management system, which key processes need to be integrated across the three companies?
3. What are the barriers to increased cooperation between the companies?

ENDNOTES

1. Churn rate is the number of existing customers who have left by the end of a given period divided by the number of existing customers at the beginning of the respective period.

2. This case was prepared by Ulrike Wiehr, the Boston Consulting Group MBA Fellow, under the supervision of Professor Werner J. Reinartz, at INSEAD.

3. "The 50 Best Companies to Work For," *Sunday Times* (2001): 9.

CHAPTER 5

Introduction to Customer-Based Marketing Metrics

Contents

5.1 OVERVIEW

Customer value management rests on the idea of allocating resources differently to different customers. The basis of this differential resource allocation is the economic value of the customer to the firm. Thus, before one can start to manage customers, one must have a thorough understanding of how to compute the value contribution each customer makes to a firm. Various economic concepts and procedures have been developed that help us do this. Some are based on simple notions, whereas some require the application of mathematical techniques. But as a precursor to understanding and applying these concepts, it is necessary to define measures or metrics of marketing activities and their outcomes. This chapter reviews traditional marketing metrics and introduces various primary customer-based metrics.

It is important at this stage to note the difference between traditional marketing metrics and customer-based metrics. Traditional marketing metrics have been in use by marketing professionals for years and are helpful in measuring performance of brands, products, and firms in a given geographical region. *Market share* and *sales growth* are popular traditional marketing metrics normally computed for the geographical area a particular market covers. These metrics were developed when individual customer data were hard or impossible to obtain and therefore do not provide customer-level insight into the market. Historically, managerial rewards and incentives have been based on how well a manager is able to deliver on these metrics. However, over the years, the availability of customer-level data has resulted in the development of a new set of metrics that reflect the need to evaluate managerial performance based on the value each individual buyer brings to the customer base of the firm. In order to arrive at some measure of customer value, various activities and their costs and returns need to be recorded and measured. *Acquisition rate* and *acquisition cost* are two primary metrics that measure the customer-level success of marketing efforts aimed at acquiring new customers. Metrics have also been developed to track customer activities after they have been acquired until they cease to be customers. *Retention rate, survival rate, probability of a customer being active—P*(Active)—and *customer lifetime duration* are some such metrics. In industries with high churn such as Internet service providers (ISPs) and telecom services, it is also possible to win back some customers who have left. *Win-back rate* is thus an important metric of marketing performance in such industries. Thus, various marketing metrics which will be discussed in the course of this chapter and the next chapter can be classified as follows:

1. Traditional marketing metrics
   a. Market share
   b. Sales growth
2. Primary customer-based metrics
   a. Acquisition rate
   b. Acquisition cost
   c. Retention rate
   d. Survival rate
   e. *P*(Active)
   f. Lifetime duration
   g. Win-back rate
3. Popular customer-based value metrics
   a. Share of category requirement
   b. Size of wallet
   c. Share of wallet
   d. Expected share of wallet
4. Strategic customer-based value metrics
   a. Past customer value
   b. RFM value
   c. Customer lifetime value
   d. Customer equity

The key for the various notations used in the formulas is given in appendix 1.

5.2 TRADITIONAL MARKETING METRICS

5.2.1 MARKET SHARE (MS)

Market share is one of the most common metrics for measuring marketing performance. It is defined as the share of a firm's sales relative to the sales of all firms—across all customers in the given market. MS is an aggregate measure across customers, and it is measured in percentage. It can be calculated either on a monetary or a volumetric basis.

$$\text{MS (\%) of a firm } (j) \text{ in a category} = 100 \times \left[S_j \middle/ \sum_{j=1}^{J} S_j \right] \tag{1}$$

where:
j = firm
S = sales
ΣS_j = sum of sales across all firms in the market
Where does the information come from?

- Numerator: Sales of the focal firm are readily available from internal records.
- Denominator: Category sales are available from market research reports or from competitive intelligence.

Evaluation

Market share is one of the most common measures of marketing performance because it conveys an important piece of information and is readily computed. It is a typical measure of a product-focused marketing approach. However, it doesn't give any information about how the sales are distributed by customers—it only gives an aggregate notion of category performance. For example, a given market share can be caused by selling large amounts to a small percentage of the customer base or by making small sales to a large proportion of the market.

5.2.2 SALES GROWTH

Sales growth of a brand, product, or a firm is a simple measure that compares the increase or decrease in sales volume or sales value in a given period to sales volume or value in the previous period. Hence, it is measured in percentage. It indicates the degree of improvement in the sales performance between two or more time periods and acts as a flag for the management. A negative sales growth or sales growth lower than the rest of the market is normally a cause for concern.

$$\text{Sales growth in period } t \text{ (\%)} = 100 \times \left[\Delta S_{jt} \middle/ S_{jt-1} \right] \tag{2}$$

where:
J = firm
S_{jt} = change in sales in period t from period $t-1$,
S_{jt-1} = sales in period $t-1$
Where does the information come from?

- Both the numerator and denominator are available from internal records.

Evaluation

Sales growth is a quick indicator of the current health of a firm. If compared with the sales growth of the other players in the market, it also provides a relative measure of performance. However, it does not tell us which customers grew and which ones did not. This information is necessary if we are to take customer-level marketing initiatives.

5.3   PRIMARY CUSTOMER-BASED METRICS

5.3.1   CUSTOMER ACQUISITION MEASUREMENT

Customer acquisition measures have been receiving more attention recently. Managers have become more sensitive toward balancing customer acquisition and customer retention activities. In order to evaluate customer acquisition activities, we use two simple concepts—acquisition rate and acquisition cost.

Acquisition Rate

When firms attempt to acquire customers, they are typically targeting a specific group of prospects. For example, a European credit card issuer might target the student market in Italy. In order to describe the success of the acquisition campaign, a key performance indicator is the acquisition rate—the proportion of prospects converted to customers. It is calculated by dividing the fraction of prospects acquired by the total number of prospects targeted. It is measured as a percentage.

$$\text{Acquisition rate (\%)} = 100 \times \frac{\text{Number of prospects acquired}}{\text{Number of prospects targeted}} \qquad \textbf{(3)}$$

For example, the target market of the credit card issuer might have been two million students in Italy. Acquisition was measured in terms of new credit cards issued. The bank issued a total of 60,000 new credit cards. Thus, the acquisition rate was $100 \times (60{,}000/2{,}000{,}000) = 3$ percent.

The acquisition rate denotes an *average probability* of acquiring a customer from a population. Thus, the acquisition rate is always calculated for a *group* of customers (e.g., a segment), not for an individual customer. The equivalent measure for an individual is the acquisition probability. An acquisition rate for an individual does not exist.

Defining What Acquisition Is   Firms have different definitions for the term *acquisition.* In the credit card example, an acquisition was recorded when a new credit card was issued to the prospect. However, it is possible that the prospect signed up for the card only because she was interested in the promotional incentive and that she will never use the card. As a solution, the bank could define two different levels of acquisition—for issuing the credit card and issuing a statement (which depends on credit card activity). For example, although 60,000 credit cards have been issued to new customers, only 55,000 of them have received a statement, indicating activity on the card account. Thus, the level 1 acquisition rate is 3 percent and the level 2 acquisition rate is 2.75 percent.

In noncontractual contexts, acquisition is typically defined as the first purchase or purchasing in the first predefined period. For example, an outdoor direct-mail merchant received 110 first-time orders from a campaign based on a new mailing list of 5,000 prospects. Thus, the firm's acquisition rate is 2.2 percent.

It is important to note that acquisition rates are typically computed on a campaign-by-campaign basis. Since acquisition rates can vary tremendously within the same firm, an average (firm-wide) acquisition rate is mostly of limited value.

Where does the information come from?

- Numerator: Number of prospects acquired is determined from internal records.
- Denominator: Number of prospects targeted is gleaned from database and/or market research data.

Evaluation   Acquisition rate is a very important metric. However, it cannot be looked at in isolation.

Acquisition Cost

The second key metric in customer acquisition is the acquisition cost. The acquisition rate measures responsiveness to a campaign, but it doesn't say anything about the cost efficiency of a campaign. Acquisition cost is defined as the acquisition campaign spending divided by the number of acquired prospects. Acquisition cost is measured in monetary terms.

$$\text{Acquisition cost (\$)} = \frac{\text{Acquisition spending (\$)}}{\text{Number of prospects acquired}} \qquad \textbf{(4)}$$

For example, the cost of the acquisition campaign of the Italian credit card issuer was $3 million. Thus, the average cost of acquiring a single new customer for this campaign was $3,000,000/60,000 = $50. Depending on the exact definition of what constitutes acquisition, the cost can be calculated for different acquisition levels.

Delineating Acquisition Spending   It is not difficult to identify acquisition spending in an organization that (1) acquires prospects in distinct campaigns and (2) is able to pinpoint its acquisition efforts quite precisely to the prospect group. In this situation, acquisition cost can be calculated with the highest accuracy. Any company targeting prospects through direct mail would fall in this category—it knows the precise target group and the acquisition spending directed toward that group. As soon as firms rely on broadcasted communication (e.g., advertising through television or print media), measurement of acquisition cost becomes less precise. For example, prospects can be persuaded by advertising that was originally not targeted at them but toward existing customers. Clearly, acquisition cost will seem lower if those customers enter the acquisition cost calculation—making the numbers look more attractive than they really are. Also, firms might not necessarily differentiate between acquisition advertising and retention advertising. Calculating the precise acquisition cost in such a case can become quite difficult.

Where does the information come from?

- Numerator: Acquisition spending comes from internal records.
- Denominator: Number of prospects acquired comes from internal records.

Evaluation   Acquisition cost is a very important metric that firms should strive to continuously monitor.

5.3.2   CUSTOMER ACTIVITY MEASUREMENT

Once a prospect has been converted into a customer, the main phase of the customer-firm relationship begins. The concept of measuring the activity status of a customer-firm relationship deals with a very fundamental issue—whether a customer is a customer! On first sight, this might appear to be obvious. If a customer buys, then the customer is, in fact, a customer—otherwise, she is not. However, digging a little bit deeper, it seems we are uncovering a quite complicated matter. It is not at all clear what constitutes a living relationship. What's more, the meaning of an active relationship differs across industries. Clearly, one has to look at more than just purchasing acts of a customer. Customers interact with the firm in multiple ways (prepurchase inquiry, post-purchase service, complaints, and so on), all of which contribute to the entirety of the customer-firm relationship. Even in a simple case such as grocery shopping where the purchase per se is of highest importance to both parties involved, a multitude of other nonpurchase interactions adds or detracts from the relationship quality (e.g., the interaction with service employees, the communication of the store toward the customer, and the shopping experience).

Thus, it becomes clear that the customer–firm interaction comprises many more elements that may contribute to the fabric of the relationship. In most cases, however, the sequence of purchase is used to define whether a relationship exists. However, even if one uses this simplification, there still is the issue of customer dormancy. Dormancy occurs when an ongoing relationship is disrupted temporarily during the period we do not observe any purchase activity. To state an example, this might occur naturally when someone loses her job and therefore must scale down consumption. Once the person finds a new position, she is likely to return to the old consumption pattern. Consequently, the person is not starting a new relationship but is continuing an existing relationship. (We admit this discussion becomes complex when the dormancy has been very long.)

The challenge from a managerial point of view is to establish whether a seemingly dormant relationship has ended or the customer will return. In practice, this is a very tough call to make. Dormancy will or will not be considered, depending on the specific measure used to estimate customer activity.

Objective of Customer Activity Measurement

The reason we want to shed light on customer activity measurement is twofold. First, knowing the status of a customer's (a segment's) activity is important for managing marketing interventions. A customer-oriented organization tries to align resource allocation with actual customer behavior. Instead of mass advertising or mass marketing, managerial action can gain tremendous efficiency by adjusting its interventions to the actual customer needs or activity status. The second reason for measuring customer activity is because it is a key input in customer valuation models such as net-present value (NPV) models. The marketing function has come under increasing pressure to demonstrate how it adds to shareholder value. This demonstration typically involves the estimation of the evolving customer value over time. Thus, measuring customer activity is a critical intermediary step in this valuation process.

This section covers these types of customer activity:

- Average inter-purchase time (AIT)
- Retention rate and defection rate
- Survival rate
- Lifetime duration
- P(Active)

Each metric has a purpose with its own strengths and weaknesses. Thus, the task of the manager will be to find the most suitable metric for a given situation.

Average Inter-Purchase Time (AIT)

AIT is the average time between purchases. It is measured in terms of time periods (days, weeks, months, etc). It is computed by taking the inverse of the number of purchase incidences per time period.

$$\text{AIT of a customer} = \frac{1}{\begin{array}{c}\text{Number of purchase incidences from the}\\\text{first purchase until the current time period}\end{array}} \tag{5}$$

Example: If a BINGO supermarket customer buys, on average, six times at BINGO during a month, then the AIT for that customer will be $1/6 = 0.1667$ months, or approximately 5 days (0.1667×30).

Where does the information come from?

- Denominator: Sales records are used, assuming individual customer records are maintained and individual customers are identified.

Evaluation AIT is an easy-to-calculate indicator which can be an important statistic of the customer's activity status, especially for those industries where customers buy on a frequent basis. As a simple rule, firm intervention might be warranted any time customers fall considerably below their AIT.

Retention and Defection

Retention and defection are like two sides of the same coin. One can be inferred from the other, and, depending on the context, it is better to use one or the other metric. Similar to the discussion for acquisition rate, retention rate is always defined for a group of customers—that is, a segment. *Retention rate* is defined as the average likelihood that a customer purchases from the focal firm in a period (t), given that this customer has purchased in the last period ($t - 1$). The defection rate is defined as the average likelihood that a customer defects from the focal firm in a period (t), given that the customer was purchasing up to period ($t - 1$). Retention rate and defection rate are measured in percentage.

$$\text{Retention rate (\%)} = \left(\frac{\begin{array}{c} \text{Number of customers in cohort buying in } (t)| \\ \text{Number of customers in cohort buying in } (t-1) \end{array}}{\text{Number of customers in cohort buying in } (t-1)} \right) \times 100 \quad \textbf{(6)}$$

This calculation is easy to perform. The resulting retention rate refers to the average retention rate of a cohort or segment of customers.

Average retention rate, lifetime duration, and average defection rate can be shown to be interrelated using the following simple formulas.

$$\text{Retention rate (\%)} = 1 - \left(\frac{1}{\text{Avg. lifetime duration}} \right) \quad \textbf{(7)}$$

or

$$\text{Avg. retention rate (\%)} = 1 - \text{Avg. defection rate} \quad \textbf{(8)}$$

Although we use the case of an average retention rate, one has to be aware that retention rates are typically *not* equal across different periods. For example, if one deals with a single cohort, proportionally fewer customers leave over time, thus making the retention rate decrease over time. One has to keep this in mind when extrapolating retention rates for one period to an entire time horizon.

Calculating the customer retention rate using equation (7) assumes knowledge of a customer's lifetime duration.[1] How to assess lifetime duration will be discussed later. Nevertheless, one can regroup equation (7) to calculate the average lifetime duration from the known average retention rate.

$$\text{Avg. lifetime duration} = \frac{1}{(1 - \text{Avg. retention rate})} \quad \textbf{(9)}$$

Example: If the average customer lifetime duration of a group of customers is four years, then the average retention rate is $1 - (1/4) = 0.75$, or 75 percent a year. This means that on average, 75 percent of the customers remain customers in the next period. If we look at the effect for a cohort of customers over time (see the following table) we find that from 100 customers who start in year 1, about 32 are left at the end of year 4.

Customers starting at the beginning of year 1:	100	
Customers remaining at the end of year 1:	75	(0.75×100)
Customers remaining at the end of year 2:	56.25	(0.75×75)
Customers remaining at the end of year 3:	42.18	(0.75×56.25)
Customers remaining at the end of year 4:	31.64	(0.75×42.18)

Assuming constant retention rates, the number of retained customers in any arbitrary period $(t + n)$ can simply be calculated with equation (10):

Number of retained customers
= Number of acquired customers in cohort $\times$ Retention rate$^{(t + n)}$ **(10)**

For the previous example, the number of retained customers at the end of year 4 is $100 \times 0.75^4 = 31.64$. If we plot the entire series of customers who defect each period, we see the variation (or heterogeneity) around the average lifetime duration of four years (see Figure 5-1).

Given a retention rate of 75 percent, many customers leave in the early years. However, a small number of customers continue to stay for a long duration. This pattern results in an average lifetime duration of four years.

Assuming a constant retention rate, customer lifetime durations and retention rates are linked; see equation (7). Figure 5-2 illustrates this link. As the retention rate increases, customer lifetime duration increases disproportionately. This pattern hints at the potential attractiveness of long-term customer relationships. One has to keep in mind, however, increasing the marginal retention rate is likely to be increasingly expensive.

Cautionary Note   A key assumption of the retention rate concept is that once customers leave the relationship, they are gone forever. The concept of retention rate does not allow for temporary dormancies. Managers have to make a judgment whether the dormancy phenomenon plays a major or a minor role in their business. Using the retention rate is fine if it plays a minor role. If dormancy plays a major role, other concepts have to be used to assess customer activity. These concepts will be dealt with in later sections (see lifetime duration, transition matrix).

Is Retention only about Buying?   Typically, retention refers to the fact that a customer continues to purchase goods or services from the company. This is always the case.

FIGURE   5-1   VARIATION IN DEFECTION RATE WITH RESPECT TO CUSTOMER TENURE

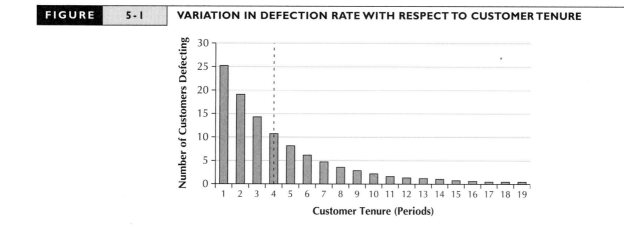

FIGURE **5-2** **CHANGE IN RETENTION RATE WITH CUSTOMER LIFETIME DURATION**

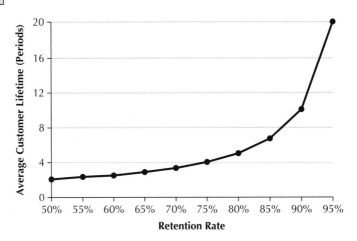

Take, for example, Yahoo.com. Most of Yahoo's services, such as basic e-mail and weather forecasts, are free. Although most of Yahoo's customers don't have any transactions in the traditional sense, one would consider site visits as the critical activity, which then would be used to measure retention for Yahoo. Thus, in the case that the customer-firm relationship is not primarily about monetary transactions, it is important to define an appropriate basis in order to measure retention.

How Is Retention Different from Loyalty? Retention is *not* the same as customer loyalty. Although retention is measured on a period-by-period basis and indicates whether customers are coming back, the loyalty construct has a much stronger theoretical meaning. If somebody is loyal toward a store or a brand, this person has a positive emotional or psychological disposition toward this brand. People might continue to purchase a particular brand or might patronize a particular store, but this may be purely out of convenience or inertia. In this case, someone might be retained, but the person is not loyal.

Defection Rate As already mentioned, the concepts of defection and retention go together. Defection rate is calculated as follows:

$$\text{Avg. defection rate (\%)} = 1 - \text{Avg. retention rate}_t \tag{11}$$

Example: The retention rate in the previous example is 0.75. Thus, the defection rate is 1 − 0.75 = 0.25, or 25 percent.

Survival Rate

Another concept closely linked with retention and defection is survival. The survival rate indicates the proportion of customers who have *survived* (or, in other words, continued to remain as a customer) until a period t from the beginning of observing these customers.

Survival rate is measured for cohorts of customers, wherein a cohort refers to a batch of customers acquired within a specified period of time.

Although retention rate and defection rate reflect retention and defection, respectively, in a given period the survival rate gives a summary measure of how many customers survived

---

CRM AT WORK 5.1

AMAZON: ACQUISITION AND RETENTION

As previously noted, Amazon is one of the leaders in implementing customer relationship management programs on the Web. These programs have helped drive both customer acquisition and retention. In 1999, Amazon acquired 11 million new customers, nearly tripling its number of customers from 1998, but its greatest success in that year was not adding customers, but keeping those that it already had. Repeat customers during the year accounted for 71 percent of all sales.

Amazon has been able to acquire and retain customers at such a high rate by striving to learn about its customers and their needs and then using this information to offer them value-added features.

SOURCE: Robert. C. Blattberg, Gary Getz, Jacquelyn S. Thomas, "Customer Equity: Building and Managing Relationships as Valuable Assets" (Cambridge, Mass.: Harvard Business School Press, 2001).

---

between the start of the formation of a cohort and any point in time afterward. It is measured in percentage. Survival rate at time (t) is equal to the product of the retention rate at time (t) and the survival rate during the immediately preceding period.

$$\text{Survival rate}_t (\%) = 100 \times \text{Retention rate}_t \times \text{Survival rate}_{t-1} \qquad (12)$$

In period 1, the survival rate $_{t-1}$ is, of course, assumed to be 100 percent.

The survival rate is of great interest, because one can conveniently calculate the absolute number of survivors in a given period t. One simply multiplies the survival rate$_t$ by the cohort size in the beginning.

Example: (Number of customers starting at the beginning of year one is 1,000.)

	Retention Rate	Survival Rate	Survivors
Period 1	0.55	0.55	550
Period 2	0.62	0.341	341
Period 3	0.68	0.231	231
Period 4	0.73	0.169	169

Computing the number of survivors:

For example,
Number of survivors for period 1 = Survival rate for period 1 × Number of customers at the beginning
Therefore,
Number of survivors for period 1 = 0.55 × 1,000 = 550

Computing survival rate:

Recall that
Survival rate$_t$ (%) = Retention rate$_t$ × Survival rate$_{t-1}$

In the table above, survival rate for period 2 can be calculated as follows:
   Survival rate for period 2 = Retention rate of period 2 × Survival rate of period 1
   Therefore, the survival rate for period 2 = 0.62 × 0.55 = 0.341, or 34.1%

Projecting Retention Rates   Very often, we find ourselves in a situation where we would like to get an idea about future retention rates of a particular cohort of customers. To do so, we use information on past retention rates to make a prediction of future retention rates. We have already discussed that retention rates tend to increase over time. As short-term customers drop out, the retention rate of the remaining (loyal) customers increases necessarily. This increase, however, is not linear. Almost always, retention rates tend to increase at a decreasing rate.

There is a simple method which allows us to forecast nonlinear retention rates—a simple exponential form. This approach models the retention rate as a function of time.

$$Rr_t = Rr_c \times (1 - \exp^{-rt}) \tag{13}$$

Rr_t is the predicted retention rate for a given period in the future. Rr_c is the retention rate ceiling, which is the maximum attainable retention rate if unlimited resources were available. Clearly, a firm will not be able to retain all customers even if they spent unlimited advertising on them. The figure for Rr_c is typically estimated through managerial judgment. The parameter r is the coefficient of retention. This parameter determines how quickly retention rates converge over time to the retention ceiling. It can easily be estimated through spreadsheet analysis based on past retention data.

Figure 5-3 shows actual retention rates for a credit card company (white bars). The time horizon is 20 quarters. Equation 13 was applied with $Rr_c = 0.95$, which means that managers believe that the maximum attainable retention rate is 95 percent. The parameter $r = 0.2$ is based on estimates that come from previous observations. Applying equation (13), the retention rates for period 11–20 were estimated (gray bars). It can be seen that the method *to approximate* the actual retention rates was very close.

If past estimates of the parameter r are not available, one can use another method. The retention rate Rr_t is observed for a number of past periods. Equation (13) can be regrouped to form equation (14):

$$r = (1/t) \times (\ln (Rr_c) - \ln (Rr_c - Rr_t)) \tag{14}$$

For example, the known retention rate in period 9 is 80 percent, while the one in period 10 is 82 percent. Thus, the parameter r for period 9 is $(1/9) \times (\ln(0.95) - \ln(0.95 - 0.8)) = 0.205$. The parameter r for period 10 is $(1/10) \times (\ln(0.95) - \ln(0.95 - 0.82)) = 0.198$. One can see that for both periods the parameter r approximates the value 0.2.

FIGURE 5-3 ACTUAL AND PREDICTED RETENTION RATE FOR A CREDIT CARD COMPANY

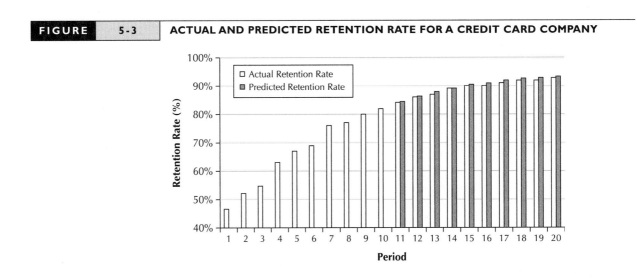

Comprehensive Example

Let's look at an actual retention pattern of a direct marketing firm. We want to illustrate the concepts of retention rate, defection rate, and survival rate. A cohort of 7,500 customers was acquired at the outset of the analysis. Table 5-1 shows the actual retention pattern for 10 periods in column 2. For example, after period 1, only 32 percent of the customers are retained into the second period. Thus, this company has a high rate of lost customers. If we are at the end of period 10 and want to make an assessment of future retention rates, we need to make a customer activity forecast.

Column 3 shows the predicted retention pattern, based on equation (13). The underlying maximum retention rate for the example is 0.80, and the coefficient of retention r is 0.5 (estimated from past data for the company). Thus, retention rates approximate the maximum rate already at period 10. This means that after period 10, the company retains approximately 80 percent of customer base from period to period. The defection rate in column 4 is simply calculated as (1 – retention rate). Finally, the survival rate, calculated with equation (12), indicates the proportion of the original cohort that survives until period t. For example, only 1.2 percent of the original cohort survives until period 11. If the survival rate is multiplied by the original cohort size—in this case, 7,500—we obtain the number of customers surviving up to period t (column 6).

Another important measure which can be derived from the information is that of lifetime duration. A simple (naïve) approach would be to calculate the mean lifetime duration from the average retention rate. The average retention rate across the 15 periods (column 2 and 3) is 71.8 percent, which results in an average lifetime duration of 3.54 periods. Since the retention rates change over time, we would have to compute an appropriate measure of average retention in order to compute average lifetime duration. More specifically, since many more customers are subject to a lower retention rate in the early periods as compared to higher retention rates in later periods, a simple average of retention rates 1 to 15 would be misleading. In the computation of an average retention rate, we need to weigh the number of survived periods accordingly. The correct average lifetime duration is calculated as follows:

| TABLE | 5-1 | | | ACTUAL RETENTION PATTERN OF A DIRECT MARKETING FIRM |

1 Period Since Acquisition	2 Actual Retention Rate	3 Predicted Retention Rate	4 Defection Rate %	5 Survival Rate	6 Expected Number of Active Customers	7 Number of Active Periods
1	32.0%		68.0%	32.0%	2,400	2,400
2	49.1%		50.9%	15.7%	1,178	2,357
3	63.2%		36.8%	9.9%	745	2,234
4	69.0%		31.0%	6.9%	514	2,056
5	72.6%		27.4%	5.0%	373	1,865
6	76.7%		23.3%	3.8%	286	1,717
7	77.9%		22.1%	3.0%	223	1,560
8	78.5%		21.5%	2.3%	175	1,400
9	79.0%		21.0%	1.8%	138	1,244
10	80.0%		20.0%	1.5%	111	1,106
11		79.7%	20.3%	1.2%	88	969
12		79.8%	20.2%	0.9%	70	844
13		79.9%	20.1%	0.7%	56	730
14		79.9%	20.1%	0.6%	45	628
15		80.0%	20.0%	0.5%	36	538

$$\text{Avg. lifetime duration} = \frac{\sum_{t=1}^{T} \text{Customers retained}_t \times \text{Number of periods}}{N} \qquad (15)$$

Where:

N = cohort size

t = time period

The result of the weighing process is shown in column 7. Intuitively, it is the number of active customer periods for every period. For example, at the end of period 1 we have 2,400 (2,400 customers $\times$ 1 period) active periods, at the end of period 2 we have 2,357 (1,178 customers $\times$ 2 period) active periods, and so on. If we add all active periods and divide by the cohort size of 7,500, the average lifetime duration will be 2.89 periods. Thus, the company needs to replace its customer base every three periods, and not every 3.5 periods, as indicated before.

Lifetime Duration

It is sometimes unclear how long a customer has been associated with a firm in a noncontractual setting, since there is no expiration date explicitly stated by the customer. In such situations, it is important to be able to predict the lifetime duration of a customer by observing buying patterns and other explanatory factors. Knowing how long a customer remains a customer is a key ingredient in the calculation of the *customer lifetime value*—a key strategic metric. Furthermore, it has implications for churn management, customer replacement, and management of lifetime duration drivers.

In calculating the lifetime duration of a customer we therefore differentiate between two cases. The first is the case of complete information. In this scenario, a customer's first and last purchases are assumed to be known. The second case is the case of incomplete information, where either the time of first purchase, or the time of the last purchase, or both are unknown. Figure 5-4 illustrates this situation.

Buyer 1 starts his relationship with the firm after the beginning of the observation window and also stops his relationship before the end of the given observation window. Buyer 2 started his relationships with the organization before his behavior was being monitored. Nevertheless, the termination of his relationship is observed. This observation is called *left-censored*. In this situation, it is unknown to the firm for how long the buyer has been engaging in the relationship *before* the start of the observation window (t_0).

The start of Buyer 3's relationship has been observed within the observation window. However, his relationships continued beyond the end of the observation window (t_1).

FIGURE 5-4 CUSTOMER LIFETIME DURATION WHEN THE INFORMATION IS INCOMPLETE

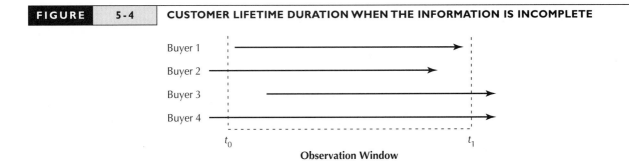

Observation Window

Thus, it is not known to the firm at t_1 how much longer the customer will in fact be a customer. This observation is called *right-censored*. Finally, Buyer 4's relationship started before the observation window and ends after the observation window. This observation is called *left- and right-censored*. Data that consist of right-censored observations require the use of survival analysis techniques.[2]

Calculating Lifetime Duration   When talking about the concept of a customer's lifetime duration, not all relationships are equal. We must take the type of product, which is subject to exchange into account. Here, we are specifying the following three cases:

1. Contractual
2. Noncontractual (or always-a-share)
3. One-off purchases

Contractual relationships are those where buyers engage in a specific commitment. This commitment may foresee duration and/or level of usage. A contractual relationship that defines length and level of usage is, for example, an apartment rental lease or a cable TV subscription. A contractual relationship, which defines only length, is, for example, a mobile phone contract. Finally, a contractual relationship which defines neither length nor usage level is a credit card. This category has also been labeled *lost-for-good* because a company uses the entire customer relationship once a client terminates the contract.

Noncontractual relationships are those where buyers do not commit in any way, either in duration or level of usage. Purchasing with a department store, an airline, or a direct-mail company are examples. Since customers may use at any given time several suppliers (e.g., go to several different supermarkets), this category has been labeled *always-a-share*.

In most situations, one can unambiguously associate a particular product category with one of the previous cases. We want to caution the reader about a number of situations where the association is not as clear and where a categorization can be subject to debate.

- *Contractual case.* A contractual relationship constitutes the most straightforward lifetime duration calculation. One simply measures the time from start of the relationship (or from start of the observation window) until the end of the relationship (or until end of observation window). Since the status of the account is known, this is straightforward to calculate. For example, a cable TV subscriber opened his account on January 1, 2002, and remained active until June 30, 2004. Thus, the lifetime duration is thirty months. This example shows a case where the duration is neither left, nor right-censored (buyer 1 in Figure 5-4). If the relationship is still ongoing, we use the right observation window to calculate the lifetime duration.

- Noncontractual case. If the relationship is such that there is no explicit contract, buyers come and go as they please. Two different approaches are used here. The first approach emulates the calculation of a finite duration, similar to the contractual case. Towards this end, one establishes for a given point in time the likelihood a customer is still active. If that likelihood falls below a certain threshold, the customer is deemed to be inactive. A consequence of that might be that the organization stops allocating resources to that customer.

P(Active)

In a noncontractual case, given a particular customer, it may be useful to know if the customer is likely to transact in a particular time period. In other words we would like to know the probability of that customer being active in time *t*, *P*(Active).

A simple approach for computing the probability of being active, $P(\text{Active})$, is via the following formula:[3]

$$P(\text{Active}) = T^n \qquad\qquad (16)$$

where

n is the number of purchases in a given period

T is the time of the last purchase (expressed as a fraction of the observation period)

Example To compute the $P(\text{Active})$ of each of the two customers in the twelfth month of activity, see Figure 5-5.

Thus for Customer 1: $T = (8/12) = 0.6667$ and $n = 4$

$$P(\text{Active})_1 = (0.6667)^4 = 0.197 \qquad\qquad (17)$$

And for Customer 2: $T = (8/12) = 0.6667$ and $n = 2$

$$P(\text{Active})_2 = (0.6667)^2 = 0.444 \qquad\qquad (18)$$

It is interesting to observe that a customer who has bought four times in the first eight months but has not bought in the last four months has a lower probability of buying in the twelfth month over a customer who has bought only twice in the same window of eight months.

There are several methods of calculating $P(\text{Active})$. For an advanced application, see Reinartz and Kumar (2000)[4] and Reinartz and Kumar (2002).[5]

5.3.3 WIN-BACK RATE

Win-back is really a part of the acquisition process. Win-back is applicable to contractual and noncontractual situations. Firms may want to measure the proportion of acquired customers in a period whom they had lost in an earlier period. This indicates either a successful communication of an important change in the product offering, service, or a change in the customer needs. *Win-back rate* is used as an indicator of success in turn-around efforts. In order to monitor win-back, a firm needs to keep track of lost customers and identify them when reentering the transacting customer base at a later time.

FIGURE **5-5** **ESTIMATION OF *P*(ACTIVE)**

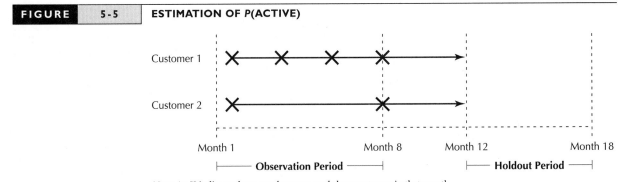

Note: An X indicates that a purchase was made by a customer in that month.

5.4 SUMMARY

Since customer value management involves allocating resources differently for individual customers based on their economic value, understanding value contribution from each of the customers to the firm is very important. In the absence of individual customer data, companies have relied on traditional marketing metrics such as market share and sales growth. Market share is defined as the share of a firm's sales relative to the sales of all firms—across all customers in the given market. It only gives an aggregate notion of category performance, but doesn't give any information about how the sales are distributed by customers. Sales growth expressed in percentage provides a relative measure of performance but fails to indicate which customers contributed more and which contributed less. The availability of customer-level data helps firms utilize a new set of metrics which enables value to be assigned to each customer. Acquisition measurement metrics measure the customer level success of marketing efforts to acquire new customers. Two important acquisition metrics are *acquisition rate and acquisition cost.* Acquisition rate is the proportion of prospects converted to customers, and acquisition cost is the campaign spending per acquired customer. Customer activity metrics, by contrast, track customer activities after the acquisition stage. Some critical customer activity metrics are retention rate, survival rate, probability of a customer being active, $P(\text{Active})$, customer lifetime duration, and win-back rate. These are important inputs for the calculation of customer value and for aligning resource allocation with customers' behavior. Average inter-purchase time is one of the preliminary customer activity metrics, and is defined as the average time between purchases. Retention rate is defined as the average likelihood a customer purchases from the focal firm in a period (t), given this customer has purchased in the last period $(t-1)$. The defection rate is defined as the average likelihood a customer defects from the focal firm in a period (t), given the customer was purchasing up to period $(t-1)$. The survival rate is another preliminary customer metric, and this indicates the proportion of customers that have "survived" (or, in other words, continued to remain as a customer) until a period t from the beginning of observing these customers. Survival rate is closely linked with retention rate. Survival rate is a summary measure of how many customers survived between the start of the formation of a cohort and any point in time afterward, while retention rate reflects retention in a given period only. It can be measured as the product of the retention rate at time t and the survival rate during the immediately preceding period. Lifetime duration is a very important metric in the calculation of the customer lifetime value—a key strategic metric. Calculation of lifetime duration is different in contractual and noncontractual situations. In a contractual case, this is the time from the start of the relationship (or from the start of the observation window) until the end of the relationship (or until end of observation window). However, in a noncontractual situation, firms are interested in the likelihood the customer is active at a given point in time. If the likelihood is less than a threshold value, the customer is considered inactive. This is given by the next metric, $P(\text{Active})$, which is the probability that a customer is active in time t. A simple formula for $P(\text{Active})$ is $P(\text{Active}) = T^n$, where n is the number of purchases in a given period and T is the time of the last purchase (expressed as a fraction of the observation period). Win-back rate is the proportion of the lost customers acquired in a later period. Win-back rate is used as an indicator of the success of the turn-around efforts of a firm.

5.5 EXERCISE QUESTIONS

1. How would you calculate the retention rate of your company's customer base? What assumptions do you need to make?

2. How will you calculate the acquisition cost per customer? Consider a mail-order catalog company, an IT services company, and a retail store. What are the underlying assumptions in each case? How precise are your calculations?
3. Try to predict retention rates using equation (13).
4. How will you determine if a customer is still your customer in noncontractual settings?

MINI CASE 5.1

AMERICAN AIRLINES USES DATABASE MARKETING FOR EFFICIENT CUSTOMER ACQUISITION

American Airlines is one of the leading scheduled air carriers in the world, running both passenger and cargo services. The company operates on a worldwide basis with services to major cities in Europe, Canada, Mexico, the Caribbean, Central and South America, Asia, and across the United States. American Airlines is headquartered in Fort Worth, Texas. The company was the first to implement a frequent flyer program (AAdvantage), and today, the program is the largest in terms of members. Besides using the program to induce current members to spend more of their flight dollars with American Airlines, the company uses the program to efficiently target new prospects and to convert patrons of competing airlines. One example of this strategy is the cooperation with the credit card company American Express. Through the collaboration with American Express, American Airlines tries to identify attractive customers who are not American Airlines flyers. Take the example of the Southeast Asian route from Los Angeles to Tokyo. American Airlines obtains data from American Express about customers who live in California and who are using their Amex card in Japan. This list of customers is compared with the actual list of AAadvantage members who are flying to Tokyo. Naturally, there will be customers who do not appear on AAdvantage's member list. These are obviously premier targets for American Airlines, as they apparently fly to Tokyo but do so with a competing carrier. These prospects will then get attractive offers inducing them to try American Airlines. American Airlines has been very successful in targeting attractive prospects fly to large number of destinations.

Questions:

1. How does American Airlines know whether this new practice works (i.e., is successful in acquiring more customers than previous methods)? Which performance indicators do you need to measure in order to document this?
2. Explain how exactly American Airlines can compute return on marketing spend with this new practice.
3. Do you think American Airlines' practice is a benefit or a cost to the consumer?

APPENDIX I

Notation Key

Notation	Explanation
i	buyer with the focal firm
I	total number of buyers with the focal firm
k	buyer in the market
K	total number of buyers in the market
n	customer in cohort
N	cohort size
j	firm
J	total number of firms
S	sales (value)
V	sales (volume)
c	category
t	time period
T	length of horizon
Ar	acquisition rate
Rr	retention rate
Dr	defection rate
Sr	survival rate
Ar_c	acquisition rate ceiling
Rr_c	retention rate ceiling
r	coefficient of retention
a	coefficient of acquisition
$P(\text{Active})$	the probability of the ith customer being alive or transacting in period t

ENDNOTES

1.   The terms *lifetime duration, customer lifetime,* and *customer tenure* are often used interchangeably.

2.   Survival analysis techniques allow us to examine the relationship of various variables that affect the lifetime duration in a firm-customer scenario when observed variables are right-censored.

3.   David C. Schmittlein and Donald G. Morrison, "Is the Customer Still Active?" *The American Statistician* 39, no. 4 (1985): 291–295.

4.   Werner Reinartz and V. Kumar, "On the Profitability of Long-Life Customers in a Noncontractual Setting: An Empirical Investigation and Implications for Marketing," *Journal of Marketing* 64, no. 4 (October 2000): 17–35.

5.   Werner Reinartz and V. Kumar, "The Mismanagement of Customer Loyalty," *Harvard Business Review* (July 2002).

CHAPTER 6

Customer Value Metrics— Concepts and Practices

Contents

6.1 OVERVIEW

In the previous chapter, we examined some traditional marketing metrics and various primary customer-based metrics. This chapter explains some surrogate metrics of customer value used in the industry and proceeds to conceptualize strategic metrics of customer value. Some of the primary customer-based metrics introduced earlier form the inputs to derive customer value—the key metric that drives decision making in the age of data-based marketing.

Size of wallet and *share of wallet* are popular metrics firms frequently apply to evaluate a customer's worth. In a frequently purchased category such as toothpaste, it is possible to observe customers frequently switching between multiple brands. A transition matrix can be used as a customer-based tool which allows us to compute the metric *expected share of wallet* for multiple brands. Metrics have been developed to keep track of marketing actions and costs related to customer acquisition. *Past customer value and RFM value* are more refined methods of computing the relative worth of individual customers. In recent times, *customer lifetime value* has emerged as the key metric needed to manage customers profitably. The aggregate of the customer lifetime value of each customer is referred to as the *customer equity* of the firm.

Customer selection strategies, which are explained in the third section of the chapter, help firms identify the right customers to optimally allocate the available marketing resources. The chapter explains two popular customer selection strategies—namely, decision tree and logistic regression. Typically, both decision tree algorithm and logistic regression identify the predictor variables that best separate the outcome of a 0/1 binary dependent variable. In the last section of the chapter, we discuss techniques companies can use to evaluate alternative selection strategies. The techniques described include lift analysis, cumulative lift analysis, and deciles analysis.

6.2 POPULAR CUSTOMER-BASED VALUE METRICS

Firms have adopted some popular surrogate measures of customer value which they anticipate will be reasonable indicators of the actual customer value. These metrics help firms prioritize their customers in a manner that helps them assign a higher proportion of resources to the customers who they expect will generate greater profits in the future. In the absence of the availability of more sophisticated mathematical techniques, these measures help firms make superior decisions.

We suggest managers attempt to correlate these surrogate measures on a selective basis with more rigorous customer value metrics. Only if these correlations yield satisfactory results (i.e., correlations are substantial) can and should the surrogate measures be used for decision making.

6.2.1 SIZE OF WALLET

Size of wallet is the amount of a buyer's total spending in a category—or, stated differently, the category sales of all firms to that customer. Size of wallet is measured in monetary terms.

$$\text{Size of wallet (\$) of customer in a category} = \sum_{j=1}^{J} S_j \qquad (1)$$

where:

S_j = sales to the focal customer by the firm j

j = firm

$\displaystyle\sum_{j=1}^{J}$ represents the summation of the value of sales made by all firms, J, that sell a category of products to the focal customer.

Example: A consumer might spend an average of $400 every month on groceries, across several supermarkets. Thus, her size of wallet is $400.

Where does the information come from?

Information about the size of wallet can be gathered in many ways. For existing customers, the information can be collected through primary market research (e.g., surveys). A typical question a firm might ask is, "On average, how much do you spend every month on category A?" For prospects, it is quite difficult to obtain the size-of-wallet information on an individual level. Therefore, segment-level information is most appropriate.

Evaluation

Size of wallet is a critical measure of the customer-centric organization. When firms attempt to establish and maintain profitable relationships, the customer's buying potential (i.e., size of wallet) is a critical piece of information. Firms are particularly interested in acquiring and retaining customers with large wallet sizes. The assumption firms make here is that large customers will bring in more revenues and profits.

6.2.2   SHARE OF CATEGORY REQUIREMENT (SCR)

SCR is defined as the proportion of category *volume* accounted for by a brand or focal firm within its base of buyers. SCR is often computed as an aggregate level metric, when individual purchase data are unavailable. However, when such data are available, SCR is computed by dividing the volume of sales (V) of the focal firm in a category by the total category volume *within the firm's buyer base.* SCR is measured as a percentage.

$$\text{SCR (\%) of firm or brand in category} = \frac{\sum_{i=1}^{I} V_{ij}}{\sum_{i=1}^{I} \sum_{j=1}^{J} V_{ij}} \qquad (2)$$

where

  j = firm
  V = purchase volume
  i = those customers who buy brand

$\sum_{i=1}^{I}$ represents the summation of volume purchased by all the i customers from a firm j

$\sum_{i=1}^{I} \sum_{j=1}^{J}$ represents the summation of volume purchased by all i customers from all j firms

The SCR ratio is sometimes calculated simply by using purchase occasions or product units as the unit of analysis. The computation discussed here is for the aggregated case. SCR can also be calculated for individual customers. At the individual level, then, this measures the percentage of a customer's SCR a given brand or store satisfies.

Example: In this example, there are three customers in the category. The category consists of three brands—SAMA, SOMO, and SUMU. Table 6-1 shows the number of purchases during a three-month period.

| TABLE 6-1 | CALCULATION OF SCR-PURCHASES DURING A THREE-MONTH PERIOD |

	Brand SAMA	Brand SOMO	Brand SUMU	TOTAL
Customer 1	2	8	0	10
Customer 2	6	0	3	9
Customer 3	0	4	1	5
TOTAL	8	12	4	**24**

The category volume in the three-month period is 24 units. Brand SAMA has a market share of 33 percent (i.e., 8 purchases out of a total of 24) and a SCR of 42.1 percent (i.e., 8 purchases out of 19, made by its two buyers). This example shows that even though SAMA's market share is already substantial, its SCR is even higher. The high SCR for SAMA indicates that once consumers buy SAMA, they tend to prefer it disproportionately more.

Where does the information come from?

- Numerator: Volumetric sales of the focal firm are readily available from internal records.
- Denominator: The total volumetric purchases of the focal firm's buyer base are typically obtained through market and distribution panels, which are quite common for certain industries (e.g., fast-moving consumer goods (FMCG)). Other industries use mainly primary market research (surveys). Since this information is costly to gather, it is typically collected for a representative sample and then extrapolated to the entire buyer base. Qualitative managerial judgment is another potential low-cost alternative.

Evaluation

SCR is one of the most commonly accepted measures of customer loyalty, at least for FMCG categories. It separates the question, "whether anyone buys the brand" from the question, "how much they buy." An important characteristic of this measure is that it controls for the total volume of the segments/individuals category requirements. In other words, regardless of the total value of purchases per period, in terms of percentage of allocated purchases (loyalty), it puts all customers on the same metric. Overall, it is an important indicator on which firms should strive to deliver. However, this metric does not necessarily indicate whether a high SCR customer will generate substantial revenues or profits—this only comes through knowing something about the size of wallet of this customer.

Case in Point

Suppose a computer manufacturer, say ABC Computers, has the following data about its annual customer purchases on Notebook Computers for the year 2003. Using Table 6-2, it can compute the SCR ratio for each of its customers and identify those customers who have a higher SCR ratio from those with a lower SCR ratio.

From Table 6-2, we can see customer 3 has the highest SCR. Therefore, ABC Computers should identify high SCR customers such as customer 3, and target more of its marketing efforts (mailers, advertisements, etc.) toward such customers and their

TABLE	**6-2**	**SCR RATIOS**		
		Total Requirement of Notebook Computers per Customer in 2003 A	**Total Number of Notebook Computers Purchased from ABC Computers per Customer per Period** B	**Share of Category Requirement for ABC Computers per Customer per Period** B/A
	Customer 1	100	20	.20
	Customer 2	1,000	200	.20
	Customer 3	2,000	500	.25

respective requirements. In addition, customer 3's size of wallet (column A) is the largest, making customer 3 even more attractive.

6.2.3 SHARE OF WALLET (SW)

SW is defined as the proportion of category *value* accounted for by a focal brand or a focal firm *within its base of buyers*. It can be measured at the individual customer level or at an aggregate level (e.g., segment level or entire customer base).

Individual Share of Wallet (ISW)

ISW is defined as the proportion of category *value* accounted for by a focal brand or a focal firm for a buyer from all brands the buyer purchases in that category. It indicates the degree to which a customer satisfies his needs in the category with a focal brand or firm.

It is computed by dividing the value of sales (S) of the focal firm (j) to a buyer in a category by the size of wallet of the same customer in a time period. ISW is measured as a percentage.

$$\text{ISW (\%) of firm to customer (\%)} = \frac{S_j}{\sum_{j=1}^{J} S_j} \tag{3}$$

where

S = sales to the focal customer
j = firm

$\sum_{j=1}^{J}$ represents the summation of the value of sales made by all the J firms selling a category of products to a buyer

Example: If a consumer spends $400 monthly on groceries, and $300 of her purchases are with Supermarket BINGO, then BINGO's share of wallet for that consumer is 75 percent in that month.

Where does the information come from?

- Numerator: Typically, sales come from internal records (assuming that information is stored on the individual level).
- Denominator: Typically, sales value across all firms comes from primary market research (surveys), administered to individual customers. Since this information is costly to gather, it is often collected for a representative sample and then extrapolated to the entire buyer base. Sometimes, firms can *infer* the size of wallet for a certain product—for example, in certain business-to-business (B-to-B) contexts. For example, BASF, one of the few manufacturers of car paint, supplies its product to Daimler-Chrysler. Based on its knowledge of how much paint it takes to paint an average sized car, it can infer Daimler-Chrysler's size of wallet for car paint based on its worldwide production output—a figure easily derived from secondary sources.

Evaluation   Just like SCR, SW is a measure of customer loyalty and can be an important metric on which firms should strive to deliver. However, SW is unable to provide a clear indication of future revenues and profits expected from a customer.

Aggregate Share of Wallet (ASW) (Brand or Firm Level)

Aggregate share of wallet (ASW) is defined as the proportion of category *value* accounted for by a focal brand or a focal firm *within its base of buyers.* It indicates the degree to which the customers of a focal firm satisfy their needs on average, in a category with a focal firm.

ASW of firm (%)

$$= \frac{\sum_{t=1}^{T} ISW_{ji}}{\text{Number of customers}} \quad (4)$$

$$= \frac{\sum_{i=1}^{I} S_i}{\sum_{j=1}^{J} \sum_{i=1}^{I} S_{ij}} \quad (5)$$

where

S = sales to the focal customer
j = firm
i = those customers who buy brand

Example: Using equation (4), BINGO may calculate its aggregate share of wallet as 60 percent among its 5,000 customers, by summing equation (3) across all customers and dividing by the number of its customers.

Or, using equation (5), the ASW is BINGO's sales in period t ($750,000) divided by the total grocery expenditures of BINGO's customers in the same period ($1,250,000); thus, 750,000/1,250,000 = 60 percent.

Where does the information come from?

- Numerator: This information comes from internal records.
- Denominator: The source is the same as for SCR.

Evaluation SW, like SCR, is an important measure of customer loyalty and an important indicator firms should strive to have.

When to Use SCR and When to Use SW

Information on share of wallet is slightly more difficult to obtain than for SCR. SCR is, in most cases, the preferred measure. This is particularly true for categories where the variance of customer expenditures is relatively small (groceries, for example). If purchases are similar in volume, a customer's lifetime value is primarily driven by his frequency of purchases. Thus, SCR is a fairly appropriate measure of loyalty. However, if the variance of consumer expenditures is relatively high (furniture, cars, or other infrequent purchases), then SW is a better measure of loyalty than SCR. In the former case, the frequency is more easily remembered. In the latter case, the customer more easily remembers the expenditures.

Share of Wallet and Size of Wallet
Hold Important Pieces of Information

Even though two buyers might have the same share of wallet, firms might find their attractiveness as customers to be different. Consider Table 6-3.

| TABLE 6-3 | SHARE OF WALLET AND SIZE OF WALLET |

	Share of Wallet	Size of Wallet	Absolute Expenses with Firm
Buyer 1	50%	$400	$200
Buyer 2	50%	$50	$25

Depending on the size of wallet, the absolute attractiveness of buyer 1 is eight times higher, even though the share of wallet is the same as for buyer 2. The example shows it is always important to consider share of wallet and size of wallet simultaneously. Figure 6-1 illustrates this.

The matrix shows the recommended strategies for the various segments differ substantively. The firm makes optimal resource allocation decisions only by segmenting the customers along the two dimensions simultaneously.

Difference of Share of Wallet to Market Share

It is important to recognize the difference between market share (MS) and share of wallet (SW). MS is calculated across buyers and nonbuyers, whereas SW is calculated *only among buyers.*

How to Convert SW to MS?

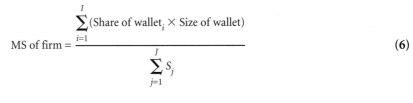

$$\text{MS of firm} = \frac{\sum_{i=1}^{I}(\text{Share of wallet}_i \times \text{Size of wallet})}{\sum_{j=1}^{J} S_j} \tag{6}$$

where
  S = sales to the focal customer
  j = firm
  i = those customers who buy the brand

| FIGURE 6-1 | SEGMENTING CUSTOMERS ALONG SHARE OF WALLET AND SIZE OF WALLET |

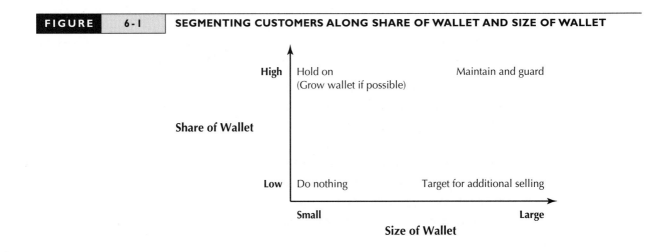

Market share is the share of wallet across all customers in the category divided by the sales across all firms in the category in period *t*. MS is measured on a percent basis and can be computed based on unit volume, $ volume, or equivalent unit volumes (grams, ounces).

Example: If BINGO has 5,000 customers with an average expense at BINGO of $150 per month (share of wallet × size of wallet), and the total grocery sales in BINGO's trade area are $5,000,000 per month, then BINGO's market share is (5,000 × $150) / $5,000,000 = 0.15, or 15 percent.

The implication here is that although BINGO has an overall low market share, it has a high share of wallet for those buyers buying at BINGO. This indicates that BINGO is a niche player with a very loyal clientele.

6.2.4 TRANSITION MATRIX

A transition matrix is a convenient way to characterize a customer's likelihood to buy over time or brand's likelihood to be bought. The assumption is that a customer moves over his/her lifetime through various stages of activity. Table 6-4 shows such a transition matrix.

In Table 6-4, the top row indicates the movement for customers who are currently brand A buyers; 70 percent of them will buy brand A next time, 20 percent will buy brand B, and 10 percent will buy brand C. The diagonals (in bold) are customer-retention probabilities computed by the company. However, we see that consumers can switch back and forth from brands. For example, the probability that a consumer of brand A will transition to brand B and then come back to brand A in the next two purchase occasions is 20% × 10% = 2%. If, on average, a customer purchases twice per period, the two purchases could be AA, AB, AC, BA, BB, BC, CA, CB, or CC. We can compute the probability of each of these outcomes if we know the brand the customer bought last. This provides us with the expected share of wallet for the three brands. This process can be continued for as many purchase occasions as desired. This information for the matrix comes from responses to questions as part of routine surveys, for example, "Which hotel did you stay in last?" or "The next time you stay in a hotel, what is the probability that you will stay at each of the hotels that you consider as options?"

6.3 STRATEGIC CUSTOMER-BASED VALUE METRICS

6.3.1 RFM

RFM stands for recency, frequency, and monetary value. This technique utilizes these three metrics to evaluate customer behavior and customer value.

TABLE 6-4 **TRANSITION MATRIX**

		Brand Purchased Next Time		
		A	B	C
Brand Currently Purchased	A	**70%**	20%	10%
	B	10%	**80%**	10%
	C	25%	15%	**60%**

Note: Customer retention probabilities are in bold.

SOURCE: Roland T. Rust, Valerie A. Zeithaml, and Katherine N. Lemon, "Driving Customer Equity" (New York: The Free Press, 2000).

1. *Recency* is a measure of how long it has been since a customer last placed an order with the company.

2. *Frequency* is a measure of how often a customer orders from the company in a certain defined period.

3. *Monetary value* is the amount that a customer spends on an average transaction.

RFM is similar to the switching matrix approach in that it also tracks customer behavior over time in what is called a state-space. That is, customers move over time through a space with certain defined activity states.

Two Methods of Computing and Applying RFM

Two popular methods of computing and applying RFM are in vogue among contemporary marketing professionals. The first method involves sorting customer data from the customer database, using the RFM criteria, and grouping them in equal quintiles and analyzing the resulting data.

The second method involves computing relative weights for R, F, and M using regression techniques, and then using those weights for calculating the combined effects of RFM.

RFM technique helps organizations significantly, not only in clearly targeting valuable customers who have a very high chance of purchasing, but also in avoiding costly communications and campaigns to customers who have a lesser chance of purchasing. RFM technique can be applied only on historical customer data available and not on prospects data.

RFM Method 1 For the following discussions about RFM coding, consider the following example of a firm with a customer base of 400,000 customers. From this customer base, a sample of 40,000 customers is chosen. In other words, every tenth customer from the larger database of 400,000 customers was picked so as to form a test group of 40,000 customers who are representative of the whole customer base.

Also, assume this firm is planning to send a marketing mailer campaign of a $150 discount coupon to be mailed to its customers.[1]

Recency Coding Assume this firm sends its $150 mailer campaign to the 40,000 customers in the test group, and assume 808 customers (2.02% of 40,000) responded. In order to determine if there is any correlation between those customers who responded to the mailer campaign and their corresponding historical recency, the following analysis is done.

The test group of 40,000 customers is sorted in descending order based on the criterion of *most recent purchase date*. The earliest purchasers are listed on the top and the oldest are listed at the bottom. The sorted data are further divided into five equal groups (20 percent in each group). The top-most group is assigned a recency code of 1, and the next group is assigned a code of 2, and so on, until the bottom-most group is assigned a code of 5. An analysis of the customer response data from the mailer campaign and the recency-based grouping data point out that the mailer campaign received the highest response from those customers grouped in recency code 1, followed by those grouped in code 2, and so on. Figure 6-2 depicts the distribution of percentages of customers who responded fell within the recency code grouping of 1 through 5.

Figure 6-2 indicates the highest response rate (4.5%) for the campaign was from those customers in the test group who had the highest recency quintile (recency code = 1). Note the average customer response rate computed for all five groups would be none other than the actual response rate of 2.02 percent achieved by the campaign. That is, (4.50% + 2.80% + 1.50% + 1.05% + 0.25%)/5 = 2.02 percent.

| **FIGURE** | **6-2** | **RESPONSE AND RECENCY** |

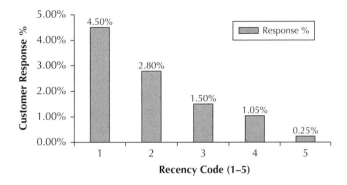

At the end of this recency coding exercise we would assign recency values of $r = 1$ through 5 for groups of customers, depending on the quintile that they fall within.

Frequency Coding   Frequency coding process is exactly same as the recency coding process just discussed. However, to sort the test group of 40,000 customers based on *frequency* metric, we need to know the average number of purchases made by a customer per month. Of course, the choice of the appropriate time period depends on the usual frequency of purchases. In this case, customers with the highest number of purchases per month are grouped at the top, while those with lesser number of purchases per month were listed below. Here again, the sorted list is grouped into five groups. Those in the top are assigned a code of 1 and those at the bottom a code of 5. The graph below depicts the same.

An analysis of the customer response data from the mailer campaign and the *frequency*-based grouping data point out that the mailer campaign got the highest response from those customers grouped in *frequency* code 1, followed by those grouped in code 2, and so on. Figure 6-3 depicts the distribution of percentage of customers who responded fell within the *frequency* code grouping of 1 through 5.

As it can be seen in Figure 6-3, the highest response rate (2.45%) for the campaign was from those customers in the test group who had the highest *frequency* quintile (frequency code = 1).

At the end of this *frequency* coding exercise we would assign frequency values of $f = 1$ though 5 for groups of customers, depending on the quintile that they fall within.

| **FIGURE** | **6-3** | **RESPONSE AND FREQUENCY** |

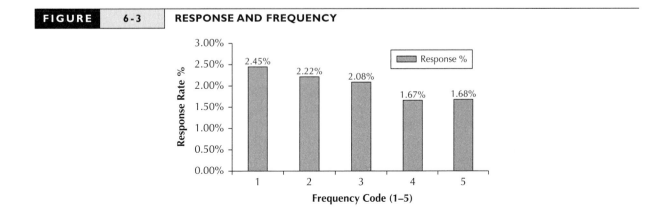

Monetary Value Coding   The *monetary value* coding process is exactly same as the recency and frequency coding process. However, to sort the test group of 40,000 customers based on *monetary value* metric, we need to know the *average amount purchased per month.* The monetary value is also an important metric driving analysis of customer behavior. As with *recency* and *frequency,* the customer data are sorted, grouped, and coded with a 1 to 5 value.

As can be seen in Figure 6-4, the highest response rate (2.35%) for the campaign was from those customers in the test group who had the highest *monetary value* quintile (monetary value code = 1).

At the end of this *monetary value* coding exercise, we would assign *monetary value* of $m = 1$ through 5 for groups of customers, depending on the quintile that they fall within.

At the end of this whole exercise, you will have individual R, F, and M scores for each customer. Each customer will be assigned to 1 of the 125 groups such as 111, 233, 432 ... 555, based on their respective RFM codes.

Limitations   This method independently links customer response data with R, F, and M values and then groups customers belonging to specific RFM codes. However, this method may not produce an equal number of customers under each RFM cell. This is because the individual metrics R, F, and M are likely to be somewhat correlated. For example, someone spending more (high M) is also likely, on average, to buy more frequently (high F). However, for practical purposes, it is desirable to have exactly the same number of individuals in each RFM cell. A sorting technique ensuring equal numbers in each RFM cell is described as follows.

RFM Sorting Technique   This is a more sophisticated sorting technique which helps to arrive at an RFM code for each customer and ensures the grouping of equal number of customers under each RFM code.

Figure 6-5 depicts a schematic diagram of the logic behind RFM sorting. Consider the list of 40,000 test group customers. The list is first sorted for recency and grouped into five equal groups of 8,000. Therefore group 1 will have 8,000 customers, and so will the other groups through group 5.

Now, take the 8,000 customers in each group and sort them based on frequency and divide them into five equal groups of 1,600 each. At the end of this stage, you will have RF codes starting from 11 through 55, with each group having 1,600 customers. In the last stage, each of the RF groups is further sorted based on monetary value and divided into five equal groups of 320 customers each. Again, we will have RFM codes starting from 111

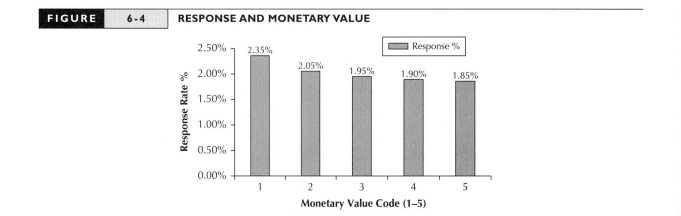

FIGURE   6-4   RESPONSE AND MONETARY VALUE

FIGURE	6-5	RFM CELL SORTING

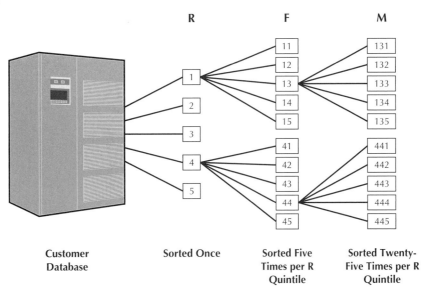

through 555, each having 320 customers. Considering each RFM code as a cell, we will have 125 cells.

5 recency divisions × 5 frequency divisions × 5 monetary value divisions = 125 RFM codes

Breakeven Value   Before proceeding to see an application of the RFM codes, it would be useful to review the concept of breakeven value. In marketing literature, *breakeven* refers to the fact that the net profit from a marketing promotion equals the cost associated with conducting the promotion.

$$\text{Breakeven value (BE)} = \frac{\text{Unit cost price}}{\text{Unit net profit}}$$

If this ratio for a particular promotion is 1, then the promotion only broke even and did not generate any net profits. This ratio also computes the minimum response rates required in order to offset the promotional costs involved and thereby not incur any losses.

Consider our example of mailing $150 discount coupons. Suppose the cost to mail each piece is a dollar, and the net profit (after all costs) is $45, then the breakeven value or breakeven response rate required can be computed as breakeven value (BE) = $1/$45 = 0.0222, or 2.22 percent. This value can be computed for every RFM cell and then can be used to compare it with the actual response rate of each cell.

The breakeven response rate just computed could be used in computing a *breakeven index*. The breakeven index is calculated using the following formula.

$$\text{Breakeven index (BEI)} = \left(\frac{(\text{Actual response rate} - \text{BE})}{\text{BE}}\right) \times 100$$

Therefore, if the actual response rate of a particular RFM cell was 3.5 percent, then BEI = ((3.5% − 2.22%)/2.22%) × 100 = 57.66.

A positive value indicates that some profit was made from the transaction. A BEI value of 0 indicates that the transaction just broke even, and a negative BEI value indicates that the transaction resulted in a loss. See Table 6-5.

TABLE	6-5	COMBINING RFM CODES, BREAKEVEN CODES, BREAKEVEN INDEX

Cell #	RFM Codes	Cost per Mail	Net Profit per Sale	Breakeven %	Actual Response %	Breakeven Index
1	111	$1.00	$45.00	2.22%	17.55%	690
2	112	$1.00	$45.00	2.22%	17.45%	685
3	113	$1.00	$45.00	2.22%	17.35%	681
4	114	$1.00	$45.00	2.22%	17.25%	676
5	115	$1.00	$45.00	2.22%	17.15%	672
6	121	$1.00	$45.00	2.22%	17.05%	667
7	122	$1.00	$45.00	2.22%	16.95%	663
8	123	$1.00	$45.00	2.22%	16.85%	658
9	124	$1.00	$45.00	2.22%	16.75%	654
10	125	$1.00	$45.00	2.22%	16.65%	649
11	131	$1.00	$45.00	2.22%	16.55%	645
12	132	$1.00	$45.00	2.22%	16.45%	640
13	133	$1.00	$45.00	2.22%	16.35%	636
14	134	$1.00	$45.00	2.22%	16.25%	631
15	135	$1.00	$45.00	2.22%	16.15%	627
16	141	$1.00	$45.00	2.22%	16.05%	622
17	142	$1.00	$45.00	2.22%	15.95%	618
18	143	$1.00	$45.00	2.22%	15.85%	613
19	144	$1.00	$45.00	2.22%	15.75%	609
20	145	$1.00	$45.00	2.22%	15.65%	604
21	151	$1.00	$45.00	2.22%	15.55%	600
22	152	$1.00	$45.00	2.22%	15.45%	595
23	153	$1.00	$45.00	2.22%	15.35%	591
24	154	$1.00	$45.00	2.22%	15.25%	586
25	155	$1.00	$45.00	2.22%	15.15%	582
26	211	$1.00	$45.00	2.22%	15.65%	604
27	212	$1.00	$45.00	2.22%	15.55%	600
28	213	$1.00	$45.00	2.22%	15.45%	595
29	214	$1.00	$45.00	2.22%	15.35%	591
30	215	$1.00	$45.00	2.22%	15.25%	586
31	221	$1.00	$45.00	2.22%	15.15%	582
32	222	$1.00	$45.00	2.22%	15.05%	577
33	223	$1.00	$45.00	2.22%	14.95%	573
34	224	$1.00	$45.00	2.22%	14.85%	568
35	225	$1.00	$45.00	2.22%	14.75%	564
36	231	$1.00	$45.00	2.22%	14.65%	559
37	232	$1.00	$45.00	2.22%	14.55%	555
38	233	$1.00	$45.00	2.22%	14.45%	550
39	234	$1.00	$45.00	2.22%	14.35%	546
40	235	$1.00	$45.00	2.22%	14.25%	541

Table 6–5 shows an excerpt from the breakeven index computations for the various RFM cells. The complete table is available in Appendix 2 of this chapter. RFM cells with a corresponding positive BEI value are the groups of customers the marketing campaign should target, and all those RFM cells with corresponding negative BEI values are those customers to be avoided for this promotion.

Rows with positive BEI values have been highlighted. It is interesting to note that of the 125 RFM cells, only customers within 56 cells have a higher chance of offering profitability to the firm, and the rest do not! Therefore, it becomes clear that a firm can save significantly by only focusing on potential profitable customers and leaving the rest.

Figure 6-6 plots the RFM cell codes and their corresponding BEI values. Customers with positive BEI values are to be chosen and the rest are to be left. Note that customers

FIGURE 6-6 **RFM CODES VS. BREAKEVEN INDEX**

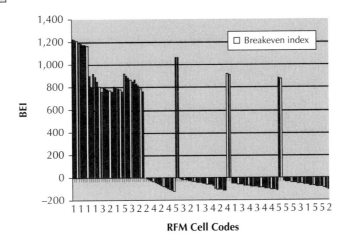

RFM Cell Codes

with higher RFM values tend to have higher BEI values. However, at the same time, customers with a lower recency value but relatively higher F and M values also tend to have positive BEI values and hence should be considered for target mailing.

Order of Importance of R, F, and M   The industry, in general, uses the RFM technique in the order of recency, frequency, and monetary value. However, the order varies for different industry segments. Although the RFM order is normally acceptable, a more accurate order of coding would depend on the rapidity of customer response rate drops. The metric (R, F, or M) for which the customer response rates drops more rapidly is likely to be the best predictor of future customer response and, hence, could be coded first. Once the metric of highest influence is determined, the same yardstick of measurement can be used to determine the order of the remaining metrics.

Referring to Figures 6-2, 6-3, and 6-4, notice that customer response rate drops more rapidly for the recency metric than the other two metrics. Similarly, the customer response rate for the frequency metric drops more rapidly than the monetary value metric. Therefore, the order of R, F, and M holds good in this case.

RFM and Profitability   From Table 6-6, it is clear the firm will benefit significantly more by sending the mailers to select customers within specific RFM cells, than by sending it to their whole customer base.

TABLE 6-6 **COMPARISON OF PROFITS**

	Test	Full Customer Base	RFM Selection
Average response rate	2.02%	2.02%	15.25%
Number of responses	808	8,080	2,732.8
Average net profit/sale	$45	$45	$45
Net revenue	$36,360	$363,600	$122,976
Number of mailers sent	40,000	400,000	17,920
Cost per mailer	$1.00	$1.00	$1.00
Mailing cost	$40,000.00	$400,000.00	$17,920.00
Profits	($3,640.00)	($36,400.00)	$105,056.00

The loss of $3,650 incurred in conducting the test is offset by the profits generated by by sending mailers to the RFM select customers.

Benefits: RFM techniques provide tangible benefits to the marketing professionals. Organizations need not mindlessly spend on contacting all their customers, but instead can smartly use the RFM selections to identify only those customers with high probabilities of purchase and target their marketing strategies and communications towards that population.

RFM Method 2   In the first RFM method, the RFM values are assigned for each customer by sequential sorting based on the RFM metrics. However, there is an alternative method which uses regression techniques to compute the relative weights of the R, F, and M metrics, and these relative weights are used to compute the cumulative points of each customer. The precomputed weights for R, F, and M, based on a test sample, are used to assign RFM scores to each customer (see Appendix 1). The higher the computed score, the more profitable the customer is likely to be in the future. This method, unlike the earlier one, is flexible and can be tailored to each business situation.

Example[2]   Three customers have a purchase history calculated over a twelve-month period (see Tables 6-7 to 6-10). For every customer, numerical points have been assigned to each transaction according to a historically derived R/F/M formula. The relative weight

TABLE	**6-7**	**RECENCY SCORE**		
Customer	**Purchases (Number)**	**Recency (Months)**	**Assigned Points**	**Weighted Points**
John	1	2	20	100
	2	4	10	50
	3	9	3	15
Smith	1	6	5	25
Mags	1	2	20	100
	2	4	10	50
	3	6	5	25
	4	9	3	15

Points for Recency: 20 points if within past 2 months; 10 points if within past 4 months; 05 points if within past 6 months; 03 points if within past 9 months; 01 point if within past 12 months; Relative weight = 5

TABLE	**6-8**	**FREQUENCY SCORE**		
Customer	**Purchases (Number)**	**Frequency**	**Assigned Points**	**Weighted Points**
John	1	1	3	6
	2	1	3	6
	3	1	3	6
Smith	1	2	6	12
Mags	1	1	3	6
	2	1	3	6
	3	2	6	12
	4	1	3	6

Points for Frequency: 3 points for each purchase within 12 months; Maximum = 15 points; Relative weight = 2

| TABLE 6-9 | MONETARY VALUE SCORE |

Customer	Purchases (Number)	Monetary	Assigned Points	Weighted Points
John	1	$40	4	12
	2	$120	12	36
	3	$60	6	18
Smith	1	$400	25	75
Mags	1	$90	9	27
	2	$70	7	21
	3	$80	8	24
	4	$40	4	12

Monetary Value: 10 percent of the $ Volume of Purchase with 12 months; Maximum = 25 points; Relative weight = 3

| TABLE 6-10 | RFM CUMULATIVE SCORE |

Customer	Purchases (Number)	Total Weighted Points	Cumulative Points
John	1	118	118
	2	92	210
	3	39	249
Smith	1	112	112
Mags	1	133	133
	2	77	210
	3	61	271
	4	37	308

based on the importance assigned to each of the three variables, R, F, and M on the basis of an analysis carried out on past customer transactions is as follows:

Recency = 5, Frequency = 2, Monetary = 3

The resulting cumulative scores, 249 for John, 112 for Smith, and 308 for Mags, indicate a potential preference for Mags. In this case, John seems to be a good prospect as well, but mailing to Smith might be a misdirected marketing effort. This example illustrates a simple application of the RFM technique. In practice, however, the number of customers to be analyzed can run into millions. Regression techniques are often employed to arrive at the relative weights for RFM. See Appendix 1 for an overview of regression models.

6.3.2 PAST CUSTOMER VALUE

Past customer value is a model which extrapolates the results of past transactions into the future. The value of a customer is determined based on the total contribution (toward profits) provided by the customer in the past. This modeling technique assumes past performance of the customer indicates the future level of profitability. Since products/services are bought at different points in time during the customer's lifetime, all transactions must be adjusted for the time value of money.

$$\text{Past customer value of a customer} = \sum_{n=1}^{n} GC_{in} \times (1 + r)^n \qquad (7)$$

where

i = number representing the customer

r = applicable discount rate (for example 15% per annum or 1.25% per month)

n = number of time periods prior to current period when purchase was made

GC_{in} = Gross contribution of transaction of the ith customer in the nth time period

Example: If we have data on the products purchased by various customers over a period of time, the value of the purchases, and the contribution margin, we can compare the value generated by each customer by computing all transactions in terms of their present value. Table 6-11 illustrates this computation for one customer.

$$\text{Gross Contribution (GC)} = \text{Purchase Amount} \times 0.3 \tag{8}$$

$$\begin{aligned}
\text{Past Customer Value Scoring} &= \\
6(1 + 0.0125) &+ 9(1 + 0.0125)^2 + 15(1 + 0.0125)^3 \\
&+ 15(1 + 0.0125)^4 + 240(1 + 0.0125)^5 = 302.01486
\end{aligned} \tag{9}$$

This customer is worth $302.01 in contribution margin, expressed in net present value in May dollars. By comparing this score to a set of customers, we arrive at a prioritization for directing future marketing efforts. The customers with higher values are normally the customers deserving greater marketing resources. This method, while extremely useful, does not incorporate other useful information which could help refine the process of selecting profitable customers. For instance, it does not consider whether a customer is going to be active in the future. It also does not incorporate the expected cost of maintaining the customer in the future. All in all, it is still a backward-looking metric.

6.3.3   LTV METRICS (NPV MODELS)

LTV stands for lifetime value and NPV stands for net present value. Evaluating the long-term economic value of a customer to the firm has seen a dramatic rise in interest. This is a direct outcome of the shift from transactional marketing to relational marketing. If a manager wants to evaluate marketing resource allocation plans targeted at improving the long-term value of customers, corresponding control measures must be put in place. Looking at profits on a per-transaction basis is not sufficient. Managers want to have an idea how the value of a client has evolved *over time*. The general term used to describe the long-term economic value of a customer is *lifetime value*. In very simple terms, it is a multiperiod evaluation of a customer's value to the firm. However, the term LTV is not without controversies. Although it is the Holy Grail for some, others call it "an elaborate fiction of presumed precision."[3] In the following section we present some of the most common ways to calculate LTV. Nevertheless, the reader should be aware that there are many specific formulations. It is important to present the principle in such a manner that readers can adapt the calculation to their own requirements. Conceptually, the principle of calculating LTV is represented in Figure 6-7.

As one can easily see, there is no a single way to arrive at each component. For example, are the recurring costs comprised only of direct product costs or also marketing, sales, and service costs? Depending on many factors, such as nature of product, data availability, and statistical capabilities, the inputs for the LTV calculation change. Is this problematic?

TABLE	6-11	SPENDING PATTERN OF A CUSTOMER				
		Jan	Feb	March	April	May
$ Amount		800	50	50	30	20
GC		240	15	15	9	6

FIGURE 6-7 **PRINCIPLES OF LTV CALCULATION**

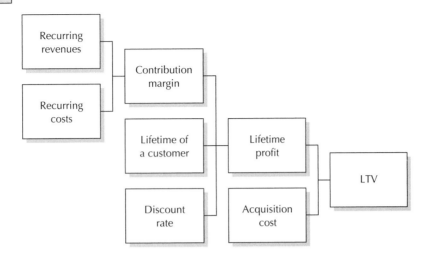

It is not. First and foremost, it is important to understand the principle. Based on the general principle, one can then start to adjust the calculation to the reliably available data. Also, one needs to adapt the formulation to the industry and company context. For example, having a defined finite lifetime duration (as for a contractual relationship such as cable subscription) makes for a different formulation as having non-finite relationship (as for a noncontractual relationship such as a supermarket).

After discussing the basic formulations, we will highlight key issues that should be considered when employing the models. In the following discussion, we will present different formulations of the same principle.

Example 1

In the most simple definition, the lifetime value of an individual customer i is the sum of the customer's discounted contribution margins over the respective observation horizon (T).

$$LTV = \sum_{t=1}^{T} CM_t \left(\frac{1}{1+\delta} \right)^t \tag{10}$$

where
  LTV = lifetime value of an individual customer in $
  CM = contribution margin
  δ = interest rate
  t = time unit
  Σ = summation of contribution margins across time periods

The resulting LTV is a measure of a single customer's worth to the firm. The contribution margin CM may vary, of course, across customers and across time units. This formulation is primarily used for pedagogical and conceptual purposes. It is typically based on past customer behavior and may have limited diagnostic value for future decision making.

Where does information come from?

The contribution margin CM and the duration T are derived either from managerial judgment or comes from actual purchase data (see previous section on how to calculate lifetime duration). The interest rate is a function of a firm's cost of capital and can be obtained from the financial accounting function.

Cautionary note: If the time unit is different from a yearly basis, the interest rate δ needs to be adjusted accordingly. For example, if the yearly interest rate is 15 percent, the quarterly interest rate is 3.75 percent.

Example 2

On the next level, one can break down the contribution margin into its constituting elements.

$$LTV = \sum_{t=1}^{T} (S_{it} - DC_{it}) - MC_{it} \left(\frac{1}{1+\delta}\right)^t \tag{11}$$

where
  LTV = lifetime value of an individual customer in $
  S = Sales to customer i
  DC = direct cost of products purchased by customer i
  MC = marketing cost of customer i
  The cost element in this example is broken down into direct product-related cost and marketing cost. Depending on data availability, it can be enhanced by including service-related cost, delivery cost, or other relevant cost elements.
  Where does information come from?
  The information on sales, direct cost, and marketing cost comes from internal company records. The key issue with direct cost and marketing cost is that they must be known on a per-customer basis. This knowledge is not necessarily common among many firms. An increasing number of firms are installing activity-based costing (ABC) schemes. ABC methods are used to arrive at appropriate allocations of customer and process-specific costs.

6.3.4 CUSTOMER EQUITY

The sum of the lifetime value of all a firm's customers represents the customer equity of a firm. This metric is an indicator of how much the firm is worth at a particular point in time as a result of the firm's customer management efforts. This metric therefore can be seen as a link to the shareholder value of a firm.

Example 3

Building on the formulation in equation (11), we can aggregate the LTV measure across customers. The resulting quantity is the customer equity (CE).

$$CE = \sum_{i=1}^{I} \sum_{t=1}^{T} CM_{it} \left(\frac{1}{1+\delta}\right)^t \tag{12}$$

where
  CE = customer equity of customer base in $ (sum of individual lifetime values)
  In this case, the CE measure gives the economic value of an entire cohort or segment of customers—subject to the same restrictions as in example 1.

Example 4

So far, an assumption was that all customers under investigation remain fully active during the period of interest. However, in reality, more and more customers stop their relationship with the firm over time. The next step is therefore to consider customer retention probabilities. This relates to the fact that customers tend to remain in the relationship only with a certain average retention rate Rr.

$$LTV = \left(\sum_{t=1}^{T} \left(\prod_{t=1}^{T} Rr \right) CM_{it} \left(\frac{1}{1+\delta} \right) \right)^t - AC \qquad (13)$$

where
  LTV = lifetime value of an individual customer in $
  Rr = retention rate
  Π = Product of retention rates for each time period from 1 to T
  AC = acquisition cost
  T = total time horizon under consideration
  The retention rate in this example is constant (i.e., it does not vary across time or customers). Although this is a common assumption, it is mostly not very realistic, as was previously discussed. Also, the acquisition cost (AC) is now subtracted from the customer's value.

Example 5

Equation (13) can be simplified to the following formula under the assumption that $T \rightarrow \infty$ and that the contribution margin CM does not vary over time.

$$LTV_i = \frac{CM}{1 - Rr + \delta} - AC \qquad (14)$$

This formulation is easy for quick calculations and, unless the retention rate is very high, produces results very close to the more precise formulation. One needs only to multiply the contribution margin with the margin multiple ($1/(1 - Rr + \delta)$) and subtract the acquisition cost.

How Long Is Lifetime Duration?

The word *lifetime* must be taken in many circumstances with a grain of salt. Although the term makes little sense with one-off purchases (say, for example, a house), it also seems strange to talk about LTV of a grocery shopper. Clearly, there is an actual lifetime value of a grocery shopper. However, given the long time span, this actual value is not practical. For all practical purposes, the lifetime duration is a longer-term duration used managerially. For example, in a direct marketing general merchandise context, managers do not look beyond a four-year time span. Beyond that, any calculation and prediction may become difficult due to so many uncontrollable factors (the customer moves, new competitors move in, and so on). It is therefore important to make an educated judgment regarding a sensible duration horizon in the context of making decisions.[4]

Comprehensive Example

The following example illustrates some aspects of the previously introduced LTV and customer equity models (see Table 6-12). The observation horizon for this example is five years (column 1). A company targets a list of 10,000 purchased addresses with an acquisition campaign. The company acquires 1,000 customers through the target mailing; thus, the acquisition rate is 10 percent. Once acquired, a customer generates on average $120 in

| **TABLE** | **6-12** | **CUSTOMER EQUITY CALCULATION EXAMPLE** |

1 Year from Acquisition	2 Sales per Customer	3 Manufacturer Margin	4 Manufacturer's Gross Margin	5 Marketing and Servicing Costs	6 Actual Retention Rate	7 Survival Rate	8 Expected Number of Active Customers	9 Profit per Customer per Period to Manufacturer	10 Discounted Profit per Customer per Period to Manufacturer
0	120	0.3	36	20	0.4	0.4	400	16	16
1	120	0.3	36	20	0.63	0.25	250	16	14
2	120	0.3	36	20	0.75	0.187	187	16	12
3	120	0.3	36	20	0.82	0.153	153	16	11
4	120	0.3	36	20	0.85	0.131	131	16	9
Total customer equity									

sales (column 2). For simplicity's sake, this level of sales is assumed to be constant over the lifetime of the customers (column 2). The margin of the firm is 30 percent, resulting in a constant gross margin (column 3). Marketing and service cost while alive are constant as well (column 5). The retention rate in the first period is 40 percent and then increases over time, as the loyal customers remain. The resulting number of remaining customers in each period is shown in column 8. The profit per customer (column 9) is computed by subtracting the marketing and service cost from the gross margin. This per-period is discounted to present value with a yearly rate of 15 percent (column 10). The remainder is to multiply yearly discounted profit times the remaining customers in each year. Then sum these values up to the total customer equity of this group or cohort of customers (column 11).

Customer equity share (CES) is an alternative metric to market share that takes customer lifetime value (CLV) into account. CES for each brand j can be calculated using the following formula.

$$CES_j = \frac{CE_j}{\sum\limits_{k} CE_k} \qquad (15)$$

where
CE = customer equity
j = focal brand
k = all brands

6.4 POPULAR CUSTOMER SELECTION STRATEGIES

Customer selection strategies are applied when firms want to target individual customers or groups of customers. The reason for targeting these customers can be manifold, for example, for sending out a promotion or for inviting them to a special event. Finding the right targets for marketing resource allocation is at the heart of any CRM strategy. Smart targeting allows firms to spend resources judiciously and allows customers to receive messages relevant to them. Dumb targeting actions destroy value by over- or underspending from the firm's perspective and by providing undesirable messages (*junk mail*). One step in the successful implementation of CRM is the smart deployment of targeting methodologies to maximize the benefits to firm and customer.

CRM AT WORK 6.1

TESCO

Tesco, the British supermarket chain has a very successful loyalty program in place. In addition, the company has built up distinct analysis and targeting capabilities, which allows Tesco to customize its promotions to a large number of different segments. Consider the following case: Using the loyalty program, Tesco builds a market basket history for each cardholder. It can then analyze basket content, and, based, on the current basket, can propose certain items via its promotions. Tesco observed that a certain group of customers never buy meat from Tesco. The underlying hypothesis could be that these customers buy their meat at the local butcher because they believe it is superior to Tesco's. This would mean Tesco could send them coupons in order to entice them to buy Tesco's meat. However, a completely different interpretation could be that these customers are vegetarians. This, then, would mean if Tesco were to send them coupons, the company would basically show it doesn't really understand its customer. In reality, Tesco plays it safe and doesn't send any coupons for meat. They might forgo some purchases from those who do buy at the local butcher, but Tesco prefers to not harm the relationships with those who are vegetarian.

This is an example where a company combines analytical skills, judicious judgment, knowledge about consumer behavior, and careful targeting of customers. It also shows that targeting always happens in a business context and is not an isolated activity.

6.4.1 DECISION TREES

Using decision trees is a methodology for finding the best predictors of a 0/1 dependent variable. For example, a company wants to know the differential demographic characteristics of loyalty program members versus nonmembers. Decision trees are especially useful when there is a large set of potential predictors for a model. In such a case, it may be difficult to determine which predictors are the most important or what the relationships between the predictors and the target (dependent) variable are. Decision tree algorithms can be used to iteratively search through the data to find out which predictor best separates the two categories of a binary target variable. Typically, this search is performed on two thirds of the available data, with one third of the data reserved for later use for testing the eventual model that develops. Example: Customer data for purchases of hockey equipment from sporting goods catalog.

Step 1: The algorithm is run. It determines that separating the customers based on gender is the optimum first step. See Figure 6-8.

Step 2: The algorithm is run again and determines the optimum approach is to separate the male customers by whether they have bought scuba equipment in the past and to separate the female customers by marital status. See Figure 6-9.

This process can be repeated for each subsegment, until all of the predictors have been applied to the model. When this process is complete, a tree will be developed in which segments are nested within segments. The profitable segments can then be identified for use as target markets.

One problem with the decision tree approach is that it is prone to over fitting, whereby segments are tailored to very small segments, (based upon the dataset that was used to create the tree) and as a result, the model developed will not perform nearly as well on a separate dataset. At this point, the one third of the data left for testing can be analyzed with the decision tree model developed. If the results show a large discrepancy with what was expected, then the model will need to be reevaluated. If the results are within range of what is predicted from the model, it is likely that the model is a good fit.

**STEP 1: CUSTOMER DATA FOR PURCHASES OF
HOCKEY EQUIPMENT FROM SPORTING GOODS CATALOG**

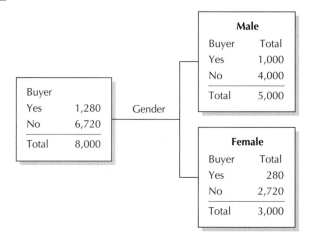

**STEP 2: CUSTOMER DATA FOR PURCHASES OF
HOCKEY EQUIPMENT FROM SPORTING GOODS CATALOG**

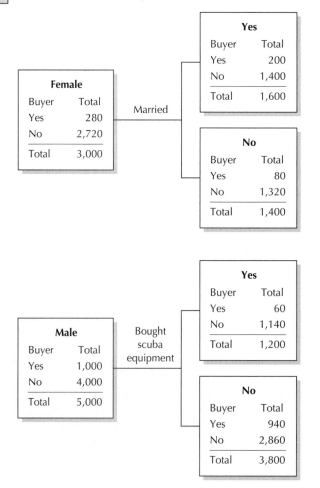

6.4.2 LOGISTIC REGRESSION

Linear regression starts with the specification of the dependent variable and the independent variable. For example the number of people entering a store on a Saturday is the dependent variable of interest and the amount of money the store spent on advertising on Friday is the independent variable. We expect to see a linear relationship between the two variables. A regression analysis creates an estimate of the coefficient that represents the effect of advertising on store traffic. In this situation we note store traffic—the dependent variable—can take on a large range of values. However, in marketing we often come across situations where the dependent variable is binary. For example, in a situation where we are interested in whether a customer bought a product or not, we assign the value 0 to this variable when the customer does not buy, and the value 1 when the customer buys. Linear regression if used when the dependent variable takes on only two values, 0 or 1, and when we interpret the intermediate values (e.g., 0.4, 0.5, etc.) as representing the probability of the desired outcome, is called a linear probability model. However, making statistical inferences using linear probability models poses problems overcome by using logistic regression. *Logistic regression* is the method of choice when the dependent variable is binary and assumes only two discrete values. For example:

1. Whether a customer responded to a marketing campaign or not
2. Whether a person bought a car or not

These observed values for the dependent variable take on only two values and are usually represented using a 0–1 dummy variable. The mean of a 0–1 dummy variable is equal to the proportion of observations with a value of 1, and can be interpreted as a probability. Furthermore, the predicted values in a logistic regression fall between 0 and 1 and are also interpreted as probabilities. For example, home ownership as a function of income can be modeled whereby ownership is delineated by a 1 and nonownership a 0. The predicted value based on the model is interpreted as the probability that the individual is a homeowner. With a positive correlation between increasing income and increasing probability of ownership, we can expect to see results where the predicted probability of ownership is .22 for a person with an income of $35,000, and .95 for a person with a $250,000 income.

Example: Credit Card Offering

Using logistic regression to identify potential targets for marketing credit cards offers to:

- Dependent variable—whether or not the customer signed up for a gold card offer
- Predictor variables—other bank services the customer used plus financial and demographic customer information

By inputting values for the predictor variables for each new customer, the logistic model will yield a predicted probability. Customers with high predicted probabilities may be chosen to receive the offer because they seem more likely to respond positively.

Unlike in linear regression where the effect of one unit change in the independent variable on the dependent variable is assumed to be a constant represented by the slope of a straight line, for logistic regression the effect of a one-unit increase in the predictor variable varies along an s-shaped curve (see Figure 6-10). This means that at the extremes, a one-unit change has very little effect, but in the middle a one-unit change has a fairly large effect. In the case of the income versus home ownership example, the difference in the likelihood that an individual owns a home may not change much as income increases from $10,000 to $30,000 or from $1,000,000 to $1,020,000, but may increase considerably if income increases from $50,000 to $70,000.

FIGURE 6-10 **LINEAR AND LOGISTIC REGRESSION**

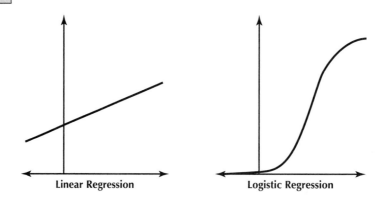

Mathematically, linear regression takes the form

$$y = \alpha + \beta x + e$$

where y is the dependent variable, x is the predictor variable, α represents a constant, β represents the effect of x on y, and e is the error term. In this sort of regression, y can take on any value between negative infinity and positive infinity. However, as we noted earlier, in many instances we normally observe only binary activity represented by 0 or 1. Hence, if the actually observed dependent variable has to be constrained between 0 and 1 to indicate the probability of an event occurring, a transformation is necessary. This transformation is the basis of logistic regression. The steps in the transformation are given as follows.

Step 1   If p represents the probability of an event occurring, consider the ratio $\frac{p}{1-p}$. Since p is a positive quantity less than 1, the range of this expression is 0 to infinity.

Step 2   Take the logarithm of this ratio $\log\left(\frac{p}{1-p}\right)$.
This transformation allows the range of values for this expression to lie between negative infinity and positive infinity.

Step 3   The value $\log\left(\frac{p}{1-p}\right)$ can now be considered as the dependent variable.

A linear relationship of this value with predictor variables in the form $z = \alpha + \beta x + e$ can be written out. The α and β_s can be estimated.

Step 4   In order to obtain the predicted probability p, the following back transformation is necessary:

$$\text{Since } \log\left(\frac{p}{1-p}\right) = z = \alpha + \beta x + e$$

$$\frac{p}{1-p} = e^z$$

This allows us to calculate the probability p of an event occurring, the variable of interest, as

$$p = \left(\frac{1}{1+e^{-z}}\right)$$

6.5 TECHNIQUES TO EVALUATE ALTERNATIVE CUSTOMER SELECTION STRATEGIES

These techniques revolve around constructing models to predict or classify customer data, with the goal of discovering a superior business method than what is already being implemented. The most common way to assess a model's performance is to compare its performance to the results expected if no model was used. This gives a baseline measure of how good the model is. The value of a predictive model can then be assessed by using the model to rank or score a sample set of customers and contacting or targeting the customers based on the results of the model.

6.5.1 LIFT CHARTS

Lifts indicate how much better a model performs than the *no model* or average performance. Lifts can be used to track a model's performance over time, or to compare a model's performance on different samples.

To calculate lifts for different deciles of data, we need the following information about a model with regard to the set of customer data.

- Cumulative number of customers: The number of total customers up to and including that decile
- Cumulative percentage of customers: The percent of total customers up to and including that decile
- Cumulative number of buyers: The number of buyers up to and including that decile
- Response rate: The actual response rate for each decile, computed by dividing the number of buyers by the number of customers for each decile

The lift = (Response rate for each decile) ÷ (Overall response rate) × 100. And the cumulative lift = (Cumulative response rate) ÷ (Overall response rate) × 100. The cumulative response rate = Cumulative number of buyers ÷ Cumulative number of customers (see Table 6-13).

TABLE 6-13 **LIFT AND CUMULATIVE LIFT**

Decile	Number of Customers	Number of Buyers	Response Rate	Lift	Cumulative Lift
1	5,000	1,759	35.18%	3.09	3.09
2	5,000	1,126	22.52%	1.98	5.07
3	5,000	998	19.96%	1.75	6.82
4	5,000	554	11.08%	0.97	7.80
5	5,000	449	8.98%	0.79	8.59
6	5,000	337	6.74%	0.59	9.18
7	5,000	221	4.42%	0.39	9.57
8	5,000	113	2.26%	0.20	9.76
9	5,000	89	1.78%	0.16	9.92
10	5,000	45	0.90%	0.08	10.00
Total	50,000	5,691	11.38%		

Lift Performance Illustration

The decile analysis in Figure 6-11 allows us to distribute customers into ten equal-sized groups. In a model that performs well, customers in the first decile exhibit the highest response rate. The response rate continues to drop as we proceed along the deciles. See Figure 6-12.

For the top decile in this case, the lift is 3.09. This indicates that by targeting only these customers we would expect to yield 3.09 times the number of buyers found by randomly mailing the same number of customers. In contrast, the last decile (decile 10) has only (.08 times) the number of buyers as one would expect in a random sample of the same size. Lift is an index that indicates the model's ability to beat the no model case or average performance. Lifts that exceed 1 indicate better than average performance, and those that are less than 1 indicate a poorer than average performance. Also keep in mind that lift is a relative index to a baseline measure.

The cumulative lifts for the model in Figure 6-13 reveal the proportion of responders we can expect to gain from targeting a specific percent of customers using the model. (If we choose the top 30 percent of the customers from the top three deciles, we will obtain 68

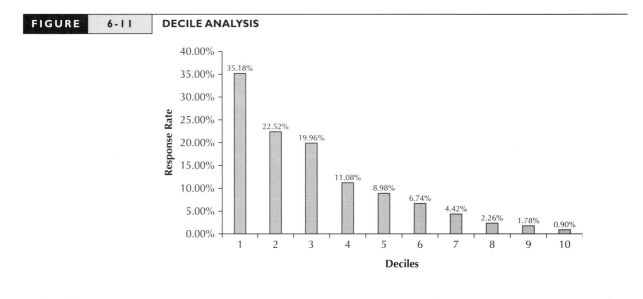

FIGURE 6-11 DECILE ANALYSIS

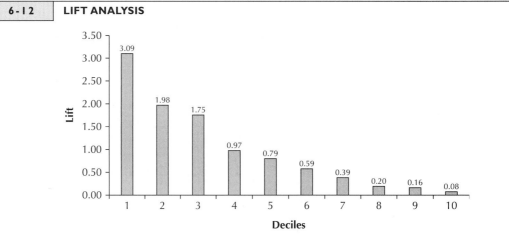

FIGURE 6-12 LIFT ANALYSIS

| FIGURE | 6-13 | **CUMULATIVE LIFT ANALYSIS** |

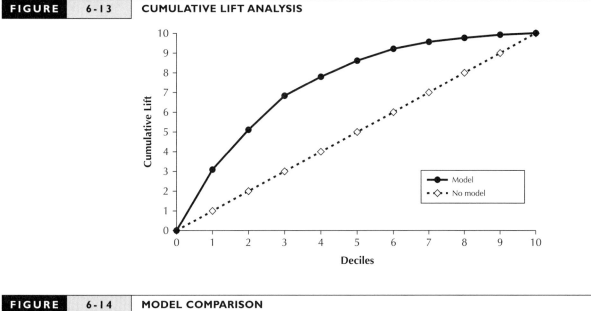

| FIGURE | 6-14 | **MODEL COMPARISON** |

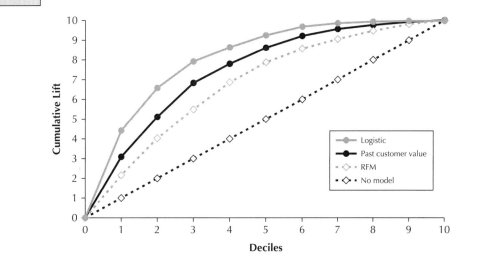

percent of the total responders.) The larger the distance between the model and no model lines, the stronger or more powerful is the model. In a nutshell, lifts can be used to compare two or more alternative models, track a model's performance over time, or to compare a model's performance on different samples.

Past experience shows logistic models tend to provide the best lift performance. This is seen from the topmost curve in the lift chart in Figure 6-14. The model is better able to identify the best customers and group them in the first few deciles. The past customer value approach provides the next best performance, whereas the traditional RFM approach, though by no means redundant, exhibits the poorest performance.

6.6   SUMMARY

Firms use different surrogate measures of customer value to prioritize their customers and to differentially invest in them. Size of wallet is the buyer's total spending in a category and usually firms are interested in acquiring and retaining customers with large wallet sizes. Share of category requirement (SCR) is an aggregate level measure of the proportion of the category volume accounted for by a brand or a focal firm. SCR is one of the most commonly accepted measures of customer loyalty for FMCG categories. Although this is an overall indicator of customer loyalty, it does not necessarily indicate whether a high SCR customer will generate substantial revenues or profits, for which the knowledge about customer's size of wallet is necessary. Share of wallet (SW) is the proportion of category *value* accounted for by a focal brand or firm *within its base of buyers*. At an *individual* level, SW is defined as the proportion of category *value* accounted for by a focal brand or firm for a buyer from all brands the buyer purchases in that category. It indicates the degree to which a customer satisfies his or her needs in the category with a focal brand or firm. Firms can use the information about size of wallet and share of wallet together for optimal allocation of resources. Expected share of wallet can be obtained by using a transition matrix. The transition matrix provides us with the probability a customer will purchase a particular brand if we know which brand the customer purchased previously.

Popular strategic customer-based value metrics are RFM, past customer value, lifetime value, and customer equity. RFM is a composite score of recency, frequency, and monetary value. Two methods used for computing and applying RFM are sorting techniques and calculation of relative weights for R, F, and M. In the sorting technique the RFM values are assigned for each customer by sequential sorting based on the RFM metrics. One of the sorting techniques independently links customer response data with R, F, and M values and then groups customers, belonging to specific RFM codes. However, this method might not produce equal number of customers under each RFM cell. A more sophisticated sorting technique ensures equal numbers in each RFM cell. This is done by first sorting the list of customers by recency and dividing them into equal groups. Each of these groups is then sorted based on frequency and divided into groups of equal size. Each of these subgroups is sorted on monetary value and divided into groups of equal size. This way, each RFM cell will have equal number of customers. Breakeven value and breakeven index can be calculated for each RFM cell. With respect to a promotion, *breakeven* refers to the fact that the net profit from a marketing promotion equals the cost associated with conducting the promotion. Breakeven value (BE) = Unit cost price / Unit net profit. The breakeven value or breakeven response rate can be used in computing a breakeven index, calculated as Breakeven index (BEI) = ((Actual response rate – BE)/BE) $\times$ 100. A positive BEI indicates some profit was made from the transaction. A BEI value of 0 indicates the transaction only broke even, and a negative BEI value indicates the transaction resulted in a loss. An alternate method for RFM metric uses regression technique to arrive at the relative weights of the R, F, and M metrics, and these relative weights are used to compute the RFM score of each customer. The higher the computed RFM score, the more profitable the customer is likely to be in the future. This method has the advantage of being flexible, and it can be tailored to each business situation.

Another important customer-based metric is past customer value, in which the value of a customer is determined based on the total contribution (toward profits) provided by the customer in the past after adjusting for the time value of money. In another metric called lifetime value (LTV), the long-term economic value of a customer is calculated as the sum of the discounted contribution margins over the respective observation horizon. The contribution margin can be computed knowing the values of sales, direct costs, and marketing costs. The sum of the lifetime value of all the customers of a firm represents the customer equity of a firm, another metric which is an indicator of how much the firm is worth at a particular point in time as a result of the firm's customer management efforts. This metric therefore can be seen as a link to the shareholder value of a firm. The formula for computing customer equity incorporates the average retention rate for a firm's customers.

Firms employ different customer selection strategies to target the right customers. Some of the popular customer selection strategies are *decision trees* and *logistic regression.* decision tree algorithm is a recursive partitioning algorithm used for finding the predictors which best separate the two categories of a 0/1 dependent variable. Typically, this search is performed on two thirds of the available data with one third of the data reserved for testing the eventual model that will be developed. Logistic regression is a statistical tool to predict the probability of a binary outcome using predictor variables.

Lift analysis, decile analysis, and cumulative lift analysis are various techniques firms use to evaluate alternative selection strategies. Lifts indicate how much better a model performs than the no model or average performance, and is calculated as (Response rate for each decile) ÷ (Overall response rate) × 100. In decile analysis, customers are grouped into deciles. For a good model, customers in the first decile have the highest response rate, and subsequently the response rate drops. Cumulative lift is calculated as (Cumulative response rate) ÷ (Overall response rate) × 100. It reveals the proportion of responders we can expect to gain from targeting a specific percent of customers using the model.

6.7   EXERCISE QUESTIONS

1. How would you implement the recommended strategies in Figure 6-1? What are some specific marketing actions you would take in the four quadrants?
2. A hotel chain wants to analyze its customer base with RFM. Describe the data fields (variables) in the database necessary to do this.
3. Whatever RFM analysis can do, regression analysis can do as well. Evaluate this statement.
4. How will you use lift charts to determine future marketing action?
5. Describe three business situations where you would consider using logistic regression as the preferred technique for analysis and decision making.
6. What is the link between customer lifetime value and the profitability of an organization?

MINI CASE 6.1

CATALINA IS CHANGING SUPERMARKET SHOPPER MEASUREMENT

Catalina Inc. is a Florida-based company specializing in supermarket shopper tracking and coupon issuing. The company has about 1,600 employees and operates in the United States, as well as in major European countries. The company built its business model on issuing coupons to grocery shoppers online when they check out. The basis for this business model is that traditional print media has long production lead times, and the response to these media is not measurable on the individual customer level. Thus, supermarkets and manufacturers cannot run and track individualized campaigns with traditional media. Catalina's system consists of a printer connected to the cashier's scanner and a database. The information on each shopping basket that checks out via the scanner is then stored in the database. Using the person's credit card number or check number, the database links individual shopping baskets over time. If the person pays cash, the system cannot link the basket. The system then allows both manufacturers and retailers to run individualized campaigns based on the information in the database. For example, Catalina could partner with the retailer to improve its cross selling. A typical issue for any given retailer is that certain customers use the store as their primary shopping location, whereas others use it as their secondary store. To improve the share of wallet with the latter group of customers, Catalina first investigates basket composition of the various buyers. It then finds that certain buyers buy, for example, baby or children products (thus, there is apparently a family behind this shopping basket), yet the number of calories in that basket does not match that of an average family. One explanation for this might be that this shopper uses this outlet as a secondary store. Given this interpretation, the decision then is to allocate to this customer a gift of say $10, for shopping for four weeks in a row spending at least $40 per week in the store. The goal is to selectively target those shoppers of whom the store captures only a low share of wallet, and to entice them to change their behavior.

Questions:

1. Explain why Catalina's approach is superior from a retailer's perspective vis-à-vis the traditional mass media approach.
2. Discuss the role of traditional metrics (such as market share) in this new CRM environment. Should they be discarded?
3. Do you think Catalina's practice (which is entirely legal) is ethically acceptable?

MINI CASE 6.2

DIFFERENTIATING CUSTOMER SERVICE ACCORDING TO CUSTOMER VALUE AT AKZO NOBEL, NV

Akzo Nobel, headquartered in Arnhem, Netherlands, is one of the world's largest chemical manufacturers and also one of the world's largest paint makers. Its chemical unit produces pulp and paper chemicals, functional chemicals (including flame retardants and animal feed additives), surfactants (used in detergents and personal care products), polymers, and catalysts. The polymer division, which serves exclusively the B-to-B market, established a tiered customer-service policy in the early 2000s. The necessity to introduce this policy came out of the recognition that customers are becoming more and more demanding when it comes to asking for additional services around the purchase of polymer products. For example, customers became increasingly aware that Akzo Nobel offers product disposal services, delivers nonstandard pallet sizes, and offers negotiable delivery times. On the one hand, Akzo Nobel did not typically charge for these services, and on the other hand, while extended services were typically offered only to medium- to high-volume clients, the relationship between service offerings and *client profitability* was not clear. When Akzo Nobel investigated more closely who received the service offerings, it found the correlation with client profitability (i.e., contribution margin) was *very* low. This finding led to the development of a formal *tiered service-level framework* within the polymer division.

In the first step, the company developed a thorough list of all possible service activities the company currently offers. Interestingly, the sales force provided a significant number of these services with little further consideration. Since the sales force was compensated on the sales volume it generated, it had all the incentive to lure in clients with little consideration for bottom-line results. Concurrently, to formalize customer service activities, the company implemented a customer scorecard mechanism. The scorecard allowed it to measure and document contribution margins per individual customer. Based on these two pieces of information, the organization then specified which customer type should be eligible for which type of service. In terms of service allocation, it designated certain services would be free for all types of customers, certain services would be subject to negotiation for lower-level customer groups, another set of services would be subject to fees for lower-level customers, and finally, certain services would not be available for the least valuable set of customers. Although the sales force was not very happy at first with these new measures, the new policy had a dramatic impact on the sales force understanding of the drivers of customer profitability.

Questions:

1. How can an organization compute client-level profitability?
2. What types of systems and processes are needed to document client profitability in a systematic and ongoing fashion?
3. Is there a way to move established clients accustomed to receiving a large number of ancillary services for free to paying for these services?

APPENDIX I

Regression Scoring Models

Scoring models is the process of evaluating potential customer behavior on the basis of test results. Typically, a test is conducted in a limited market or in an experimental set up on a small sub-set of customers. This subset of customers is exposed to a marketing campaign and a product offering. The purpose of this test is to assign to each of the remaining customers a *value* which is extrapolated from the results of this test. These values typically reflect the prospective customer's likelihood of purchasing the test marketed product. The process of regression scoring can be represented in the following steps:

1. Draw a random sample from the overall population of prospective customers.
2. Obtain data from the sample that profiles individual consumer characteristics. The R, F, and M scores are variables which profile behavioral characteristics of a customer and are typically used in this procedure, along with other relevant variables.
3. Initiate a marketing campaign directed at the random sample, and record the individuals who become customers.
4. With that information, develop a regression scoring model to obtain a series of weighted variables that either predict which prospects are more likely to become customers or the value of profits that each customer is likely to provide, based on their individual characteristics.
5. By applying these weights to individual characteristics of prospective customers, we can arrive at a value for each customer which indicates how likely it is that the customer will purchase a product, or how much profit the customer will generate, if exposed to the tested marketing campaign.

Often, a model is fitted on a training sample and then validated on a holdout sample.

APPENDIX 2

RFM Values versus BEI Table

Cell #	RFM Codes	Cost per Mail	Net Profit per Sale	Breakeven %	Actual Response %	Breakeven Index	Cell #	RFM Codes	Cost per Mail	Net Profit per Sale	Breakeven %	Actual Response %	Breakeven Index
1	111	$1.00	$45.00	2.22%	17.55%	690	64	334	$1.00	$45.00	2.22%	0.54%	−76
2	112	$1.00	$45.00	2.22%	17.45%	685	65	335	$1.00	$45.00	2.22%	0.50%	−78
3	113	$1.00	$45.00	2.22%	17.35%	681	66	341	$1.00	$45.00	2.22%	0.46%	−79
4	114	$1.00	$45.00	2.22%	17.25%	676	67	342	$1.00	$45.00	2.22%	0.42%	−81
5	115	$1.00	$45.00	2.22%	17.15%	672	68	343	$1.00	$45.00	2.22%	0.38%	−83
6	121	$1.00	$45.00	2.22%	17.05%	667	69	344	$1.00	$45.00	2.22%	0.34%	−85
7	122	$1.00	$45.00	2.22%	16.95%	663	70	345	$1.00	$45.00	2.22%	0.00%	−100
8	123	$1.00	$45.00	2.22%	16.85%	658	71	351	$1.00	$45.00	2.22%	−0.03%	−101
9	124	$1.00	$45.00	2.22%	16.75%	654	72	352	$1.00	$45.00	2.22%	−0.06%	−103
10	125	$1.00	$45.00	2.22%	16.65%	649	73	353	$1.00	$45.00	2.22%	−0.09%	−104
11	131	$1.00	$45.00	2.22%	16.55%	645	74	354	$1.00	$45.00	2.22%	−0.12%	−105
12	132	$1.00	$45.00	2.22%	16.45%	640	75	355	$1.00	$45.00	2.22%	−0.15%	−107
13	133	$1.00	$45.00	2.22%	16.35%	636	76	411	$1.00	$45.00	2.22%	11.25%	406
14	134	$1.00	$45.00	2.22%	16.25%	631	77	412	$1.00	$45.00	2.22%	11.22%	405
15	135	$1.00	$45.00	2.22%	16.15%	627	78	413	$1.00	$45.00	2.22%	0.55%	−75
16	141	$1.00	$45.00	2.22%	16.05%	622	79	414	$1.00	$45.00	2.22%	0.52%	−77
17	142	$1.00	$45.00	2.22%	15.95%	618	80	415	$1.00	$45.00	2.22%	0.49%	−78
18	143	$1.00	$45.00	2.22%	15.85%	613	81	421	$1.00	$45.00	2.22%	0.46%	−79
19	144	$1.00	$45.00	2.22%	15.75%	609	82	422	$1.00	$45.00	2.22%	0.43%	−81
20	145	$1.00	$45.00	2.22%	15.65%	604	83	423	$1.00	$45.00	2.22%	0.40%	−82
21	151	$1.00	$45.00	2.22%	15.55%	600	84	424	$1.00	$45.00	2.22%	0.37%	−83
22	152	$1.00	$45.00	2.22%	15.45%	595	85	425	$1.00	$45.00	2.22%	0.34%	−85
23	153	$1.00	$45.00	2.22%	15.35%	591	86	431	$1.00	$45.00	2.22%	0.31%	−86
24	154	$1.00	$45.00	2.22%	15.25%	586	87	432	$1.00	$45.00	2.22%	0.28%	−87
25	155	$1.00	$45.00	2.22%	15.15%	582	88	433	$1.00	$45.00	2.22%	0.25%	−89
26	211	$1.00	$45.00	2.22%	15.65%	604	89	434	$1.00	$45.00	2.22%	0.22%	−90
27	212	$1.00	$45.00	2.22%	15.55%	600	90	435	$1.00	$45.00	2.22%	0.19%	−91
28	213	$1.00	$45.00	2.22%	15.45%	595	91	441	$1.00	$45.00	2.22%	0.16%	−93
29	214	$1.00	$45.00	2.22%	15.35%	591	92	442	$1.00	$45.00	2.22%	0.13%	−94
30	215	$1.00	$45.00	2.22%	15.25%	586	93	443	$1.00	$45.00	2.22%	0.10%	−96
31	221	$1.00	$45.00	2.22%	15.15%	582	94	444	$1.00	$45.00	2.22%	0.07%	−97
32	222	$1.00	$45.00	2.22%	15.05%	577	95	445	$1.00	$45.00	2.22%	0.04%	−98
33	223	$1.00	$45.00	2.22%	14.95%	573	96	451	$1.00	$45.00	2.22%	0.01%	−100
34	224	$1.00	$45.00	2.22%	14.85%	568	97	452	$1.00	$45.00	2.22%	−0.02%	−101
35	225	$1.00	$45.00	2.22%	14.75%	564	98	453	$1.00	$45.00	2.22%	−0.05%	−102
36	231	$1.00	$45.00	2.22%	14.65%	559	99	454	$1.00	$45.00	2.22%	−0.08%	−104
37	232	$1.00	$45.00	2.22%	14.55%	555	100	455	$1.00	$45.00	2.22%	−0.11%	−105
38	233	$1.00	$45.00	2.22%	14.45%	550	101	511	$1.00	$45.00	2.22%	10.88%	390
39	234	$1.00	$45.00	2.22%	14.35%	546	102	512	$1.00	$45.00	2.22%	10.85%	388
40	235	$1.00	$45.00	2.22%	14.25%	541	103	513	$1.00	$45.00	2.22%	0.78%	−65
41	241	$1.00	$45.00	2.22%	14.15%	537	104	514	$1.00	$45.00	2.22%	0.73%	−67
42	242	$1.00	$45.00	2.22%	14.05%	532	105	515	$1.00	$45.00	2.22%	0.70%	−69
43	243	$1.00	$45.00	2.22%	13.95%	528	106	521	$1.00	$45.00	2.22%	0.67%	−70
44	244	$1.00	$45.00	2.22%	13.85%	523	107	522	$1.00	$45.00	2.22%	0.64%	−71
45	245	$1.00	$45.00	2.22%	13.75%	519	108	523	$1.00	$45.00	2.22%	0.61%	−73
46	251	$1.00	$45.00	2.22%	13.65%	514	109	524	$1.00	$45.00	2.22%	0.58%	−74
47	252	$1.00	$45.00	2.22%	13.55%	510	110	525	$1.00	$45.00	2.22%	0.55%	−75
48	253	$1.00	$45.00	2.22%	13.45%	505	111	531	$1.00	$45.00	2.22%	0.52%	−77
49	254	$1.00	$45.00	2.22%	13.35%	501	112	532	$1.00	$45.00	2.22%	0.49%	−78
50	255	$1.00	$45.00	2.22%	13.25%	496	113	533	$1.00	$45.00	2.22%	0.46%	−79
51	311	$1.00	$45.00	2.22%	12.95%	483	114	534	$1.00	$45.00	2.22%	0.43%	−81
52	312	$1.00	$45.00	2.22%	12.91%	481	115	535	$1.00	$45.00	2.22%	0.40%	−82
53	313	$1.00	$45.00	2.22%	0.98%	−56	116	541	$1.00	$45.00	2.22%	0.37%	−83
54	314	$1.00	$45.00	2.22%	0.94%	−58	117	542	$1.00	$45.00	2.22%	0.34%	−85
55	315	$1.00	$45.00	2.22%	0.90%	−60	118	543	$1.00	$45.00	2.22%	0.31%	−86
56	321	$1.00	$45.00	2.22%	0.86%	−61	119	544	$1.00	$45.00	2.22%	0.28%	−87
57	322	$1.00	$45.00	2.22%	0.82%	−63	120	545	$1.00	$45.00	2.22%	0.25%	−89
58	323	$1.00	$45.00	2.22%	0.78%	−65	121	551	$1.00	$45.00	2.22%	0.22%	−90
59	324	$1.00	$45.00	2.22%	0.74%	−67	122	552	$1.00	$45.00	2.22%	0.19%	−91
60	325	$1.00	$45.00	2.22%	0.70%	−69	123	553	$1.00	$45.00	2.22%	0.10%	−96
61	331	$1.00	$45.00	2.22%	0.66%	−70	124	554	$1.00	$45.00	2.22%	0.01%	−100
62	332	$1.00	$45.00	2.22%	0.62%	−72	125	555	$1.00	$45.00	2.22%	−0.08%	−104
63	333	$1.00	$45.00	2.22%	0.58%	−74							

ENDNOTES

1. All numerical figures mentioned in the discussions below are hypothetical data created for instructional purposes only. However, due care has been exercised to ensure these data are fairly closer to real life experiences of many firms.

2. David A. Aaker, V. Kumar, and George S. Day, *Marketing Research,* 8th ed., (New York: John Wiley & Sons, 2003).

3. D. R. Jackson, "In Quest of the Grail: Breaking the Barriers to Customer Valuation," *Direct Marketing* 54, no. 11 (1992): 44–48.

4. For details on various forms of LTV models, see: Dipak Jain, and Siddhartha Singh, "Customer Lifetime Value Research in Marketing: A Review and Future Directions," *Journal of Interactive Marketing* 16 (March 1, 2002); and Paul D. Berger and Nada I Nasr, "Customer Lifetime Value: Marketing Models and Applications," *Journal of Interactive Marketing* 12 (Winter 1998): 17–30.

PART

II

Implementation of Database Marketing

Using Databases

Contents

7.1 OVERVIEW

Companies gather information about their customers, store it in databases, analyze the data, make marketing decisions, and implement marketing programs based on the results of the data analysis. Interactive marketing programs develop two-way communication with customers to get their feedback, tailor products and services to meet customers' expectations, and develop a unique and profitable relationship with each of these customers. In other words, effective database marketing drives successful CRM. Without a database, marketers rely on traditional mass marketing, which is indifferent to the individual customers. Wastages from mass advertising, postage, and printing costs are avoided by making efficient use of marketing databases. In this chapter, we provide an overview of different types of databases and how they differ in terms of their function, information included, and technology. We also illustrate how companies use different types of databases and how they benefit from using different databases effectively.

7.2. TYPES OF DATABASE

The types and nature of databases depend on the criteria we use to group databases. If we do not limit the discussion to marketing or customer database, databases used in companies can first be categorized using their main business functions. By doing so we would have the following:

- Databases managing business operations (e.g., account payable database, cost accounting database, order processing database, payroll database)
- Databases supporting decision-making activities (e.g., marketing databases, product development database, and advertisement/promotion databases)

Databases can also be categorized according to the following criteria:

- The information included in the databases
- The nature of the underlying marketing activities
- Database technology

7.2.1 CATEGORIZATION BASED ON THE INFORMATION INCLUDED IN THE DATABASES

There are four types of databases: (1) customer databases; (2) prospect databases; (3) cluster databases; and (4) enhancement databases. Let's look at each of these in turn.

Customer Database

The customer database is the core of any marketing database. It is a collection of information about a company's customers. For each company, a customer database is an invaluable asset. Marketers usually use customer databases to identify and profile the best customers and communicate with them in ways likely to elicit a customer response. In general, the following information may be included in customer databases:

- Basic information: name, address, ZIP code, and telephone number
- Demographic information: age, gender, marital status, education, number of people in household, income, and so on
- Psychographic information: values, activities, interests, preferences, etc.
- Transaction history: What transactions have the customers conducted? How frequently do they purchase? How much did they spend? How were they acquired?
- Other relevant information: inquiries and referrals, satisfaction, loyalty

Several companies gather and sell data from public and private sources across the United States. These data allow the companies (buying them) to market their products to specific customer segments to achieve higher net marketing contribution. Some companies selling databases and database solutions are Acxiom, D&B, and Prizm. The following examples of customer databases provide an insight into how businesses in the real world use data:

- *D&B's U.S. Marketing File.* This customer database comprises telemarketing, direct mail, competitor analysis, and other types of data pertaining to 18.5 million small, privately owned, as well as large, publicly owned businesses.
- *InfoBase® eProducts.* E-mail marketing is the most inexpensive profit-generating marketing tool to augment companies' direct mail or other channels of communication with their customers. E-mail marketing is used today in cross-selling and customer retention initiatives. Newsletters, discount

offers, sneak previews, and so on are common inducements communicated through e-mails. InfoBase® eProducts from Acxiom provides the user companies with the e-mail addresses of their customers thereby enabling the companies to achieve the following:

- ☐ Targeted personalized offers
- ☐ Reduced direct mail costs and therefore increased net marketing contribution
- ☐ Additional customer touch point
- ☐ Larger number of customers visiting the company's Web site

Case study CRM at Work 7.1 highlights the effective use of e-mail marketing.

We should note that not only active customers, but also inactive customers should be included in customer databases. Data from active customers help marketers learn what has been done well in the past, and data from inactive customers help to identify what needs to be improved. For inactive customers, the following additional information would be important to document:

- How long have the customers been inactive?
- How long have they been active?
- What was their purchasing pattern when they were active?
- How much did they spend?
- How were they initially acquired?
- Why are they inactive?

Prospect Database

Prospects are noncustomers with profiles similar to those of existing customers. The prospect database should include as much information about prospects as the customer database does about customers. For obvious reasons, however, the prospect database does not contain any transaction history data. Marketers can use a prospect database to

---

CRM AT WORK 7.1

E-MAIL MARKETING AT BLOCKBUSTER

Quris, an e-mail marketing company, has helped several companies like Charles Schwab and Blockbuster use e-mail as relationship-building tools to help these companies improve revenues, build stronger brands, and cut expenses.

Quris helped Blockbuster create its e-mail newsletter. The newsletter marketed Blockbuster's new movies (on DVD/VHS) and games to its customers via e-mail. In the e-mail, customers received a bar-coded coupon to print out and then later redeem at the store. The customers could also subscribe to the newsletter on the Internet. A simple e-mail marketing newsletter like this produced great results for blockbuster. According to reports,

- The total return on investment for the program was 96 percent higher than the ROI for direct mail.
- For customers receiving electronic coupons, it was 144 percent higher.
- Active Blockbuster customers showed the greatest sustainable increase in ROI% relative to a control—providing quantitative evidence of the viability of e-mail as a retention tool.

The success of this project highlighted the use of e-mail as a long-term marketing channel.

SOURCE: www.quris.com, May 17, 2003.

design marketing campaigns to target prospects with the intent of acquiring them as new customers. Marketers should carefully analyze the channels through which the prospects prefer to receive information—whether they are newspaper/magazine readers, TV viewers, radio listeners, or catalog purchasers. By doing this, marketers can effectively utilize all advertising media to achieve a higher response rate.

In order to achieve the best response rate, marketers also need to segment prospects just as they segment customers, so that they can position the company's differentiated products to the prospects' specific needs. Large-scale promotions to all the prospects should be implemented only after the prospect list has been tested on an experimental basis and has proved to be promising.

Examples of some prospect databases used in the industry follow:

- *InfoBase® List.* Companies interested in marketing their products to new prospective customers would find this useful. The InfoBase® list offers a collection of U.S. consumer data available in one source for list rentals covering 111 million households and 176 million individuals.
- *Harris Selectory Online.* This is a prospect database from D&B that helps companies find new customers. Such a database allows companies to:
  - ☐ Qualify developing leads
  - ☐ Contact the decision maker best suited to hear their sales pitch
  - ☐ Research potential opportunities

Cluster Database

Cluster databases include information about relatively small *clusters.* These clusters could be defined based on geographic reference groups (such as a ZIP code area), affinity groups (e.g., clubs and associations), and lifestyle reference groups. People in the same cluster tend to have common or similar interests, attitudes, purchasing habits, and preferences. Based on the proportion of existing customers in each of these clusters, companies can identify the clusters to which prospective customers belong. Also, depending on the membership of prospective customers in specific clusters, firms can customize their marketing communications, thereby increasing the efficiency of marketing efforts. Prizm is a good example of cluster databases.

The Prizm database segments every U.S. neighborhood into sixty two distinct areas. Companies can use these databases to identify their potential future customers, locate them, and determine how to reach them in the most effective way. Every Prizm database is categorized into groups, each group having several clusters. Some of the groups in the Prizm databases follow:

- *S1 (Elite Suburbs).* The five clusters in group S1 are the nation's most affluent social people.
- *U1 (Urban uptown).* These clusters include high concentration of executives and professionals.
- *C1 (City Society).* The three clusters of group C1 make the upper crust of America's second and satellite cities.
- *T1 (Landed Gentry).* The clusters in this group are made of multi-income families having school-age kids and are headed by well-educated executives and professionals. This is the fourth most affluent group in the United States.

The following case study, CRM at Work 7.2, highlights the use of cluster databases.

CRM AT WORK 7.2

GLOBE AND MAIL

Globe and Mail is a popular Canadian national newspaper. A major chunk (almost 75 percent) of the revenues for *Globe and Mail* comes from advertisements, and the rest from newspaper readers. As with other newspapers, the revenue stream coming from advertising is dependent upon the circulation of the newspaper. Also, as not all readers are alike from the advertiser's standpoint, advertisers prefer more urban middle class subscribers than rural blue-collar subscribers.

After trying some discount strategies, *Globe and Mail* adopted database marketing techniques to target urban customers and gained urban market share, thereby improving not only readership but also the revenue stream through advertisers.

To start with, *Globe and Mail* created a marketing database of prospective subscribers. Then it enhanced its existing customers' data with Canadian cluster codes and demographic data, provided by Compusearch. Using this cluster data, it could target customers in the prospect database, since it knew the combination of demographics which represented customers more likely to purchase *Globe and Mail*. Some of the postal walks (ZIP code equivalent in Canada) the earlier program sent offers to did not have any subscribers in them. Also, the old telemarketing program dialed almost all numbers in the telephone book. These deficiencies in the old marketing program were addressed by the new database-driven marketing program. The offers were now sent to prospective customers whose demographics matched that of the current customers. Also, *Globe and Mail* used a predictive dialing method that doubled its prospective customer contacts per hour.

SOURCE: http://www.dbmarketing.com/articles/Art107.htm, "Building Circulation with Database Marketing", Arthur Middleton Hughes, January 20, 2005.

Enhancement Database

An enhancement database is used to transfer additional information about customers and prospects. An overlaying process is used that eliminates duplications. Enhancements may include demographic and psychographic data, transaction history, changes in address, changes in income levels, privacy status, and new product categories bought recently.

For example, InfoBase® Enhanced—InfoBase® provides a large collection of U.S. customer information such as telephone and address data, mailing lists including hotline files, e-mail data, and so on in one single source. The InfoBase® Enhanced provides the ability to append the latest demographics, socioeconomic and lifestyle data to your existing in-house customer database. A consumer goods company could use this data to better target its advertising and marketing campaigns, expand brand reach, improve acquisition and retention rates, and increase profitability.

This Bass Pro Shops' study in CRM at Work 7.3 illustrates how firms use an enhancement database.

7.2.2 CATEGORIZATION BASED ON THE NATURE OF THE UNDERLYING MARKETING ACTIVITIES

There are two types of marketing databases—passive and active.

Passive Marketing Database

A passive marketing database involves generating a customer list and then storing this list in the database. Future marketing efforts target the same customers in the list. The database is only a mailing list passively storing information about acquired customers, and has

CRM AT WORK 7.3

BASS PRO SHOPS

Bass Pro Shops is a business with twelve retail locations and a special outlet store where fishermen, hikers, hunters, and golfers come to buy fishing poles, boats, guns, and backpacks. The stores are popular enough for customers to travel across states to get to them. With such a widely scattered customer base, it is critical for Bass Pro Shops to capture customer information at the point of sale. With this information, the company knows where to send mailings about its special promotions—mailings which will bring those scattered customers back into the store to buy more merchandise.

Its main problem was having an inadequate name and address match rate from an earlier telephone data supplier. According to Carl Kendrick, director of corporate database marketing for Bass Pro Shops, "On the retail side of the business, we were only able to append mailing addresses to roughly 30 percent of the phone numbers we were getting at the point of sale. We knew this was substandard. What's more, a number of the addresses that were being appended were actually undeliverable. The mailings we sent to those addresses simply ended up in the postal dumpsters because the addresses weren't good."

Bass Pro Shops chose InfoBase TeleSource from Acxiom to solve this problem. InfoBase TeleSource data is multisourced, giving them more names, with more complete addresses and a higher level of accuracy. As a result, Bass Pro Shops is able to send their mailings to deliverable addresses, which cuts wastage and helps increase mailing efficiency.

SOURCE: http://www.acxiom.com/subimages/12112001160207basspro_telsource.pdf, January 20, 2005.

no active influence on the company's strategic marketing decisions. This may be a suboptimal use of the company's data resources. As Figure 7-1 shows, the database uses the same customer list for different marketing campaigns.

Any of the customer databases can be used as a passive database wherein a company keeps buying a new and updated customer database every time it needs customer information for campaigns. The campaign results from a past campaign hold no significance in this case.

Active Marketing Database

In contrast, marketers can use an active database to develop strategic marketing plans. Every individual marketing program designed to carry out the plan will then be data-driven. After

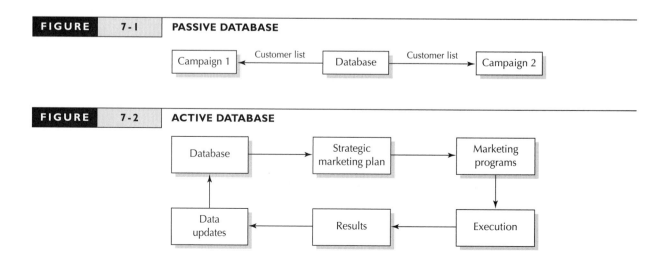

FIGURE 7-1   PASSIVE DATABASE

FIGURE 7-2   ACTIVE DATABASE

marketing programs are executed, the results are used to update the database. The updated database can then be used to help marketers adjust or redesign the strategic marketing plan.

The Travelers case study in CRM at Work 7.4 highlights the use of active databases.

7.2.3 CATEGORIZATION BASED ON THE DATABASE TECHNOLOGY

Third, databases can be categorized according to their underlying technology. Please note that the term *database,* in this context does not refer only to marketing databases.

Hierarchical Database

A hierarchical database is useful when the queries are standard and routine, but high-speed processing is required. Hierarchical databases are preferred in the banking, airline, and hotel industries. In hierarchical databases, all information pertaining to a customer will be in a master record. Hence, cross-referencing from other data sources is not needed.

Databases used in mainframe technology typically are hierarchical databases. They are huge in size and are still used as databases supporting critical applications in some medium- to big-sized corporations.

Inverted Database

Inverted databases are suited for direct marketing applications because they have the speed of a hierarchical database and also the flexibility to respond to unanticipated questions. It is also easy to add new elements to an inverted database as and when updated information is acquired.

CRM AT WORK 7.4

TRAVELERS

In the insurance industry, it takes a number of years before a customer becomes profitable. Travelers knew this fact but until recently was not able to do much about it. Travelers, like other insurance companies, works through several independent agents. The challenge was to build profitable relationships with customers though these independent agents.

A recent program implemented by Travelers took care of this problem by using a customer database effectively. The program used customer data to create a series of customized interactions with the customer to engage them in a relationship that lasts a lifetime. The program was essentially a retention program built from their customer database to interact with the customer in a systematic and low cost way. These interactions were five *touches* (an annual review, a thank you card, a cross-sell post card, a newsletter, and a seasonal greeting) over various times during a year. Depending on the customer, the message, frequency, channel, and the timing varied. Independent agents performed these interactions without much additional effort. The program was also used to calculate customer profitability, enabling Travelers to determine which customers it would want to keep, and thereby manage its communications effectively. This program reduced the number of customers lost by participating agents by almost 5 percent. Therefore, effective use of the customer database led to an increase in Travelers' customer retention rate. This database is a good example of an active database since the frequency, channel, and timing of the future interactions (with a customer) is based on the touch the customer responded to.

SOURCE: http://www.dbmarketing.com/articles/Art179.htm, "How Travelers Retain Their Best Customers", Arthur Middleton Hughes, January 20, 2005.

Some of the commonly used inverted file systems are Model 204, Adabas, and Computer Associates' Datacom/DB. These vary in their processing speeds and flexibility in the implementation environments.

Relational Database

Relational databases are composed of many simple tables. Users can create queries to extract information from these tables and recombine it. This capability means that when compared to other types of databases, relational databases have the greatest flexibility. However, this flexibility also means the speed of processing is somewhat slower.

Databases like Oracle, SQL Server, and Microsoft Access are all relational databases. Each one of these has different interfaces and capacities. Its use in organizations today depends on the size of the database marketing initiative. Oracle and SQL Server are capable of handling medium- to large-sized companywide marketing programs while Microsoft Access is used for smaller-sized database marketing initiatives.

7.3 THE BENEFITS OF MARKETING DATABASES

Companies that efficiently use their marketing databases can expect the following benefits.

7.3.1 THE ABILITY TO CARRY OUT PROFITABLE SEGMENTATION

Customers can be classified into different groups, depending on their buying behaviors. Frequent buyers need to be treated differently than occasional buyers. First-time users should be approached differently than repeat buyers. Marketing databases allow us to analyze customers and classify them into different groups. Different marketing programs can then be executed and implemented for different groups or segments.

7.3.2 RETAINED CUSTOMERS AND REPEAT BUSINESS

Retaining existing customers has become one of the important goals of many companies' marketing practices. Marketing databases enable marketers to determine the critical factors which influence the degree of customer satisfaction, and to develop effective campaigns accordingly to retain as many existing customers as possible at the lowest possible cost.

7.3.3 THE ABILITY TO SPOT POTENTIALLY PROFITABLE CUSTOMERS

With marketing databases, the company can profile its own customers, and then use lists and media surveys to locate potential customers with the same profile, and are therefore expected to contribute significantly to the company's revenues because of their higher response rates and willingness to buy premium products.

7.4 THE USES OF MARKETING DATABASES

7.4.1 USES THAT DIRECTLY INFLUENCE THE CUSTOMER RELATIONSHIP

- *Identify and profile the best customers.* By tracking customer transaction data, marketers can conduct recency, frequency, and monetary value (RFM) analysis or develop sophisticated models to identify customers who are of greatest value to the company.

- *Develop new customers.* Armed with the profile of the company's best customers, the company can find new customers with the characteristics of the best customers. Marketers could target not only the new users of the product/service but also competitors' existing customers.

- *Deliver customized messages consistent with product/service usage.* With customer transaction history data and customer service data, marketers can track customers' feedback to the specific products and services, and find out what pleased or displeased them. Then, the company can design specially customized marketing messages consistent with the product/service to promote their products and/or services.

- *Send follow-up messages to customers for post-purchase reinforcement.*

- *Cross-sell products/services.* The company can identify customers' other needs based on their demographic, lifestyle, and behavioral characteristics, and then sell them other products/services that satisfy their needs.

- *Ensure cost-effective communication with customers.* A marketing database enables marketers to classify customers into high potential, medium potential, and low potential groups. After evaluating the monetary value of these customers' potential, marketers will be able to determine how much the company should invest on communicating with these customers.

- *Improve promotion result.* Marketers can achieve better promotion results by targeting the customer groups who are most likely to respond (e.g., loyalists, prospects with best customer profiles).

- *Personalize customer service.* Knowing when, where, and what the customers purchased, the company can communicate with the customers to get their feedback, and then personalize the customer service delivered to them.

- *Stealth communication with customers.* Marketing databases provide the opportunity for one-on-one communications with each customer without the competitors' knowledge.

7.4.2 USES THAT DIRECTLY INFLUENCE OTHER BUSINESS OPERATIONS

- *Evaluate and refine existing marketing practices.* By analyzing customer data, marketers can assess the effectiveness of all the aspects of the existing marketing practice, including strategy, planning, budgeting, campaign design, implementation, customer communication, and so on, to identify shortcomings and suggest improvements.

- *Maintain brand equity.* Match brands with customers who fit the brand profile and keep communicating with those customers using specially designed brand-building messages.

- *Increase effectiveness of distribution channels.* Customers' transaction data and customer service data can tell how existing distribution channels work and how to make them more effective.

- *Conduct product and market research.* In a customer-centric company, product and market research must focus on customer needs. Marketing databases provide a unique resource of information on customer needs.

- *Integrating the marketing program.* A complete and integral marketing database can track all marketing efforts toward a customer. Marketers will be able to avoid duplicate, supplemental, and misdirected communications. It also helps marketers determine any overlapping between marketing programs targeted at different customer groups.

■ *Create a new valuable management resource.* A marketing database could be used to support not only the traditional marketing practices, but also a wide range of other business functions such as advertising, product R&D, distribution, customer service, and so on.

7.5   SUMMARY

Effective database analysis is important for successful CRM. Databases can be categorized based on their main business function—databases managing business and databases supporting decision-making activities. In addition, databases can also be categorized based on the information included in the databases, the nature of the underlying marketing activities, and database technology. Based on the information included in the databases, databases can be classified as customer, prospect, cluster, and enhancement databases. Customer databases identify and profile the best customers and communicate with these customers to elicit a response. These data allow the companies to market their products to specific customer segments to achieve higher net marketing contribution. Data from active and inactive customers are important to ensure efficient marketing function. The prospect database includes information on noncustomers with profiles similar to those of existing customers. It can be used by marketers to design marketing campaigns to target prospects with the intent of acquiring them as new customers. This is done after carefully analyzing the channels through which the prospects like to receive information. Cluster databases include information about small clusters based on geographic reference groups, affinity groups, and lifestyle reference groups. An enhancement database is used to transfer additional information on customers and prospects avoiding duplications.

Based on the nature of the underlying marketing activities, marketing databases are categorized into active and passive. A passive database is a customer mailing list that passively stores information about acquired customers for targeting future marketing efforts, and has no active influence on the company's strategic marketing decisions. An active database is used by marketers to develop strategic marketing plans. After marketing programs are executed, the results are used to update the database. The updated database can be used to help marketers adjust or redesign the strategic marketing plan. According to the underlying technology, databases can be categorized into hierarchical, inverted, and relational databases. A hierarchical database is useful for routine and standard queries which need high-speed processing. These have all the information pertaining to a customer in a master record and are typically used in mainframe technology. Inverted databases are suited for direct marketing applications on account of their speed, flexibility, and ease of updating. Relational databases have the greatest flexibility but lower speed of processing. Marketing databases allow marketers to analyze customers and classify them into different groups and, accordingly, implement different marketing programs for each group. These databases also enable marketers to determine the critical factors influencing customer satisfaction and take measures to retain existing customers at lowest cost. They also aid the company in locating potentially profitable customers using lists and media surveys. Using marketing databases, marketers can identify individual customers of greatest value to the company. Other uses of marketing databases include developing new customers, delivering customized messages consistent with product/service usage, and effectively communicating with customers in the form of feedbacks on purchases, promotions, stealth communications, and so on. Maintaining brand equity, increasing effectiveness of distribution channels, as well as conducting product and market research are other uses of marketing databases that directly influence business operations.

7.6 EXERCISE QUESTIONS

1. What are the various ways to categorize databases?

2. How are databases classified based on the information they contain? Are these different classes of databases complements or substitutes?

3. Assume you are the marketing manager for a local U.S. bank in Texas. Your assignment is to target prospects in Oklahoma (small- to medium-sized businesses). Go to the Web site of Axciom (http://www.acxiom.com) or Dun & Bradstreet (http://www.dnb.com) and determine the cost of obtaining ten variables of firmographic information on these firms.

4. List some key uses of marketing databases. Provide an example for each.

CHAPTER 8

Designing Loyalty Programs

Contents

8.1   OVERVIEW

In order to retain customers, many firms have focused their attention on increasing customer satisfaction levels. The degree of customer satisfaction is indeed a key measure. However, to what extent customer satisfaction leads to loyalty and profitability is an important issue to be examined. Traditionally, customer satisfaction is expected to lead to greater retention or loyalty, which, in turn, leads to greater profit. This satisfaction-loyalty-profitability chain is discussed in the first part of the chapter. Although customer satisfaction and loyalty are key mediators of profits, these measures cannot be taken as simple predictors of profit. From a business point of view, what is more important is to identify and nurture relationship with *profitable* customers. This is where loyalty programs come in. Loyalty programs (LP) have become an important CRM tool to identify, reward, and retain profitable customers. We discuss the objectives and design of various loyalty programs. We also illustrate many LP failures to gain insights into what differentiates a successful program from an unsuccessful one. We conclude the discussion about loyalty programs by reviewing LP characteristics to systematically investigate outcomes and determinants of LP success, and to provide guidelines for designing optimal programs. The key dimensions of LP design, such as reward and sponsorship, are explained in detail and illustrated using relevant case studies.

8.2 SATISFACTION-LOYALTY-PROFIT CHAIN

The satisfaction-loyalty-profit-chain (SPC) is a key concept requiring a thorough understanding because of its link to CRM (see Figure 8-1). It has been popular since the early 1990s, when companies realized the importance of measuring and managing customer satisfaction.[1] The key underlying idea is that improving product and service attributes will lead to an improvement in customer satisfaction. Increased customer satisfaction is expected to lead to greater customer retention, which is often used as a proxy for customer loyalty, which then is expected to lead to greater profitability. Despite the almost self-evident nature of these positive links, the empirical evidence from a number of years of research shows only mixed support.[2] Likewise, translating the conceptual framework into practical reality has been problematic for many firms. For example, a firm may have improved its performance on a key attribute, only to discover that the overall satisfaction score did not noticeably increase. At other times, changes in overall satisfaction scores have failed to show a demonstrable impact on customer retention.[3] We believe, therefore, that it is critical to have a complete understanding of the entire satisfaction-profit chain in order to manage customers in an efficient manner.

8.2.1 ISSUES TO CONSIDER

The Level of Analysis

When employing the SPC concept, it is worthwhile to consider the level of analysis. Most of the empirical studies have looked at aggregate, *firm-level* results. For example, a series

| FIGURE | 8-1 | **THE SATISFACTION-PROFIT CHAIN** |

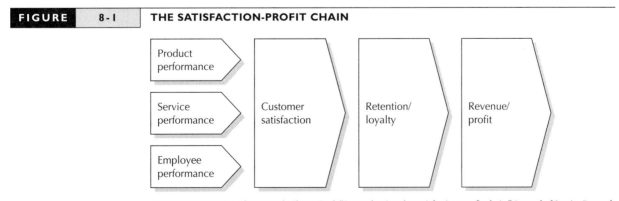

SOURCE: Eugene W. Anderson and Vikas Mittal, "Strengthening the satisfaction-profit chain," *Journal of Service Research* 3, no. 2 (November 2000): 107.

of studies[4] looked at how firm-level customer satisfaction indices are linked to firm-level performance. The finding from this and similar studies indicate a positive association between the companywide satisfaction score and company's overall performance. However, in a world where resources are allocated on the individual customer level, the chain needs to be implemented at a *disaggregate level*. There is much less hard evidence of the nature of the SPC on the individual customer level. Although one would expect a correlation between firm-level and individual-level results, it is not clear how strong this correlation really is.

The Direct Link between Customer Satisfaction and Profits

The direct link between customer satisfaction and profits suggests that as customers experience greater satisfaction with a firm's offering, profits rise. For example, in a study[5] it was found that the *stated sales satisfaction* of Volvo customers is significantly linked to *new car profitability* (e.g., through closing financing and insurance deals, Volvo card membership, and workshop loyalty).

What do we know, in general, about this direct link between satisfaction and profitability? Although early proponents of the SPC argued customer satisfaction always has a positive bottom-line impact, we have a much more complete picture today. It is interesting to note research on the direct relationship between satisfaction and profits has shown both positive effects in a limited number of studies,[6] and no effects in other studies.[7] On one hand, a study found a variety of quality strategies failed to deliver anticipated business performance. On the other hand, a positive correlation has been documented between customer satisfaction and return on assets.

What is important to understand and explains some of the seemingly contradictory findings, is that it is simply not enough to link satisfaction and revenues. Improving customer satisfaction comes at a cost, and once the cost of enhancing satisfaction is factored in, it may well be that offering "excessive satisfaction" doesn't pay. This is because the marginal gains in satisfaction decrease, while the marginal expenses to achieve the growth in satisfaction increase. This falls in line with what is said about the vastly improved product quality offered by many firms today. As the general level of quality reaches high levels, it becomes more and more costly to improve satisfaction with a further rise in quality. For example, is an investment in another ride justified for an amusement park, given the expected incremental traffic? Although the additional ride is likely to increase customer satisfaction, the question is whether it generates enough additional revenues to offset the investment. In addition, increasing customer satisfaction leads, in many cases, to an adaptation of expectation levels; consumers quickly get used to a better service level without necessarily rewarding the firm with additional purchases. What this probably means is that there is an optimum satisfaction level for any firm, beyond which increasing satisfaction doesn't pay. To find such an optimum level, firms need to conduct longitudinal satisfaction studies to investigate changes in customer satisfaction *over time* and link them to improvements in their offering.

The Link between Satisfaction and Retention

Given some of the difficulties associated with establishing unequivocal links between customer satisfaction and company performance, managers turned during the 1990s increasingly to customer retention as a long goal. By focusing on customer retention, managers move closer to the ultimate dependent variable—profits. Figure 8-2 shows a typical shape confirmed by a number of studies (even though there can be considerable

FIGURE **8-2** **ILLUSTRATION OF THE SATISFACTION-RETENTION LINK**

Note: The dotted line represents a linear approximation of the nonlinear relationship shown.

SOURCE: Eugene W. Anderson and Vikas Mittal, "Strengthening the satisfaction-profit chain," *Journal of Service Research* 3, no. 2 (November 2000): 114.

departures from this shape). The data are typically derived on the firm level, not the customer level.

The data show the link between satisfaction and retention is asymmetric: dissatisfaction has a greater impact on retention than satisfaction. A satisfied customer is influenced by many factors when making a purchase and has many options. Even if the level of satisfaction is high, retention is not guaranteed, as there may be another product that would satisfy the customer to the same extent. Conversely, if the customer is dissatisfied, then the other product becomes more enticing. The link is nonlinear; the impact of satisfaction on retention is greater at the extremes. The flat part of the curve in the middle has also been called the *zone of indifference*.[8] As seen in the industry-level databases (such as the ACSI from the University of Michigan), a number of factors—including the aggressiveness of competition, degree of switching cost, and the level of perceived risk—influence the shape of the curve and the position of the elbows (the two points in the graph where there is a sharp change in the shape of the curve).

An example of the variable link between satisfaction and retention can be demonstrated. Figure 8-3 shows the variability in the relationship across industries.

In Figure 8-3, in the competitive automotive industry, very high levels of satisfaction are necessary for a customer to repurchase the same brand again. On the contrary, consumers may incur considerable switching costs when utilizing an airline. This cost might increase due to bonus-point build-up in frequent-flyer programs or limited airline choice at any given airport. Thus, consumers tend to re-patronize an airline even though satisfaction might only be moderate.

The same caveats that apply to the satisfaction-profit link also apply to the satisfaction-retention link. First, firms should thoroughly investigate the nature of the link for a specific industry, category, or segment. For example, two firms operating in two different industries might have identical satisfaction levels, yet the relationship between customer satisfaction and retention might be quite different for the two firms. To assess the impact of satisfaction on retention in a better manner, firms must account for the attractiveness of alternatives in addition to what they offer. Another aspect to consider is that the link might change, depending on the measurement employed for the loyalty measured. For example, a study[9] found that repurchase behavior is a better measure than repurchase intent. Finally,

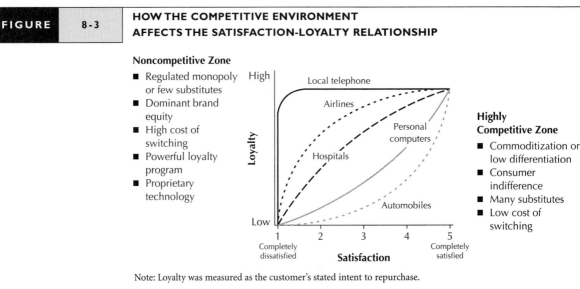

FIGURE 8-3

HOW THE COMPETITIVE ENVIRONMENT AFFECTS THE SATISFACTION-LOYALTY RELATIONSHIP

Noncompetitive Zone
- Regulated monopoly or few substitutes
- Dominant brand equity
- High cost of switching
- Powerful loyalty program
- Proprietary technology

Highly Competitive Zone
- Commoditization or low differentiation
- Consumer indifference
- Many substitutes
- Low cost of switching

Note: Loyalty was measured as the customer's stated intent to repurchase.

SOURCE: Thomas O. Jones and W. Earl Sasser, Jr., "Why satisfied customers defect," *Harvard Business Review* 73, no. 6 (November/December 1995).

we know comparatively less about the link on an individual customer level as compared to a company or industry level analyses.

The Link between Loyalty and Profits

Due to the complexity and specificity of the links, taking customer satisfaction as a proxy measure for customer loyalty or for customer profits is not a viable solution. Therefore, it is not surprising to see increasing interest in examining the direct link between customer retention and a firm's performance. The key proponent of looking at this link is Frederick F. Reichheld, who, in a series of writings, stresses the importance of managing customer retention.[10]

Long-term customers supposedly do the following, according to the principal hypotheses of Reichheld:

- Spend more per period over time
- Cost less to serve per period over time
- Have greater propensity to generate word-of-mouth customers
- Pay a premium price when compared to that paid by short-term customers

The underlying argument is that customers are acquired at a cost, which then gets recovered over time, thus becoming more and more profitable over time. Although this might hold true in a contractual relationship (e.g., magazine subscription, cable TV contract) it hardly holds true in a noncontractual relationship (such as shopping in a department store). In a noncontractual relationship, the revenue stream must be balanced by the cost of constantly sustaining the relationship and fending off competitive attacks. However, managing these constant investments in customer relationships can be quite tricky. Obviously, a high retention rate is very desirable, but increasing the marginal retention comes at an increasing cost. Blindly increasing retention spending will eventually lead to overspending. Clearly, efforts at increasing customer satisfaction and retention not only consume a firm's resources, but are subject to diminishing returns. In addition, be aware that Reichheld's propositions are derived from *asking managers about what they believe* the benefits of relation are. Since managerial opinions can be biased and self-serving, it is important to consequently investigate actual customer behavior in order to investigate the true, more underlying, link.

Reichheld's propositions have been tested recently by Reinartz and Kumar, who investigated the profitability of a sample of more than 16,000 individual customers across four industries.[11] Their results bring out a different picture. Essentially, the researchers found the relationship between customer retention and customer profits is not as strong as anticipated. Reinartz and Kumar demonstrate, for example, that, across different firms, there is a segment of customers who are loyal but not very profitable (due to excessive resource allocation), and a segment that generates very high profits although it has only a short tenure. Since these short-term customers can be very profitable, it is clear that loyalty is not the only path to profitability. As the following figure illustrates, the overall trend shows a direct correlation between loyalty and profitability. However, outliers on the graph who generate high profits while not having high loyalty will outperform those customers with a high level of loyalty but low profitability (see Figure 8-4).

The key implication of Reinartz and Kumar's finding is that caution must be exercised when equating customer retention with customer profitability. Firms ultimately have to make an effort to obtain information on individual or segment profitability (see Figure 8-5).

What Does It All Mean?

Although the SPC is conceptually sound, measuring and managing customer satisfaction is not enough. By not understanding the exact nature (e.g., strength, symmetry, and nonlinearity) of the various links, many companies have seriously misallocated resources based on an incorrect understanding of the underlying mechanics. The key conclusion from this section's discussion is the importance of moving to the ultimate end of the satisfaction-profit chain (SPC). Moving to the ultimate dependent variable, customer profits are ultimately required for making good marketing decisions.

This does not mean that knowing the status of customer satisfaction or customer loyalty is no longer important. However, it is important to assess the various links in the SPC in a correct manner. As we know today, these links are almost always nonlinear,

FIGURE 8-4 **LIFETIME DURATION-PROFITABILITY ASSOCIATION**

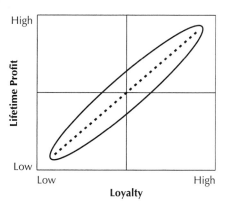

SOURCE: W. Reinartz and V. Kumar, "On the Profitability of Long-Life Customers in a Non-Contractual Setting: An Empirical Investigation and Implications for Marketing," *Journal of Marketing* 64 (October 2000): 17–32.

FIGURE	8-5	**ASSOCIATION OF PROFITABILITY AND LONGEVITY OF CUSTOMERS**

	Percentage of Customers			Percentage of Customers	
High Profitability	Corporate service provider	20%		Corporate service provider	30%
	Grocery retail	15%		Grocery retail	36%
	Mail-order	19%		Mail-order	31%
	Direct brokerage	18%		Direct brokerage	32%
	Percentage of Customers			Percentage of Customers	
Low Profitability	Corporate service provider	29%		Corporate service provider	21%
	Grocery retail	34%		Grocery retail	15%
	Mail-order	29%		Mail-order	21%
	Direct brokerage	33%		Direct brokerage	17%
	Short-Term Customers			**Long-Term Customers**	

SOURCE: W. Reinartz and V. Kumar, "The mismanagement of customer loyalty," *Harvard Business Review* 80, no. 7 (July 2002): 86.

asymmetric, and certainly segment- and industry-specific. As such, taking customer satisfaction or customer loyalty as a simple proxy measure for customer profits is not sufficient, and we therefore need to make every effort to measure customer-level profitability. However, since firms cannot influence profits per se, but do so via product and service quality, the impact of customer satisfaction and customer loyalty as key mediators cannot be neglected.

8.3   WHAT IS LOYALTY?

It was thought that more loyal customers would do more repeat business and develop a larger tolerance to price increases, and therefore are more profitable to the firm. We've seen this was not always the case. A very loyal customer may also be consuming the firm's resources by utilizing services and discounts, and therefore may not be *profitable*. The current focus of marketers is in locating and enticing new customers who will be *profitable*, and finding appropriate strategies for identifying unprofitable customers to take appropriate marketing action or eventually let go of such customers.

In Chapter 1, we came across the concept of *customer value*. We defined customer value as the economic value ($-metric) of the customer relationship to the firm—expressed on the basis of contribution margin or net profit. Customer value is a marketing metric proving to be an important decision aid, in addition to evaluating marketing effectiveness. A firm can both measure and optimize its marketing efforts by incorporating the concept of customer value at the core of its decision-making process.

It must be noted that customers' loyalty to a product or service by way of repeat purchases can be due to their natural satisfaction and preference for the products' features and benefits. Alternatively, loyalty can also be induced through marketing plans and programs from the firm. For example, a wireless cellular phone service requiring a contractual relationship of one or two years with the customer is an indirect way of ensuring repetitive and profitable transactions from the customer for a predictable period of time.

Whether contractual or motivated through incentives, the success or failure of a loyalty program (LP) is determined by the profitability from the customer. Further, it is also clear that longevity of the customer relationship does not automatically translate into tangible profitability.

Many different forms of customer loyalty programs are being practiced, and their primary objectives are to identify, reward, and retain profitable customers. In the following sections, we will discuss the various aspects of customer loyalty programs and their design.

8.4   DIFFERENCE BETWEEN BEHAVIORAL AND ATTITUDINAL LOYALTY

Before looking at loyalty programs per se, it is important to understand a significant difference between behavioral and attitudinal loyalty of customers. Broadly speaking, *behavioral loyalty* refers to the observed action customers have demonstrated towards a particular product or service. *Attitudinal loyalty,* by contrast, refers to the perceptions and attitudes a customer has toward a particular product or service. Ideally, a strong correlation between a customer's attitude and behaviors can be expected. However, there are instances when customer behaviors can be quite different from their attitudinal perceptions about the product or service.

8.4.1   CASE IN POINT

A frequent flyer member of ABC airlines may be continuing her relationship only because she has accrued many points and wants to redeem her miles. Though her attitudinal preference is for traveling with XYZ airlines because of its superior quality of service and experience, she is compelled to continue transacting with ABC. In this situation, her relationship with ABC reflects a strong behavioral loyalty. But her negative perceptions toward ABC reflect poor attitudinal loyalty. Attitudinal loyalty is extremely important, as customers who are not attitudinally loyal are likely to cease the relationship at the earliest available opportunity. As we see later, not all loyalty programs tend to focus on creating attitudinal loyalty with the target customers.

8.5   WHAT IS A LOYALTY PROGRAM?

In recent years, many companies have introduced loyalty programs (LPs), frequency reward programs, and customer clubs, and they are currently available in many consumer markets. A loyalty program (LP) can be defined as a marketing process that generates rewards to customers based on their repeat purchasing. The term *LP* is used here to subsume the many different forms of frequency reward programs. Consumers who enter a loyalty program are expected to transact more with the focal company, thereby giving up the free choice they have otherwise. In exchange for concentrating their purchases with the focal firm, they accumulate assets (e.g., points), which are exchanged for products and services, typically but not necessarily associated with the focal firm. Therefore, LPs have become an important CRM tool used by marketers to identify, award, and retain profitable customers.

LPs are certainly not a new instrument in the relationship marketer's toolkit. Sainsbury (UK) archives show how, in the 1970s, its managers wrote to customers who had not made their usual shopping trip in an effort to maintain patronage. Later, the store used Green Stamps, which were well supported by customers, despite the need to paste them into many books.[12]

8.6 KEY OBJECTIVES OF LOYALTY PROGRAMS

The key objectives of introducing LPs fall into the following four categories:

1. Building true (attitudinal and behavioral) loyalty
2. Efficiency profits
3. Effectiveness profits
4. Value alignment

- *Building true (attitudinal and behavioral) loyalty.* This refers to a greater commitment to the product or organization through the building of true loyalty, that is, a combination of attitudinal and behavioral customer loyalty. The consequences of true loyalty—greater commitment, greater word of mouth (WOM), or greater share of category requirements (SCR)—are somewhat difficult to observe. This objective is also not easy to achieve because consumers are fickle and economic benefits are very important to them. Building true loyalty is the goal of many customer clubs.
- *Efficiency profits.* This refers to immediate profit consequences as compared to profit consequences without loyalty programs—net of the LP cost.
- *Effectiveness profits.* Effectiveness profits are long-term profit consequences realized through better knowledge of customer preferences over time. This learning allows sustainable value creation for customers through, for example, customization of products or communication (this is likely to provide competitive advantage since it produces higher profits in the long run).
- *Value alignment.* The goal is to align the cost to serve a particular customer with the value he/she brings to the firm. This allows firms to serve their most valuable customers in the best manner.

Any loyalty program may or may not pursue all these goals at the same time.

8.6.1 BUILDING TRUE LOYALTY

True loyalty will always encompass both components—attitudinal and behavioral loyalty. According to this logic, customers may exhibit behavioral loyalty (i.e., they purchase a product repeatedly) but they may do so for many reasons, for example, convenience or price. Clearly, behavioral loyalty may be a result of attitudinal loyalty, but it may be driven by other factors as well.

Many LPs have been set up with the goal of "making customers more loyal." This goal is very hard to reach. Enforcing loyalty by enticing customers with rewards and bonuses is unlikely to create true loyalty. True loyalty is a function of true value provided to the customers. It also encompasses many other factors, such as the degree of involvement in the product category, the visibility of the product when using it, or the value expressive nature of the product. These aspects are hard to control from a firm's perspective.

Take, for example, the case of a low-involvement category—grocery shopping. As CRM at Work 8.1 shows, inducing real loyalty is a tough proposition. Purchases are driven by tangible considerations, such as value for money.

CRM AT WORK 8.1

SUPERMARKETS LOSING LOYALTY BATTLE

Despite spending hundreds of millions of pounds on price-cutting campaigns and loyalty card schemes, UK supermarkets have only persuaded a small minority of shoppers to stay loyal. Only 15 percent of all grocery shoppers are completely loyal to the store where they do their main grocery shopping, according to a report from Mintel Research, while 29 percent use one other store and 22 percent use two others. Men are more likely than women to be loyal to a single store, with 46 percent of men shopping in just one or two main stores. Overall, people in the United Kingdom are increasingly shopping at the top three supermarkets—Tesco, Sainsbury's, and Asda, which now account for 59 percent of main grocery trips, an increase from 48 percent in 1994. Between 1994 and 2001, all three supermarkets increased their share, with Asda adding on the most additional share. Safeway and Morrison's maintained their positions as the fourth and fifth most popular choices for main grocery shopping. Food retailing is the largest of all retail sectors in the United Kingdom, with sales accounting for £97.2 billion in 2000—almost 45 percent of all retail expenditure.[13]

Depending on the product category, true loyalty finds its expression in community building as well. Taking the brand as a reason to share experiences in a community is a very powerful expression of loyalty. Therefore, it is not surprising that many companies attempt to build communities around their brands. Often, brand communities are linked to special benefits unavailable outside the community. For example, the German company *Steiff*, the venerable maker of teddy bears, has a customer club which offers a limited-edition teddy bear exclusively to its members once a year.

8.6.2 EFFICIENCY PROFITS

Efficiency profits are profits resulting from a change in customer's buying behavior due to the loyalty program. This change in buying behavior can be measured in various ways:

- Basket size
- Purchase frequency acceleration
- Price sensitivity
- Share of category requirements (SCR) or share of wallet
- Retention
- Lifetime duration

The most widely used measure of behavioral loyalty is SCR, that is how much of the purchases in a category are served through the focal brand or retailer. Naturally, efficiency profits are net of LP cost. The key idea of an LP aiming at efficiency profits is that customers build up switching cost by accumulating assets in the LP. By accumulating assets, customers forego their free choice, yet the expected reward seems to make this reduction in free choice worthwhile. The key criticism to this viewpoint has been as follows: First, for a customer to engage in an LP, the overall utility of being in an LP should be higher than that of not being in an LP. This means that the cost for the firm to entice the customer to change his behavior accordingly may be, in fact, higher than that without the LP.

Scrapping Safeway's (UK) ABC loyalty card scheme saves it £50 million this year, money that will be invested in cutting prices.[14]

The second criticism of the goal of efficiency profits is the hypothesis that the customer segment most likely to join the LP consists of truly loyals anyway, and their business would have been certain in the first place. The question that arises is whether LPs actually change buying behavior. It is possible that it does not change behavior as much as it reinforces existing behavior, and at a much higher cost to the firm.

Loyalty cards have been criticized for rewarding heavy spending rather than true loyalty, and indeed the segments most interested in them are the affluent groups who can afford to build up their points, even if they hold cards from more than one store group.[15]

In spite of the difficult nature of achieving efficiency profits, many, if not most, LPs are introduced with this goal in mind.

8.6.3   EFFECTIVENESS PROFITS

Effectiveness profits refer to the medium- to long-term profit consequences realized through better knowledge of customer preferences. The LP is designed to cumulatively gather information about individuals, their behavior, and their preferences and to derive knowledge from this information. This process of learning allows the firm to continuously improve on its knowledge of customer preferences and to increasingly offer a better value proposition to its various customers. The improvement in the value proposition comes through effective product and communication offerings. Effectiveness profits are, more than any other type of LP outcome, likely to generate sustainable competitive advantage since they produce the highest profits in the long run.

Achieving Effectiveness Profits in a Grocery Store

Achieving effectiveness profits means implementing an information-based strategy: gathering and analyzing information about every transaction. For example, in grocery retailing, this includes information on every single item purchased, down to the color of ink in a pen, along with the time of day, weather, and even the checkout operator's name.

Data mining is used to generate personalized promotions and recommendations. For instance, a vegetarian would not receive a promotion for steak. The knowledge that a customer is a vegetarian is either derived from surveys or from the customer's buying behavior. If the store's computer sees that a customer is not buying meat, it assumes that customer is a vegetarian, and not that she is buying her meat elsewhere. Although such an assumption could be wrong, a store would rather not bother a customer with costly promotions for categories from which that customer has never bought anything in the first place.

To promote new products, an *ideas list* is populated from new launches, as well as from existing products that the data-mining algorithms suggest customers might desire. For example, if a customer is buying a lot of California Chardonnay, the list may suggest the customer try white Burgundy which is on special because it is made from the same grape.

The strategy of using an LP to *learn about customer preferences* may result in impressive gains for both customers and organizations. Customers get more of what they truly want, and firms are safe in terms of not having to engage in a costly mass marketing exercise.

The possible downside to a learning strategy is the relative process sophistication necessary for its implementation. While the collection of massive amounts of data is an all too easy step, the analysis, learning, and implementation of the learning is much more difficult. Few companies have actually mastered this strategic capability.

8.6.4   VALUE ALIGNMENT

Value alignment refers to the goal of aligning the cost to serve a particular customer with the value that a customer is bringing to the firm. The concept underlying this goal is that for any industry, customers do have differential monetary value to the firm, and they are typically differentially expensive to serve. For example, if a provider of wireless services were to arrange its customers from highest to lowest value to the firm, it would find a great variance. Clearly, a business user would be more likely to rack up higher phone bills than an occasional private user. Likewise, if it were to arrange the same customers from highest to lowest cost-to-serve it would find considerable variance. Some customers are easy to satisfy whereas others exploit the customer service function to a great extent.

If a firm pursues value alignment it simply attempts to align the profits it receives from a given customer with the cost incurred to serve that same customer. Clearly, this means not every customer is treated equally—a notion some managers find discomforting. However, it allows firms to ensure their best customers are also getting the best service. The goal of value alignment is particularly critical when there is great heterogeneity in the customer's value and cost to serve. Some industries where this is the case are the airline business, the hospitality industry, and the financial services industry.

Example

Figure 8-6 illustrates an example of a firm with a highly heterogeneous customer base. It indicates the profitability of a bank, showing three very different customer profiles. On the left, Tier A, represents 71 percent of the customer base. In the middle, Tier B, represents 42 percent of the customer base, and on the right, Tier C, represents the remaining 27 percent. More than one quarter of the customers are unprofitable and need to be subsidized by the highly profitable ones—a condition not uncommon to find in banks.

As can be seen from the previous discussion, there are potentially four different LP goals. Given a particular goal for LP, how can it be achieved most effectively? Clearly, to make this assessment, we need to know and investigate the impact of the drivers of LP success.

Having understood the goals of an LP, it may be useful to understand some of the characteristics of LPs. Characteristics such as suitability of the goal, cost structures, challenges involved, and the degree of competitive advantage created are summarized in Table 8-1 and also correlated with the corresponding LP goal.

8.7 EXAMPLES OF LOYALTY PROGRAMS

- *Frequent-buyer programs.* The most simple initiatives are based on punch-cards that offer, for example, a free complimentary product. City Bagels, a sandwich retail chain, offers customers who have nine stamps from previous purchases every tenth sandwich free. The purpose of CityBagel's program is to increase both sandwich consumption and customer retention. Stores like BigY, Kroger, and CVS offer discounts on certain store merchandise to store-cardholders to ensure customer loyalty and retention.

- *Volkswagen Club and Card.* The Volkswagen Club and Card concept attempts to establish a direct relationship with the end customer. Customers collect points

FIGURE **8-6** **REVENUE AND PROFITABILITY OF CUSTOMERS**

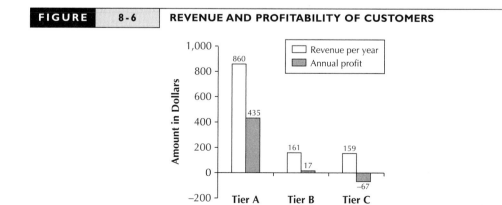

TABLE   8-1   KEY CHARACTERISTICS OF LOYALTY PROGRAMS

Goal of LP	Commitment, WOM, Building Communities (True Loyalty)	Efficiency Profits	Effectiveness Profits	Value Alignment
Most suited for	All branded products (however, the larger the brand, the more difficult it becomes to uniquely differentiate the brand and the more difficult to manage customer interactions consistently)	Many industries	■ Firms with access to large amounts of information about customers. ■ Firms who communicate directly with end customer	All industries with skewed customer value distribution. Within this constraint, particularly well suited for industries with product perishability (airlines, hospitality industry, rental car business)
Cost of LP may be mitigated by	—	Contributions from manufacturers (promotions)	Contributions from manufacturers (promotions)	Low marginal cost of rewards
Key challenges	■ Providing meaningful value to create differentiation in consumer's minds ■ Brand building	■ Providing acceptable incentives to customers and at the same time, controlling cost ■ Program differentiation	Capability of handling, analyzing, learning from, and deploying knowledge from large databases	■ Implementing the customer differentiation scheme (deployment automation) ■ Having fair and equitable relationships in general and still ensure that best customers are treated best
Degree of competitive advantage created	*High* (having a truly loyal customer base is hard and costly to replicate because it can only be built over time)	*Low* (because it is easy to replicate hard benefits and program cost creates major challenges)	*High* (capability of learning from customer behavior and using it is very difficult to copy and unique to a company's context)	*Low-Medium* (because LPs have become standard industry practice)

from Volkswagen (VW) for servicing their car or buying accessories and from partners of car rental companies and tour operators. The points can be redeemed for dealer services, price reductions on car purchases, and catalog merchandise. The purpose of the program is to establish a better communication between VW, VW dealers, and the customers and to bind customers to the brand.

■ *Star Alliance Frequent-Flyer Program.* The Star Alliance is a group of airlines across all continents that cross-list flights, share facilities, and recognize their respective frequent-flyer programs. Any flight on any Star Alliance airline counts towards a member's frequent-flyer program. With 900 airports in 129 countries worldwide, the Star Alliance has become the largest airline network in the world.

■ *Webmiles.de.* Webmiles.de, founded in 1999, operates an LP that differs from most company-specific programs. Webmiles allows its members to collect and redeem assets in a network of retail partners. Thus, the retailers become members in Webmiles' partner network. Webmiles manages the program and the communication with more than 1 million customers. It claimed to be the largest LP in Europe in 2003.

- *Neimann Marcus.* Neiman Marcus, the luxury retailer based in Dallas Texas, offers its LP 'InCircles' to all customers. Using a shopping card, customers accumulate points that can be redeemed for exclusive rewards.

- *Buitoni Pasta Club:* Buitoni (UK) has created a club for pasta lovers. While the members do not accumulate points, Buitoni offers a platform for exchange among pasta enthusiasts: sharing recipes, sharing cooking experiences, and testing innovative product concepts. The club offers an opportunity for Buitoni to get closer to heavy end users.

8.8   LOYALTY PROGRAMS: INCREASING IN POPULARITY

Interest in loyalty programs exploded in the late 1990s. Building mainly on the premise that it is cheaper to market to existing customers than to acquire new ones; firms across a multitude of industries have raced to implement loyalty schemes of one form or another. Recently, the Internet service provider AOL and American Airlines created the world's biggest loyalty programs with 1.5 million and 78 million members, respectively, and more than 2,000 partners. In Europe, an estimated 350 million loyalty cards were issued in 1999 for the retailing sector alone.[16]

The growth in LP usage has been staggering (See Figure 8-7 for growth in LP membership across different countries and Figure 8-8 for membership growth in the U.S. over three years.) The following numbers attest to this growth.

- The Australian FlyBuy program had a membership of 7 million Australians in 1996—one in four Australian households.[17]

- By 2002, there were more than 120 million airline frequent-flyer members worldwide, with most residing in the United States (74 million), Europe (24 million), and Asia (21 million).[18]

- American AAdvantage is the largest frequent flyer program in the world. As of November 2003, it had grown to a membership of more than 45 million members.[19]

- In 1997, Marriott International replaced its Honored Guest Awards and launched *Marriott Rewards,* the world's largest multibrand frequent guest program, comprising 9 million members, six Marriott Lodging brands and 1,000 hotels in 70 countries. By October 2003, *Marriott Rewards* had grown to 19 million members and more than 2,700 participating hotels worldwide.[20]

- In the highly competitive UK retail industry, Tesco has managed to double its earnings by taking market share from rivals like Sainsburys. Tesco's success has been credited to its popular customer loyalty program, which enables shoppers to earn points and redeem them either during future visits or with airlines.[21]

- French retailer E.Leclerc spends approximately $21.2 million each year for LP marketing and management.[22]

- According to Gartner analyst Adam Sarner, U.S. companies spent more than $1.2 billion on customer loyalty programs in 2003.[23]

The most well-known examples of loyalty programs are frequent-flyer programs in the airline industry. American Airlines was the first company to establish its AAdvantage frequent flyer

| FIGURE | 8-7 | **LOYALTY PROGRAMS MEMBERSHIP GROWTH** |

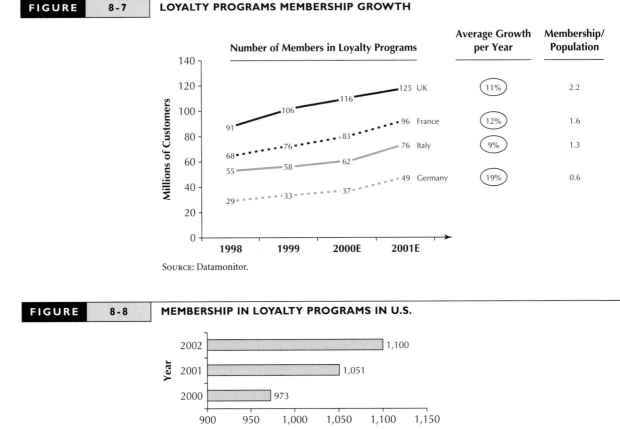

SOURCE: Datamonitor.

| FIGURE | 8-8 | **MEMBERSHIP IN LOYALTY PROGRAMS IN U.S.** |

program in 1981. During the 1990s, many supermarket chains and general merchandise retailers established loyalty programs—for example, the "Carte Iris" program of the French retail chain Champion or the "ClubCard" of the British retailer Tesco. The latest form of loyalty programs finds its expression in point collection schemes initiated by third parties (e.g., Webmiles or PayBack), where users collect points across a network of member companies.

Although LPs have become immensely popular, it is far from clear whether LPs are effective in helping firms engender greater customer loyalty and higher profits, partly because of the considerable cost associated with managing an LP, and partly because management of LPs can be tricky. See CRM at Work 8.2.

8.9 PROBLEMS WITH LOYALTY PROGRAMS

Although LPs have become widely popular, the benefits are not clear. Many companies who invested millions of dollars into this CRM tool have found it is costing them without providing any obvious return. An example for such a company is ANZ.

- In May 2003, ANZ Bank of Australia increased its annual fees by $50 on its credit cards linked to reward programs. This increase was primarily due to the increased point acquisition by frequent flyers and the potential fee reduction for inter-bank credit card transactions.[24]

CRM AT WORK 8.2
FREQUENT-FLYER PROGRAMS

In the airline industry there are five main factors driving a customer's choice of airline. These factors are market coverage, price, schedule, frequent-flyer programs, and product attributes. For many years, the belief in the airline industry was that loyal customers are more profitable, and that by rewarding customers based on the miles they fly with an airline, the airline could increase their loyalty. However, there were shortcomings in this approach. By rewarding all passengers equally, the airline was not maximizing the value of its most profitable customers. The seat class type and fare type were ignored with regard to the reward system. Having realized this, the airline industry has moved away from simply basing rewards on miles flown. American Airlines, United, Continental, and USAir now multiply the miles flown by a customer by a coefficient derived from the type of seat class the customer has paid for.

Passengers willing to pay to upgrade to business or first class will, in turn, earn more miles and thus be rewarded sooner and more often. Delta uses a similar system, and accounts for the fare type of the passenger. Customers who hunt for bargains and purchase deeply discounted tickets far in advance or at just the last minute are rewarded less miles than those who pay the full fare. This practice makes sense conceptually, as bargain-hunting customers will most likely be more loyal to finding a bargain than to a reward card program. All these airlines increase the reward to passengers willing to pay more per seat than the average passenger. Effectively, this maximizes the reward for the most profitable customers, while minimizing rewards for bargain-hunting passengers.

Southwest Airlines does not reward customers in such a manner because there is no seat differentiation on its planes. Southwest's reward program is based on the number of flights an individual takes. Every eight round-trip flights are worth one free round-trip flight. Thus, a flight from Providence, Rhode Island, to Baltimore, Maryland, is worth the same as a flight from Baltimore to Las Vegas in terms of points/rewards. Even though the distance is much less, Southwest has determined the reward value should be the same. This makes sense conceptually when one considers a large percentage of operating a plane is independent of the distance flown. Flight crew costs, airport desks, and luggage handling are all constant costs. Customers who fly longer distances tend to pay more for their flight since fare often depends on the distance. However, this extra revenue is offset by the cost of the extra fuel used during the flight and the fact that a plane on a longer flight route flies fewer times per day than a plane that makes quick hops from relatively close airports.

Additionally, Southwest rewards customers who fly fifty round trip flights in a year with a free companion pass. This pass allows the customer to designate a companion and receive a free ticket for that companion each time the customer flies during the next year. By doing so, Southwest can capture the business of high-value customers who fly at least once a week, on an average. Credits for flights are deleted from a customer's reward account after a year, so if the customer takes less than eight round trip flights in a year, the customer will not earn a free flight. Customers can double the credit they receive for purchasing a ticket, by using Southwest's Web site. This presents a win-win situation for both the customer and the airline. The customer can more quickly acquire enough credits to redeem for a free flight, and Southwest cuts down on the sales by middlemen (such as travel agents and online discount ticket sites). By reducing the role of the middleman, Southwest is able to capture the revenue these intermediate services would normally collect. It is interesting to note that Southwest has been the only major airline with a positive net income since 2000.

- ANZ Bank (Australia's third-largest bank) planned to raise fees of credit card holders paying their balance monthly (taking advantage of the interest free period). This was a wake-up call for corporations investing marketing dollars in LPs.[25] The primary reason for the price hikes seems to stem from the cost of running the credit-card–related reward programs. The costs have risen to a point where these programs are not sustainable in their current form. Therefore, it seemed that banks needed to choose between reducing reward program benefits or increasing annual fees and pass on some of the costs to the customer.

These examples seem to be the beginning of a trend wherein large corporations spending millions of marketing dollars on LPs will closely evaluate their costs and tailor reward programs to achieve better profitability.

Most companies need to revisit their business model not only to reflect on the impact of loyalty programs on their bottom line, but also to determine how customer service initiatives add value to the future revenue streams.

The LP test run of Asda Supermarket (purchased by Wal-Mart) cost £8 million for a year. The company did not decide to go for a full rollout, which would have cost £60 million.[26]

> We decided we didn't have to invest in points and plastic to make our customers loyal.
>
> — Nick Agarwel, spokesperson for Asda

Asda did not seem to have suffered from this move. At the time it did the pilot, its market share was at an all-time high of 17.2 percent. A year later, it had risen 17.6 percent.

Safeway terminated its LP in April 2000. Its decision saved the company approximately $85 million per year.[27]

> People have lost interest in (loyalty card) points and don't think they give value. What they really appreciate are straightforward product offers at great prices.
>
> —Safeway's CEO Carlos Criado-Perez, May 2000

A few years ago, Continental Airlines downgraded its liberal upgrading policy because it was too expensive. It estimated a $100 million loss in revenue from upset frequent flyers. A class action suit followed. What was designed to be a customer LP turned out to be a disappointing failure.

In 2000, customers had an average of three memberships in frequent-flyer programs.[28]

Thus, although being immensely popular, it is far from clear what sets a successful LP apart from an unsuccessful one. The goal of the following discussion is to review LP characteristics, to systematically investigate outcomes and determinants of LP success, and provide guidelines for designing optimal programs.

8.10 What Are the Design Characteristics of Loyalty Programs?

The multitudes of LPs that exist attest to the discretionary choices in program design. LPs differ substantially both within and across different industries. This section describes the structure and key dimensions of LP design. Managers can exercise discretion on the choice of included dimensions in their LP design, and also the corresponding assigned weights for each of the included dimensions.

LPs can be described along the following key dimensions:
- Reward structure
    - Hard versus soft rewards
    - Product proposition support (choice of rewards)
    - Aspirational value of reward
    - Rate of rewards
    - Tiering of rewards
    - Timing of rewards

- ■ Sponsorship (existence of partner network, network externalities)
  - ☐ Single versus multiform LP
  - ☐ Within sector versus across sector LP
  - ☐ Ownership (focal firm versus other firm)

8.10.1   REWARD STRUCTURE

The principal motivation for consumers to enroll in LPs is to accrue benefits from rewards that can be attributed to their purchase transactions over time. Thus, from a consumer's perspective, rewards are the key design benefit.

Hard versus Soft Rewards

One can distinguish between financial or tangible rewards (hard rewards) and those that are based on psychological or emotional benefits (soft rewards). Hard rewards comprise the gamut of price reductions, promotions, free products, and preferred treatment. For example, a member of the Flying Dutchman frequent-flyer program of KLM Airlines may receive a free ticket for traveling within Europe after collecting 20,000 miles—a hard reward. Soft rewards are typically linked to special recognition of the buyer. It is the psychological benefit of being treated special or having special status that creates the benefit to the buyer. For example, many frequent travelers with Silver or Gold status consider belonging to this category of travelers as something special (often called the *badge effect*). Naturally, the psychological recognition of somebody's loyalty status often comes with tangible benefits such as preferred customer service (e.g., special service phone number).

Product Proposition Support

The reward of a loyalty program may be directly linked to the company's product offering. The reward can also be entirely unrelated. For example, the U.S. bagel franchise Finagle-A-Bagel has an LP which allows participants to redeem their accumulated bonus points for the firm's own products—sandwiches and drinks. Clearly, the reward directly supports the firm's product proposition. Other LPs may allow the LP member to redeem points for products completely unrelated to the focal firm's offering. For example, British Petroleum's LP users may redeem points from their gasoline-related purchases for merchandise such as first-aid kits, photographic films, coffee mugs, and Barbie dolls.

Aspirational Value of Reward

Consumers may engage from time-to-time in *hedonic consumption*. Hedonic products are those whose consumption is associated with pleasure and fun. An interesting result from research of consumer psychology is that consumers prefer hedonic goods to utilitarian goods when receiving a gift. Consumers indulge more easily in luxury consumption when getting "something for nothing," as in the case of a gift or an LP reward. For example, a free flight to an exotic destination might be worth more for a buyer (at least perceptually), as compared to vouchers for the local supermarket of the same face value. Companies try to differentiate their LPs on the basis of the inspirational or hedonic value of their rewards. For example, the LP of PRO7, the German TV channel, is the PRO7 Club. One of its most popular rewards is the VIP service, which offers preferred access to becoming a talk show visitor, or to meet actors backstage. Mercedes Benz's LP makes it possible to transform points into a flight in a MIG 29 combat aircraft. Neimann Marcus, the U.S. luxury retail chain, generates a new list of "wow and cool" rewards each year. These unique rewards include a world-famous photographer visiting to a customer's home to take pictures.

Rate of Rewards

The *rate of rewards* refers to the ratio of reward value (in monetary terms) over transaction volume (in monetary terms). In other words, it tells you how much a consumer is getting in return for concentrating his or her purchases. Needless to say, consumers generally prefer higher reward rates, and reward redemptions are a key cost factor for firms in running LPs. Rate of rewards is one of, if not *the* key driver, to determine LP enrollment and use.

Tiering of Rewards

Rewards are given based on the asset accumulation response function. This describes how assets or rewards are accumulated as a function of spending behavior. In Figure 8-9, two different response functions are depicted.

In case 1, the buyer receives the same amount of rewards per dollar spent, regardless of the spending level. In case 2, the buyer receives a larger amount of rewards per dollar spent, with increasing spending level. Clearly, in case 2, the program is relatively more attractive for high spending buyers. For example, many airline programs follow the pattern depicted in case 2. See CRM at Work 8.3 and 8.4.

Timing of Rewards

The timing of reward redemption is an important design feature of an LP. It is more attractive for the firm to create redemption rules that favor long accumulation periods, thereby impacting customer retention. This effect is also called *lock-in.* Customers build up assets which function as switching cost. Naturally, customers favor the opposite, immediate rewards or short accumulation periods. Managers must ask themselves how long it takes to accumulate assets for a representative reward, given a certain buying pattern (average inter-purchase time). The timing of rewards is determined by minimum redemption rules, type of reward given, and the reward rate. Also, the longer it takes to build up a certain reward level, the greater the *breakage,* which is the amount of rewards never redeemed.

| **FIGURE** | **8-9** | **CHANGE IN CUMULATIVE SPENDING WITH TWO DIFFERENT RESPONSE FUNCTIONS** |

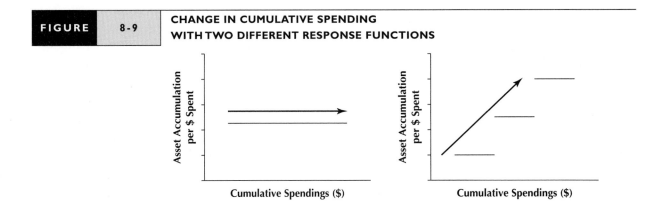

CRM AT WORK 8.3

REWARD PROGRAMS IN THE GAMING INDUSTRY

Harrah's Entertainment has consistently had rising revenues year after year (see example graph) in the highly competitive casino/entertainment industry. Gary Loveman, president and CEO of Harrah's, summed up the importance of Harrah's loyalty reward program when he stated, "The cornerstone of our growth strategy is 'Total Rewards.' This three-tiered loyalty program is one of the most advanced customer-relationship-management (CRM) systems found in any industry today." The tiered structure offers different levels of reward services and privileges to customers of differing tiers. These rewards range from cash back at slots/tables to complimentary offers for shows, meals, and hotel stays at any Harrah's location. Members can also draw benefits from Harrah's alliance with partner firms such as Sony, Royal Caribbean, and Warner Brothers.

The three-tiered structure allows Harrah's to specifically target the most profitable customers with the most desirable rewards. This places Harrah's in a position to maximize profit from these customers. This program sets Harrah's apart from its competition in the gaming industry. In 2002, when revenue growth for the industry was flat, Harrah's had revenue growth of 12.2 percent. It was also the only major casino group whose revenue went above 2.7 percent.

Revenue Growth (from 2001 to 2002)

Harrah's Entertainment:	12.2%
Trump Hotels & Casino Resorts:	2.7%
Park Place Entertainment:	1.5%
MGM MIRAGE:	1.5%
Mandalay Resort Group:	0.7%

Harrah's Entertainment

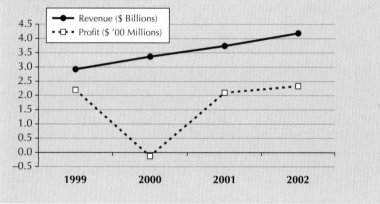

8.10.2 SPONSORSHIP

The second dimension by which LPs can be described are that of sponsorship. Sponsorship refers to supply side features of the LP owner.

Single versus Multi-Firm LP

Organizations may establish LPs to reflect only the transactions with its own customers. For example, the frequency program of BP France reflects only the transactions of members made at BP stations in France. By contrast, the LP member may also accumulate assets at organizations associated with the focal firm's LP. For example, members of Tesco's

---

CRM AT WORK 8.4

BLOOMINGDALES REWARDS PLUS PROGRAM

Bloomingdales Rewards Plus program is broken down into three tiers, which offer increasing levels of rewards to customers based on their annual spending level. Regardless of their spending level, all members with a Bloomingdales credit card receive the benefits of the Premier Insider program. Premier Insider members have access to exclusive travel and entertainment offers, preview days before sales begin, and receive extra savings for using their card during membership days. Women's shoe purchases by Premier Insider members are also automatically tracked, and members receive savings on future shoe purchases through the insider shoe club.

The second tier, Premier Plus Insider, is reserved for members who spend more than $1,000 annually. These customers receive the same rewards listed for the Premier Insider program, as well as a host of other benefits. Members of the Premier Plus Insider tier earn certificates toward future Bloomingdales purchases. This rebate is earned at a rate of 3 percent for all purchases made at Bloomingdales, and at 1 percent for all purchases made elsewhere with the credit card. During special double and triple reward events, the 3 percent rebate is increased to 6 percent and 9 percent. Premier Plus members also receive twelve free gift wraps each year and a free subscription to Bloomingdale's B lifestyle magazine. This magazine is a convenient way for Bloomingdales to disguise what would otherwise be considered an advertising and promotions campaign as a special reward.

The pinnacle of the three membership rewards tiers is Ultimate Premier Insider. These major customers spend more than $2,500 each year at Bloomingdales. They are, in turn, exclusively offered some of the very best rewards, including unlimited free gift-wrapping and free local delivery of their purchases. Ultimate Insiders are also granted access to a customer service line exclusively reserved for their use, as well as access to exclusive events and offers.

By offering a differentiated rewards program, Bloomingdales is seeking to distribute the highest amount of rewards to its best customers. The rebate system, in effect, pays for itself by generating revenue from customers who carry a balance on their card. However, some of the other benefits, such as free delivery, could prove to be costly to Bloomingdales.

ClubCard may accumulate points at the British utility TXU Energi. The introduction of partners is currently one of the major axes of growth in LP design. The advantage of bringing in partners is the increased attractiveness for LP members due to more opportunities for asset accumulation. The disadvantage is that the LP of the focal company loses meaning when there are too many partners. Transaction with the focal vendor and consumer asset accumulation may become completely unrelated.

Within Sector/Across Sector

Another supply side dimension of multi-firm LP design is the degree of cross sector partners. The design variable is whether customers accumulate assets within the same sector or across different sectors. For example, the STAR Alliance of SAS, Lufthansa, United Airlines, Varig, and various others airlines is an example of an LP structure that covers the same sector. However, the LP of AOL and American Airlines, with its 2,000 or so partners, spans many different industries.

Ownership

In case of multiform LPs, the ownership dimension characterizes who owns the LP within the network. Is it the focal firm, a partner firm, or a firm whose sole purpose it is to manage an LP? An example for the latter case is Webmiles, an organization that draws together a network of partners across many industries and whose sole purpose is LP management.

8.11 <u>SUMMARY</u>

The satisfaction-profit-chain (SPC) is based on the idea that improving product and service attributes will lead to an improvement in customer satisfaction, which in turn will lead to greater customer loyalty, and thereby profitability. Although empirical studies concentrate on aggregate, *firm-level* results, the chain needs to be implemented at a *disaggregate level* or individual level.

Improving customer satisfaction comes at a cost and may not often deliver anticipated business results. There is an optimum satisfaction level for any firm, beyond which increasing satisfaction doesn't pay. In order to find such an optimum level, firms need to conduct longitudinal satisfaction studies to investigate changes in customer satisfaction *over time* and to link them to improvements in their offering. By focusing on customer retention, managers move closer to the ultimate dependent variable—profits. Graphical representation of data showed the link between satisfaction and retention is asymmetric (i.e., dissatisfaction has a greater impact on retention than satisfaction). It is also nonlinear; the impact of satisfaction on retention is greater at the extremes with a flat part in the middle of the curve called the *zone of indifference.*

According to the hypothesis proposed by Frederick F. Reichheld, long-term customers spend more per period over time, cost less to serve, have greater propensity to generate word-of-mouth, and pay a premium price when compared to that paid by short-term customers. However, Reinartz and Kumar tested the hypothesis and demonstrated that, across different firms, there is a segment of customers who are loyal but not very profitable (due to excessive resource allocation), and a segment that generates very high profits although it has only a short tenure. Since these short-term customers can be very profitable, it is clear that loyalty is not the only path to profitability. It is important to move to the ultimate end of the satisfaction-profit chain (SPC). In other words, customer profits are ultimately required for making good marketing decisions.

Behavioral loyalty refers to the observed action the customers have demonstrated towards a particular product or service. Attitudinal loyalty refers to the perceptions and attitudes a customer has towards a particular product or service. Customers who are not attitudinally loyal are likely to cease the relationship at the earliest available opportunity. A loyalty program (LP) can be defined as a marketing process that generates rewards to customers based on their repeat purchasing. In exchange for concentrating their purchases with the focal firm, they accumulate assets (e.g., points), which are exchanged for products and services. The success or failure of a loyalty program (LP), whether contractual or motivated through incentives, is determined by the profitability from the customer. Also, the longevity of the customer relationship does not automatically translate into tangible profitability. Therefore, LPs have become an important CRM tool used by marketers to identify, award, and retain profitable customers.

The key objectives of introducing LPs include building true (attitudinal and behavioral) loyalty, efficiency profits, effectiveness profits, and value alignment. True loyalty is a function of true value provided to the customers. Efficiency profits, which are net of LP cost, are the profits that result from a change in customer's buying behavior due to the loyalty program. The most widely used measure of behavioral loyalty is share of category requirements (SCR), or share of wallet. Possibly, LP does not change behavior as much as it reinforces already existing behavior and at a much higher cost to the firm. Effectiveness profits refer to the medium to long-term profit consequences realized through better learning about customer preferences and are likely to generate sustainable competitive advantage since it produces the highest profits in the long run. Value alignment refers to the goal of aligning the cost to serve a particular customer with the value a customer is bringing to the firm. Its role is particularly critical when there is great heterogeneity in the customer's value and in the customer's cost to serve. Although LPs have become immensely popular, it is not clear whether LPs are effective in helping firms engender greater customer loyalty and higher profits, because of the cost of managing an LP, as well as because management of LPs can be tricky. Most companies need to revisit their business model, not only to reflect on the impact of LPs on their bottom line, but also to determine how customer service initiatives add value to the future revenue streams.

LPs can be described according to reward structure and sponsorship. From a consumer's perspective, rewards are the key design benefit. Hard rewards comprise the gamut of price reductions, promotions, free products, and preferred treatment. Soft rewards are linked to the psychological recognition of somebody's loyalty status and often come with tangible benefits such as preferred customer service. The reward of a loyalty program may or may not be directly linked to the company's product offering. Consumers prefer hedonic goods as opposed to utilitarian goods when receiving a gift. Therefore, companies have been trying to differentiate their LPs on the basis of the inspirational or hedonic value of their rewards. The rate of rewards (the ratio of reward value over transaction volume) is one of the key drivers to determine LP enrollment and use. Rewards are given out based on the asset accumulation response function (i.e., the accumulation of assets or rewards based on spending behavior). The tiered structure of rewards offers different levels of reward services and privileges to customers of differing tiers. Timing of reward redemption, another important design feature of an LP, is determined by minimum redemption rules, type of reward given out, and the reward rate.

Sponsorship refers to supply side features of the LP owner. The introduction of partners is currently one of the major axes of growth in LP design. In such case, LP members may also accumulate assets at organizations associated with the focal firms LP. Another supply-side dimension of multifirm LP design is the degree of cross sector partners. Customers may accumulate assets within the same sector as in the case of Lufthansa, United Airlines, and so on, or across different sectors, as for AOL and American Airlines, with its 2,000 or so partners, which spans many different industries.

8.12 EXERCISE QUESTIONS

1. Explain what we have learned in the last few years about the satisfaction-profit chain.
2. Explain the difference between behavioral and attitudinal loyalty. Provide an example for each.
3. What are the key objectives for establishing loyalty programs? Which of these objectives provide the strongest competitive advantage?
4. You are a consultant to a credit card organization who wants to establish a loyalty program. The CEO has just read about how most loyalty programs result in money-losing propositions. How do you alleviate the CEO's concerns?

ENDNOTES

1. James L. Heskett, Thomas O. Jones, Gary Loveman, W Earl Sasser Jr., and Leonard A Schlesinger, "Putting the Service-Profit Chain to Work," *Harvard Business Review* (March 1, 1994).

2. Valarie A. Zeithaml, "Service Quality, Profitability, and the Economic Worth of Customers: What We Know and What We Need to Learn," *Academy of Marketing Science* 28, no. 1 (Winter 2000).

3. C. D. Ittner and D. F. Larcker, "Coming Up Short on Non-financial Performance Measurement". *Harvard Business Review* (November 2003): 88–95.

4. C. Fornell, E. W. Anderson, R. T. Rust, "Customer Satisfaction, Productivity, and Profitability: Differences Between Goods and Services," *Marketing Science* 16, no. 2 (1997): 129–45 and E. W. Anderson and D. R. Lehmann, "Customer Satisfaction, Market Share, and Profitability: Findings from Sweden" *Journal of Marketing* (July 1994): 53–66.

5. Bo Edvardsson, Michael D. Johnson, Anders Gustafsson, and Tore Strandvik, "The Effects of Satisfaction and Loyalty on Profits and Growth: Products versus Services." *Total Quality Management & Business Excellence* 11, no. 7 (September 2000).

6. Christopher D. Ittner and David F. Larcke, "Are Nonfinancial Measures Leading Indicators of Financial Performance? An Analysis of Customer Satisfaction," *Journal of Accounting Research* 36, no. 1 (1998): 1–35.

7. Zeithaml, p. 67.

8. Thomas O. Jones and W. Earl Sasser Jr., "Why Satisfied Customers Defect," *Harvard Business Review* 73, no. 6 (November/December 1995).

9. Mittal Vikas and Wagner A. Kamakura, "Satisfaction, Repurchase Intent, and Repurchase Behavior: Investigating the Moderating Effect of Customer Characteristics," *Journal of Marketing Research* 38, no. 1 (February 2001): 131.

10. Frederick F. Reichheld, Robert G. Markey Jr., and Christopher Hopton, "The Loyalty Effect—the Relationship between Loyalty and Profits," *European Business Journal* 12, no. 3 (2000): 134.

11. Werner Reinartz and V. Kumar, "The Mismanagement of Customer Loyalty," *Harvard Business Review* 80, no. 7 (July 2002): 86.

12. J. Passingham, "Grocery Retailing and the Loyalty Card," *Journal of the Market Research Society* 40, no. 1 (1998): 55–67.

13. Julia Day, http://media.guardian.co.uk/marketingandpr/story/0,7494,568752,00.html, accessed October 12, 2001; Media.Guardian.co.UK.

14. Carlos Criado Perez, CEO Safeway (UK), May 2000, from BBC News (May 4, 2000).

15. Richard Caines, Retail Consultant with Mintel Research UK (Spring 2001).

16. David Pringle, "Retailers Scrap High-Tech Ideas For Marketing—Safeway of Britain Finds Loyalty-Card Program Generated Useless Data," *Wall Street Journal* 1 (Eastern edition) (June 19, 2000): 1.

17. Sharp Byron and Anne Sharp, "Loyalty Programs and Their Impact on Repeat Purchase Loyalty Patterns," *International Journal of Research in Marketing* 14 (1997): 477–486.

18. http://www.webflyer.com.

19. http://www.webflyer.com.

20. http://www.marriottnewsroom.com.

21. http://www.abc.net.au/businessbreakfast/content/2007/s887177.htm, accessed June 2007.

22. 1 Euro = 1.1780 USD Conversion rate, November 25, 2003. 11.44 A.M. EST, USA. http://finance.yahoo.com.

23. Margaret L. Young and Marcia Stepanek, "Trends: Loyalty Programs", http://www.cioinsight.com/article2/0,3959,1458960,00.asp, accessed December 1, 2003.

24. http://moneymanager.smh.com.au/banking/guides/articles/cc07.html.

25. Niels Kjellerup, "The Myth of Customer Loyalty Programs and Customer Retention," http://www.callcentres.com.au/ Ashgrove, accessed May 25, 2003.

26. Direct Marketing.

27. 1 British Pound = 1.7 USD Conversion rate, November 25, 2003. 11.44 A.M. EST, USA. http://finance.yahoo.com.

CHAPTER 9

Effectiveness of Loyalty Programs

Contents

9.1 OVERVIEW

The past two decades have seen many firms establishing some type of customer loyalty program (LP). Typically, these programs offer financial and relationship rewards to customers. In most cases, the aim of these programs is to increase sales revenue by increasing the usage/purchase level and by up-selling and cross-selling. Loyalty programs are also a means for developing a strong relationship with the customers. But for companies, the benefits of loyalty programs do not come without a cost. Hence, it is important to ask a few pertinent questions before establishing a loyalty program. What is the cost-effectiveness of the loyalty program? What differentiates an effective LP from an ineffective one? What are the key drivers of effectiveness of loyalty programs? We address these questions in this chapter.

Understanding the goals and the design characteristics of an LP is critical to design and implement an effective loyalty program. At the same time, it is equally important (if not more) to understand and monitor the key drivers of the effectiveness of an LP. Four key drivers of effectiveness of loyalty programs are discussed in the first section. The effect of these drivers on LP effectiveness is summarized schematically. We also present some empirical evidence about the performance of LPs across various industry segments. In a subsequent section, we discuss how firms can create competitive advantage through loyalty programs geared toward attaining effectiveness profits and also by value alignment with the help of two case studies. Finally, we present a seven-point checklist for successful design and implementation of loyalty programs.

9.2 DRIVERS OF LOYALTY PROGRAM EFFECTIVENESS

The factors that drive the effectiveness of a loyalty program can be structured into the following categories:

1. LP design characteristics
2. Customer characteristics
3. Market characteristics
4. Firm characteristics

The configuration and interaction of these four drivers determine whether an LP achieves its desired objective(s).

9.2.1 LOYALTY PROGRAM DESIGN CHARACTERISTICS

LP design characteristics as discussed previously can be classified on the basis of:

- Reward structure
- Sponsorship (existence of partner network, network externalities)

Three key questions must be answered to know if a LP is effective:

1. From the consumer's perspective, are rewards attainable?
2. From the consumer's perspective, are rewards relevant?
3. From the firm's perspective, is the LP design aligned with the desired goal(s)?

The first question asks how attractive is the payoff from the LP from the consumer's point of view. If the LP does not provide sufficient value (timing of rewards, rate of rewards) for the customer to concentrate his/her purchases, no change in behavior will follow. For example, the degree to which a traveler can redeem miles for a free flight depends on the minimum mileage necessary. The level at which the airline sets this minimum mileage will determine how many lower-end customers will enroll in the program.

The second question is whether an LP is relevant for a consumer, regardless of attainability of rewards. It looks at the degree to which an accumulation of assets in the program is relevant to the consumer in terms of type of rewards (hard/soft, aspirational value). For example, if a consumer does not care for recognition and cares only for hard rewards but the LP program offers few hard rewards, it is clearly not relevant. The question here is whether the firm designs its program in such a fashion that it aligns with the desired benefits of a particular target segment.

The third question is whether the LP's design is aligned with the desired firm goals. For example, if an LP offers hard rewards and promotions that focus on change in short-term behavior, it is most likely that the LP has a bigger impact on behavioral loyalty and less so on attitudinal loyalty. If effectiveness profits are the declared goal, then the LP must be designed such that it allows the firm to collect a maximum of information about the customer.

9.2.2 CUSTOMER CHARACTERISTICS

The key customer characteristic relevant to the effectiveness of LPs is the skewness of customer value distribution (or value heterogeneity).

The skewness of the distribution of the customer's value to the firm varies greatly between industries. In some industries, the values of individual customers or accounts tend to be similar. In other industries, the values of individual customers or accounts tend to be highly different. An example for the former case is the gasoline industry. For the average driver, the monthly consumption of gasoline varies moderately within limits. However, an example for the latter case is the financial services or the telecom industry. Usage and thus customer profitability of financial services and telecoms varies widely between customers or accounts.

How does it affect the effectiveness of LPs? If an LP is designed to achieve value alignment, then this is most likely to succeed in an environment where customers exhibit high-value heterogeneity. Thus, the goal of value alignment is potentially feasible in industries such as airlines, hotels, rental cars, pharmacies, telecom, and financial services.

9.2.3 MARKET CHARACTERISTICS

The key factor relevant to LP effectiveness in terms of market characteristics is market concentration (supply side).

Studies from market researchers Ehrenberg et al.[1] have shown the existence of a phenomenon called *double jeopardy*. Double jeopardy refers to the fact that small-market-share brands suffer because of two threats (therefore, *double* jeopardy). First, low-share brands are purchased by fewer customers than high-share brands, and second, among those who buy the brand, they purchase it less often. Ehrenberg has demonstrated this effect across a number of different categories. What does this mean for the concept of loyalty? It simply means that brand loyalty is more natural to obtain for large-share brands. It does not mean that low-share brands cannot obtain loyal customers. There are examples of low-share brands with highly loyal customers. However, on average the effect of double jeopardy seems to hold (see Figure 9-1).

Thus, if markets are concentrated or if a brand has high market share, it is easier to achieve, at least, behavioral loyalty. As already mentioned, it is possible to achieve loyalty with a low-share brand—a case in point is BodyShop, a British cosmetics chain. However, *on average* behavioral loyalty is easier to achieve with high share brands.

9.2.4 FIRM CHARACTERISTICS

Factors relevant to LP effectiveness in terms of organizational characteristics are:

- Perishability of a product
- Breadth and depth of the firm offering the product at the store/retail level

Key aspects in the success of LPs are the specific characteristics of the product a firm sells. In particular, whether a product is perishable plays a critical role. In fact, this characteristic drives the fact that LPs are so widespread in the airline and hospitality industry. For example, a crucial feature of hotel LPs is that frequent users get upgrades to "better" rooms

FIGURE 9-1 DOUBLE JEOPARDY

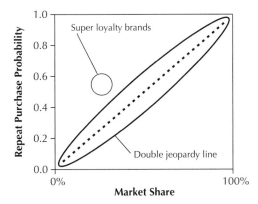

SOURCE: Graham Dowling and Mark Uncles, "Do Customer Loyalty Programs Really Work?" *Sloan Management Review* (Summer 1997): 71–82.

subject to availability. Upgrades are only given when there is excess capacity that night. Because the rooms would not be sold otherwise, the reward of an upgrade comes at very low marginal cost. Given this perishability characteristic of the product, the hotel is able to economize its LP on this industry-specific fact. Whenever a firm cannot capitalize on the perishability of its products, the expenses for rewards come directly from the bottom line—thus making the economics of an LP harder to justify.

Another important aspect of LP effectiveness is the variety of products and brands offered on the retail level. There should be more opportunities for efficiency profits with greater breadth and depth of offerings at store level for the following reasons:

■ Buyers are more likely to fulfill their needs.

■ Buyers have more opportunity for one-stop shopping (attributed to more time saving).

■ Buyers have more opportunity for behavioral loyalty (attributed to more purchase occasions).

Thus, one would expect in environments of greater choice greater effectiveness of LPs in terms of behavioral loyalty. In addition, there should be opportunities for effectiveness profits with greater breadth and depth of offerings at store level because the latitude of purchases allows the firm more opportunities for learning about customer preferences and for cross selling of products. Figure 9-2 summarizes how the drivers of the effectiveness of LP affect the outcomes of an LP.

9.3 EMPIRICAL EVIDENCE ON LOYALTY PROGRAM EFFECTIVENESS

There are more and more reports on empirical evidence from the markets about how good LPs really are in achieving their stated goals. However, there is limited empirical evidence on the success or failure of loyalty programs. It is particularly difficult to get unbiased information about the performance of firm specific LPs, partially because proper metrics are not in place, and partially because low performance is unlikely to be admitted. Appendix 1 summarizes a few studies. One should keep in mind that only selected industries are covered in these studies. In addition, the few number of studies clearly limits our ability to make strong

FIGURE **9-2** **DRIVERS OF EFFECTIVENESS**

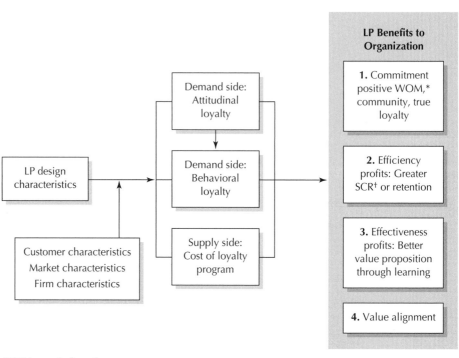

*WOM = word of mouth.

†SCR = share-of-category-requirements.

CRM AT WORK 9.1

THE STARBUCKS CARD

In fall 2003, Starbucks rolled out a new customer loyalty program called the Starbucks Card, which combines the company's existing prepaid card program with a credit card which offers rewards in the form of Starbucks products. The credit card offers a 1 percent rebate on all purchases made with the card. At the end of each month, this rebate is loaded onto the customer's prepaid account for use at any Starbucks location. The benefits of this program to both the company and customers are quite clear. Since the cost of purchasing a coffee is so small even people who use the card sparingly will receive free products on a fairly regular basis. Meanwhile, when a customer uses the card to make a purchase, Starbucks will be earning money from its share of the debt servicing that its partners (Bank One and Visa) are performing when customers carry a balance. An additional benefit arises because most transactions are far less than ten dollars at Starbucks stores and are therefore most often paid for in cash. Traditionally, this has made it difficult for Starbucks to gather information on its customers. By encouraging customers to use a unique card for making payments, Starbucks will be able to build a much better database of customer information.

It remains to be seen just how successful this program will be. From a profitability standpoint, it seems to be a good approach. Discover is able to remain profitable while offering a card with a 1 percent cash rebate. Since the Starbucks card offers its rebate in the form of store dollars, the actual cash value to Starbucks of each one-dollar rebate is much less than a dollar. In the future Starbucks hopes to reward its most frequent and experienced customers, by allowing them to swipe their own card and enter their own order as soon as they walk into the store. The idea is to retain customers by offering the fastest ordering process in the business. The focus of this plan will be the Starbucks Card.

empirical generalizations. However, the conclusions we can draw from these published studies are summarized as follows:

- There is no published evidence that LPs create attitudinal loyalty (i.e., real loyalty), although firms might have proprietary information on this.
- There is evidence for an impact of LPs on behavioral loyalty. LPs seem to have an impact (to varying degrees) on changing purchase behavior.
- We have very little information on the cost efficiency of LPs. We speculate that companies don't have the knowledge themselves due to lack of proper accounting or that they are reluctant to reveal it. Individual cases (e.g., Safeway, Asda) point to the expensive nature of LPs.
- Using LPs as a value alignment tool seems viable.

9.4   ACHIEVING COMPETITIVE ADVANTAGE

The key reason a firm develops an LP is to create competitive advantage. Competitive advantage is defined as the ability to operate more profitably over a sustained period of time. In this case, we are focusing, of course, on the competitive advantage created by the LP. In a 1999 survey conducted by McKinsey of 1,200 customers across 16 product categories, it was found the effect of LPs could vary, depending on the industry category implementing a loyalty program. First, it seems as if a highly frequented category like grocery stores is more likely to attract members to its LP compared to casual apparel. Second, a far larger percentage of customers admit to spending more as a result of the LP in the grocery stores category than in the casual apparel category. From the evidence we have so far, we know that LPs with the goal of creating efficiency profits provide the smallest basis for achieving competitive advantage. The following case study (CRM at Work 9.2) on Kodak in Poland illustrates that once every major firm in the market matches the first mover, all are back to square one, *except that every firm now has higher cost.*

Thus, the key challenge when pursuing efficiency profits is to keep the costs of the LP under control. For the supermarket industry, which operates on razor-thin margins, this is a big problem. This is why LPs of groceries are most often cofunded by manufacturers. Without manufacturer's funding in the form of promotions and rebates, a supermarket LP would hardly be able to offer decent rewards. Clearly, organizations must be ingenious to keep LP costs under control. As mentioned earlier, the value provided to the customers participating in an LP must be greater than for customers not participating—otherwise, there

---

CRM AT WORK 9.2

KODAK EXPRESS: HARD TO GET A COMPETITIVE EDGE

Kodak Express was one of the first to introduce a loyalty program in the Polish market. Since 1992, the company has been issuing *frequent customer cards,* which make customers eligible for discounts on the services of Kodak photo laboratories. Kodak frequent customer cards have become popular among Polish customers, with more than 200,000 cards issued annually. Marian Cholewiński, director of Empik Kodak Express laboratory, estimates about 80 to 90 percent of his company's customers have club cards, carrying a 10 percent discount for laboratory services and a discount for the purchase of certain company products. However, Agfa and Fuji, Kodak's biggest rivals in the Polish market, followed suit and have been issuing similar cards for several years now.[2] This blunted the advantage Kodak hoped to gain.

is no reason for customers to be interested. The case study on Harrah's in the previous chapter shows how some firms manage LP cost efficiency.

LPs designed to create effectiveness profits have the highest chance of creating competitive advantage. It is probably the effectiveness profits goal that has the greatest appeal to most (large) firms. The latest and continuous developments in IT make information-based strategies possible in the first place. The capability of learning from customer behavior through continuous monitoring, analyzing this information appropriately, and using the newly found insights for designing and deploying LPs is quite challenging. Thus, although technology and concepts are widely available, we see great differences in a firm's ability to implement LPs with a goal to improve effectiveness profits. See CRM at Work 9.3.

Finally, the goal of value alignment might yield low-to-medium competitive advantage. In certain industries such as the airline or hotel industry, value alignment has become a standard industry practice—it is a necessity. Thus, not much of a competitive advantage can be expected from the program itself. However, industries such as financial services or telecom can expect to reap competitive advantage when pursuing this goal because execution matters and firms differ on their capability to execute such programs.

9.5 THE SEVEN-POINT CHECKLIST FOR SUCCESSFUL LP DESIGN AND IMPLEMENTATION

A checklist for developing, designing, and implementing a successful LP can be summarized in seven points.

1. *Clearly determine your LPs goals.* Is this goal compatible with your marketing strategy? With the positioning of your organization in the market?

2. *Make sure the design of your LP is aligned with the characteristics of your market, your customer base, and your firm.* Knowing the customer base is important since customer segments' preferences for LP benefits may vary. For example, senior citizens may not value accumulation of redeemable points as much as the price discounts on a product.

3. *Manage the costs of LPs.* LPs are expensive. Thus, cost management of LPs is a critical component. Make sure to consider all the costs involved (e.g., the opportunity cost of the time of the managers involved). Can costs be mitigated via low marginal cost rewards or contributions from manufacturers?

4. *Measure the predicted benefits of the LP for your organization.* Although it is difficult to specify these benefits well, you should attempt a trade-off analysis between cost and gains of the LP program. Also consider the time horizon (short versus long term).

5. *Once introduced, avoid withdrawal of LP as it can have negative consequences for the firm in the form of customer dissatisfaction and customer defection.* Customers don't like it when LPs are withdrawn, once they are accustomed to the benefits. Thus, design faults will not only result in losses, but they will also haunt you later in the form of customer dissatisfaction.

6. *Ensure the LP is designed in such a way to achieve maximum effectiveness in marketing operations through the program.* This can be achieved by learning the customer preferences and responding to these preferences through your offering.

7. *Make sure your firm has the necessary capabilities for managing LP effectively.* This can be in terms of data storage, data analysis, and empowerment of employees.

CRM AT WORK 9.3

TESCO: FROM PRICE PROMOTIONS TO MARKETING EFFICIENCY

The British supermarket chain Tesco is an example of a company that successfully implemented an LP aimed at achieving effectiveness profits. In 1997, Tesco was ranked third among grocery retailers in the United Kingdom, operating on the traditional model of promotion-based and price based competition. Although data about customer's purchase behavior were, in principle, available via its scanner checkouts, these data were not collected on the individual customer level but rather at the store level. In February 1995, Tesco launched the first LP in the British super-market industry. In the first years, Tesco relied mostly on the incentive aspect of the loyalty scheme. Tesco was very successful in capturing both market share and share-of category require-ments in the subsequent years, but it remains unclear whether these gains came from the sales area expansion, improved service, or from the LP.

Supermarket Group's Market Share

	1995	1996	1997
Tesco	17.7	20.9	22.0
Sainsbury	20.2	19.0	19.6
Asda	11.1	12.1	17.2
Safeway	8.6	9.5	10.0

SOURCE: Taylor Nelson AGB Superpanel, 1995, 1996, 1997.

Over time, Tesco made more use of the sales data to target benefits with the objective of steering customers into new areas of consumption. In addition, Tesco established a segmenta-tion scheme of its customer base and determined which segments ought to be primarily served. The LP reflects this segment approach by offering tailored cards to students, families, top cus-tomers, and seniors. Within the LP, Tesco found ways to provide value for special groups such as families with babies. For example, in Tesco's Baby Club, parents can meet, can obtain informa-tion about infant health and food, enroll in courses, and get special rebates on baby-related products. Thus, Tesco tries to align its LP offering closely with the specific member's needs, as opposed to giving out general incentives.

Knowledge about individual customers' and/or segments' preferences is derived from an analysis of the data gathered within the LP. In addition, Tesco merges information on customer transactions within Tesco's Web site and with point of sale data (products, which store, time of the day, basket size). This knowledge about customer preferences allows Tesco to customize its product offerings and communications, based on specific customer needs and economic cus-tomer value to Tesco. Tesco's segmentation is such that it sends eighty different versions of its mailing to members, and publishes four versions of its Clubcard magazine. Thresholds of reward are linked to spending behavior.

As a result, Tesco's loyalty program (Clubcard) has few of the incentive scheme characteris-tics it started with. Today, it is all about increasing the efficiency of Tesco's marketing efforts—having happier consumers *and* being more profitable.

9.6 CONCLUSION: LOYALTY PROGRAMS, SHACKLE OR REWARD—TO WHOM?

There is convincing evidence that loyalty programs as they exist today fall short in terms of creating attitudinal loyalty. The name *LP* is a misnomer in that sense. Furthermore, loyalty programs focusing on incentives, deals, and promotions are often a costly propo-sition for the firm—unless there is a way to offer underutilized, perishable assets such as in the hotel or rental car industry. For example, giving out costly rewards on top of the razor-thin margins in the grocery industry hardly seems sustainable in the medium to long run. Surviving LPs will be those that are *saving* companies money by replacing other communication tools, as opposed to being drains on resources. Done properly, an LP can act as a method to gather data which can then be used to improve efficiency and effectiveness of the marketing function:

> LPs that are most likely to provide sustainable competitive advantage are those that leverage data obtained from consumers into more effective marketing decisions and thus result in true value creation for customers. Loyalty is likely to follow.[3]

Interestingly, some firms with admirable true customer loyalty do not have loyalty programs (Saturn, Harley). For them, it seems that LPs and being loyal do not go hand in hand, because true loyalty does not need hard incentives—it is merely based on attitudes.

9.7 SUMMARY

The factors driving the effectiveness of an LP can be categorized into LP design, customer, market, and firm characteristics. The configuration and interaction of these four drivers determine whether an LP achieves its desired objective(s). To know if an LP is effective, issues to be addressed include attractiveness of LP from the consumer's point of view, the degree to which an accumulation of assets in the program is relevant to the consumer in terms of type of rewards, and whether the LP's design is aligned with the desired firm goals.

The customer characteristic relevant to the effectiveness of LPs is the skewness of customer value distribution (value heterogeneity). If an LP is designed to achieve value alignment, it is most likely to succeed in an environment where customers exhibit high value heterogeneity—as in industries such as airlines, pharmacies, or financial services. The relevant key factor in LP effectiveness in terms of market characteristics is market concentration (supply side). Ehrenberg et al. have shown the existence of a phenomenon called *double jeopardy* where small market share brands suffer because of two threats. Low-share brands are purchased by fewer customers than high-share brands, and among those who buy the brand, frequency of purchase is less, meaning that brand loyalty (mainly behavioral loyalty) is more natural to obtain for large-share brands.

Factors relevant to LP effectiveness in terms of organizational characteristics are perishability of a product and breadth and depth of the firm offering the product at the store/retail level. When a firm cannot capitalize on the perishability of its products, the expenses for rewards come directly from the bottom line—thus making the economic viability of LP much harder. There should be opportunities for effectiveness profits with greater breadth and depth of offerings at store level because the latitude of purchases allows the firm more opportunities for learning customer preferences and for cross selling products. There is no published evidence that LPs create attitudinal loyalty, though there is evidence for an impact of LPs on behavioral loyalty. There is very little information on the cost efficiency of LPs, although using LPs as a value alignment tool seems viable.

The key reason a firm develops an LP is to create competitive advantage—the ability to operate more profitably over a sustained period of time. The key challenge when pursuing efficiency profits is to keep the costs of the LP under control. LPs designed to create effectiveness profits have the highest chance of creating competitive advantage, and it is the effectiveness profits goal that probably has the greatest appeal to most (large) firms. The goal of value alignment may yield low to medium competitive advantage. In certain industries such as the airline or hotel industry, value alignment has become a necessary standard industry practice. However, industries such as financial services or telecom can expect to reap competitive advantage when pursuing this goal since execution matters and firms differ on their capability to execute such programs.

There is convincing evidence that loyalty programs as they exist today fall short in terms of creating attitudinal loyalty. Done properly, an LP can act as a method to gather data which can be used to improve efficiency and effectiveness of the marketing function.

9.8 EXERCISE QUESTIONS

1. Do companies profit by introducing loyalty programs? Is the success of a company's loyalty program dependent on the industry category in which it operates?

2. How can you measure loyalty? How is loyalty linked to the profitability of a company?

3. Would low-ticket items (coffee, candy, sodas) benefit from loyalty programs? What kind of incentives would work?

4. Design a loyalty program for your neighborhood gas station. Describe the incentives. Determine the cost structure. Set benchmarks and evaluate the profitability of the program across possible scenarios.

5. What are the ethical issues that surround loyalty programs? Should the gaming industry be allowed to use loyalty instruments?

MINI CASE 9.1

LOYALTY PROGRAM MANAGEMENT AT STARWOOD HOTELS

Starwood is one of the world's largest hotel and leisure companies. The company's service ranges from exclusive hotels such as the St. Regis and the Luxury Collection, to its key five-star hotels Sheraton and Westin, down to the moderately priced Four Points hotel chain. With a total of approximately 750 properties, Starwood is represented in most major markets around the world. The company operates a customer loyalty program called Starwood Preferred Guest (SPG), which allows customers to accumulate points for staying and spending with Starwood. The program is somewhat unique in the industry in that its points never expire and that Starwood does not have so-called *black-out dates* (i.e., dates when customers cannot use their points for redemption).

Even though the program has these advantages over those of major competitors, the company is struggling to utilize its program to its fullest potential. In particular, the company must address a number of challenges. First, while it collects information on individual customer behavior (movie watching, minibar use, room service use, restaurant use, etc), it is not clear how they can easily use that information. Although some customers like that the company learns about their preferences, many customers are concerned about a possible privacy invasion. They simply want to be left alone, or, at least have more control over the kind of information the company uses. Second, although roughly 7 million Starwood customers are members of the loyalty program, 6 million customers are not. Thus, the company has very little knowledge about a large portion of its customer base. Third, although the company targets existing program members with customized offerings and communications, it yet has to figure out how much customers can be bothered. That is, although Starwood wants to maximize its cross-selling and up-selling opportunities, it recognizes customers will react negatively if they get too many offerings.

Questions:

1. How could a large company like Starwood address the issue of exploiting customer data while at the same time safeguarding and respecting customer privacy?

2. How can Starwood attract the loyalty program nonusers into the program or find out more about the behavior and preferences of this large group?

3. How far should Starwood push its direct offerings toward its program members? How can they find the limit?

APPENDIX I

Empirical Findings from Various Studies Conducted on LPs

Number	Organization Details	Industry	Findings
1	Six partner companies of the FlyBuy program in Australia	General retail	■ LP has hardly any effect on repeat purchase pattern (behavioral loyalty).[4]
2	Credit card firms (single firms) in three European countries	Credit cards	■ LP members are more likely to overlook negative experiences with the focal company. ■ LP members have higher usage level and higher retention. ■ There is no information on cost efficiency.[5]
3	Single firm	Hospitality	■ 20% of LP member stays are because of LP. ■ Strategy of using LP as a value alignment tool is successful. ■ LP is profitable.[6]
4	—	Grocery industry in France	■ Being a LP member does not modify purchase behavior. ■ Events and promotions associated with LP seem to have clear effect on purchase behavior (e.g., purchase acceleration). ■ The effects of LP are mostly short term rather than long term. Thus, they seem to work as a promotional tool rather than a means to induce loyalty. ■ There is no information on cost efficiency.[7]
5	U.S. direct marketing firm	General merchandise	■ LP membership is associated with the longer duration of customer–firm relationship. ■ No information on cost efficiency.[8]
6	—	U.S. grocery industry	■ LP is operationalized as a shocker program (e.g., Turkey bucks), not the traditional long-term card program. Thus, it can be better described as a long promotion. ■ There is significant increase in spending (market basket). ■ LPs seem to affect "cherry-pickers" most. ■ Program is profitable.[9]
7	—	Cross-sector sample of 71 LPs	■ LPs are classified according to their objectives and characteristics. ■ The two main purposes of LPs are either customer heterogeneity management or creating switching cost (behavioral loyalty).

ENDNOTES

1. A.S.C. Ehrenberg G. J. Goodhardt, and P. Barwise, "Double Jeopardy Revisited," *Journal of Marketing* 54 (July 1990): 82–91.

2. http://www.warsawvoice.pl/v578/Busi00.html.

3. Prof. Werner J. Reinartz, 2002.

4. Kannan Bolton and Bramlett, "Implications of Loyalty Program Membership and Service Experience for Customer Retention and Value," *Journal of The Academy of Marketing Science* 28, no. 1 (2000): 95–108.

5. John Deighton, Stowe Shoemaker, *Hilton HHonors Worldwide: Loyalty Wars,* Harvard Business Online (October 2000).

6. Dominique Crié, Lars Meyer-Waarden, and Christophe Benavent, "Analysis of the Efficiency of Loyalty Programs," Working Paper, University of Pau, France, 2000.

7. Werner Reinartz and V. Kumar, "The Impact of Customer Relationship Characteristics on Profitable Lifetime Duration," *Journal of Marketing* 67 (January 2003): 77–99.

8. Lal Rajiv, "Retail Loyalty Programs: Do They Work?" Presentation at the Marketing Science Conference, Wiesbaden Germany, June.

9. Lars Meyer-Waarden and Christophe Benavent, "Loyalty Programs: Strategies and Practice," Working Paper, University of Pau, France, 2001.

10 Data Mining*

Contents

10.1 OVERVIEW

The way in which companies interact with their customers has changed dramatically over the past few years. Customers' expectations have gone up, and it is becoming increasingly difficult to satisfy them. Customers have access to an array of alternative products to choose from and customers' loyalty is difficult to gain. At the same time, companies need to retain the profitable customers to succeed in a competitive and dynamic marketplace. As a result, companies have found they need to understand their customers better, and to respond to their wants and needs faster. The time frame in which these responses need to be made has been shrinking. More customers, more products, more competitors, and less time to react means understanding the customers is now much harder to do.

To succeed, companies must be proactive and anticipate customer desires. Many firms have realized this and are collecting information about their customers and their preferences. Firms collect, store, and process vast amounts of highly detailed information about customers, markets, products, and processes

*We thank Frank Block, Ph.D., of FinScore Corporation (Switzerland) for his collaboration on this chapter.

through different programs. *Data mining* this information gives businesses the ability to make knowledge-driven strategic business decisions to help predict future trends and behaviors and create new opportunities. Data mining can assist in selecting the right target customers or in identifying (previously unknown) customer segments with similar behavior and needs.

This chapter provides an overview of the benefits of data mining and the data-mining process. The data-mining procedure breaks down into five subsections: namely, defining the business objectives, getting the raw data, identifying relevant variables, gaining customer insight, and acting. The discussion of these steps will help the reader understand the overall process of data mining. Finally, we present a case study, "Yapi Kredi—Predictive Model–Based cross-sell Campaign," to illustrate the practice of data mining.

10.2 THE NEED FOR DATA MINING

Today, most companies do not suffer from lack of data about their customers, products, transactions, and markets. To the contrary, *data deluge* is a problem for many industries. This is especially challenging for information-intensive businesses, such as banking, telecommunication, and e-commerce. The sheer amount of raw data is, for many, an obstacle to using it for extracting knowledge and for making critical business decisions. By default, educated guessing becomes the primary decision-making tool. It does not have to be that way.

Availability of computers and mass storage, statistical and data analysis methods, sophisticated reporting platforms, and more, now give companies access to a powerful asset: information. Data have become a company's most important—and in many cases, untapped—asset. To extract customer intelligence and value from that data, companies must implement a standardized data-mining procedure. A successful data-mining infrastructure consists of technology, human skills, and tight integration with enterprise operations to allow transforming new knowledge into business action and value. It is important to standardize the data-mining process to assure the required quality of results, make it a repeatable process,[1] better maintain and keep the knowledge inside the company, and train new employees more quickly.

10.3 THE BUSINESS VALUE OF DATA MINING

In the context of CRM, data mining brings science into the relationship game. Marketing is still frequently associated only with creative and soft skills. But by scientifically enhancing targeting, we can obtain more impressive cost reductions and revenue enhancements than by working only with the creative aspects of marketing. Data mining can assist in selecting the right target customers or in identifying (previously unknown) customer segments with similar behavior and needs. A good target list developed by using data-mining techniques is likely to increase purchase rates and have a positive impact on revenue.

Applications of data mining include the following:

- Reducing churn with the help of predictive models, which enable early identification of those customers likely to stop doing business with your company
- Increasing customer profitability by identifying customers with a high growth potential
- Reducing marketing costs by more selective targeting

This chapter introduces a systematic approach to data-mining projects.

10.4 THE DATA-MINING PROCESS

10.4.1 OVERVIEW

A complete data-mining process does not *only* consist of building analytical models using techniques such as logistic regression, neural networks, or even genetic algorithms. It includes assessing and specifying the business objectives, data sourcing, transformation, creation of analytical variables, and much more. Figure 10-1 presents an overview of the process.

In many instances of current data-mining projects we find data preparation steps easily take from 60 to 70 percent of the total project time. This is not due to the weaknesses of any specific data-mining methodology. It is due to issues regarding unavailability of relevant variables describing customer behavior. An example of which is, difficult access to legacy data source systems managed by different departments which do not possess the customer centric views required for data mining projects. These departments are more likely geared towards transaction, product, contract or other type of views more suited to fulfill the needs of their current operational systems. The graph shown in Figure 10-2 helps us understand the timeframe of the methodology.

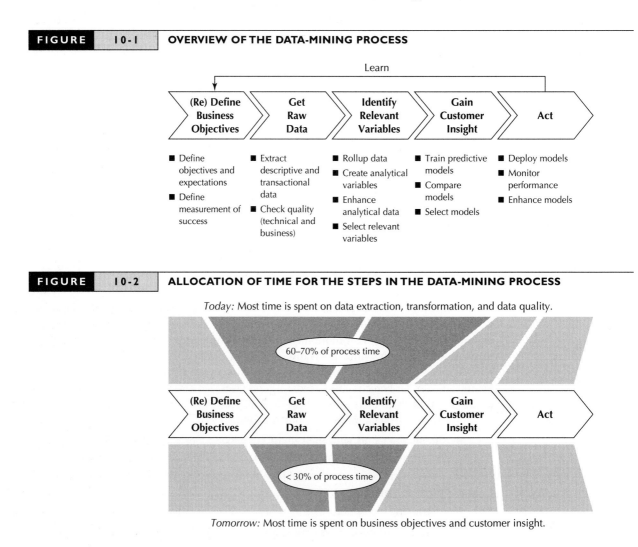

FIGURE **10-1** **OVERVIEW OF THE DATA-MINING PROCESS**

Learn

| (Re) Define Business Objectives | Get Raw Data | Identify Relevant Variables | Gain Customer Insight | Act |

- Define objectives and expectations
- Define measurement of success

- Extract descriptive and transactional data
- Check quality (technical and business)

- Rollup data
- Create analytical variables
- Enhance analytical data
- Select relevant variables

- Train predictive models
- Compare models
- Select models

- Deploy models
- Monitor performance
- Enhance models

FIGURE **10-2** **ALLOCATION OF TIME FOR THE STEPS IN THE DATA-MINING PROCESS**

Today: Most time is spent on data extraction, transformation, and data quality.

60–70% of process time

| (Re) Define Business Objectives | Get Raw Data | Identify Relevant Variables | Gain Customer Insight | Act |

< 30% of process time

Tomorrow: Most time is spent on business objectives and customer insight.

It is important to automate the time-consuming data extraction and manipulation, and the data quality monitoring and enhancement steps. To achieve this goal, it is necessary to sequentially and systematically code data knowledge into programs that can be executed, for instance, in batch mode. This will free up time of highly qualified quantitative data analysts (data miners) to concentrate on the value-generating tasks such as the precise definition of business objectives, extraction of customer insight, and effective actions based on gained knowledge.

Figure 10-3 shows the extent of involvement of the three main groups participating in a data-mining project—business (e.g., marketing, product management), data mining, and IT—during the different process steps.

The data-mining group must understand the business objectives and support the business group in refining and sometimes correcting the scope of the project and aligning their expectations to fit the limitations posed by the available data. IT resources are required for the sourcing and extraction of the required data used for modeling. The data-mining group is most active during the variable selection and modeling phase. It will share the obtained customer insights with the business group, who are strongly involved at this point to check the plausibility and soundness of the solution in business terms. Finally, the business group takes the lead when it comes to deploying the new insights into corporate action such as a call center or direct mail campaign.

As we move through the data-mining process, the dimensionality of the data used may change dramatically. In a simple, two-dimensional data table, we think of the columns as being the descriptive variables and the rows as being single observations, each pertaining to a collection of variables about the same primary object (e.g., customer identification number, transaction identification number).

Manipulations on columns can take several forms:

■ *Transformation.* Transform birth date to age.

■ *Derivation.* Create new variables based on existing ones (e.g., compute monthly profits from sales and cost information).

■ *Elimination.* A whole variable may be excluded from further processing due to a variety of possible reasons (e.g., a variable that does not help in predicting or a variable that is correlated to one or more variables already in the model could be eliminated).

The number of variables used changes drastically during the data-mining process. Figure 10-4 illustrates a typical example of the changes in the number of variables used at each step.

FIGURE 10-3   **LEVEL OF INVOLVEMENT OF BUSINESS, DATA MINING, AND IT RESOURCES IN A TYPICAL DATA-MINING PROJECT**

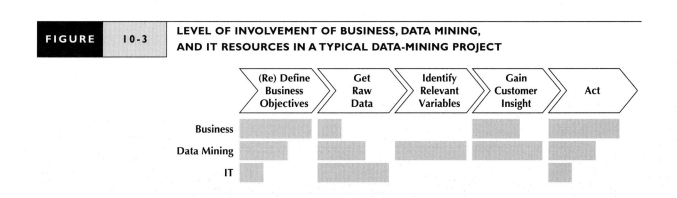

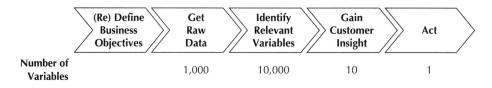

	(Re) Define Business Objectives	Get Raw Data	Identify Relevant Variables	Gain Customer Insight	Act
Number of Variables		1,000	10,000	10	1

If we also take into consideration that we usually work with up to several millions of rows it becomes obvious that scalability and good sampling methods are essential for any data mining environment.

There are also several types of row manipulations, including:

- *Aggregation.* Examples include counts, mean, standard deviation of the number of transactions of a specific type over a given time period, for a specific customer, product type and many more.

- *Change detection.* This is used to detect when and if certain variables change their value such as ZIP code of customer's domicile, or his/her credit rating.

- *Missing value detection.* It is common that raw data come with many data fields either totally missing or with some missing values. The reasons for this may be nonmandatory input fields in front-office systems, incomplete data migration from one system to another, and so on. There are various ways of treating a variable with missing values, including eliminating the whole row from further processing when a missing value is detected, replacing the missing value with a constant value, or replacing it with a randomly generated value based on the distribution of this data field's nonmissing values or based on correlations with other data fields.[2]

- *Outlier detection.* Many distributions of data fields show the existence of outliers, meaning values far away from the bulk of the distribution. Sometimes these outliers are real; sometimes they are the consequence of bad data quality. Outlier detection is in its simple form univariate: we just look at one variable and try to find values that stand out. In its more sophisticated form we look at many variables at the same time and watch for multivariate outliers (a data point might look like an outlier in the univariate case but not in the multivariate case). Outliers can be mapped to other values or the corresponding rows and be excluded from further processing.

When preparing the data for modeling, it is common to sample and split the incoming data into various streams for different purposes:

- *Train set.* Used to build the models.
- *Test set.* Used for out-of-sample tests of the model quality and to select the final model candidate.
- *Scoring data.* Used for model-based prediction. Typically, this data set is large as compared to the previous ones.

The data sets must be carefully examined and designed to assure statistical significance of the results obtained.

10.4.2 DEFINE BUSINESS OBJECTIVES

Data mining finds application in many situations. Profitable customer acquisition requires modeling of expected customer potential, in order to target the acquisition of those customers

FIGURE   10-5   (RE)DEFINE BUSINESS OBJECTIVES

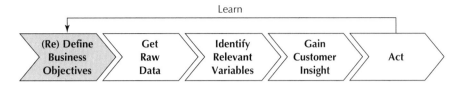

who will be profitable over the lifetime of the business relationship (they might be unprofitable in the beginning and turn into very profitable customers later—e.g., a medicine student). In a cross-selling or up-selling model, we model the customer's affinity with a set of products or services translated into her purchase likelihood. In churn management, it is crucial to correctly model a customer's likelihood to defect based on past behavior. Some applications require predicting not only who will purchase which product or service, but also the expected amount spent on the transactions.

Once it has been identified which customer behavior has to be predicted, we need to mathematically define this target variable or dependent variable. While up-selling platinum credit cards to customers already owning a standard credit card, we might find several types of standard and platinum cards exist. The business objective might, in fact, only be to up-sell platinum cards of types P2 and P3 to customers not owning a card yet, or those already owning standard cards of type S1, S3, and S4. The target variable has to reflect these conditions when calculated. This has a later direct impact on the modeling process. To prepare the modeling data sets we will look for two types of customers in the customer database and set the value of the target variable accordingly:

- FOR all customers who (own a standard card of type S1, S3 or S4) AND until today did not purchase any platinum card of flavor P2 or P3) OR (neither own a standard nor a platinum card) SET target variable=0.

- FOR all customers who (first purchased a standard card of type S1, S3 or S4 and then purchased a platinum card of type P2 or P3) SET target variable=1.

- Once these restrictions and considerations have been applied to the data, the model will be trained to distinguish between customers with a target variable equal to zero and customers with a target variable equal to one. After training, the model will be applied to predict if a given customer is likely to buy the platinum cards. The business group must establish likelihood threshold levels above which they think a prospect should be included in the marketing campaign.

Another aspect of the campaign which should be defined during this project phase is the set of business or selection rules for a campaign. Rules define the customers that should be excluded from or included in the target groups: certain products or services might not be available for specific customer groups. Suppose that in certain countries only customers at least 18 years old are eligible to purchase a credit card. Credit products in general have restrictions with respect to the customer's credit rating. Companies have "blacklists" containing customers who should not receive any new offerings, either due to bad debt indicators (they do not have a good credit rating) or persons explicitly asking not to be contacted for marketing purposes. Some countries have centrally managed lists with all persons not wanting to receive unauthorized direct mails or calls. By contrast, there might also be customer groups that should be included at any price in the campaign—for instance, due to strategic issues such as need to gain market share in a specific region or otherwise defined group. In those cases, it is not relevant if members of that group get high model scores; they are included anyway.

To ensure a successful project, we need to define at this point the details of its execution. Therefore, we should create a project plan specifying, for instance, the start and delivery dates of the data-mining process, as well as the responsible resources for each task. For the final model selection the business group must be available for reviewing the data-mining results, perform consistency checks with the data-mining group, and make the final decision about the model selected for deployment. Delivery dates for the final model or scores also need to be defined, along with dates for start and end of the supported campaign, which is essential later for accurate campaign success assessment.

We need to carefully define the chosen experimental setup for the campaign; this is critical for correctly evaluating its success later. It is highly recommended to spend a significant amount of time getting this right. Usually, we split the target group into various cells. In the simplest case there will be only two cells:

1. *The control group contains only randomly selected customers.* This group will be needed to measure the baseline effect (i.e., what would have been the normal customer behavior without the influence of the campaign).

2. *The other cell will contain only the best customers according to the model used.* This simple setup allows measuring how the model-based selection is doing with respect to the average customer behavior.

More refined setups may generate more than two cells. As an example, take the control group and two target groups to which we communicate different content about the same offering during the campaign. This will show the impact of the communication content on the purchase behavior.

To get the business context into the data-mining project, describe the nature of the business involving the data-mining project, and the cost and revenue drivers of the business. This knowledge will affect the final model and target group selections. It is helpful to define a cost/revenue matrix describing how the business mechanics will work in the supported campaign and how it will affect the data-mining process. As an example, consider a call center campaign to sell a mobile phone contract. Table 10-1 shows an example of the associated cost/revenue matrix.

Here, we assume the average cost per call is $5. Each positive responder (purchaser) will generate additional cost including administration work required to register him as a new customer and the cost of the delivered phone handset of, say, $100. Customers who respond positively will generate average revenue of $1,000 a year. Putting all these factors together defines the cost/revenue decision matrix, which will subsequently have an impact on the choice of model parameters such as the cut-off point for the selected model scores. It will also give business users an immediately interpretable table.

Finally, we need to establish the criteria for evaluating the success of the campaign. This is a key aspect for the success or failure of the whole project. Often there is a misunderstanding

| **TABLE** 10-1 | **COST/REVENUE MATRIX** |

Cost/Revenue Matrix	Prospect Did Not Purchase	Prospect Did Purchase
Model predicts prospect will not purchase (not contacted)	Cost: $0 First year revenue: $0 Total: $0	Lost business opportunity of +$895
Model predicts prospect will purchase (contacted)	Cost: −$5 First year revenue: $0 Total: −$5	Cost: −$5 to $100 First year revenue: +$1000 Total: +$895

on both sides—business and modelers—with respect to what is feasible from a business and statistical perspective. Clearly defining the expectations helps. If, for example, gaining market share is more important than obtaining high purchase rates, the measure of success changes from "percentage of sold cards per contacted customer" to "absolute number of cards sold during the campaign." In this context, it is crucial to specify how the campaign results will be tracked and analyzed. Depending on the type of business, how it is structured into customer segments, regions, products, and others, we could be interested in measuring purchase rates per region, per sales channels, per product type, and many more as a function of time. When we consider a situation where we have defined various target groups (cells) for different communication contents or product offers in one campaign, it is worth measuring the purchase rates for each group.

Sometimes it is useful to look for a benchmark to compare results obtained in the past for the same or similar campaign setups using traditional targeting methods and not predictive models. We have to be careful when comparing the result of the old and new methods because there could be hidden differences due to different business (market) conditions, changes in the products or services, and so on. In this chapter, we examine the French company Credite Est, a regional bank that implemented a data-mining process. CRM at Work 10.1 looks at how Credite Est defined its business objectives.

10.4.3   GET RAW DATA

Overview

Now that we have a clear understanding of the business objectives, we need to translate them into requirements for the data-mining project, and—to start with—into data requirements (i.e., which data are available that appropriately and accurately describe the problem thereby allowing us to model the targeted behavior?) Once the required data have been identified, extract and consolidate it in a database (often called *analytical data mart*) so it is readily available for subsequent data manipulation and data-mining steps. Another important step is to check the quality of the analytical raw data. This includes technical

---

CRM AT WORK 10.1

DEFINING BUSINESS OBJECTIVES AT CREDITE EST

Credite Est is a regional mid-tier bank in France, serving roughly 600,000 million customers. The company, which has been growing organically since its inception in 1965, has a quantitative approach to operations. Therefore, the use of quantitative methods in marketing via data mining is second nature to the company. The following example highlights a specific data-mining project of the bank.

As is typical for financial services operations, the bank has a very diverse set of customers in terms of customer profitability. Besides using segmentation scheme based on behavioral characteristics (e.g., product ownership), the company has an activity-based-costing system in place that allows individual customer-level contribution margin to be identified.

The project in question had the business goal to acquire new prospects. Specifically, the objective was to identify the characteristics of profitable customers in Credite Est's mass-market segment. Once these characteristics are more closely identified, it could then efficiently target similar profiles in the prospect pool. The nature of this project required the bank to go beyond using firm-level data because behavioral (transaction) data are not available for prospects by definition. Since the company does all data-mining projects in house, it has considerable experience in the process management of such a project.

FIGURE | **10-6** **GET RAW DATA**

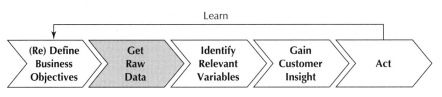

checks as well as ensuring the data make sense in the given business context and that correct deductions can be obtained.

During this phase of the project, database administrators and IT professionals with knowledge of the data source systems will be asked to extract and provide all the data fields required for the data-mining project, in close cooperation with the data miners to ensure the extracted data corresponds to the initial requirements. Then, we also need to involve business resources to ensure and cross-check data quality.

Step 1: Looking for Data Sources

To start this we look into data sourcing, a mixed top-down and bottom-up process, driven by business requirements (top) and technical restrictions (bottom). Its main objective consists of searching for available data sources in your company (or externally) which describe the problem at hand. The availability of a data warehouse can sometimes speed this process. Conflicting and bad quality of addresses and other demographic information is common. For example, you might find the same or similar information field resides in various source systems, but with contradictory content (e.g., in one database the gender code for a given customer is "male" and in another database it is "female" for the same customer). Data warehouse infrastructures with advanced data cleansing processes can help ensure you are working with high-quality data. It is also a good idea to ask for small sample data extractions from the sources to examine if the information represents what you thought it would. Make sure that you talk to many people from business and data management to understand which data sources are commonly used in certain contexts, but also to detect possible new sources that may contain valuable information. Collect all metadata available to fully understand data types, value ranges, and the primary/foreign key structures.

Once there is a better understanding of the data sources that need to be loaded, build a (simple) relational data model onto which the source data will be mapped. This model should be kept as simple and as close to a business data model as possible. Remember: there is no need for highly normalized data models. This is not the right format for data mining and analysis. Later in the process we will *denormalize* (flatten) the model to enable easier data analysis and predictive modeling.

Step 2: Loading the Data

After specifying where and how the required data will be extracted, we still need to define further query restrictions because we might want to model only subsets of the full data (e.g., specific customer segments, geographical regions, time periods, etc.). Then it is time to request data management (IT) to deliver the specified data needs.[3] IT teams will prepare the necessary data queries, which will be executed at predefined time windows in batch mode (such as each night at midnight or each Sunday after completion of the accounting batch process).

Depending on the data miner's needs they might also get direct *asynchronous* access to the data so they can run extraction when necessary. The extracted data are then delivered to the data-mining environment in a predefined format such as database tables in native format, or simply flat files in ASCII or XML (text) format with fixed or variable record lengths. In fact, flat files are still the most commonly used format for data mining due to their simplicity, enhanced definition of system boundaries, and interfaces. Data miners define how the data will be imported into the data-mining environment. Delivery using an ftp protocol is common, or data may also be put onto a common file server to be accessed directly through the network. If a DB-link is preferred, a direct database connection from the data-mining system to the source systems (or vice versa) will be established. After the data have been delivered to a defined landing area, they will be further processed and used to fill the previously defined data model in the data mining environment. The involved steps are part of the *ETL process* (Extract-Transform-Load) supported by dedicated software packages. Some data-mining tools also offer quite advanced and comprehensive utilities for ETL.

Step 3: Checking Data Quality

It is often underestimated how seriously bad data quality may affect business decisions. We need to ensure that once the data for the data-mining project have been loaded, we assess and understand their limitations resulting from their inherent quality (good or bad) aspects. We have to create an analytical database that all involved parties (business, data mining, IT) feel comfortable with, as it is the basis for subsequent analyses. Only then can the generated customer insights be trusted and applied in practice with maximum confidence of their effect on the organization.

When checking data quality, we focus not only on technical aspects of the data (primary keys, duplicate records, missing values, etc.) but also on quality issues related to the business context (a customer should not be 200 years old or have a future birth date, customers should not be purchasing nonexisting or expired products, etc.).

A preliminary data quality assessment is carried out to ensure an acceptable level of quality of the delivered data and to ensure the data mining team has a clear understanding of how to interpret the data in business terms. All parties—business, data mining, and IT—are involved in this important task. Thus, the data available for the mining project must be analyzed to answer to the following questions: (1) Does the data correspond to the original sourcing requirements? (2) Is the quality sufficient? and (3) Do we understand the data?

Several iterations of data extractions may be necessary to satisfy the data requirements. The data miner represents the link between business and IT requirements. Miscommunication between business and IT can lead to incorrect data extractions.

As already mentioned, data should have sufficient quality for achieving the project's objectives. A data field does not always have a clearly defined meaning (although available metadata might initially give you that impression). Sometimes the information it carries is different from its official description. This is a consequence of the accumulation of undocumented system changes over many years. Another common issue is missing data, which means that in some cases (i.e., for some records) a data field is not filled. We might also find wrong or contradictory information in a data field.

Finally, data miners must demonstrate they understand the data. To this end, it is useful to have them carry out some basic data interpretation and aggregation exercises where two things can be shown: (1) the data quality and (2) the ability to correctly interpret the data. As simple data interpretation examples, consider correctly counting the number of customers per region, customer segment, product ownership, total transaction volume per time periods, etc. Choose to include aggregations familiar to the business group and that can be easily cross-checked. We see an example of data gathering in CRM at Work 10.2, a further study of Credite Est.

10.4.4   IDENTIFY RELEVANT PREDICTIVE VARIABLES[4]
Overview

The raw data, now available for analysis, is not yet in a format suited to powerful predictive modeling. This is due to data formatting aspects, since the sourced data are still in a relational format, and do not yet represent a customer-centric view. During this step, we will create a flattened view of the extracted raw data aggregating all facts about the customer behavior

CRM AT WORK 10.2
GATHERING RAW DATA AT CREDITE EST

Since the objective is to acquire prospects likely to be high-value customers, Credite Est must rely on customer characteristics common to both customers (the basis for establishing the critical profile) and the prospects (scored on the basis of their profile). The process is shown in the following figure.

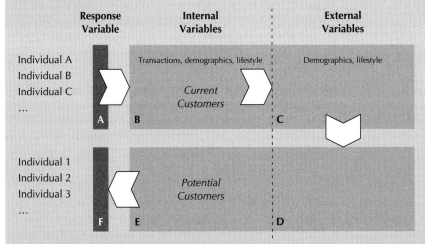

The response variable for current customers is customer contribution margin (field A). The company sorted customers by operating contribution and chose to profile the top 20 percent of customers. Transaction information (field B) is not available for prospects. This is why the bank has to rely on information available for both existing customers and prospects. One type of information is geodemographic information, such as socioeconomic status of a region, average age, type of housing, and so on. These data are provided from direct marketing agencies that specialize in the collection of geodemographic data. They can be purchased and then appended to individual records of existing customers. That is, depending on name or Zip code, geodemographic data are added to existing customer records. The model attempts to predict customer operating margin as the dependent variable with geodemographic information as the independent variables. The rationale behind this process is to find the profile that best characterizes high-value clients, which is subsequently applied to prospects' information. Credite Est appended a total of sixty-five variables to existing customer records. They were procured from the French list manager CIFEA, as well as from Claritas.

FIGURE   **10-7**   **IDENTIFY RELEVANT VARIABLES**

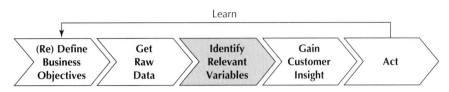

over time in a single observation (also called record or row). Also, it is a good practice to include a priori business knowledge by creating new analytical variables which might have predictive power. This part will require imagination and participation from the business group. As a result, we might end up with thousands of variables describing each customer. Further analysis is likely to reveal that most variables do not possess predictive power at all. Therefore, we will finally identify and select only those few variables with sufficient explanatory power for the modeled target behavior.

Step 1: Create Analytical Customer View—Flattening the Data

In the context of CRM, very often the individual customer is the central object analyzed by means of data mining. All data available for an individual customer must be gathered and consolidated because the individual customer constitutes an observational unit for data analysis and predictive modeling. The historical behavior of customers is obtained from the corresponding data queries in a time series–oriented relational transaction database.

Usually, we choose a simple, flat data model as the basis for predictive modeling. In this representation all data pertaining to an individual customer are contained in one observation (row, record). Individual columns (variables, fields) represent the conditions at specific points in time or a summary over a whole period. Creating such a customer view requires denormalizing the original relational data structures (*flattening*).

This task will involve data miners to define the details of the flattening process and use IT resources to obtain the targeted form of data.

The business objectives for the data mining project determine which features of the customer's record need to be aggregated from the analytical raw data and how. The detail levels for calculating grouped sums (e.g., sum of monthly cash withdrawals from a bank account) and counts (e.g., number of address changes within a certain year) need to be defined. This includes specification of the temporal granularity of the time series in the flattened data table. Descriptive statistics such as sums, mean, median, and standard deviation will be employed to capture features of the related time series. As an example, consider raw data describing one year of customer transactions and create four new variables containing the average transaction volume per quarter. Different kinds of global transformations, combinations, or arithmetical operations can also be applied to selected variables such as currency exchange calculations, scaling factors, logarithmic transforms, and so on.

Many new variables will be created through these types of operations, leading to very wide data tables. Later, we will use the newly created variables in addition to the raw data variables, as predictors during the predictive modeling step.

Another key variable to be created during this step is the target or dependent variable. Its correct definition is extremely important for predictive modeling. In the example of modeling customer defection, a target value of zero is assigned if the customer was still maintaining a business relationship and a target value of one if the customer already terminated the business relationship. The definition of the target variable is not always as straightforward as it might seem. In the previous examples, we could also think about a customer who is inactive since a defined time period as a *lost* customer. There might be a multitude of business rules specifying the conditions under which the target variable is either one or zero. Once we've found a satisfactory definition of the target variable, its values should be generated for all customers and added to the existing data tables.

Step 2: Create Analytical Variables

The basic set of variables resulting from the previous flattening might not be enough to fully explore the data potential for predictive modeling. We might want to introduce additional variables derived from the original ones. For example, consider a variable resulting from the product of customer age and salary. This is often referred to as an *interaction term.* Transforming variables is another operation that might lead to new and more predictive variables. We could transform customer birth date into age, or use the number of days between two customer transactions instead of the absolute dates of each transaction. Variable *binning* (or categorization) is also often encountered. Here we take highly skewed variables (such as salary) and map the distribution to a few discrete classes such as low, medium, and high salary, each defined by its boundary values. More refined methods help to increase normality of variable distributions, which in turn help the predictive model training process. Many data-mining tools provide support for increasing normality of the analytical variables. Finally, missing value management is key for enhancing the quality of the analytical data set. Numerous methods are available, including deleting each row with at least one missing value (the least preferred strategy), replacing a missing field with a constant value, randomly generating a value based on the variable's distribution, and randomly generating a value based on the variable's correlation with the other variables (such as the expectation maximization algorithm).

Step 3: Select Predictive Variables

At this point, we have a wealth of variables describing customer behavior; probably too much to enter the subsequent modeling phase of the data-mining project. We now need to reduce the dimensionality (i.e., exclude variables) to get a more parsimonious model. Presenting all predictor variables to a neutral network, for instance, might make the modeling phase extremely time consuming and sometimes results in *overfitting*—that is, the model gives good results on the training data (in sample) but fails to be generally applicable to previously unseen data (out of sample). Exclusion of variables is usually possible without deteriorating the predictive power of the obtained models since many variables have no predictive power at all. To this end we inspect the descriptive statistics of all univariate distributions associated to all available variables. We can immediately exclude those variables, which take on only one value (i.e., the variable is a constant), since they will certainly not have any predictive power. We might also exclude variables with mostly missing values. A threshold missing value count level should be defined above which the field would be excluded from further analysis (e.g., more than 95 percent missing values).

Variables directly or indirectly identifying an individual customer represent another type of candidate for exclusion. Examples are primary keys such as the customer ID number or name and address fields. Later, when deploying predictive models (i.e., when scoring customers), identifiers will usually be required. Otherwise you wouldn't know whom to address with an offering. In some cases, collinear predictive variables can have a negative impact on the convergence and performance of the estimation process of certain types of models such as logistic regression. These collinearities must be identified and the respective variables excluded before proceeding. Finally, we also exclude variables showing little correlation with the target variable. To identify them we may carry out pair-wise chi-square tests, linear correlation analyses, pair-wise simple linear regressions, and other tests. Other frequently used techniques to support the variable selection process are histograms, scatter plots, box plots, and frequency tables.

Also notice that excluding variables from further processing must not automatically imply that the respective columns are deleted from the data sets. It could only mean flagging the respective columns to be temporarily ignored for further analysis. The exclusion should be easily reversible to readily test other variable scenario selections.

Before concluding the variable selection step, we should carefully check if all variables have been mapped to the appropriate data types. Some data fields might represent the data in an inappropriate format (e.g., Zip codes stored as numerical integer variables should rather be categorical (or nominal) for the purpose of data mining, unless you have a Zip code–based distance measure associated for your analysis). CRM at Work 10.3 examines this issue.

10.4.5 GAIN CUSTOMER INSIGHT

Overview

Once we've obtained a credible, good-quality set of descriptive data, the next step is to extract the knowledge about customer behavior and/or other properties needed for carrying out the planned campaign. There are two steps of predictive modeling:

1. The rules (or linear/nonlinear analytical models) are built based on a training set.
2. These rules are then applied to a new dataset for generating the answers needed for the campaign.

Frequently, we distinguish between different types of predictive models obtained through different modeling paradigms: supervised and unsupervised modeling. In the case where we want to predict the likelihood of a customer purchasing a certain product, we would build a predictive model on a predefined test set containing customers who already

---

CRM AT WORK 10.3

IDENTIFYING RELEVANT VARIABLES AT CREDITE EST

Upon creating a single data file including all appended information, the next step is to start with exploratory analyses. A key concern with appended data is the amount of potentially missing information. All appended variables had almost 50 percent missing data. The next step was to assess whether the missing data could be meaningfully replaced. These operations improved the overall rate of missing values from 42 percent to 21 percent. The next step was to investigate univariate statistics (means, standard deviations, frequencies, outliers) for all variables to ensure the included variables have sufficient integrity. This step brought a reduction in variables from 65 to 54. The next step was to calculate all bivariate correlations (or mean analyses in case of categorical variables) of the existing independent variables with the dependent variable—customer value. This was an iterative process where independent variables were subjected to transformations and where new variables were created. For example, there were three variables which indicated whether a household has children in age brackets 0 to 4, 5 to 11, and 12 to 18. From that, a new variable was created that was a simple dummy indicator: children versus no children. In the end, this data evaluation process resulted in a total of seventeen variables that had a reasonable correlation with the dependent variable. These were retained for the next step, the response model.

FIGURE **10-8** **GAIN CUSTOMER INSIGHT**

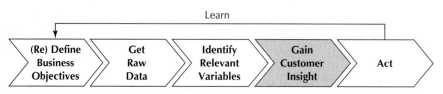

purchased the product and customers who did not. In this case, we are applying the super-vised learning paradigm, because for each customer in the modeling data set we know the correct answer to the question—that is, did the customer purchase or not?

Building a model means finding the right relationships between the variables describing the customers to predict their respective group membership likelihood: purchaser or non-purchaser. This is usually also referred to as scoring (e.g., between 0 and 1). Since we know the purchase behavior for each customer in the train set, we can also measure the model's prediction quality—that is, its misclassification rate. A different situation arises in the context, for instance, of a customer segmentation problem. Suppose you want to identify groups of customers having a similar general behavior, not only with respect to purchase behavior. In the beginning you don't know which groups will be identified. It is a process purely driven by the data and relationships between variables. Here, we would apply unsupervised model-ing where group membership is not known beforehand. We're looking for new and unex-pected patterns. Typical examples of statistical models in this context are self-organizing neural networks (Kohonen networks) and clustering algorithms.[5]

The output of this project phase can either consist in the predictive model itself, which is later applied in an online production environment (i.e., to predict next product recom-mendations for customers calling a call center), or directly in the customer score values (e.g., to select all customers with a score value above 90 percent purchase likelihood and send them a direct mail).

Step 1: Preparing Data Samples

Before we start building (or training) the models, it is necessary to analyze if sufficient data are available to obtain statistically significant results. There are cases where there is only very little data available such as when modeling purchase behavior for a recently intro-duced product, with only very few customers having bought the product until now. If we have enough data available we split the data into two samples: the train set to fit the mod-els and the test set to check the model's performance on observations that have not been used to build it. This will give an objective assessment of the model's generalization capa-bility—a critical requirement before launching a product or campaign.

Step 2: Predictive Modeling

Based on the training set, we develop predictive models that should minimize the predic-tion error. In the course of this process a set of optimal model parameters are obtained. Usually, several alternative models are trained together, applying different statistical methodologies such as neural networks, linear or logistic regression, survival analysis, prin-cipal component analysis, factor analysis, decision trees, and clustering.

Step 3: Select Model

When all alternative models have been trained, we start comparing their relative quality of prediction by comparing their respective misclassification rates obtained on the test set.

Some models will have more predictive power than others, and we will select the model we think generalizes best from the train to the test data.

A misclassification error rate or confusion matrix could look like Table 10-2.

Lift charts are also often used for getting an idea about model performance. It shows how much better the current model would perform against a random selection–based model. As an example, consider you have a total of 1,000 prospects, of which 100 have purchased. A good predictive model helps increase the relative amount of purchasers in the selected group: a random-based selection of 100 prospects would contain about 10 purchasers, whereas a model-based selection of 100 prospects could result in 30 purchasers. This is what lift charts help to visualize. The models with the highest *lift* are candidates for final selection.

We will also include the economic implications of a model by applying the previously defined cost/revenue matrix. Predictive models, for instance, deliver a score value, or likelihood, for each customer to show the modeled target behavior (e.g., purchase of a credit card). Nevertheless, determining the threshold level score to use for a given campaign is a business decision. It could be that you want to set it to the break-even point, or you may have a fixed budget for the campaign you want to fully use. This might lead to lowering the threshold until the point where your costs equal the budget. We continue to look at this issue in CRM at Work 10.4.

CRM AT WORK 10.4

GAINING CUSTOMER INSIGHT AT CREDITE EST

The methodology chosen by the modelers was logistic regression. Since the goal was to either target or not target a certain individual in the prospect pool, classifying the dependent variable as 0/1 was appropriate. In the previous step, only those variables were retained with a minimum level of bivariate correlation. However, now the issue of multicollinearity came into play. Multicollinearity occurs when two variables convey essentially the same information, making one of them redundant. Thus, an important step was to make a theory-based elimination of those highly collinear variables. The final model was chosen on grounds of predictive ability while containing a low number of missing values. The final model contained five predictors of customer value: bourgeois cluster, technology cluster, children index, house value index, and managerial job position. The ability of the model to correctly classify in a holdout sample was 75.5 percent in the estimation sample and 69.8 percent in the holdout sample—that is, roughly 20 percent higher than based on chance alone. This result was deemed successful, and thus it was decided to utilize this model for a prospecting campaign.

TABLE	**10-2**	**CONFUSION MATRIX**

**Input Node—Classification
Neural Network (10)**

		Predicted		
		1	*0*	Totals
Observed	*1*	726	56	782
	0	173	504	677
Totals		899	560	1,459

10.4.6   ACT

The final objective of a data-mining project should be to act on its results. Sometimes we also refer to this as deployment of the results. This is crucial to the success of the whole project. The planning phase of the project must have addressed the issue of implementing the project's results into the respective business processes. The project plan must foresee involvement and availability of IT resources required to feed data-mining results back into the process supporting IT systems (databases, Web sites, call centers, etc.). In practice, deployment can have numerous applications: score-based selection of customers to be addressed through a direct mailing campaign, score-based next-product recommendation on an e-commerce Web site, optimization of marketing spending according to the model-based customer lifetime value prediction, choice of the appropriate communication channel for each customer, and so on.

This section presents the steps at this stage.

Step 1: Deliver Results to Operational Systems

The final goal in prognostic modeling within the context of CRM is to select a subset of customers for a campaign to determine which customers are more likely to be responsive than other customers. To find this subset, we apply the selected model to the entire customer base (unless restrictions have been previously defined that limit the total universe of modeled and targeted customers, such as geographical regions, a subset of customer segments, etc.). The obtained score value for each customer and the defined threshold value (already described) will determine whether the corresponding customer qualifies to participate in the campaign. We can either deploy the customer scores or, alternately, the scoring model itself, which implies that it is applied *on demand*—for example, when a customer calls the call center or visits the company's Web site.

Before scoring customers we need to prepare the score data set containing the most recent information available for each customer with the variables required by the model. This implies the score set variables go through exactly the same variable transformation, derivation, and selection process as did the train and test data sets used for building the model. Data recency is an important requirement because otherwise we are scoring customers based on old information, which may, in turn, lead to wrong conclusions.

Imagine we're scoring customers for a direct mail campaign to sell a credit card to all those customers not yet owning one. If the scoring data are not reasonably current, we might be scoring customers although they've recently purchased a credit card and potentially (if the model works well) include them in your target group. As a result, we end up offering these customers a product they have just purchased, giving a rather poor image of how much our company knows about its customers.

Finally, when delivering the results to the operational systems, make sure to also provide the necessary customer identifiers required by those systems to unambiguously link the model's score information to the correct customer.

FIGURE   10-9   ACT

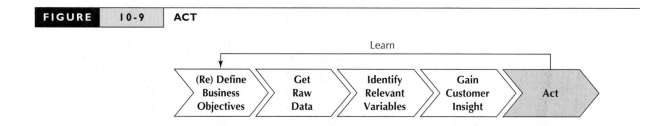

Step 2: Archive Results

The data-mining group is responsible for archiving all information related to each data-mining project it executes. This is an important and often neglected or poorly followed a piece of advice. Companies that do not archive their models cannot expect to learn from past experience as fast as those who do.

Each data-mining project will produce a huge amount of information:

- Raw data used
- Transformations for each variable
- Formulas for creating derived variables
- Train, test, and score data sets
- Target variable calculation
- Models and their parameterizations
- Score threshold levels
- Final customer target selections

Knowing this information and having it readily available helps in understanding anomalies in model performance, and in learning what worked well and what didn't (and why). It is also useful to preserve the details of the model when scoring has been done. The same model might be used to score different data sets obtained at different times.

Step 3: Learn

Learning from a data-mining project is an integral part of the process. This is also sometimes referred to as *closing the loop*. It means learning from the actions you have executed to improve performance the next time.

To learn from the data-mining project, we must first obtain the facts describing its performance and business impact. In the ideal case, we would provide return on investment figures for the data-mining project at hand.

Usually these facts are obtained by monitoring the campaign performance while it is running and from the final campaign performance analysis after the campaign has ended. Campaign monitoring is an important capability the data-mining group must provide, since it avoids blind piloting of the campaign until its end, without any intermediate performance feedback. In rapidly changing environments, it is also required for detecting when a model should be retrained. Usually, monitoring provides some key performance indicators, such as the response and/or purchase rates by region, customer segment, product, and so on. These parameters will give early indication of undesired irregularities in model performance and enable early intervention. The final campaign performance analysis will produce similar performance indicators as the monitoring function. The main difference is that it is more complete and has a determined final time horizon of influence.[6]

Following are just two of the many examples of learning from the campaign evaluation:

1. Revealing that purchase rates depend on the choice of the communication channel
2. Discovering that a direct mail with a colorful and detailed product brochure sells less than one with a black and white one-page flyer

Thus, the learning step requires data miners to generate the facts about campaign performance, and business resources to put them in context for correct interpretation. Our study of Credite Est concludes with CRM at Work 10.5, which shows how the company acted on the information it gleaned in the data-mining process.

The chapter concludes with CRM at Work 10.6, a look at Yapi Kredi, a company that put the data-mining tools to use to create a cross-selling campaign.

CRM AT WORK 10.5

ACTING ON THE INFORMATION AT CREDITE EST

The final model was rolled out in a sequential fashion to the target prospect audience. The goal was to iteratively refine the model in future rounds. As a first step, Credite Est purchased addresses from list brokers that had nonmissing values for at least three out of five variables in the final model. The prospects were scored with the model and then ranked by likelihood of being a high-value customer. From the resulting pool of 10,000 prospects, half were targeted with a money-market product, and half with a lending product. The objective was to assess the receptivity of the two samples for the respective products. In addition, a baseline scenario was conducted whereby the same prospecting campaigns were conducted for a random sample of households. Although both target mailings were significantly more successful than the base-line scenario, this was only the first step in a further refinement of the model and the offer. In particular, besides assessing response rate, it was now important to track and document the value of the acquired customers—the original goal of the project.

CRM AT WORK 10.6

YAPI KREDI—PREDICTIVE MODEL–BASED CROSS-SELL CAMPAIGN

Company Overview

Established in 1944 as the first private bank in Turkey, Yapi Kredi has always been a pioneer in the Turkish financial sector. The bank has more than 420 domestic branches and various other subsidiaries, as well as affiliated companies active in leasing, factoring, investment banking, insurance, brokerage and new economy companies. Yapi Kredi's retail services rank top on the Turkish marketplace, and has a market share above 20 percent. The bank ranks number one with respect to the number of issued credit cards and respective card business volume, number of POS terminals, and related business volume, and it ranks number two with respect to the number of available ATMs.

The Challenge

To continue Yapi Kredi's development as the fastest-growing retail bank in Turkey, in terms of assets under management and retail profitability, it targets to maintain an intimate banking relationship with the top customer segment to fully explore the potential of its 5+ million customer base, and to increase the contract per customer ratio to five.

To this end, Yapi Kredi introduced a modern retail banking approach to enable serving all customers according to their specific needs through individual product packages. The capabilities required to achieve these goals were as follows:

- Advanced analytical customer segmentation
- Segment-specific offering of product bundles
- Conversion of customers to more profitable segments via targeted campaigns using advanced CRM tools such as predictive modeling

Solution

To increase the product per customer ratio, to attract new money from customers, and to demonstrate the efficacy of the new analytical CRM methods, Yapi Kredi decided to carry out a set of pilot projects for cross-selling of consumer banking products. A reduced selection of target customers with a high propensity to positively respond would be included in a multichannel, two-step campaign. To illustrate the methodology we briefly describe the outcomes of the various project phases.

Define Business Objectives

Various cross-departmental workshops were held to define the business objectives, operational aspects of campaign execution, the basics of relevant data availability, and to measure the success of the campaign.

The first step was to find which product would be best suited for cross selling from a customer and bank perspective. After a deep analysis of potential products to be offered during this first predictive model based cross-selling campaign, it was decided to choose Yapi Kredi's B-type mutual funds, characterized by being low risk investment instruments based on fixed income securities. These funds can be easily purchased via the ATM, Web, and telephone channels.

Cross selling these mutual funds was considered to have a two-fold positive business impact. It served the purpose of acquiring new money from customers, and even those customers transferring their existing investments from other Yapi Kredi products into mutual funds (*cannibalization effect*) was still considered beneficial to the bank. It was decided to offer this product to both customer groups:

1. Customers already having invested into B-type mutual funds to stimulate an increase of the assets
2. Customers not yet owning any B-type fund to help increase product ratio and attract new money

After fixing the product details, how the campaign would be carried out had to be defined. The workshops helped define the start and end date of the campaign: a total duration of five weeks was considered appropriate.

Communication channels for offering the product were agreed upon. A two-channel approach was deemed feasible since Yapi Kredi had just finished the implementation of a project integrating the call center and the bank's branch network. These were considered the right channels for the campaign.

Given the pilot project character of the campaign and the available resources, it had been decided to contact 3,000 customers by branch based on out-bound calls and active marketing during customer branch visits. A total of sixteen branches in the Istanbul area were selected for participation in the campaign. Additionally, 1,200 target customers were to be contacted by the call center.

It was decided to run a two-step campaign, where customers were first contacted with the B-type mutual fund offer. Then, positive responders received a follow-up call if they had not purchased one week after their initial positive response.

Response and purchase rates by contact channel (branch or call centre) were chosen as measures of the campaign's success.

Get Raw Data

A data mart was developed for supporting the activities of the CRM department. To this end, data were extracted from more than fifty source system tables, and about twenty database tables were produced with thirty gigabytes of disk space for the initial project phase. The data mart included data most urgently needed for high-priority business activities (such as the pilot campaign) and easily available in a short time frame.

Identify Relevant Variables

Various aggregations and transformations were required to obtain the right customer-centric data format as needed for analysis and predictive modeling. Basic data-quality crosschecks were performed to assure the validity of the data and its suitability for further data-mining activities.

Different types of attributes were found to be relevant and used to obtain a complete picture of customer behavior and preferences. This included customer attributes describing the following:

- *Demographics.* Age, gender, marital status, group memberships, address, profession, and other identifying characteristics belong in this category.

- *Product ownership.* This relates to product portfolio held by each customer, opening/closing dates, derived variables related to customer's tenure such as maximum tenure of owned products, and so on.
- *Product usage.* Variables are related to a customer's frequency of usage such as the average number of banking transactions.
- *Channel usage.* Variables are related to customer's automatic payment behavior, average amount of automatic payments, ratios of different channels' usage, and so on.
- *Assets.* Variables are related to savings and investment products such as the average balance invested in securities, time deposits, demand deposits, and so on.
- *Liabilities.* Variables are related to loan usage such as average balance on loans, average balance on credit cards, and so on.
- *Profitability.* For the pilot project, a profitability index was created, since profitability was not available for all customers at that time. The index was used for ranking customers according to their profitability without giving its absolute value.

Gain Customer Insight

Based on six months of historical customer data, five different predictive models were developed to estimate a customer's propensity to invest into a B-type mutual fund during the following three-month period. The best model was found to be a logistic regression yielding a lift value of 29 and a cumulative response rate of 14 percent for the top customer percentile. The lift value measures the effect of the predictive model, and expresses the fact that in this case the logistic regression reaches 2.9 times more responders for the top customer percentile than a random selection of the same size.

All customers were then scored using this model, and a set of 4,200 customers with the highest propensity to purchase was selected as the target group for the pilot campaign.

Act

To roll out the campaign through the call center and the branches, each channel had to know exactly which customer to contact. Each channel needed a clear assignment of their respective target customers. A subset of 3,000 customers was assigned to the 16 branches holding the responsibility for the respective relationships. The remaining 1,200 customers were assigned to the call center. The target list with the corresponding channel assignment was then made available to the campaign management system. After preparing call scripts and training the staff involved in its execution, the campaign could start.

The following table summarizes the results obtained. Impressive response rates of 6.5 percent and 12.2 percent, respectively, were obtained with the branch-based and call-center–based part of the campaign. The pilot campaign could acquire more than £1 million into B-type mutual funds.

	Response Rate (%)	Amount of Funds Sold, €
Branches	6.5	582,000
Call center	12.2	452,000
Total	8.2	1,034,000

It is interesting to observe that although the branches obtained a lower response rate than the call center, they still acquired significantly more investment into the funds. This reflects the advantages of the more personal branch-based customer relationship. As a consequence of this successful pilot campaign, a large-scale rollout to a larger part of Yapi Kredi's customers looked very promising.

10.5   SUMMARY

Data mining can assist in selecting the right target customers or in identifying previously unknown customers with similar behavior and needs. A good target list is likely to increase purchase rates and have a positive impact on revenue. A complete data-mining process comprises assessing and specifying the business objectives, data sourcing, transformation and creation of analytical variables, and building analytical models using techniques such as logistic regression and neural networks. The number of variables used changes drastically during the data-mining process. Types of row manipulation include aggregation, change, missing value, and outlier detection. Profitable customer acquisition requires modeling of expected customer potential over the lifetime of the business relationship. In a cross-selling or up-selling model, we model the customer's affinity with a set of products or services translated into the customer's purchase likelihood.

Another aspect of the campaign that should be defined is the set of business or selection rules for a campaign, which specifies the customers who should be excluded from or included in the target groups. To measure how the model based selection is doing with respect to the average customer behavior, the target group can be split into various cells like the control group—containing only randomly selected customers and another cell containing only the best customers according to the model used. It is helpful to define a cost/revenue matrix describing how the business mechanics will work in the supported campaign and how it will impact the data-mining process. Once, the required data have been identified, extract and consolidate the data in a database (often also called *analytical data mart*) so they are readily available for subsequent data manipulation and data-mining steps. Another important step is to check the quality of the analytical raw data. Data warehouse infrastructures with advanced data cleansing processes can help ensure you are working with high-quality data. A preliminary data quality assessment is carried out to assure a good level of quality of the delivered data, and that the data-mining team has a clear understanding of how to interpret the data in business terms. It is important to identify and select only those variables with good explanatory power (relevant predictive power) for the modeled target behavior. In the context of CRM, very often the individual customer is the central object analyzed by means of data mining methods. Usually a very simple, flat data model is chosen as the basis for predictive modeling. In this representation, all data pertaining to an individual customer is contained in one observation (row). Individual columns (variables, fields) represent the conditions at specific points in time or a summary over a whole period. Descriptive statistics such as sums, mean, median, and standard deviation will be employed to capture features of the related time series.

Another key variable to be created during this step is the target or dependent variable, needed for predictive modeling. Once a satisfactory definition of the target variable is achieved, its values will be generated for all customers and added to the existing data tables. Many data-mining tools provide support for increasing normality of the analytical variables. Missing value management is a key element for enhancing the quality of the analytical data set. We also need to reduce the dimensionality (i.e., exclude variables) to get a more parsimonious model. Different methods are employed for selecting the predictor variables. These methods help us drop collinear variables and those with very low correlation with the target variable. The next step is to select the best model to predict the dependent variable. The performance of different competing models is compared using lift charts and classification tables. The final step in the data-mining project is acting based on final results. In this step, customers and prospects are scored and ranked to identify the right customers and prospects to target. Archiving is also an important activity of the data-mining process.

ENDNOTES

1. In the exact sciences, this is similar to a situation where the results obtained from an experiment not repeatable by another group of scientists will not be considered as being meaningful (as happened for instance in the 1990s when cold fusion had been mistakenly announced).

2. An example would be the expectation maximization algorithm (EM) that takes into account the correlation of the data field for which a nonmissing value is to be generated with other data fields.

3. Sometimes, obstacles such as lacking authorization of the data mining team for accessing the required data might emerge. Data miners frequently work with data which other business departments do not have access to. There is a high level of secrecy and trust involved.

4. Here we only have one output variable since we are assuming this to be a customer score of any type. Besides the customer identification number (not counted here) this is all we need to act

5. Kohonen networks belong to the family of neural network techniques. These are powerful data modeling tools able to capture and represent complex input/output relationships for example in target marketing, financial forecasting, or process control. In particular, the objective of a Kohonen network is to generate, out of complex input patterns of arbitrary dimension, a simplified (discrete) map with very few dimensions, say 1 or 2. Thus, the Kohonen network is an approach to quickly understand complex data as a result of a simplification of the structure. For a good overview of neural networks and Kohonen networks please refer to: Principe, Jose C., Neil R. Euliano and Curt Lefebvre (2000), "Neural and Adaptive Systems: Fundamentals Through Simulations" John Wiley and Sons.

6. This is required to ensure a correct measurement of the cause and effect of a campaign. It would, for instance, be unrealistic to positively attribute advertising to a customer's behavior when the customer purchases a product one year after seeing the advertisement in a campaign's direct mail.

CHAPTER 11

Campaign Management

Contents

11.1   OVERVIEW

One important goal of customer value management is to profile the existing customers on the basis of their value and use this information to identify and acquire prospects matching this profile. A marketing campaign helps firms acquire prospects and retain and reward existing customers. For many prospects, the campaign is the first opportunity for engaging in a dialogue with the firm. A dialogue between the firm and customers can effectively change customers' attitudes and behavior toward the firm. Hence, it is very important for the firms to develop, plan, and execute these campaigns effectively and analyze the campaign results carefully.

   A marketing campaign may be executed through one or more channels of customer interaction: phone, direct mail, the Web, wireless devices, e-mail, direct sales, and partner network. The success of a campaign involves reaching out to the right customer with the right offer at the right time and through the right channel. The campaign acts as a rich source of information, and once the campaign is completed, both the marketing manager and sales manager should evaluate the effectiveness of the campaign and use what they have learned for future planning.

In this chapter, we explain the different phases of campaign management processes such as campaign planning and development, campaign execution, and analysis and control. The subphases in each of these main phases are shown in Figure 11-1. In the discussion about campaign planning and development phase, we include issues such as identifying customers, developing communication strategies and media mix, developing an offer, and testing. The campaign execution phase involves actual implementation and subsequent fine-tuning of the campaign. The last phase consists of measurement of campaign results, profile, and response analysis.

11.2 CAMPAIGN MANAGEMENT

A campaign is a series of interconnected promotional efforts designed to achieve precise marketing goals. Managing a campaign encompasses planning, developing, executing, and finally analyzing the campaign results. A campaign is composed of one or more promotions, each of which is an initiative or a device designed to attract the customers' interest. It can be aimed at prospects or existing customers and usually is undertaken within a defined timeframe (such as a season, and generally not exceeding a calendar year). Marketers could use the customer value metric as a means to profitably target campaigns.

As a general rule, a successful campaign management process comprises four connected stages:

1. *Planning.* Strategic process by which decisions are taken. The purposes and objectives of the campaign should be defined and rationalized at this stage.
2. *Development.* Tactical process that takes care of creating the offer, choosing the support and design, choosing the media, and selecting the customer names.
3. *Execution.* Operational process of running the campaign in the media chosen and controlling all related aspects.
4. *Analysis.* Evaluation process of the campaign results in light of the original objectives.

In practice, these stages do not have well-defined boundaries between them and are performed at the same time. Very often, planning and development go together. In the next few sections, we will take a closer look at how each stage is managed.

11.3 CAMPAIGN PLANNING AND DEVELOPMENT

At the campaign planning stage, marketers make strategic decisions that help define the overall objectives of the campaign, the best communication message, and the best target audience. Once these strategic issues are defined, the development phase starts.

11.3.1 SETTING OBJECTIVES AND STRATEGIES

Campaigns have a central role in annual marketing plans, so campaign objectives should be in line with overall marketing and corporate objectives. These objectives are often from the four following categories: market penetration (increase usage or market share); market extension (find new user groups or enter new segments); product development (new products or services); and diversification (new markets and products, new strategies).

FIGURE   11-1   THE CAMPAIGN MANAGEMENT PROCESS

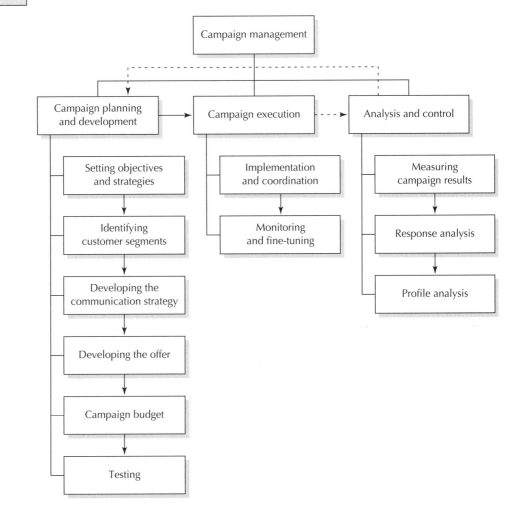

The different marketing strategies already in place should be examined. Questions asked should pertain to the product strategy (What is the product mix?), the pricing strategy (Is price important for market positioning?), the distribution strategy (Which channels does the firm use?), and the promotion strategy (Is the creative strategy consistent with product positioning?).

When defining the campaign strategy, marketers should be able to answer the following additional questions:

1. Who do you want to target? (i.e., Who are the targeted customer segments?)
2. Where should you target? (i.e., What are the channels, and points of contact?)
3. How do you get to them? (i.e., What is the communication strategy and offer?)
4. When is the best time? (i.e., When should you schedule the campaign?)

Who Do You Want to Target?

To answer this question, the company has three options: focusing on existing customers (*retention strategy*), concentrating on getting new customers (*acquisition strategy*), or targeting existing and new customers at the same time (*mixed strategy between retention-acquisition*).

When pursuing a customer retention strategy, ideally the company should target its most profitable customers via LTV (lifetime value) and RFM (recency, frequency, and monetary) analysis. Here are some approaches to target these segments:

- Develop loyalty from the existing customers, via a strong relationship or superior quality or service (e.g., loyalty programs, one-to-one relationships)
- Develop tailor-made products adequate for the needs of the existing customer profiles
- Sell additional products to existing customers also known as cross selling. (e.g., selling an insurance policy to an existing bank customer)
- Sell a superior product (with more features or additional services) to customers who already use similar products, also called *up-selling* (e.g., selling a gold credit card to a regular credit-card holder)
- Merchandise different brands from different categories to the same customer, also known as cross-merchandising (e.g., sell the gold credit card with the best interest rate)

If the company pursues a customer acquisition strategy, it has two options: If it wants to sell the same product to new customers, it should target prospects based on the profile and behavior model of existing customers; if it wants to offer different products to new customers, it should develop new markets.

Where Should You Target?

The company either chooses to act in the markets it already knows (pursue market penetration or extension) or it can choose new markets (market diversification or new product development). It may choose a multichannel strategy (selling the same product in multiple channels like Internet, store, phone, etc.) or a single-channel strategy (selling products in a single channel, like in a store).

How Do You Get to Them?

Getting your customers' and prospects' attention will be one of the goals of the company's communication strategy. Choosing the most effective media (for retention and acquisition strategies) will allow the company to efficiently reach its target segments. The offer proposition will also have a predominant role. What kind of incentives—coupons, gifts, loyalty schemes, and so on—suit a particular customer group? The company should develop the offer according to customer preferences, with the campaign budget being a constraint.

When Is the Best Time?

When preparing a campaign, marketers should be aware that some seasons are better to promote products and services than others. For example, new computer games are released and campaigned during November and December just before Christmas season. Retail banks may campaign for credit cards or personal loans in January, because people are expected to be short on money due to Christmas and New Year expenses. In addition to these examples, the product itself can be seasonable or it can have a short life cycle. For example, sunscreen lotions are sold during summer. Similarly, outdoor sports equipment is advertised before summer time.

Figure 11-2 highlights the core market and product decisions for customer retention and/or customer acquisition strategies.

| **FIGURE** | **11-2** | **CUSTOMER RETENTION AND ACQUISITION STRATEGIES** |

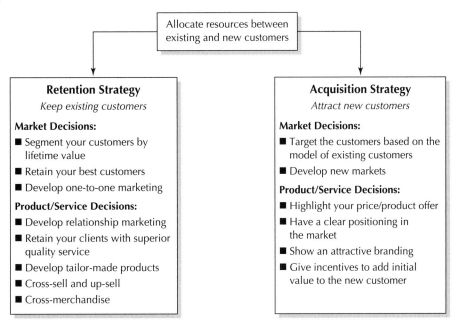

11.3.2 IDENTIFYING CUSTOMER SEGMENTS

Once the campaign objectives are established, the next step involves identifying the customer segments the campaign will target. Customer segments are homogenous groups of individuals that have similar tastes, wants, and needs with respect to the company's products or services. Lifetime segmentation and profiling should guide in targeting the specific customer segments most likely to respond to the company's offer.

Customer segments can be identified in two ways: purchase behavior and profile data. Purchase behavior is recorded in the CRM database and will allow the marketer to segment by product need and by LTV. Profile data will relate the individual customer to his or her response to past campaigns, allowing the implementation of an ROI-driven marketing campaign. Profile data also identify tastes, needs, and preferences of customers, and therefore can be used to target new customers accurately.

Obtaining a successful campaign involves a careful choice of customer segments. Marketers can focus on a strategy-mix of three types of customer groups: the existing customers, the prospects, and the defectors. The existing customers are an important source of information. They provide information about their purchasing behavior, attitudes, and tastes. Their interests, motivations, multichannel usage, and profile can be used to target prospect clients who exhibit a similar profile. The CRM database should record all the information from transactions, surveys, focus groups, complaint records, loyalty card data, Web traffic analysis, and other external sources. Identifying profiles of existing customers will help identify new customers on the market. Defecting customers also provide enlightening information. When defecting, these clients have a reason to do so. Customers can be dissatisfied with the product itself, with the quality of the service offered, or with the company channel management. Paying attention to these customers will help the company learn from past errors. This information is very useful because it allows product improvement and development, better targeting, and better service. If the company listens to what its customers are saying, then it will be able to better satisfy their needs and consequently be profitable in the long run.

How Are Customer Segments Targeted?

Segmentation, as obvious as it sounds, is in many cases not straightforward. The CRM database plays a central role in this step of the campaign process. Effective use of the information on customer behaviors and profiles, channel preferences, and brand awareness will allow the accurate definition of the target segments. Of course, the segmentation can only be as good as the quality of the underlying data.

If the campaign is aimed at retaining existing clients, the firm's CRM system is central to analyzing the recorded purchase behaviors and profiles which will help the marketer adjust the offer to meet the unsatisfied needs of customers. Several analyses could be performed at this stage (e.g., lifetime value segmentation, profiling and RFM).

11.3.3 DEVELOPING THE COMMUNICATION STRATEGY

Marketing communications (marcom) are targeted interactions between the company and its customers and prospects, using one or more media, such as direct mail, newspapers, and magazines, television, radio, telemarketing, and the Internet. A *marcom campaign* may use a single approach (e.g., direct mail) or it can combine several approaches (e.g., direct mail with advertising in television, radio, and newspapers).

When defining the communication strategy, the company identifies and defines to whom the campaign is directed (the target audience), what the campaign message is (content), and which are the best contact channels or media to deliver the content. The marketing team frequently develops the marketing communication plan, but a marketing communication agency (such as an advertising agency or a direct marketing agency) may help in its preparation. If the company chooses to outsource, it hires an agency to execute the marketing communications plan.

The campaign communication strategy will be more effective if planned in an integrated manner. Integrated marketing communications (IMC) is a process that involves the management and organization of the marketing communication tools (media, messages, promotions, and channels) in a way that delivers a clear and consistent message about the company and about the product. The CRM database system allows the effective use of IMC because it stores information about customer and prospect preferences and allows the firm to focus marketing activities toward specific targets.

Marketing communication activities can vary from very small discrete pieces of promotion (such as a mailer), to the development of a larger campaign, which involves many promotional tools (direct mail, press inserts, TV spots), and to the coordination of multiple campaigns to achieve a global objective (increasing the level of cross-selling, customer retention, etc.) It is important to build one or more interlinked databases of each medium as part of the CRM database.

Which Communication Strategy?

Generally, marketers use hybrid combinations of strategies when developing the communication strategy. Some of these strategic approaches are enumerated in Table 11-1.

Prioritizing the target segments that provide a higher potential yield is one objective of the marcom strategy. Targeting these customers in an effective way should maximize the marketing communications ROI. Naturally, some media are more effective at targeting certain groups of customers than others. The challenge is to choose those media that are both effective in achieving the campaign objective and cost-efficient.

The choice of media depends in part on whether existing customers or prospects are targeted. If customers are nonaddressable, broadcast media are used for acquisition. If the prospects' addresses are known, direct-to-customer media may be more effective. In

TABLE   11-1   **COMMUNICATION STRATEGIES**

Strategy	Description	
Generic strategy	No distinction is made between brands. The emphasis is placed on category need rather than brand awareness (e.g., promotions for a product category).	
Preemptive strategy	A generic claim is made about the superiority of the company's brand (e.g., promoting a product that is protected by a patent).	
Unique selling proposition (USP)	It emphasizes the superiority of the brand based on a unique feature or benefit (e.g., promoting a product with a new feature).	
Brand image strategy	It relies on the development of mental or psychological associations through the use of signs, symbols and images.	
Resonance strategy	It attempts to recall events or feelings by evoking meanings, experiences, thoughts, or aspirations relevant to target audiences.	
Affective or emotional strategy	It attempts to invoke involvement and emotion with a powerful message.	
Informational strategy	It is based on the view that an important element of the creative theme is to convey information (e.g., an educational campaign).	
Push promotional strategy	The focus is on a promotional effort by manufacturers of goods and services that encourages the trade channel members to stock, promote, and sell its products.	
Pull promotional strategy	The focus is on a promotional effort that encourages end customers and consumers to demand goods and services.	
Positioning strategies	Positioning by attribute, product characteristic, or consumer benefit	The brand is perceived to be better than others in a particular way. Marketing communications emphasize these features.
	Positioning by price/quality	Positioning can be sought in high price/high quality, prestige positions, low price/acceptable quality positions.
	Positioning by use or application	Segmentation and targeting can be carried out based on usage occasion (e.g., fast food is for people who have little time to eat).
	Positioning by product user	It focuses on the requirements of target customers and consumers.
	Positioning with respect to product category	Rather than competing with another brand, a brand or product category might be positioned against another product category. The competitive focus is placed on substitutes.
	Positioning against a competitor	Brands are promoted with a full understanding of their relative competitive position in the minds of the target audience.
	Cultural positioning	Positioning by cultural reference, where the brand is clearly associated with a particular culture, country, religion, ethnic group, or sense of heritage or tradition.

SOURCE: David Pickton and Amanda Broderick, *Integrated Marketing Communications* (Englewood Cliffs, NJ: Prentice-Hall, 2001).

the case of retention, the firm may spend more on personalized contacts (salesperson, telephone) with high-value clients. For low-value relationships, companies might opt for lower-cost contact channels such as the Internet or mail. In practice, customer acquisition and retention strategies are often mixed. If a company is launching a new product directed at existing customers and new customers, it will use both kinds of media. A brief description of these media is available in Table 11-2. The effect of using media-mix in acquisition and retention strategies can be seen in CRM at Work 11.1.

Marketing Media Tools Most of the media referred in the earlier sections are known as direct marketing media tools. Table 11-3 (pp. 224–225) gives a brief description of what they are and how they are used, together with their advantages and disadvantages. It provides a snapshot of different advertising mediums and their principal characteristics.

11.3.4 DEVELOPING THE OFFER

Developing the offer consists of offering the customer some kind of incentive which will induce him to buy or to ask the company for more information. This offer may range from a free product sample (e.g., getting a free sample of a shampoo in the mail) to price-related incentives (e.g., buying two CDs for the price of one), or an item providing information on the firm (e.g., a free promotion video about the firm's new products).

When developing the offer, the company must keep in mind the established objectives. Some examples of these objectives may be to attract new customers or members, obtain repeated business from existing customers, reactivate lapsed customers, produce sales leads, or acquire new customers. The offer planning should develop upon the required elements.

- What is the product positioning?
- What is the price?
- What is the length of commitment?
- What are the payment terms?
- What are the risk reduction mechanisms?

TABLE 11-2 RETENTION AND ACQUISITION MEDIA

Retention Media	Acquisition Media
Direct Mail:	*TV:*
Mailings:	■ Direct response TV (DRTV)
■ Single-product	■ TV spots
■ Multi-product	■ Home shopping channels
Miscellaneous:	■ Digital TV
■ Birthday cards	*Radio:*
■ Thank-you notes	■ Direct response radio (DRR)
■ Invitations	■ Radio spots
Enclosures:	*Telemarketing:*
■ Statements	■ Outbound
■ Parcels	■ Inbound
Telemarketing:	*Print Media:*
■ Outbound	■ Press/newspapers
■ Inbound	■ Magazines
Catalogues	■ Inserts
Newspapers/bulletins	*Direct mail:*
	■ Mailings
	■ Inserts
	Internet
	Exhibitions/field marketing

CRM AT WORK 11.1

PRO-MARK: COLLECTING INFORMATION ON THE END USERS

Often, manufacturers don't get to know the people who ultimately use their products. Their database can be filled with retailer names but not with the final customer names. This was also the case with Pro-Mark, a $10-million drumstick maker in Houston. Recently, however, this forty-year-old family business developed a database with information on end users by pursuing a print media strategy in different specialized magazines. Pro-Mark wanted to obtain information on its end-user customers in order to know their preferences, so they could build brand-loyalty and perform tests when developing new products.

Pro-Mark advertises regularly in trade publications like the *Modern Drummer.* The company won five awards in the magazine's 1995 reader poll, including the most interesting advertising/marketing campaign. Here are a few of Pro-Mark's campaigns and their payoffs.

Recruiting Test Marketers

One ad, offering free product samples in return for customer feedback, generated more than 3,000 responses. The respondents' names were entered into a database, and each received a catalog in addition to the sample drumsticks. The new test marketers proved to be conscientious reviewers. For example, when Pro-Mark tested a product prototype, it sent samples to 125 drummers. Only one failed to return the detailed questionnaire. For the first two years of the project, the company achieved a remarkable 100 percent response rate.

Profiling End Users

In June 1995, Pro-Mark ran a simple black-and-white ad asking readers to nominate themselves to be selected as the "Not Yet Famous Drummer." Readers sent their photograph and filled out a survey form indicating preferences in drumsticks, music styles, and bands—information that helps Pro-Mark target future ads. The contest not only made stars of the winning unknown drummers, whose pictures appeared in subsequent ads in *Modern Drummer,* but more importantly doubled Pro-Mark's database of names. Five thousand people entered the contest and the company received 100 calls a week for several months.

Promoting New Products

When Pro-Mark wanted to draw attention to former Pearl Jam drummer Dave Abbruzzese's new autographed drumsticks, it printed a coupon allowing readers to buy them for $5 and enter a contest to win a chance to meet Abbruzzese in person. More than 3,500 people sent back coupons, and Pro-Mark had a chance to add these names to its catalog mailing list. The company's only costs were the black-and-white ad and the famous drummer's fees.

At the same time as marketers look at these elements, they should also be seeking answers to the following questions:

- How much can they afford to spend on the incentive? For example, what is the allowable marketing cost?
- Which promotion type should be used as an incentive? (price-incentives, free samples, coupons, etc.)
- What should be the promotional package? (creative message, design, materials, etc.)
- Which promotional media should be used? (television, radio, direct mail, etc.)
- Does it involve one-stage or several stages?

| TABLE 11-3 | MEDIA CHARACTERISTICS (PART 1 OF 2) |

Medium	Principal Characteristics
DIRECT MAIL (letters, catalogues, price lists, brochures, leaflets, booklets, circulars, newsletters, cards, samples, etc.)	Direct mail consists of mailing pieces that can range from a postcard to a sophisticated package. A classic direct mail package is composed of an envelope, a letter, a brochure, a reply device and/or other inserts. *Advantages* — *Disadvantages* Accurate targeting — High cost per contact Unique capacity to involve the recipient — Long start-up time Creative flexibility / Unlimited formats — Demands a large variety of knowledge and skills Discrete — Limited potential Ease of reply No direct competition Highly testable Most controllable
DIRECT MAIL CATALOGUES	Direct mail also includes *catalogues,* which are small booklets that give a complete enumeration and description of the company's products and services. *Advantages* — *Disadvantages* Summarizes the company product range — Hazard acquisition of new names Distinctive positioning — Associated with "junk mail" Creative flexibility Timeliness Cost controllable Has a repurchase cycle Database construction and manipulation
TELEMARKETING	Telemarketing is approaching customers via telephone. Its use led to the creation of call centers as a distribution channel. Telemarketing can be used in two ways: outbound and inbound. In the outbound version the company contacts the customers with a special motive (a promotion, a survey, or a follow-up). In the inbound mode it is the customer that is induced to initiate the contact. *Advantages* — *Disadvantages* Highly targeted — Expensive Efficient and direct — Number of prospects reached is limited Immediate feedback — Difficult to retain good employees Fast response time — No visual appeal Easily tested — Intrusive Builds and maintains customer relationships — Associated with "cheap selling" Incremental effectiveness Increased levels of customer service
PRINT MEDIA	Print media consists of advertisements or inserts in written communication media, such as newspapers and magazines. This media focuses on media reach (i.e., reaching as many readers as possible). Classical uses in print media are: advertisements in magazines, newspapers or newspaper supplements and freestanding inserts.
Newspapers (local, regional, international, daily, weekly, weekend)	*Advantages* — *Disadvantages* Low cost per thousand circulation — Often poor color Rapid, predictable response — Poor selectivity Moderate lead time, late deadlines — No personalization Wide variety of formats — Newspaper rates vary Broad local coverage — Sometimes affected by local conditions Inexpensive testing — Less selectivity than mail or phone Frequency, immediacy and reach Year-round availability
Magazines (local, regional, national international, weekly, monthly, annual, consumer, business, trade, technical, professional, etc.)	*Advantages* — *Disadvantages* Low cost per thousand circulation — Slower response Easily controlled costs — Less space to tell story Moderate lead time, late deadlines — Less personal Excellent research data on readers — Less selectivity than mail or phone Wide coverage of all markets Wide choice of readers profiles Good color reproduction Long ad life Test inexpensively Advertising in a trust environment Frequency, immediacy, and reach Year-round availability
Inserts	*Advantages* — *Disadvantages* High volumes — Reduced flexibility Cost efficient — Not very popular Flexible design — No proof on insertion Impact on customers Informative Testable

TABLE	11-3	MEDIA CHARACTERISTICS (PART 2 OF 2)

Medium	Principal Characteristics	
BROADCAST MEDIA **(Analog/digital)**		
TV (terrestrial, satellite, cable, local, regional, national, international)	TV media methods are: direct-response television (DRTV) (interacts with the viewer inviting him to buy), infomercials (TV spots) that inform or describe the products and home shopping channels.	
	Advantages	*Disadvantages*
	Powerful demonstration capability	Limited copy time
	Fast response	Limited response options
	Wide choice of time buys	Difficult to perform split tests
	Total market coverage	Expensive (production costs and airtime cost)
	Strong support medium	Can take a long time to produce
	Brand awareness and differentiation	Information content limited
Radio (local, regional, national, international)	Radio can either use direct response radio (DRR) or radio spots that merely describe and advertise the product or service.	
	Advantages	*Disadvantages*
	Excellent targeting	No response device
	Cost efficient	Limited copy time
	High frequency	No visual appeal
	Involvement, friendliness, and loyalty	Creative treatment and quality often very mixed/poor
	Short start-up times	Audience passive receivers of information
	Powerful support medium	
INTERNET (www, Web page, e-mail)	Advertisement on the Web can be via: banner ads, button ads, sponsorships or co-branded ads, keyword ads, and affiliate marketing.	
	Advantages	*Disadvantages*
	Attracts customers and prospects to the site	Diminishing returns
	Engaging and interactive	Involves Web site maintenance
	Personalized	Involves investment in IT
	Builds database on customer preferences	Audience not guaranteed
	Cost efficient	Relies on browsers to find pages
	Interactivity possible	Hits may not represent interest (casual browsers)
	Message can be quickly and easily changed	
DOOR-TO-DOOR	Advertising door-to-door consists in selecting a residential area to promote or sell a product. Usually is delivered in each household with the normal mail by the postal services or in the form of insert in a local free newspaper.	
	Advantages	*Disadvantages*
	Targeted	Poor personalization
	High penetration	Diminishing returns
	No duplication of coverage	Insufficient customer knowledge
	Versatile/no format restrictions	
	Test possibilities	
	Low cost	
	Ideal primary medium	
POSTERS (outdoors-boards, outdoor-transports, inside)	Posters can be placed on boards in the streets, in railway stations, in buses or taxis, or even in shopping centers and underground trains.	
	Advantages	*Disadvantages*
	Reaches broad audience	Creative limitations
	High repeated exposure	Short exposure time
	Relative low cost	Limited audience selectivity
	Strong impact	Message must be simple
	High geographic selection	
	High visibility	
CINEMA	Advertising in cinemas can be made via advertising spots before the movie and during the breaks. It's usage varies across countries.	
	Advantages	*Disadvantages*
	High quality production	High cost of production
	Captive audience	Limited audience size
	High selectivity via movie and cinema choice	Limited response options
	High creative flexibility	

Answers to these questions will help estimate campaign costs and profitability. These answers should be recorded in the CRM system. They will be used as a model to fine-tune the campaign results.

Table 11-4 provides a list and a brief description of what kind of options a company can offer its customers and prospects.

CRM at Work 11.2 gives an example of a company that used a successful retention strategy to do repeat business with its existing customers.

11.3.5 CAMPAIGN BUDGET

The campaign budget allocates resources and coordinates expenditures across the marketing activities associated with the campaign (advertising fees, testing costs, list rentals, etc). When calculating the campaign budget, the marketer will use a mix of estimates for both

TABLE 11-4	OFFER OPTIONS
Offer Option	**Description**
Price incentives	The customer gets a discount off the regular purchase price (a specific dollar amount or a percentage discount).
Payment options	Makes it easier for customers to buy. These can be company's credit cards, easy pay plans, and so on.
"You have been specially chosen"	Recognition is a motivating factor for customers. If they feel special, they are more willing to buy. Offering something special to regular customers or inviting them to be part of a special club are some variations of this offer type.
Premiums	A premium is usually a free item or a nominal fee offered as an incentive to purchase a particular product or service (free information, gifts, etc.)
Samples	Offer samples of the product or service to be sold.
Free trial	Offer the customers a free-trial period to try the product.
Automatic shipment	Keep sending out merchandise to customers until they cancel their order. Many publishing companies do this in order to renew subscriptions.
"Member gets member"	One effective way of getting new customers is offering regular customers a gift or a dollar incentive to introduce others to the company's product or service.
Early bird offer	Customers who buy before the deadline pay a special low price.
Contests and sweepstakes	Effectiveness is attributed to the possibility of the customer building an association between purchasing a product and increasing the chances of actually winning a prize or a gift.
Multiple discount offers	Customers who spend a lot of money with the company like to receive special treatment, so companies can offer discount on big volume purchases, for example.
Multiple product offer	Companies group related products under one price and entice customers to buy the whole package.
Deluxe edition	The company offers the regular product at a specific price and then it offers the deluxe edition or the enhanced version of the product at a promotional cost.
Bounce-back	When a customer puts in or makes an order, the company includes another offer in the package it sends.
Money-back guarantee	The manufacturer or retailer offers a guarantee or warranty—an oral or written promise—that it will stand behind a product or service.

SOURCE: Nicholas J. De Bonis and Roger S. Peterson, *The AMA Handbook for Managing Business to Business Marketing Communications* (Chicago: NTC Business Books, 1997).

CRM AT WORK 11.2

CALIFORNIA COSMETICS, INC.

California Cosmetics, Inc. is a mail-order company that sells specialized skin cleaners and toners. The firm decided on a retention campaign for existing customers, since the company is able to achieve net profit margins of more than 25 percent on these clients.

When designing the campaign, California Cosmetics, Inc. used a demographic database that it had compiled while receiving orders. Usually, the company call operators would ask for the birth dates of the customers who called in and would add this information to the database.

Knowing the birthdate provided the creative idea for the campaign offer. Each existing customer was offered a birthday present. The gift consisted of a set of three small makeup brushes that cost the company 45¢. With the brushes were enclosed a $5 gift certificate and a birthday card. The whole package cost, including postage, was $1. The campaign results were impressive: 40 percent of the people who got birthday presents placed an order within days. That amounted to a 40 percent customer repeat rate, well above the 12 percent level the company had been averaging.

directly measurable and less easily measured activities (e.g., the long-term effect of advertising). In reality, the estimates for these less measurable activities come from similar past experiences, benchmarking, or plain guesswork. Although this might look unconventional, it is still better to make an educated guess than to neglect these estimates. In general, allocating the optimum financial resource level to each activity is a difficult task, and that is why arriving at a campaign budget should be a balance between measurement, financial calculations, competitive analysis, and good judgment.

There are many ways to calculate a budget. Some companies think of the campaign budget as a percentage of turnover derived from the sales forecast of a particular product or service (e.g., the general management establishes a sales objective of $2 million and states that the marketing department can only afford $500,000 on marketing activities with this product). Other firms may look at the previous year's budget and adjust it for the campaigns for the current year (e.g., the company spent $500,000 on last year's marketing activities and this year is going to adjust it for the price increase of advertisement fees, inflation, etc.)

While there are no right or wrong ways to calculate a budget, we will present seven common methods to calculate a budget and present their main advantages and disadvantages:

1. Preset budgeting
2. Budgeting for an allowable marketing cost
3. Budgeting with the competitive parity method
4. Budgeting with the objective and task method
5. Budgeting with the percentage of sales method
6. Budgeting with key performance indicators
7. Budgeting using the lifetime value method

Preset Budgeting

Most companies determine a given year's marketing expenditure on the basis of what they spent the year before, by applying a ratio that adjusts media cost inflation, projected sales increase or decrease, market conditions, and so on.

Advantages   The campaign budget won't be drastically cut over the years, so it will follow a more or less steady expenditure flow.

Disadvantages   Working with a preset budget that doesn't take into account last year's sales is the least effective way of calculating a budget. Companies treat marketing as an expenditure instead of as an investment to boost future sales. As a consequence, working with this kind of budget planning may be hazardous for the firm, rendering its business less competitive and slower to change.

Although this is the least effective way to establish a budget, it is in fact one of the most commonly adopted.

Budgeting for an Allowable Marketing Cost

Budgeting for an allowable marketing cost (AMC) consists of determining the amount that can be spent on campaign marketing activities, while preserving the required profit margin. Each potential expenditure is given priority according to its forecast for return on investment, and each investment is given equal consideration. Its objective is to achieve the optimum revenue per customer and maximize sale profits. The AMC is obtained by subtracting the costs (cost of goods + distribution costs) and the required profit margin from the total sales value.

Advantages   When using the AMC there is no preset limit to the campaign budget unless a cash-flow constraint is imposed. By using this method the company controls costs.

Disadvantages   Many activities are hard to accurately forecast, and some activities may not pay back in a given year. These intricacies lead to a degree of conservatism that inhibits the aggressive pursuit of an AMC marketing policy.

Example   One of the main sources of revenue for "Old Books Limited" comes from the subscription fees of its monthly magazine, *Rare Books*. In order to preserve this source of revenue, it has two choices: either put in place a cold mailing to obtain new subscribers or a mailing to existing subscribers, inviting them to renew their subscription. It calculated the allowable marginal cost of each activity and discovered that sending four invitations (i.e., four direct mailings) to existing customers had a lower marginal cost than doing a cold mailing.

Budgeting with the Competitive Parity Method

Competitive parity tries to equate budget allocation with those of competitors. Organizations in competitive environments may opt for this budget technique.

Advantages   In this method, emphasis is on competitor intelligence. By checking out what the competition is doing, the company is adapting itself to the market conditions.

Disadvantages   It is difficult to be precise as to who your competitors are. It is also difficult to estimate the relative size of competitors, because a company's nearest competitor may be significantly bigger or smaller than your company. Next, marketing communication strategies are certainly different for market leaders and for market followers and budgeting based on parity may thus not be very wise. This method cannot satisfactorily take into account sudden changes in the competitive activity or objectives. It does not take into account the company's own objectives.

Budgeting with the Objective and Task Method

This method focuses on, first, determining the marketing objectives, and then deciding on the marketing communication tasks needed to achieve those objectives. By calculating the costs of these tasks, a budget can be set.

Advantages This method focuses on marketing objectives. The resources are expended according to the objectives.

Disadvantages Implementing this method is a difficult task because it is not always easy to define the objectives and to quantify their implementation costs. This method also makes an important presumption: It assumes that the relationship between objectives and tasks is well known and understood.

Budgeting with the Percentage of Sales Method

A fixed percentage of turnover is allocated to marketing communications. The marketing communication expenditure is directly linked to sales level. In order to determine the exact percentage to be allocated, the company looks at competitor allocations and industry averages. To define the turnover, the company can look at historic sales.

Advantages This method incorporates a series of alternatives, and it allocates costs to the objectives.

Disadvantages It may be difficult to determine the percentage of sales that must be allocated. Competitors may have a small advertising budget and concentrate their budgets on the sales force, and this would be a deceiving benchmark.

Budgeting with Key Performance Indicators

Determining the campaign budget via some key performance indicators is a process that allows the company to figure out, in a quick way, how much it can afford to spend on a special promotion. Sometimes this analysis is called *front-end analysis*. This analysis is done with simple performance measures such as the *cost per sale,* the *conversion rate,* the *cost per inquiry,* the *marketing cost ratio,* or the *return on investment.* These performance indicators are summarized in Table 11-5.

E-mail presents itself as an effective way to engage customers in a dialogue. As a flexible and consumer-preferred communication vehicle, e-mail has applications across acquisition, retention, and customer service. Messages can be tailored to each customer based on her/his stage of the buying process. E-mail also allows customers to opt in with their own preferences.

Table 11-6 and 11-7 show the key performance indicators from a study performed by Forrester research, "the e-mail marketing dialogue," which shows that in 1999, e-mail was the second-most effective technique for driving traffic to a Web site.[1] Retention e-mail generated 10 percent click-through rates on in-house lists. But, using e-mail as a customer acquisition tool is expensive because rented lists are also expensive.

Budgeting with the Lifetime Value Method

Budgeting in the most effective and efficient way would imply reducing expenditures to a unit cost basis in order to focus on the value of individual customers and on the different values per customer. Given the data recorded in the CRM database, the company may

TABLE 11-5 **KEY PERFORMANCE INDICATORS**

Performance Measure	Formula	Definition	Example Case of a Direct Mailing to 10,000 Customers that Costs $12,395
Cost per thousand (CPM)	CPM = (Total promotion expense/Total quantity) × 1,000	Relates the total cost of a promotion with the quantity produced	The CPM is (12,395/10,000) × 1,000 = $1,239.50
Cost per response (CPR)	CPR = (Total promotion expense/number of responses)	Ratio between total campaign costs and the number of responses obtained	The number of responses to the mailing was 340. Therefore, the CPR was $36.50.
Cost per enquiry (CPE)	CPE = (Total promotion expense/total orders)	Ratio of the total campaign costs by the total inquiries	If the number of orders was 252, then the CPE was $49.20.
Cost per sale (CPS)	CPS = [Total promotion expense/(total orders – Returns and bad debts)]	Ratio between the total costs and the enquiries that were converted into sales, net of returns and bad debts	From the 252 enquiries or orders received, the company had 16 returns and 3 cases of bad debt; therefore, the CPS was $12,395/ (252 – 16 – 3) = $53.20.
Conversion rate (CR)	CR (%) = (number of buyers/number of responders) × 100	Calculated by comparing the number of buyers with the number of responders to the campaign	In this case, the CR would be (233/252) × 100 = 92%, which means that the company converts 9 of 10 customers with this campaign.
Return on Investment (ROI)	ROI = Sales Revenue/ Total promotion expense	Ratio between sales revenue and the campaign cost	Each sale represents $75 and since the company made 233 sales, the ROI will be a ratio of 7/5 (1.4), which means that for each $5 spent in the campaign you obtain $7 from your customers.

TABLE 11-6 **E-MAIL CAMPAIGN KEY PERFORMANCE INDICATORS**

	CPM	Click-Through Rate	Purchase Rate	CPS
Rented lists	$200	3.5%	2.0%	$286
Sponsored e-mail	$93	2.5%	0.8%	$465
In-house lists	$5	10.0%	2.5%	$2

SOURCE: Forrester Research, Inc.

predict ongoing customer value rather than only the individual sales revenue. Knowing the lifetime value of each customer will allow the company to compare returns on alternative marketing expenditures and to compare return on expenditure from obtaining business from existing customers or from new ones. This gives the opportunity to efficiently allocate the budget using the most profitable strategies.

Advantages   Using the CRM database information allows the company to predict, in a more accurate way, the cost of the campaign. At the same time, it efficiently allocates

TABLE	11-7	E-MAIL CAMPAIGN CUSTOMER ACQUISITION AND RETENTION PARAMETERS

	Customer Acquisition			Customer Retention	
	Direct Mail to Rented List	**Banner Advertising**	**E-mail to Rented List**	**Direct Mail to House List**	**E-mail to House List**
CPM (cost per thousand)					
Production	$462	N/A	N/A	$462	N/A
Media	$118	$15	$200	N/A	N/A
Delivery	$270	$1	N/A*	$270	$5
Total	$850	$16	$200	$686	$5
Click-through rate	N/A	0.8%	3.5%	N/A	10%
Purchase rate	1.2%	2.0%	2.0%	3.9%	2.5%
Cost per sale	$71	$100	$286	$18	$2

*Delivery costs for rented lists are incorporated into list media costs.

SOURCE: Forrester Research, Inc.

resources between strategies because it allows a comparison between the returns of alternative marketing campaigns.

Disadvantages   It is very difficult to keep track of customer values because most companies lack transactional data from customers. Forecasting the customer LTV as a budgeting measure is still in its infancy. Also, if the company doesn't keep track of the performance results of past campaigns, it won't be able to compare these results with similar campaigns and learn from past errors. Sometimes the strategy that produces the highest ROI does not provide the fastest return and therefore, it can be replaced by faster strategies with lower ROI.

Ideally, budgeting should use LTV forecasts to determine the cost of a campaign. In practice, this may be hard to implement. So in this case, the marketer should proceed with both front-end analysis and with the allowable marketing cost analysis. Keep in mind that no budget should be done without estimation of the return of marketing investment (ROI rates). Unfortunately, the preset budgeting is still a very common practice among companies, but it should ideally be replaced by the other methods discussed.

11.3.6   TESTING

Testing involves conducting a comparison between different ways of proceeding with a campaign. In general, it is performed under a simple rule: You test individual campaign elements, other elements remaining constant, and you measure the resultant change in the performance of the campaign. Testing should concentrate first and foremost on the most important variables and parameters. More importantly, one should aim to test all the key parameters, not just one of them.

Testing is based on a basic principle. Take the current set-up of the campaign and use it as the *control* for the test. Then select the element you want to test and change it. Next, select a sample of your target customers and run a test with the changed element. Comparing the performance results of the test version with the control will illustrate the impact of this variable on the overall campaign objectives.

What Are the Benefits of Testing?

Testing has value-added benefits that can improve your campaign success and performance. Some of the most important ones are listed as follows:

- Testing shows real behavior, because it provides a (close to) real environment in which behavior is validated.
- Testing augments and validates research.
- Testing also stimulates creativity, since it not only provides healthy internal competition but also presents a challenge to the creative team to find ways to beat the control campaign.
- Tests protect the company's greatest asset (the customers): By using only small samples with each test you will finally give your customers the proven offer.
- Tests minimize financial risk and avoid costly errors.
- Tests uncover ways to reduce costs.

In general, tests help maximize the performance of the campaign. They are low cost (when compared with the overall campaign costs) and fast in providing results. They are reliable (as you resort to quantitative analyses), simple to execute, and easy to prepare (as there are less customers involved). It is important that tests be done on an ongoing basis, and not be looked at as a one-time task.

What Should You Test?

We can test almost everything in a campaign. A key variable is the target audience, which is in the form of a list of targeted customers and prospects. We can also test the offer variables (prices, incentives, proposition), the format (physical shape, the *feel,* and the size), the creative element (the appeal, the tone, and the message), the media, and/or the timing.

When determining the budget, the company should consider the importance it wants to give to testing, since this has a cost. If the marketing campaign is based on a well-known process (e.g., the company uses past designs of campaigns to promote similar products or services), then testing could be carried out with one or two tests, in order to make minor improvements. If the campaign aims at something new, like product or market development, then testing should be more exhaustive.

Does Testing Predict the Future?

Testing allows you to do a small-scale measurement of the potential campaign results. It can accurately give you the performance results for the overall campaign, through the testing of the following performance measures:

- *Response to the campaign, in percentage.* Running a test campaign will generate results from the customers selected to participate in it. The number of responses obtained (e.g., customer subjects who responded positively to the incentive), divided by the total number of customers selected, will give the response rate, in percentage. This number will serve as an indicator of the success that the particular campaign being tested can achieve.
- *Campaign profitability.* The performance results of the test allow you to do an estimate of the revenues of the real campaign. From this, you should deduct the total campaign costs (expenses of preparing the campaign, testing costs plus those of running the campaign). This gives you a prediction for the profitability of the campaign.

CRM AT WORK 11.3

TESTING THE MEDIA BEFORE THE ROLL-OUT

The Executive Corner, Limited produces executive accessories such as leather briefcases, business card cases, binoculars, golf scopes, desktop accessories, leather mouse pads, and other corporate gifts.

The company is launching a campaign to promote a cigar case to new customers. The campaign customer objective is to acquire 1,000 customers. The company can afford $30 per customer (AMC = $30), and the gross margin per sale will be $50. The campaign budget for this program is $30,000 ($30 × 1,000).

The proposed campaign strategy is to run in four types of media: Internet, direct mail (a mailing), telemarketing, and magazine advertisement. The company will run a test with some customers (test target audience) to assess the most effective media. The firm has acquired customer lists for the different media and will conduct the test using a 5 percent sample for each, as shown in Table 11-8. For testing, the firm decided to send promotion e-mails to 3,000 and a mailing to 3,000 prospects. Telephone calls will be made to 500 prospects from a rental list. It also opted to insert an ad in the magazine *Top Management* whose readers are mostly top executives. The test campaign is an actual campaign resulting in effective sales, but conducted in a smaller scale with respect to the final campaign.

The first step is to determine the test budget and its size relative to the total campaign budget. Multiplying the cost per medium by the audience size gives the total test budget cost, which is $10,800. This figure represents 36% of the campaign budget (calculations are shown in Table 11-9).

Breakeven target response rates, which quantify the number of customers needed to cover the testing costs, can be obtained . This is calculated as the ratio between test costs ($10,800) and the AMC ($30) for each medium (e.g., 40 customers would be needed to respond to the cold mailing, representing 1.3 percent of the 3,000 target audience size, to cover the mailing costs).

Having run the test, the firm gets actual response rates. These will help estimate the effectiveness of each medium, by comparing the target response rates (needed to break even on campaign costs) and the actual test response rate (which is an estimate for the campaign roll-out results). Table 11-9 presents the results.

Next, with the actual test response rate, the firm can calculate the total gross margin of running the test, which is obtained by multiplying the actual number of customers who made a purchase by the gross margin per sale ($50). The net profit margin will consist of subtracting the test costs from the total gross margin. At this stage the firm has all the necessary elements to determine the ROI of each medium. The ROI is the ratio between the net profit margin and the test cost, expressed as a percentage. Table 11-10 shows the results.

Given these results, the firm should run the campaign with the media that presented the highest ROI: e-mail to prospective customers.

After the test campaign, there is a remaining budget of $19,200 of the original $30,000. This will be used to send e-mails to the remaining 57,000 e-mail addresses not used by the test. Total cost for the e-mail campaign will be $17,100, which leaves $2,100 for the next best ROI-medium: an ad in *Top Management* magazine. However, the cheapest ad insertion available in this magazine costs $5,000, well over the remaining budget. It is still possible to use the third-best ROI medium: direct mail using a rental list. A total of 5,250 promotional letters can be sent.

| **TABLE** | **11-8** | **TEST AUDIENCE SIZES PER MEDIUM** |

Medium	Customer Lists Held (Total Target Audience)	Test Target Audience
Internet	60,000 prospects	3,000 prospects
Mailing	60,000 prospects	3,000 prospects
Telephone	10,000 prospects	500 prospects
Magazine advertisement	2,000,000 prospects	100,000 prospects

| TABLE | 11-9 | COSTS OF TESTING, BREAKEVEN TARGET RESPONSES, AND TEST RESULTS |

Medium	Cost ($) per 1,000	Target Audience Size	Test Cost ($)	Number of Customers Needed to Break Even	Target Response Rate (%)	Actual Number of Test Respondents	Actual Response Rate
E-mail using a rental list	300	3,000	900	30	1.0%	33	1.1%
Direct mail using a rental list	400	3,000	1,200	40	1.3%	40	1.3%
Telemarketing to existing customers	6,200	500	3,100	103	20.7%	61	12.2%
Top Management magazine	56	100,000	5,600	187	0.2%	200	0.2%
Total			**10,800**	**360**		**334**	

| TABLE | 11-10 | NET PROFIT MARGIN AND ROI PER MEDIUM OF TEST |

Medium	Actual Response Rate (%)	Actual Number of Customers	(A) Total Gross Margin ($)	(B) Test Cost ($)	(C) = (A) – (B) Net Profit Margin ($)	(D) = (C)/(B) Return on Investment (%)
E-mail using a rental list	1.1%	33	1,650	900	750	83%
Direct mail using a rental list	1.3%	40	2,000	1,200	800	67%
Telemarketing to existing customers	12.2%	61	3,050	3,100	–50	–2%
Top Management magazine	0.2%	200	10,000	5,600	4,400	79%
Total		**334**	**16,700**	**10,800**	**5,900**	

Testing in Different Media

Direct Mail   Just about any element in the direct mail is testable, ranging from the format and the package, the message, the creativity concept, the distribution lists to the offer itself. This is possible for direct mail because the direct marketer controls every aspect of the campaign, including the timing and the budget.

Telemarketing   In one call session, the telephone operators can promote a particular product or service, can test a different script, or can test a promotion. In a single day direct marketers can have enough responses to obtain a fairly good indication about the success of the offer. The time of response to a phone call is one of the unquestionable advantages of telemarketing.[2]

Press and Inserts   When testing in print advertisement, the direct marketer can test almost everything about the editorial fit: the audience composition, the magazine/newspaper circulation, the ad placement cost, the timing of the ad placement, its frequency, and the position of the ad or its color. Although testing is possible, it is not as easy and inexpensive as telemarketing or direct mail. The most used tests are split-run testing, A/B splits, and cross-over testing.

Split-Run Testing Split-run testing is usually used for inserts. It compares the same title or message in two different insert formats, by alternating them in the print run. Basically, you insert a different code or a different phone number in each format so as to track which version has the best response rate.

Example of a Split-Run Test A company that produces crystal glasses for different types of wine is going to test four different ads (B, C, D, and E) against a control ad A to find out which ad performs better. This test will be performed in four different wine magazines with different audiences.

Magazines	Cost ($)	Control	Control Response	CPR Control	Test	Test Response	CPR Test	Lift* (%)
World Wine	1,736	A	331	29.6	B	396	24.7	20%
Wine Magazine	2,756	A	277	35.4	C	356	27.5	29%
Wine Enthusiast	2,960	A	308	31.8	D	282	34.8	–8%
Food & Wine	2,348	A	325	30.2	E	400	24.5	23%
Total	**9,800**		**1,241**	**7.9**		**1,434**	**6.8**	

*Lift is the variation, in percent, between the CPR control and the CPR test.

Analyzing the test results, ads B, C and E reveal a greater lift than ad A. In this particular test, ad C will be chosen to run the campaign because it presents the greatest lift of all the ads tested.

A/B Splits You run two versions of the print run (A and B) in alternative copies of the same publication. Usually, creative or color changes are tested this way. As in split-run testing, you should devise a mechanism for tracking response.

Cross-Over Testing You run two versions of the same advertisement: one version changes the creative message (A), the other changes the color (B). Then you insert version A in the first issue of magazine 1 and in the second issue of magazine 2. You then insert version B in the second issue of magazine 1 and in the first issue of magazine 2. This enables you to compare the response improvement when creative elements or color were changed. The response change in magazine 1 assesses the creative elements change, while response change in magazine 2 evaluates the color effect.

Example of a Cross-Over Test Following the preceding example, imagine that the company wants to cross-over test ad A with ad B in two wine magazines.

	World Wine		*Food & Wine*	
	Control	Control Response	Control	Control Response
First issue	A	331	B	308
Second issue	B	277	A	325

In this case it is possible to compare the results of each issue of both magazines and compare creative concepts. Ad A performed better in the first issue of *World Wine* than in the second issue of *Food & Wine*. Ad B performed better in the first issue of *Food & Wine* than in the second issue of *World Wine*. If we compare the creative concepts, we realize that ad A always obtains higher responses than ad B. The test conclusion would be, always roll out with ad A.

How Reliable Are the Test Predictions?

Testing is meant to allow the marketer to make inferences using established methods of analysis. It is beyond the scope of this book to explain in detail the statistical models used to analyze test results. Some of the statistical techniques that can be used for this purpose are hypothesis testing, confidence intervals, and analysis of variance. For more on these techniques, readers can refer to *Marketing Research* by Aaker, Kumar, and Day.[3]

What Are the Potential Problems in Testing?

For testing to support profitable campaigns, one should be aware of the following potential errors:

- *The marketer should avoid performing several tests with the same set of customers.* If you keep using the same group of customers for several runs of one campaign test, you should expect lower response rates. The same thing happens if you use the same fixed group for several campaigns in a short period of time. You must be aware of the extent to which there are diminishing returns. Therefore, you should plan the ideal frequency with which a customer is approached (i.e., the point where the marginal cost of testing exceeds the marginal revenue generated by the test).
- *Testing results have limited time validity.* Since customer preferences change over periods of time, conclusions drawn from tests are sometimes short-lived. Ongoing tests may provide adequate responses which reflect these changes.
- *Don't test the same things all over again.* As testing means only changing one or few variables, other things equal, change the analysis variable so you can see what changes in the results.
- *Overall marketing objectives should drive your testing.* More important than optimizing a particular campaign is to have a successful marketing program.

11.4 CAMPAIGN EXECUTION

The campaign execution stage is the operational process by which a campaign is implemented. There are two important aspects at this stage: implementation and monitoring.

11.4.1 IMPLEMENTATION AND COORDINATION

A thin line separates the development from the implementation stage. This difference arises from the fact that implementation summarizes everything that was developed and identifies all that has to be done before actually running the campaign. In order to implement the campaign, an action plan should be prepared to guide this process and all the resources involved. This plan should be divided into three subplans:

1. The campaign program
2. The campaign schedule
3. The activity schedule

Campaign Program

The campaign program is a summary of everything to be executed to run the campaign. It should lay out the list of tasks to be accomplished. These are to be assigned to a list of team members. It should contain the campaign briefing forms designed for members of the team and outside suppliers (e.g., advertising agency, merchandise suppliers, etc). In order to coordinate the tasks between all persons involved, each task should have a defined completion deadline. The summary of all these deadlines should result in the campaign timetable. Once the media and the promotion offer are chosen, the marketing team should create a description of all materials to be produced (the format, the color, the creative message) and events to take place (if it is a one-stage or a two-stage campaign).

Campaign Schedule

The campaign schedule lists the events planned, as well as their respective timing. If this campaign is planned to coincide with other marketing activity, a clash schedule should be created to identify potential conflicts of resources, timing, and customer targets.

There are two key differences between the campaign and the activity schedule. The first one is directly related to the campaign components, and the second one relates to the operational activity of the company itself.

Activity Schedule

It is important to organize your company's activity during a campaign. Interdependent actions should be identified and time should be efficiently allocated for the completion of activities. It is at this stage that the critical path method can be applied. The critical path technique involves placing a time factor in each phase of the campaign, figuring out the necessary precedent activities for each one and sequencing all the campaign phases (basically, it works as a backward timetable). One advantage of this method is that it identifies potential bottlenecks and allows revision.

One important feature of activity scheduling is that not only does it allow sufficient time for completion and approval of the tasks, but also it keeps the information up to date. Even when the campaign is running, its status will continue to be reported. The example of a Gantt chart[4] is shown in Figure 11-3.

11.4.2 MONITORING AND FINE-TUNING

Monitoring is an ongoing process. Adjustments such as scheduling modifications should be made throughout as part of the ongoing process. However, the full effect of the campaign cannot be totally known until all the results have been received and analyzed. If the company is running an integrated campaign where results can be tracked through response, then the first status report will show the preliminary results that should be compared with the forecast results. Acting on the first results will allow a timely corrective action, and the more up-to-date the report, the more useful the corrections will be.

One question that should arise is, "How can this process be fine-tuned?" Depending on the first measurable effects of a campaign, fine-tuning can be done in the following cases:

- The planning may be revised based on inquiry or orders performance alone. This adjustment is done based on the assumption that the conversion rate stays close to the forecasted level.

| FIGURE | 11-3 | A GANTT CHART IN A DIRECT CAMPAIGN |

ID	Task Name	Dec 01	Jan 02	Feb 02	Mar 02	Apr 02	May 02	Jun 02	Jul 02	Aug 02	Sep 02	Oct 02	Nov 02	Dec 02
001	Define market													
002	Campaign plan													
003	Produce brief													
004	Agency response													
005	Agree strategy													
006	Confirm budget													
007	Go/no go													
008	Contact strategy													
009	Media plan													
010	Determine lists													
011	Creative work													
012	Plan fulfillment													
013	Do selections													
014	Order lists													
015	Order media													
016	Creative submit													
017	Creative agreed													
018	Copy/artwork													
019	Copy/artwork agreed													
020	Pack finalized													
021	Production begins													
022	Printing													
023	Lasering													
024	Packs made up													
025	Ads appear													
026	Mailing begins													
027	Fulfillment													
028	Campaign close													

Legend:
- Critical
- Critical milestone
- Noncritical
- Float/delay
- Milestone

■ The media selection may be adjusted. The first media results will determine if the advertising space in a specific media is profitable and if the media booking or cost should be cancelled or renegotiated.

■ If the campaign included a first sequence of creative and offer testing, then corrective action should be undertaken as quickly as possible.

11.4.3 PROBLEMS TO TAKE INTO ACCOUNT

Campaign management and particularly campaign execution involves the marketing team, other departments (sales force, call center, operations department, etc.), top management, and outside suppliers. Many things can go wrong during the process. On one hand, if the marketer runs a direct mail to customers requiring them to call the company's call-center and if the telemarketing team is not adequately informed about the campaign features, then the most probable outcome is that the campaign will be a failure. On the other hand, suppliers should be briefed on the campaign program (the delivery dates, paper quality, color process, package dimensions, the script, etc.) in order to avoid rush work or imperfections. Then again, briefing every actor involved in this process is fundamental to the campaign's success.

We have identified some causes of campaign failures:

- When the marketing planning is undertaken at a functional level and does not integrate with other functional areas of the company, then the campaign will be largely ineffective.
- Separating the responsibilities of operational marketing and strategic marketing planning will lead to a divergence of short- and long-term objectives. Concern over short-term results at the operational level will make the company less competitive in the long term.
- If top management doesn't take an active role in marketing planning, then it will probably not be an effective system.
- If the degree of formalization of campaign management is not adapted to the diversity of operations within the company and its size, then campaign execution process won't be effective.

11.5 ANALYSIS AND CONTROL

Analysis and control end the campaign management cycle. In this phase, marketers should be able to draw some conclusions about the campaign success and use these results not only to improve their customer knowledge but also to improve future campaigns. This is an important stage because it evaluates campaign results in light of the original objectives and determines the campaign level of success or failure. Features that run well should be used as best practices for other campaigns. For features that didn't perform well, marketers should search the reasons why this has happened. This research should be recorded in the CRM database to serve as a *learning lesson* for future campaigns.

Campaign analysis can be done in many ways. Marketers can use campaign key performance indicators (KPI) and compare them with budgeted KPIs and campaign objectives. They can also perform back-end performance analysis to determine the purchase behavior of campaign respondents. Finally, more elaborate analysis can be performed, such as profile and response analysis, to link profiles and behavior with the campaign.

11.5.1 MEASURING CAMPAIGN RESULTS

Marketers can start measuring campaign results while the campaign is still running. As discussed in the previous section, the sooner the results are known and analyzed, the faster action can be taken to fine-tune the campaign execution. Standard performance measures are the key performance indicators (KPI) discussed in the budget section. Comparing the CPM, CPS, ROI, and the CR with the budgeted KPI will give an intuitive idea about the campaign results. Marketers should look deeper though, and try to understand which target segment is driving the campaign success or what medium performed better and why. Back-end performance analysis is one of the ways to evaluate campaign results. It relates the behavior of a group of respondents with sales, contribution, and profit achieved in the campaign. It also relates this group of respondents with the advertising medium that converted them into customers.

In order to measure back-end performance, it is necessary to maintain a system in which each customer is identified as coming from a specific advertising medium. Only then it is possible to analyze the behavior of all customers coming from the same initial source medium and calculate average sales, contribution, and profits. Back-end performance will vary significantly from one advertising medium to another. For example, results from some direct marketing campaigns show buyers acquired from direct mail buy more often than customers acquired through a magazine or newspaper insertion. Then it becomes vital to track customer performance in terms of its original medium source group, so that the decision to reinvest in a particular medium can be made on the basis of proven performance.

Back-end performance can be measured in many ways. For example, in a direct mailing, the measurement of back-end performance is simply the statement of profit or loss for the campaign promotion. For a loyalty program, this measurement should be done in terms of the allowable marketing cost and the breakeven. These two indicators will then be compared with the customer acquisition cost to determine customer contribution. Contribution is a formula that deducts from the gross margin the campaign costs and then divides the resulting value by the number of new customers. In the case of loyalty campaigns, it is more adequate to calculate contribution in terms of the new customer lifetime value, because it can forecast future sales and profits from the newcomers. Another measure to take into account is the attrition rate. This measure is used to determine the rate at which customers defect. When evaluating the profitability, for example, of a newspaper or magazine campaign to increase subscriptions or renewals, the KPI to take into account are the conversion rate, the renewal rates, and the response rate to promotions.

In all cases, when running a promotions campaign, marketers should always calculate the *return on promotion* (ROP). ROP is a way of calculating the return on investment of a particular promotion:

$$\text{ROP} = \frac{\text{Contribution} - \text{Cost per order}}{\text{Cost per order}} \times 100$$

The return is measured by the difference between the contribution that results from all the purchases that occur due to the promotion and the cost of acquiring the purchase.

11.5.2 RESPONSE ANALYSIS

Response analysis calculates the up-to-date campaign results, projects its final results such as responses, inquiries, and leads, and analyzes these results. Response analyzes can be performed with customer and market segments, product lines, campaigns, offers and promotions, media, or advertising agencies. To be able to perform this type of analysis, responses should be summarized by time—that is, by arrival date. Each response should be recorded at the CRM database and should have the calendar date it arrived. Results can then be analyzed as soon as the first campaign responses are known, and if needed, they can alter the campaign progression accordingly. Response analysis uses statistical models such as regression analysis models to determine the impact of several variables of interest (age, gender, level of income, etc.) on probability of response.

11.5.3 PROFILE ANALYSIS

Profile analysis is used to define and compare the profile of campaign responders with the actual profile of the company's customers and prospects. This comparison will allow marketers to verify if the initial targeted profile actually corresponds with the responder's profiles (i.e., if the customer segments were well targeted). Profile analyses can and should be performed at different stages of the campaign. It should be performed at the campaign planning stage, when defining the target segments, as part of designing tests, as campaign results are received, and after a campaign is completed to verify attrition.

The profile characteristics are recorded in the CRM database. They are used in this type of analysis if they can be related to the customer or prospect name. These characteristics may be fundamental (birth date, gender) or derived (age, score). Profile analysis considers the input (generally geographic, demographic, or psychographic) and clusters names into groups with similar tastes and preferences. Two other statistical techniques used in profiles analysis are *automatic interaction detection* (AID) and *chi-square automatic interaction detection* (CHAID). These are not discussed in this text; for more information on these techniques, see *Marketing Research* by Aaker, Kumar, and Day.[5]

By predicting the actions of customers or prospects by using these analyses, the company is refining and improving its marketing strategy.

11.6 CAMPAIGN FEEDBACK

Everyday practice shows it is far more valuable to have a reliable assessment of the measurable effects of marketing campaigns upfront. The effective registration of past marketing activities and their results—combined with modeling methods, different media, and customer segments—enable the marketer to support campaign decisions in advance and to optimize them at the implementation stage. Information on successes, failures, and the circumstances under which the campaigns were carried out should be stored. Patterns can be found, and correlation between historical successes and campaign elements can be used as learning to ensure future success.

Companies should compile detailed information about the main aspects of campaigns, such as concepts, target groups, media used, and campaign performance, into their CRM database. This way models can be designed to describe causal relationships between the variables under the marketer's control and criteria for success. The use of this stored information supports informed future action because it allows the prediction of the market environment in which certain campaigns will succeed. Recording and analyzing the success and failures of past campaigns improves the profitability of future campaigns. Deviations between achieved and desired results are minimized through the correct use of this compiled knowledge.

Keep in mind that three steps should be implemented in order to ensure successful campaigns and to enhance knowledge for the company:

1. Record all relevant data about campaign planning, implementation, and results.
2. Model relationships between the data gathered, the controllable variables, and the campaign results.
3. Apply this knowledge to future campaigns. If information is not sufficient, test the important variables to fill the gaps in knowledge.

11.7 SUMMARY

A campaign is a series of interconnected promotional efforts usually undertaken within a defined timeframe, designed to capture the customers' interest, and thereby achieve precise marketing goals. A successful campaign management process comprises planning, development, execution, and analysis. At the campaign planning stage, marketers make strategic decisions that define the overall objectives of the campaign, the best communication message, and the best target audience. The objectives often are market penetration, market extension, product development, or diversification. When pursuing a customer retention strategy, ideally the company should target its most profitable customers via LTV (lifetime value) and RFM (recency, frequency, and monetary) analyses. The company can choose to pursue market penetration or extension, market diversification, or new product development. Communication strategy involves choosing the most effective message and media (for retention and acquisition strategies) to efficiently reach its target segments.

Identification of the customer segments (homogenous groups of individuals with similar tastes, wants, and needs regarding the company's products or services) that the campaign will target can be done using lifetime segmentation and profiling, and on the basis of purchase behavior and profile data. The CRM database plays a central role in the segmentation process by providing information on customer behaviors and profiles, channel preferences, and brand awareness. Marketing communications (marcom) are targeted interactions between the company and its customers and prospects using one or more media. Integrated marketing communications (IMC) involves the management and organization of all the marketing communication tools to deliver a clear and consistent message about the company and the product. Targeting customers who provide a higher potential yield should be done in a way that maximizes the marketing communications ROI. Developing the offer consists of offering the customer some kind of incentive that will induce him/her to buy or to ask the company for more information. The campaign budget allocates resources and coordinates expenditures across the marketing activities associated with the campaign. Making a campaign budget should be a balance between measurement, financial calculations, competitive analysis, and good judgment. There are several methods to calculate a budget. Preset budgeting determines a given year's marketing expenditure on the basis of what the company spent the year before, by applying a ratio that adjusts media cost inflation, projected sales increase or decrease, market conditions, and so on. Budgeting for an allowable marketing cost (AMC) consists of determining the amount that can be spent on campaign marketing activities, while preserving the required profit margin. The AMC is obtained by subtracting the costs (cost of goods + distribution costs) and the required profit margin from the total sales value. Competitive parity method tries to equate budget allocation with those of competitors. Budgeting with the objective and task method focuses on determining the marketing objectives and then deciding on the marketing communications tasks needed to achieve those objectives. In the percentage of sales method, the company looks at the competitor allocations and on the industry averages, to determine the exact percentage that should be allocated. *Front-end analysis* allows the company to figure out, in a quick way, how much it can afford to spend on a special promotion.

Preset budgeting should ideally be replaced by LTV forecasts, front-end analysis, allowable marketing cost analysis and estimation of the return of marketing investment (ROI rates) because this will allow the company to compare returns on alternative marketing expenditures.

Tests help maximize the performance of the campaign. Key variables in testing are the target audience, the offer, the format, the creative element, the media, and/or the timing. Testing can accurately predict performance measures such as response to the campaign in percentage and campaign profitability.

Campaign implementation plans should be divided into three sub-plans: the campaign program, the campaign schedule, and the activity schedule. In the analysis and control stage, marketers should be able to draw conclusions about the campaign success and use these results not only to improve their customer knowledge but also to improve future campaigns. Campaign analysis can be done using campaign key performance indicators (KPI) and comparing them with budgeted KPIs and campaign objectives, by using back-end performance analysis, or even profile and response analysis, to link profiles and behavior with the campaign. When running a promotions campaign, marketers should always calculate the return on promotion (ROP). Response analysis calculates the up-to-date campaign results, projects its final results, such as responses, inquiries and leads, and analyzes these results. By contrast, profile analysis is used to define and compare the profile of campaign responders with the actual profile of the company's customers and prospects. Recording and analyzing the success and failures of past campaigns improves the profitability of future campaigns.

11.8 EXERCISE QUESTIONS

1. Explain the three key steps in the management of campaigns.

2. Imagine you are the manager of a chain of twenty-five seafood restaurants in Virginia. The restaurant has a mainstream positioning. You are planning a campaign to attract new clients, and your available budget is $30.000. Describe how you would go about implementing this campaign.

3. Explain the ideas revolving around the concept of campaign testing. Do you think testing in general will become more important in the future? Why or why not?

4. Give examples for key performance indicators for the evaluation of campaign success.

5. Explain the advantages and disadvantages of the various campaign budget-setting methods.

MINI CASE 11.1

Z4 LAUNCH CAMPAIGN AT BMW

BMW, the Munich-based luxury carmaker, is a strong believer in CRM practices across dealers and end customers. Traditionally, customers communicated with dealers and dealers with the BMW Group. Today, many end customers expect to communicate directly with the BMW Group. The challenge, therefore, for BMW (and any carmaker) is to establish the relationship between BMW Group and end customers and yet strengthen the traditional relationship between end customers and dealers. BMW Group's CRM approach is therefore very integrated in nature, both in terms of spanning dealers and end customers, as well as in terms of customer service, new customer attraction, and loyalization.

The launch of the Z4 roadster in 2002/2003 is a prototypical example for BMW Group's approach. The objectives were to position the car in the premium segment, to conquer new customers, and to loyalize owners of the previous model Z3. An integrated communications campaign was launched that coordinated TV and print campaigns, direct marketing, preview events, electronic media, as well as dealer marketing. The goal of the entire campaign was to select relevant prospects for the actual launch in March 2003. In practice, this meant the addresses of the most interested set of prospects were known at launch and these individuals were then invited for closed room and preview events. The selection was made based on prospects' reaction to the mailings, e-mails, Short Message Service (SMS), and Internet offers. The activities started with bulk-mail activities, followed by TV and print inserts. These initial teasers set off a second wave where interested parties would call or e-mail a service center that then forwarded information material to these qualified prospects. These address data and e-mail addresses formed a key part of the prospect database. Prospects could then also sign up for preview events where the actual car was shown. Using feedback from these preview events, information on the hottest prospects was then given to the dealers who followed up on the prospects for landing the sales. The effectiveness of the prelaunch activities was measured in terms of number and quality of prospects, response rate of activities, and cost per contact. Overall, the campaign was extremely successful, not only in achieving the desired premium positioning but also in terms of leading sales in the segment of premium roadsters.

Questions:

1. Explain the likely issues (as discussed in the chapter) that might come up during the Z4 campaign management process.

2. Should the campaign stop here? Are there opportunities for BMW to proceed campaigning with the new owners of the Z4? What are some of those opportunities?

ENDNOTES

1. "The email marketing dialogue," Forrester Research, Inc. (January 2000).

2. However, the federal do-not-call implementation has made it mandatory for telemarketers to scrub their contact lists against the national do-not-call registry every thirty-one days.

3. David A. Aaker, V. Kumar, and G. Day, Eighth ed. (Hoboken, N.J.: John Wiley & Sons, 2004).

4. Gantt chart is a graphical representation of the duration of tasks against the progression of time.

5. *Ibid.*

PART III

Advances in CRM Applications

CHAPTER 12

Applications of Database Marketing in B-to-C and B-to-B Scenarios

Contents

12.1 OVERVIEW[1]

Delta Airlines had long been operating a customer loyalty program that computed the accumulated frequent-flier reward points solely on the basis of the total number of miles flown by a customer. The loyalty program did not differentiate between those customers who pay economy class fares and those who pay business class fares, to fly the same distance. From a profitability viewpoint, this program was misaligned. Delta Airlines' loyalty program was clearly not based on the customer's value to the firm. No wonder, then, this program was recently replaced with one that differentiated between customers paying for different fare classes. Now, a customer flying business class gets 50 percent more points than does a customer traveling economy class. This new approach recognizes customers who are more profitable to the firm need to be rewarded more.

General Motors revised the redemption scheme on its ten-year-old GM card in 2002. The maximum amount of earnings a customer can redeem toward the purchase or lease of a new GM car, truck, or SUV *now depends on the year, make, and model* chosen. This move is similar to the one adopted by Delta, in that a customer who spends on a premium product is rewarded more than a customer who purchases a low-end product.

There seems to be two complementary reasons why firms are becoming unabashedly profit-oriented in their approach toward customer rewards programs. First, firms are in a better position, thanks to technology, to record customer actions and ascertain their individual profitability levels. Thus, firms no longer use surrogate measures like unit volume of business, share of wallet, and duration of association to reward their customers. Let us examine the share of wallet measure some firms use to decide on customer-level investments. Share of wallet (SW) is defined as the ratio of the total customer spending with the firm to the total category spending (the firm plus its competitors) for that customer. It is clear that achieving a large SW of a low-spending client may not be as good as achieving a low SW of a high-spending client. Thus, firms do not need to continue using surrogate measures because the drawbacks inherent in these measures can now be overcome by concentrating directly on individual customer profitability. Second, customers realize they can no longer expect a firm to believe they are special if they are not genuine high-value buyers. Differential treatment of customers is therefore being accepted as a way of life by both firms and customers. However, differential treatment can work for a firm in the long run, only if it has an eye on the future. The challenge for a firm today is to develop an optimal blend of differential levels of treatments such that over every customer's lifetime, the profits earned by the firm are maximized. Not every firm understands how to develop a strategy which balances customer relations and profitability.

The level of sophistication of the adoption of the customer value metric approach into a firm's marketing program could vary. A firm operating a loyalty program can start using the customer value metric to examine whether the customers being rewarded are indeed the profitable ones. It should take corrective action if it finds that such is not the case. At the next level, a firm can begin to observe when its customers are beginning to turn unprofitable. The firm can decide to let go of these customers without wasting further efforts on them. Moving up another level, a firm could determine the factors likely to affect how long a customer is likely to stay profitable. This enables the firm to control and manage the variables necessary to increase a customer's profitability. At the next level, a firm can plan investments in marketing initiatives on the basis of an analysis of expected profits from its customers during a given planning period. A firm can achieve the next level of sophistication by understanding the impact of changing the frequency of its marketing communication elements on the profitability of each customer. In this manner it can allocate its resources optimally across marketing initiatives, by cutting down on wasteful efforts and increasing the frequency of effective efforts, one customer at a time. At the next level, a firm can predict the timing of purchase of each of the products in its portfolio and tailor the communication message around the product likely to be next purchased by a customer. Mathematical models necessary to carry these levels of analyses and predictions have been developed in the CRM literature.[2] This, as well as the next chapter illustrate how seemingly divergent marketing decisions can be integrated using these models, all of which utilize the customer value metric.

12.2 Customer Value—A Decision Metric

Customer value is an important metric used to help firms address marketing issues with greater confidence. Kumar et al. (2004)[3] outline these as follows:

> How do firms decide the customers to whom they should provide preferential and sometimes personal treatment, that clearly costs more money and resources, to which customer they should interact through inexpensive channels like the Internet or the touch tone phone, and which customer to let go? How do firms decide the timing of an offering to a customer? How do firms decide which prospect will make a better customer in the future, and is therefore worthwhile to acquire now? Having got the customer to transact with the firm, what kind of

sales and service resources should the firm allocate, to conduct future business with that customer? How should firms monitor customer activity, in order to readjust the form and intensity of their marketing initiatives?

Depending on the relevance and criticality of a firm's CRM decisions to its survival and growth, a firm can decide either to adopt the customer value metric in a step-by-step manner or integrate it as the guiding principle for all future marketing actions. In this chapter, we discuss two empirical studies which demonstrate the importance of the customer value metric in evaluating and monitoring a firm's profitability.

12.2.1 STUDY 1: THIS STUDY EXAMINES THE LINK BETWEEN CUSTOMER LIFETIME DURATION AND CUSTOMER PROFITABILITY

Although the link between customer lifetime duration and customer profitability has been emphasized in relationship marketing, empirical evidence is scarce, particularly in noncontractual settings—relationships between buyers and sellers not governed by a contract or membership. Here, we present the results of two recent studies conducted by applying database-marketing analytics in B-to-C and B-to-B scenarios, on lifetime duration and profitability in noncontractual relationships. In Study 1, we will offer four propositions and subsequently test each of them in a noncontractual context, using the data obtained from a large catalog retailer. The four are propositions related to whether (1) there exists a strong positive relationship between customer lifetime duration and profitability (referred to in this chapter as lifetime-profitability relationship), (2) profits increase over time, (3) the cost of serving long-life customers is less, and (4) long-life customers pay higher prices. The findings from the study challenge the expectations derived from the literature—long-life customers are not necessarily profitable customers.

12.2.2 STUDY 2: THIS STUDY ATTEMPTS TO UNDERSTAND THE FACTORS THAT AFFECT THE PROFITABLE LIFETIME DURATION OF CUSTOMERS

We develop plausible explanations for findings which go against the available evidence in the literature and identify three indicators to help managers focus their efforts on more profitable customers. We develop a metric which incorporates projected profitability of customers in the computations of lifetime duration, leveraging the findings of Study 1. We identify factors under a manager's control which explain the variation in the profitable lifetime duration, and we also compare other metrics with the traditional methods such as the recency, frequency, and monetary value metric and past customer value, and then illustrate the superiority of the proposed metric. Finally, we develop several valuable key implications for decision makers in managing customer relationships.

12.2.3 STUDY 3: A MODEL FOR IDENTIFYING THE TRUE VALUE OF A LOST CUSTOMER

This study argues for the inclusion of the social effects such as word of mouth and imitation influencing the future acquisition while valuing the customers especially for markets involving new products or services. It examines the impact of a lost customer on the profitability of the firm because of defection and disadoption. It also shows how the value of a lost customer changes throughout the product life cycle.

12.3 Study 1: The Lifetime-Profitability Relationship in a Noncontractual Setting[4]

12.3.1 BACKGROUND AND OBJECTIVE

A basic tenet of relationship marketing is that firms benefit more from maintaining long-term customer relationships as compared to short-term customer relationships. Convincing conceptual evidence for this argument has been advanced by a number of authors.[5] Also, it has been shown that the relationship-marketing payoff to the firm comes only when relationships endure.[6] In a widely quoted HBR article, Reichheld and Sasser state, "Customer defections have a surprisingly powerful impact on the bottom line. As a customer's relationship with the company lengthens, profits rise."[7]

While anecdotal evidence on the lifetime-profitability relationship seems to be plentiful, Reichheld and Teal's 1996 study seems to be the only well-documented empirical evidence to substantiate the hypothesized positive lifetime-profitability relationship.[8] Contrary to the anecdotal evidence that long-life customers are most profitable to the firm, Dowling and Uncles caution, "In short, the contention that loyal customers are always more profitable is a gross oversimplification."[9]

In particular, this study questions the existing contentions that the costs of serving loyal customers are presumably lower, that loyal customers presumably pay higher prices, and that loyal customers presumably spend more with the firm than nonloyal customers. Obviously, the study shows concern with the widespread assumption of a clear-cut positive lifetime-profitability relationship and underlines the importance of a differentiated analysis. Consequently, there seems to be a need for more rigorous empirical evidence on the lifetime-profitability relationship.

Lifetime analyses have typically been conducted in contractual settings.[10] Examples for this type of relationships are magazine subscriptions, cable service subscriptions, and cellular phone services. In contractual settings, expected revenues can be forecasted fairly accurately and, given a constant usage of the service, one would expect increasing cumulative profits over the customer's lifetime. However, in *noncontractual* settings, the firm must ensure the relationship stays alive because the customer typically splits his category expenses with several firms.[11] Examples of *noncontractual* settings are department-store purchases or mail-order purchases in the catalog and direct marketing industry.

Catalog marketing involves selling through catalogs mailed to a select list of customers. Consumers can buy almost anything from a catalog. More than 14 billion copies of more than 8,500 different consumer catalogs are mailed out annually, and the average household receives some 50 catalogs a year. According to a study by the Direct Marketing Association, in 2001, catalog sales increased at more than twice the rate of overall retail sales.[12]

Direct marketing industry is important because, in 1998, U.S. sales revenue attributable to direct marketing was estimated to reach close to $1.4 trillion. In 1999, approximately 13.2 million workers were employed throughout the U.S. economy as a result of direct marketing activity.

In a noncontractual setting such as the catalog industry, specifically, a customer who starts to purchase in a given time period may then buy repeatedly at some irregular time intervals. If the time intervals are relatively longer, is it wise for the firm to assume this customer is likely to purchase again in the near future, and, if so, to expect him to spend a certain amount of dollars? This is a necessary element for estimating customer lifetime value. Although duration seems like a simple concept, it can be complicated. The customer portfolios of many companies are composed of a small number of active customers—people who have regular and frequent interactions with the provider—and a large number of inactives. Drawing the line is not easy, as inactives can be a source of future actives.

In many cases, the actual duration of the relationship is not especially revealing due to normal fluctuations in customer activity over time. For example, direct mail publishers may learn more from the seasonal and life-stage variations in customer buying patterns than from the specific number of years the customer has been in the database. What appears on the surface to be dormancy actually may be a naturally occurring pattern which will trigger purchasing when the next cycle comes around. Different customer segments may exhibit different patterns of attrition, switching, and reactivation.[13] The firm dealing with limited/finite resources must decide when it is appropriate to make contact (through mailing of catalogs or other means) with the customer or stop contacting the customers. Given the cost implications, is it worthwhile to chase the dollars from some customers with longer lifetime duration?

The research takes place in the context of the catalog and direct marketing industry. Given the contradictory statements and sparse empirical evidence available in the literature, the main objective of this study is a rigorous and differentiated empirical analysis of the lifetime-profitability relationship in a *noncontractual* context. In order to achieve this objective, we test for the following:

- The strength of the lifetime duration–profitability relationship
- Whether profits increase over time (lifetime profitability pattern)
- Whether the costs of serving long-life customers are actually less
- Whether long-life customers pay higher prices

Once we understand what happens in the marketplace, then we can address *why* it happens that way. As data become available across different situations, empirical generalizations can be advanced. This is important, especially in the noncontractual setting, as the uncertainty for a firm is maximum here. An additional objective is to derive marketing implications from the findings. That is, if distinct lifetime and profitability segments can be delineated, what implications can be derived for a customer management strategy (i.e., tailored communication, early warning indicators, and so on)?

12.3.2   CONCEPTUAL MODEL

Individual customer lifetime profits are modeled as a function of a customer's lifetime duration. Revenue flows over the course of a customer's lifetime, and firm cost is associated with the marketing exchange. We want to investigate the consequences of customer retention—namely, profitability.

Customer Lifetime and Firm Profitability

We offer the following four propositions and subsequently test each one of the propositions in a non-contractual scenario.

Proposition 1: The Nature of the Lifetime-Profitability Relationship Is Positive   Ongoing relationships in consumer markets have received substantial attention in recent years.[14] The building of strong customer relationships has been suggested as a means for gaining competitive advantage.[15] The underlying assumption of much of the existing research is that long-term relationships are desirable because they are more profitable for the firm, as compared to short-term relationships. Following this line of reasoning, we would expect a substantial positive association between the duration of a customer–firm relationship and the firm profits derived thereof.[16] This is true for a contractual case; where there is no repeated cost to entice customers into buying. Figure 12-1 summarizes this situation. In line with the argument, one would expect the majority of relationship outcomes to fall along the diagonal, as shown in Figure 12-1. In other words, one would expect a substantial positive correlation between the two variables. Thus, an assessment of the numbers of customers falling into each quadrant, along with a simple measure of association between lifetime profits and lifetime duration, would readily yield some insight into the nature of the lifetime-profitability relationship.

A factor that complicates the firm's objective of establishing long-term relationships with its customers is that of intrinsic retainability of customers. Not all customers want to engage in a long-term relationship with the firm for many possible reasons. For example, in the long-distance telephone service market, many 10-10-xxx companies have emerged. There is no need to sign any contract with the service providers. Here, customers use a particular 10-10-xxx company, depending on the quality of service, unit price, and the speed of connection. As discussed before, to retain customers, it is important to satisfy the customers. The satisfaction of customers may come at a significant cost to the company. In a noncontractual case like catalog shopping, a household might have to be sent many catalogs over a period of time before they decide to buy again. Thus, when the costs of satisfying customers exceed the profit margin offered by the customer, the expected positive lifetime profitability relationship need not hold good. Also, some customers may be buying less from a catalog company due to competitive offerings, need for limited spending, or other reasons over a period of time. This forces companies in a noncontractual scenario to look at the spending levels of each of their customers.

Firms should partition their customer base into behaviorally and attitudinally homogenous groups that spend at different levels (see Figure 12-2) and then estimate the profitability characteristics for each group. This grouping is considered appropriate by many managers in the direct marketing industry as they focus on the revenue generated by each customer over a period of time. Thus, the two dimensions—lifetime duration and revenues—may help managers to make better decisions. Irrespective of the segmentation scheme, conventional wisdom argues for a positive relationship between profitability and time. Although the available evidence suggests a positive lifetime-profitability relationship, it need not be true if the cost of serving the customer is greater than the profit margin generated by the customer. In fact, there could be many customers who may be receiving catalogs on a regular basis because they bought at least one item in the recent past, even though it may be of lower dollar value.

FIGURE 12-1 LIFETIME-PROBABILITY ASSOCIATION

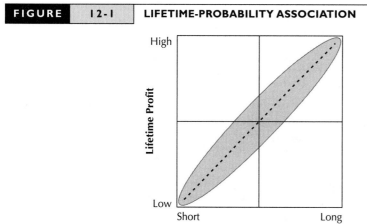

Lifetime Duration

| FIGURE | 12-2 | **SEGMENTATION SCHEME** |

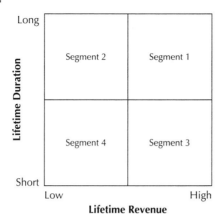

Proposition 2: Profits Increase over Time

Although a correlational measure is important and insightful, it presents only a *static* picture of the lifetime-profitability relationship. While related to proposition 1, the analysis of the *dynamic aspects* of the lifetime-profitability relationship yields further important insights. The important difference is that we analyze profits dynamically across time, whereas in proposition 1 we analyze profits in a single lifetime measure across subjects. Recall that we mentioned finding evidence for *increasing* profits per time unit over the length of the customer's tenure. These arguments can be true for a contractual setting but need not hold good for a noncontractual scenario. In the case of catalog shopping or direct mail offerings, the customer may end up buying once a year and spending a small amount. If this pattern prevails, then the cost of serving this customer can easily exceed the profit margin brought in by the customer. Therefore, profits may not increase over time.

Using the same long distance telephone service example discussed under Proposition 1, there are several instances where the overhead costs of serving long-life customers are higher as compared to the percentage of profit margin offered by the customer. It is necessary for a firm offering the 10-10-xxx service to send monthly bills to all the customers who have started to use their service. Even if a customer does not use the service in a given month, that customer receives a bill. Here, the cost of serving the customer clearly exceeds the profit margin from the customer, and this loss becomes significant for the firm over a period of time and across many such customers. This type of phenomenon occurs in the credit card industry also. Thus, it is not obvious that profit for the firm increases over time. Therefore, it is worthwhile to test this relationship.

Proposition 3: The Costs of Serving Longer-life Customers Are Lower

Another commonly held contention is that long-life customers are less costly to serve than short-life customers. This is possibly true for contractual setting. But, for the broad retail sector, we would hardly expect lower transaction costs for longer-life versus shorter-life customers. For example, there is little reason to believe that transaction costs for a piece of garment in the second purchase encounter with a firm is different from, say, the tenth purchase encounter.

Other costs incurred over the course of a relationship are the costs of the promotional mix directed at each customer. In a noncontractual scenario such as the direct marketing context, promotional costs are typically the largest nonproduct cost factor in a customer–firm relationship. Following the commonly held contention, we would expect the cost of promotional expenditures per dollar sales revenue is lower for longer-life customers. The reason would be that the promotional mix has a greater efficiency in relation to the longer-life customer. This is possibly due to cumulative effects or a more favorable attitude toward the firm's communication. Thus, we propose that the cost of promoting to a customer, in relation to her revenues, is lower for long-life customers. Yet, to our knowledge, there is no empirical evidence in the literature to substantiate this claim. Therefore, it will be interesting to test whether the costs associated with promotional expenditures directed at longer- and shorter-life customers actually differ.

Proposition 4: Longer-life Customers Pay Higher Prices Previous research[17] has argued that in most industries, existing customers pay effectively higher prices than new ones, even after accounting for possible introductory offers. This would imply that the average price paid by customers and the customer lifetime duration could be positively related.

However, company managers told us that their informal experience suggests a higher value consciousness (i.e., lower average prices paid) for long-term customers. That is, if a customer buys more product units for a given dollar amount, the customer exhibits a higher degree of value consciousness (i.e., wants more "bang for the buck"). If this observation were true, it would contradict the existing evidence. A possible reason for higher-value consciousness of long-term customers might be that customers learn over time to trust lower-priced items or brands rather than established name brand products.

Thus, there seems to exist some reasonable evidence for both possibilities. Therefore, instead of proposing a directional effect, we suggest to test this proposition empirically.

12.3.3 RESEARCH METHODOLOGY

Data

Data from an established U.S. catalog retailer were used for the empirical estimation in this study. The items sold by the firm cover a broad spectrum of general merchandise. The firm's products are offered and can be purchased all year round. The data for this study cover a three-year window and are recorded on a daily basis. Two key characteristics of this data set are that the customers are tracked from their very first purchase with the firm, and these households have not previously been customers of the company. Consequently, the observations are not left-censored.

A Model for Measuring Customer Lifetime for Noncontractual Relationships

A critical component in our model is customer lifetime duration. The modeling process of a customer's lifetime is contingent on a valid measurement framework that adequately describes the process of *birth, purchase activity,* and *defection.* Toward that end, we empirically implement and extend a procedure previously suggested.[18] Once the lifetime duration is computed for each customer, we can develop testable propositions dealing with lifetime duration based on conventional wisdom and past literature.

We are using the *negative binomial distribution* (NBD)/Pareto model, which has been proposed and validated in a previous study. The key result of the NBD/Pareto model is an answer to the question: "Which individual customers are most likely to represent active or inactive customers?" This is a nontrivial question because the purchase activity is a random process and the defection is not directly observed. Based on the customer-specific probability of being alive, the model can be used to determine which customers should be deleted from active status. The outcome of the NBD/Pareto model, the probability that a customer with a particular observed transaction history is still alive at time T since trial, is of key interest to our modeling effort.

Given that the outcome of the NBD/Pareto model is a continuous probability estimate, the continuous $P(\text{Alive})$ estimate is transformed into a dichotomous alive/dead measure. Knowing a person's time of birth (when the person became a customer) and given a specified probability level (threshold), we can approximate when a customer is deemed to have left the relationship. The time from birth, t_0, until the date associated with the cut-off threshold, $t_{cut-off}$, then constitutes the lifetime of the customer. Figure 12-3 illustrates the procedure. This procedure allows us to calculate a finite lifetime for each customer, which then can be used for the profitability analysis.

This discussion has been based on the assumptions that the time t_0 when the customer came on file or when she executed the first purchase is known. Given the widespread existence of customers' databases in organizations, this assumption is not difficult to meet.

Establishment of Cut-off Threshold The choice of cut-off of the $P(\text{Alive})$ threshold c determines the length of the lifetime estimate for each customer. The cut-off threshold that produces the highest percentage of correct classifications is obviously the choice most consistent with the data.

In this study, the threshold of 0.5 produces the highest percentage of correct classifications. As a result, for the purpose of the lifetime analysis, we use 0.5 as the cut-off threshold.

Lifetime Estimation Based on the model and the implementation of the validation process, the final step in the analysis is the calculation of a finite lifetime estimate for each customer. The average lifetime across Cohort 1 is 28.7 months, and the average lifetime across Cohort 2 is 27.9 months (Table 12-1). A cohort is a group of customers who started their relationship at the same point in time (e.g., a particular month or quarter). Cohort 2 consists of customers who started the relationship with the firm one month after Cohort 1. The consistency between the two cohorts is very high. In both cohorts, about 60 percent of the sample has a lifetime less than the observation window. Thus, the available observation window is obviously adequate for describing lifetime purchases of the given sample.

| **FIGURE** | **12-3** | **ILLUSTRATIVE LIFETIME DETERMINATION OF INDIVIDUAL HOUSEHOLD** |

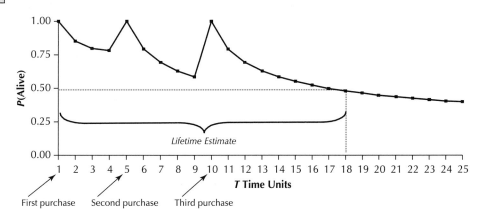

SOURCE: W. Reinartz and V. Kumar, "On the Profitability of Long-Life Customers in a Non-Contractual Setting: An Empirical Investigation and Implications for Marketing," *Journal of Marketing* 64 (October 2000): 17–32.

TABLE	12-1	FINITE LIFETIME ESTIMATES

	Mean Lifetime (Months)	Standard Deviation	Right-Censored (%)	Minimum	Maximum
Cohort 1	28.7	7.8	41.1	11	36
Cohort 2	27.9	7.9	41.7	12	35

Profit Calculation   Net-present value of profit is calculated on an individual customer basis for the period of thirty-six months using the following equation:

$$LT\pi_i = \sum_{t=1}^{36} (GC_{ti} - C_{ti}) \left(\frac{1}{1 + 0.125} \right)^t \tag{1}$$

where $LT\pi_i$ = individual net-present lifetime profit for thirty-six months, GC_{ti} = gross contribution in month t for customer i, C_{ti} = mailing cost in month t for customer i, and 0.0125 = monthly discount rate (based on 0.15 rate per year). The discount rate is set to 15 percent, which equals U.S. prime rate in 1999 plus 7 percent. Gross contribution GC_{ti} is calculated from the monthly revenue, which is the total household purchase amount for every month of the observation period. The monthly gross contribution is calculated on average as 30 percent profit margin of the monthly revenues. This is a rather conservative figure and reflects the firm's managerial judgment. Due to the wide assortment the firm offers, the calculation of an average profit seems reasonable. Furthermore, estimates of individual-item direct cost are not available within the firm. The cost component C_{ti} constitutes the total cost of mailing catalogs and solicitations per month and per customer. These costs include catalog production cost, letter shop, and mailing costs. Individual customer mailing costs in the observation window vary between $2.5 and $111.1 for Cohort 1 (mean = $53.3) and $3.3 and $108.5 for Cohort 2 (mean = $57.6). Acquisition costs are not included since the company does not track them on a per-customer basis. Now that lifetime duration and profitability have been computed, we can proceed to test the propositions offered in this study.

Test of the Propositions[19]

Proposition 1: The Nature of the Lifetime-Profitability Relationship Is Positive
As Figure 12-2 shows, using *Profit* as the dependent variable, one can segment the customer base with a median split of the independent variables *Lifetime Duration* and *Lifetime Revenues*. Thus, we will employ a median split and create a shorter and a longer *lifetime half* and a higher and a lower *revenue half*.

Obviously, we would expect the longer a customer's tenure with the firm and the higher the revenues of a customer, *ceteris paribus*, the more profitable that customer would be. In line with the relationship marketing literature, we would expect the customers falling into segment 1 to generate the highest profits. Likewise, customers in Segment 4 would be expected to yield the lowest profits. However, in addition to providing empirical evidence for these expectations, this segmentation scheme lets us test the importance of the off-diagonal segments to the firm. An analysis of the off-diagonal quadrants could provide an answer to an important question. Could we possibly encounter a situation where customers with shorter tenure might actually be more profitable than long-term customers, a claim which runs counter to the theoretical expectations of a relationship perspective? Furthermore, which group of customers is of more interest to the firm, the one that buys heavily for a short period (Segment 3) or the one with small spending but with long-term commitment (Segment 2)? This is a particularly important question in combination with the size of the segments. That is, for example, if the total number of customers in Segment 1 were comparably small, it is imperative for the firm to pay very close attention to the characteristics of their second-most profitable segment. Naturally, the answer to this question is driven by whether revenues and contribution margin are similar or dissimilar.

Proposition 2: Profits Increase over Time   To test the proposition of increasing profits over time, we will (a) examine the profitability evolution visually and (b) analyze the sign of the slope coefficient. If profits were to increase over a customer's tenure, we would expect a positive slope parameter for the same variable. In addition to the linear effect, a dummy variable is included for the first purchase period to reflect the large first month purchase amount. The exact specification of the regression is as follows:

$$\text{Profit}_{ts} = a_s + b_{1s} \times \text{Dummy} + b_{2s} \times t_s + \text{error}$$

where t = month

b_{1s} = regression coefficient

s = segment

Dummy = 1 if first purchase month, else 0

The profit figures are derived for those customers who either have purchase activity in a given month and/or incur cost due to mailings in a given month. The dummy variable was included to achieve a better fit of the estimation because purchases in month 1 were considerably higher for all groups. This higher purchase could be the reflection of the novelty of the situation—such as the new vendor, new goods, or new deals. As a result, the estimation better reflects the actual profit pattern beyond month 1.

Proposition 3: The Costs of Serving Long-life Customers Are Lower   To test this proposition, we will compute the ratio of promotional costs in a given period over the revenues in the same period. Promotional costs are the total cost of producing and mailing promotions and catalogs, starting with the birth of the customer. This varies for each customer, depending on the purchase transaction history. Within each segment, the mean promotional costs are computed across all households, and then the costs are compared across segments to see if the costs of serving longer-life customers are actually lower.

Proposition 4: Longer-life Customers Pay Higher Prices   We test in our study whether longer-life customers do pay higher prices, as compared to shorter-life customers. Therefore, we will compare the average price paid across products and purchase occasions for each of the four segments. Next, we discuss the findings from the test of propositions.

12.3.4   EMPIRICAL FINDINGS

What Is the Nature of the Lifetime-Profitability Relationship?

To test the strength of the lifetime-profitability relationship, the bivariate Pearson correlation between lifetime duration (in months) and lifetime profit ($) is calculated. The correlation coefficient r is 0.175 for Cohort 1 and 0.219 for Cohort 2, which means that only a moderate linear association between lifetime duration and lifetime profits exists. Although a significant positive association (at $\alpha = 0.05$) in line with theoretical expectations clearly exists—overall, it seems weak. Clearly, lifetime duration alone does not explain very well overall lifetime profitability. Furthermore, when segmenting the customers in Cohort 1 using a median split, we find that 2,530 out of 4,202 households fall in the diagonal of Figure 12-2 (1,322 in the upper right quadrant; 1,208 in the lower left quadrant). That means a very substantive 39.9 percent of the customers fall into the off-diagonal quadrants.

Thus, the large percentage in the off-diagonal quadrants signals a sizable segment (18.7 percent) that generates high profits even though the customer tenure is short, and another segment (21.2 percent) that generates low profits even though they exhibit long lifetime. Although our findings moderately support the theoretical predictions from the relationship marketing perspective, additional analyses seem warranted to explain the apparently counterintuitive results. Specifically, we are interested in how much *each segment* contributes to overall profits. The goal is to optimally uncover the underlying relationship of lifetime with profitability. Table 12-2 summarizes these results.

Several results in Table 12-2 are remarkable. The first finding is that the average net present lifetime profit per customer is highest for Segment 1 ($289.83). That is, customers who have long lifetimes and generate high revenues represent the most valuable customers to the firm. Of key interest however is the comparison of Segments 2 and 3. Clearly, it can be found for this setting that customers in Segment 3 are, on average, *far* more profitable ($257.96) than customers in Segment 2 ($50.85). The mean profit for segment 3 is significantly ($\alpha = 0.01$) different from the mean profit of segment 2. In terms of total segment profitability, the short-lived Segment 3 generates 29.2% of the total cohort profits. Thus, while long-term customers in Segment 1 are obviously important to the firm, short-term customers in Segment 3 are also important because they generate more than a quarter of the total cohort profits.

Thus, this is a case where both long-term customers (Segment 1) *and* short-term customers (Segment 3) constitute the core of the firm's business. Likewise, we find the relationship between lifetime and profits can be far from positive and monotonic. Consequently, an implication for managers is that a firm strategy focusing on relational buyers only as opposed to transactional buyers would clearly be disadvantageous.

Another very interesting outcome of the analysis is that in terms of relative profit (i.e., profit per month), customers in Segment 3 are the *most* attractive of all (Table 12-2, Figure 12-4). Segment 3 customers purchase with high-intensity, thus generating higher profits in a relatively shorter period of time. Thus, in terms of sustaining cash flow, they play a vital

---

TABLE 12-2 **TESTS OF PROPOSITIONS—RESULTS (COHORT 2 RESULTS IN PARENTHESES)**

		Segment 2					Segment 1			
	1	2	3	4	5	1	2	3	4	5
Long Lifetime	Number of Customers	Lifetime Profit per Customer ($)	Relative Profit ($/Month)	Mailing Cost/ Sale Ratio	Average Item Price	Number of Customers	Lifetime Profit per Customer ($)	Relative Profit ($/Month)	Mailing Cost/ Sale Ratio	Average Item Price
	889	50.85	1.43	0.128	47.74	1,332	289.83	8.18	0.063*	58.43**
	(973)	(55.26)	(1.56)	(0.124)	(48.72)	(1,546)	(322.03)	(9.31)	(0.062)*	(58.25)**
		Segment 4					Segment 3			
	1	2	3	4	5	1	2	3	4	5
Short Lifetime	Number of Customers	Lifetime Profit per Customer ($)	Relative Profit ($/Month)	Mailing Cost/ Sale Ratio	Average Item Price	Number of Customers	Lifetime Profit per Customer ($)	Relative Profit ($/Month)	Mailing Cost/ Sale Ratio	Average Item Price
	1,208	50.49	2.41	0.141	47.97	783	257.96	11.67	0.065	63.54
	(1,504)	(53.67)	(2.67)	(0.143)	(46.80)	(942)	(284.20)	(12.57)	(0.064)	(64.47)

Low Lifetime Revenue   **High Lifetime Revenue**

*Difference between Segment 1 and Segment 3 is not significant.

**Difference between Segment 1 and Segment 3 is significant at $\alpha = 0.05$.

role for the firm. The mean relative profit for each segment is significantly different from the other segment at least at $\alpha = 0.05$ (using the multiple comparison test). The profits per month for longer-life segments are shown in Figure 12-5, which capture the implications discussed so far.

One needs to speculate on the reasons for this interesting pattern of results. Obviously, Segment 1 customers are the most desirable set for the firm—representing the loyalty effect at its best. These customers' desires are likely to be matched well by the firm's offerings over time, and they are more likely to be habitual mail-order buyers. For Segment 3 customers (high revenue but short lifetime), we still suspect a good match between offerings and desires, but we assume that their relationship duration is complicated by several moderating factors. For example, consumer factors such as an intrinsic transactional buying behavior, the execution of a limited set of planned purchases, being less of a typical mail-order buyer, or a higher susceptibility to competitor's offers. We suspect that it has less to do with product or service dissatisfaction since they spend at a high level. Dissatisfaction might rather occur for Segment 4, whose customers spend the lowest amount. Although we highlight the speculative nature of these inferences, it seems worthwhile to search for the underlying consumer motivations.

Do Profits Increase Over Time?

To test the proposition of increasing profits over time, we first examine the profitability evolution visually. Figures 12-4 and 12-5 show the lifetime profitability plots for the four segments. A visual inspection of the charts reveals three of the four segments actually exhibit *decreasing profits* over time. Only for Segment 2 (long life, low revenue) we find a slightly positive trend in the profitability evolution.

For a more formal test, we compare the sign and significance of the time coefficient from the regression analysis of profits as a function of time. The results are presented in Table 12-3. With the exception of Segment 2, we generally find that the coefficient for the

---

FIGURE 12-4 **AGGREGATE PROFITS ($) FOR SHORT-LIFE SEGMENTS**

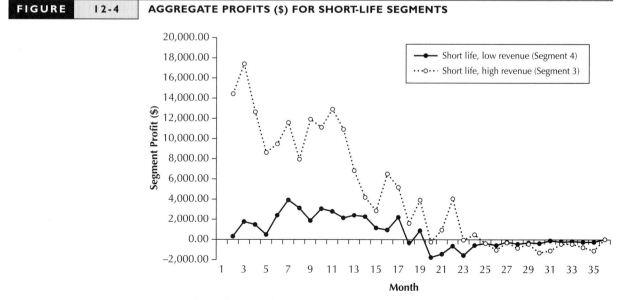

Note: Month 1 profits omitted from chart.

FIGURE | **12-5** | **AGGREGATE PROFITS ($) FOR LONG-LIFE SEGMENTS**

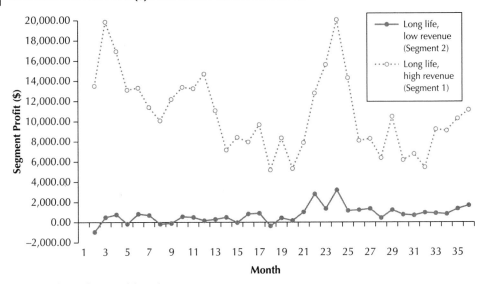

Note: Month 1 profits omitted from chart.

linear effect has a negative sign, thus highlighting the negative profit trend over time for the three segments. All the coefficients for time are significant at $\alpha = 0.01$.

It is not uncommon that proponents of relationship marketing mention that profits due to loyal customer are higher in each subsequent period. This is typically the case for contractual settings where a firm derives most or all of the business of a customer—for example, for life insurances or health club memberships. However, for noncontractual settings this might be different. For some products and services this is clearly not the case (e.g., there is no reason to believe people bring more and more clothes to their dry cleaner over time).

The theoretical claim is that loyal customers enter a virtual cycle where satisfaction with transactions in previous periods feed not only into loyalty in future periods but also a reinforcement and growth in firm profits. The counterforces to this virtual cycle are, for example, variety seeking across firms, customers getting tired of interacting with the same firm, firms' competitive actions, and the fact that no contracts exist. This negative relationship is also possible if the customer contact costs through mailing catalogs are high compared to the potential revenue from the sales realized from each customer. If costs exceed

TABLE | **12-3** | **REGRESSIONS RESULTS FOR T = 1 TO 36 MONTHS (COHORT 1), VALIDATION RESULTS IN PARENTHESES (COHORT 2)**

Segment	Intercept (a)	Dummy Coefficient for $t = 1$ (b_1)	Coefficient for t (b_2)	R^2
1	12.11 (12.73)	45.77 (46.38)	−0.13 (−0.14)	0.85 (0.85)
2	n.s. (n.s.)	30.24 (30.91)	0.07 (0.071)	0.92 (0.91)
3	19.40 (20.9)	57.85 (58.29)	−0.70 (−0.75)	0.95 (0.94)
4	3.25 (3.69)	29.53 (31.45)	−0.14 (−0.15)	0.94 (0.95)

Notes: All coefficients are significant at $p < 0.01$ except n.s.; n.s. = not significant.

revenue, then over time, this gap can increase to a point where the negative relationship is prevalent. Obviously, these counterforces are strong enough to block the theoretically existing virtuous cycle, thereby leading to decreasing profits over time. Even for Segment 1, the long-life, high-revenue group, the theoretical expectation does not hold. Thus, our finding questions the general claim that loyalty is always desirable to achieve, because we do not find support for the underlying argument (i.e., that profits of long-life customers increase over time). However, loyalty might lead to increased profit over time if there is a forced ongoing relationship, an inertia-driven relationship, or if cost of maintenance decreases over time at a faster rate than revenue falls off.

Are the Costs of Serving Long-Life Customers Lower?

The objective was to test whether the cost associated with promotional expenditures directed at longer- and shorter-life customers differ. To test this argument, we compute the ratio of promotional costs in a given period over the revenues in the same period for each segment. The segment mean represents the dollar amount promotional cost necessary to sustain a dollar amount of revenue. Results are shown in Table 12-2 for Cohort 1 and Cohort 2.

The notion that customers with long tenure are associated with lower promotional costs is clearly rejected. The ratio of mailing cost per dollar sales in the longer-life segment (Segment 1) is statistically not different from the mailing cost per dollar sales in the shorter-life segment (Segment 3). This means, in terms of cost efficiency, that Segments 1 and 3 are the most attractive to the firm, although they have very different lifetime properties. Our findings show that the ratio of mailing cost and revenues—which is one measure of efficiency—need not necessarily be lower for long-life customers.

Do Long-Life Customers Pay Higher Prices?

We wanted to empirically test whether longer-life customers pay, on average, higher or lower prices for their chosen products as compared to customers in the short-life segments. We compute for each transaction the ratio of dollar spending over number of items purchased and average this figure across purchase occasions and customers within segments. Results are shown in Table 12-2 for Cohort 1 and Cohort 2. The average price per item for segment 3 is significantly ($\alpha = 0.05$) different from (and greater than) that of segment 1.

The highest average price paid for a single product item is encountered in Segment 3, the short-life segment. Segment 3 spends, on average, 8.04 percent (Cohort 1) and 10.6 percent (Cohort 2) more on a single product as compared to Segment 1. As a result, our observation of the higher value consciousness of Segment 1 customers goes counter to the argument that long-life customers are less price-sensitive. It is, in fact, the highly profitable short-term customer who seems to be less sensitive to the product's price. One possible explanation for the behavior of Segment 3 customers could be that these are heavy users of the catalog but not all that brand focused. Thus, they might shop heavily from more retailers and switch more easily for smaller benefits, since for these customers even a small benefit may have a large value. Therefore, the higher spending (average prices paid) by Segment 3 customers may be due to some other benefit sought by them.

Thus, our empirical evidence showed four things:

1. A strong linear positive association between lifetime and profits does not necessarily exist.

2. A static and a dynamic lifetime-profit analysis can exhibit a much-differentiated picture: Profitability can occur for the firm from high *and* low

lifetime customers. We discovered that, for our case at least, profits do not increase with increasing customer tenure, thereby adding new empirical evidence to the domain.

3. The cost of serving long-life customers is not lower.

4. Long-life customers do not pay higher prices.

12.3.5 IMPLICATIONS

In this study, we showed a context where managers cannot simply equate a long-life customer with increased lifetime spending, with decreasing costs of serving, and with lower price sensitivity. When a firm examines its customer database, it should not be too surprised to find a significant set of customers who transact with the firm for a short while, but in that duration contribute handsomely to the firm's profits. A firm focused purely on rewarding and retaining customers on the basis of how long they have been with the firm may thus miss out on the opportunity to maximize returns from the higher-value, but shorter-lifetime customers. Similarly, rewarding customers simply because they keep coming to your firm for most of their needs and do not conduct much business with your competitors might also not be the shrewdest strategy to adopt in terms of profits.

12.4 STUDY 2: A MODEL FOR INCORPORATING CUSTOMERS' PROJECTED PROFITABILITY INTO LIFETIME DURATION COMPUTATION[20]

12.4.1 BACKGROUND AND OBJECTIVES

No firm would want to waste its resources by chasing customers who are not likely to be transacting profitably in the future. Deciding when to let go of an unprofitable customer is critical. From a managerial standpoint, it would be extremely desirable to know, at any given time, whether it will be profitable to mail a catalog or send a salesperson to a given customer. If it is profitable, then the manager decides to mail the catalog or initiate a personal contract, otherwise not. Based on this decision metric, it is possible to compute lifetime durations for each customer. Once profitable lifetime duration is obtained for each customer, managers are interested in knowing the factors that drive the profitable lifetime duration. In response to this phenomenon, we conducted a study which presents an integrated metric for measuring profitable customer lifetime duration and assessing antecedent factors. The key research tasks were as follows:

- Empirically measure lifetime duration for *noncontractual* customer-firm relationships, incorporating projected profits.

- Understand the structure of profitable relationships and test the factors which impact a customer's profitable lifetime duration.

- Develop managerial implications for building and managing profitable relationship exchanges.

The research took place in the context of the direct marketing industry. Specifically, our research was conducted for one of the leading general merchandise direct marketers (business-to-consumer, or B-to-C, setting) in the United States. Furthermore, we validated the results with a customer sample from a high-technology firm (business-to-business, B-to-B, setting) selling computer hardware and software.

12.4.2   A DYNAMIC MODEL OF THE ANTECEDENTS OF PROFITABLE LIFETIME DURATION

In this section, we offer a metric to identify, for each customer, the time periods beyond which they may not be profitable. Toward that end we want to suggest a procedure for estimating the lifetime of customers and implementing this procedure empirically.

Since the model describes and analyzes how and why duration times differ systematically across customers, it is a customer-level analysis. Since our approach exploits longitudinal information obtained *within* customers, we refer to it as a *dynamic* model.

Figure 12-6 details the conceptual framework that centers on the focal construct of profitable lifetime duration of customers. *Profitable lifetime duration* is conceptualized to be a function of the characteristics of the relationship. Figure 12-6 not only illustrates how the current study differs from the previous one, but also shows how the current study incorporates the findings of the previous study in the proposed framework—through the incorporation of revenues and cost in measuring lifetime duration. In a nutshell, our research in the last section focuses on the consequences of lifetime duration, while the study in this section focuses on the antecedents of profitable lifetime duration. Once managers understand the important consequences of both longer and shorter lifetime duration (described in the first study), this study tells them how to incorporate those findings when deciding to stop chasing a customer.

The first step involves determining the contribution margin expected from each customer in future periods based on the average of the contribution margins in the past. The second step is to determine for each future period, the probability that the customer will be alive and will transact with the firm. The third step is to combine these two components. The fourth step is to discount the expected contribution margin in each future period to its *net present value* (NPV) using the cost of capital applicable to the firm. If, in a given month, the cost of additional marketing efforts turns out to be greater than the NPV, we determine that the profitable lifetime duration of the customer has ended.

Although it is useful to know the profitable lifetime duration of each customer to determine when to withdraw marketing efforts directed at that customer, it is also important to understand the antecedents of profitable lifetime duration. This provides a manager

FIGURE   12-6   CONCEPTUAL MODEL OF PROFITABLE CUSTOMER LIFETIME

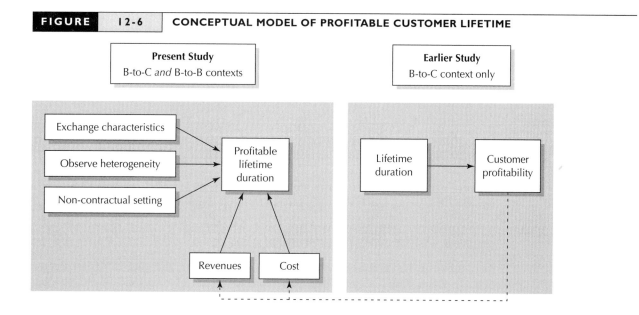

with knowledge about the controllable and environmental variables that explain systematic differences in profitable customer lifetime durations. With this information, a manager is able to focus on appropriate marketing initiatives likely to improve profitability during the tenure of every customer. By analyzing and modeling variables for which data are readily available, a firm can determine which factors are significant in affecting customers' profitable lifetime durations.

The focus of our inquiry is on variables which determine the nature of the customer–firm exchange. Typically, we would need to choose predictor variables of two types to incorporate into the model:

1. *Exchange variables:* Amount purchased, degree of cross-buying, degree of focused buying, interpurchase time, number of product returns, ownership of loyalty instruments, and mailing efforts undertaken by the firm are some variables that can be expected to contribute significantly.
2. *Customer heterogeneity variables:* Location and income of the customer can be expected to add explanatory power to the lifetime duration model.

Conceptually,

Profitable lifetime duration = f (Exchange characteristics, Customer heterogeneity)

Exchange Characteristics

The model provides intuitive explanations for the expected effects of some of these variables. For instance, it is likely that the profitable lifetime duration of a customer is higher for a customer who has spent more than the others and thus has a higher value for the variable *Amount purchased.* Similarly, we can expect a customer who has a tendency to buy across the product line of a firm and therefore exhibits a high *Degree of cross-buying,* should exhibit sustained profitability compared to other customers. Customers who demonstrate a moderate but stable time interval between successive purchases (*Interpurchase time*) are likely to be profitable for a longer duration than customers who have long interpurchase intervals or those who burn out after a rapid series of purchases. Surprisingly, *Number of product returns* can relate positively to profitable lifetime duration, because heavier buyers are also likely to return more merchandise, and a positive experience during the return procedure is likely to boost the buyer–seller relationship.

Customer Heterogeneity

Demographic variables that capture observed customer heterogeneity have been used consistently in response modeling. The main motivation to include these variables is for statistical control purposes, as well as for potential segmentation purposes.

Spatial Location of Consumer We would expect a higher proportion of long lifetime customers to live in low-density areas as opposed to high-density areas (i.e., cities).

Income In general, customers with higher incomes are less susceptible to higher price sensitivity[21] and are expected to keep buying from the firm for the added convenience.

12.4.3   RESEARCH METHODOLOGY

The data we use for this research are the same data we used for the study in the last section. The use of the same data set is critical because we are trying to evaluate if our previous findings can be implemented successfully to determine which customers to let go and when to let go. In addition to the data from the two cohorts used in the last study, data from an additional cohort were also used. Thus, we can validate the results across three different sets of customers. Although the data are partially the same for both studies, the studies have entirely different objectives.

Database

The data are provided by the same U.S. general merchandise catalog retailer, of which the characteristics have been described in the last section. The data for this study also cover a three-year window and are recorded on a daily basis. The database for the three cohorts consists of a total number of observations of 11,992 households. The sample of households belongs to three different cohorts, the structure of which is depicted in Figure 12-7.

The customer-firm interaction of Cohort 1 households is tracked for a 36-month time period, the behavior of Cohort 2 households for a 35-month time period, and the behavior of Cohort 3 households for a 34-month time period. The households are sampled randomly from all households that started in January, February, and March 1995, respectively. The number of purchases ranges from 1 to 46 across the sample with a median number of five purchases, the median interpurchase time is 117 days, and the median transaction amount is $91 for each purchase.

12.4.4 DETERMINING PROFITABLE CUSTOMER LIFETIME DURATION

Lifetime Duration Calculation

Calculate Net Present Value (NPV) of Expected Contribution Margin (ECM$_{it}$)   Given the nature of our data (and the data structure in the direct marketing industry in general), managers can easily determine past purchase and spending activity for each customer. Likewise, an estimate of the P(Alive) status, using the NBD/Pareto model, can be obtained for both past and future periods. This allows us to establish the following decision rule: If the sum of the expected discounted future contribution margin were smaller than a currently planned marketing intervention, we would establish the death event for the customer (A managerial consequence would be to stop mailing to that customer, even though this is not our primary concern.) More formally, we compute the estimated future contribution margin:

$$NPV \, of \, ECM_{it} = \sum_{n=t+1}^{t+18} P(\text{Alive})_{in} \times AMCM_{it}\left(\frac{1}{1+r}\right)^n \tag{2}$$

FIGURE   12-7   DATABASE STRUCTURE FOR B-TO-C SETTING

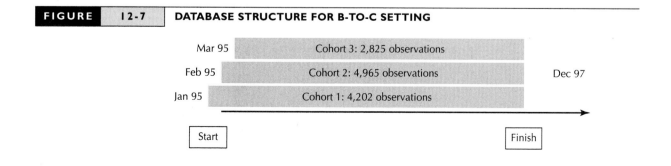

where ECM_{it} is the estimated expected contribution margin for a given month t, $AMCM_{it}$ is the average contribution margin in month t based on all prior purchases since birth (updated dynamically), r is the discount rate (15 percent on a yearly basis), i is the customer, t is the month for which NPV is estimated, n is the number of months beyond t, and $P(\text{Alive})_{in}$ is the probability that customer i is alive in month n.

For example, the *NPV of expected contribution margin* for customer i in month 18 is calculated as follows: For each month and for each customer, we observe the total purchases in dollars. Then, we multiply the purchase amount by 0.3 to reflect the gross margin. In other words, the *Cost of goods sold* is accounted for, and what we have is gross margin. Next, we subtract the *Cost of actual marketing efforts* (in this case, the cost of catalogs plus the mailing costs) to obtain the monthly contribution margin. If a decision is made at the end of month 18, then we take the average ($AMCM_i$) of months 1 to 18 by summing up all the 18 contribution margins and dividing the sum by 18. If we are at the end of time period 36, then we take the average (AMCM) of the previous 36 months' contribution margins by summing up all the 36 contribution margins and dividing the sum by 36. Thus, the AMCM estimate is updated monthly—in other words, dynamically modeled and used as a baseline for future purchases (i.e., purchases between t and N). The past purchase level at time t is projected into the future and multiplied monthly with the predicted $P(\text{Alive})$ estimate. It thus endogenously contains the information about the mailing process as well. The future time horizon is limited to 18 months because the associated $P(\text{Alive})$ estimate becomes only marginally different from zero after 18 months. For example, according to the NBD/Pareto model, if a customer hasn't bought in a long time, his probability of being alive is small. Since the predicted $P(\text{Alive})$ for the next 18 months will be even smaller, the net present value of the expected future contribution margin stream will be very low. Thus, having to decide whether to invest in this person (i.e., marketing intervention), chances are that this person would not be deemed as a lucrative future customer—given the cost of mailing.

Decision of Relationship Termination Formally, if *NPV of ECM_{it} < Cost of mailing*, then the firm would decide to terminate the relationship. Using this decision rule, we establish for every customer at what point he is subjected to the proposed termination policy. The decision rule incorporates the cost of mailings and an average flat contribution margin before mailings of 25 percent. The discount rate is assumed to be 15 percent.

Calculation of Finite Lifetime Estimate Based on the decision of relationship termination, the average lifetime across Cohort 1 is 29.3 months, across Cohort 2 is 28.6 months, and across Cohort 3 is 27.8 months (Table 12-4). The consistency between the three cohorts is very high. In all the cohorts, little more than 60 percent of the samples have a lifetime less than the observation window. Households clearly show variability in lifetime duration. This is evidenced through several factors, such as the wide range

| **TABLE** | **12-4** | **NBD/PARETO MODEL CHARACTERISTICS AND FINITE LIFETIME ESTIMATES** |

	Sample Size	Pearson Correlation of P(Alive)*	Mean Average Percentage Error**	Mean Lifetime (Months)	Lifetime Standard Deviation	Percentage Right-Censored
Cohort 1	4,202	0.9981	5.83%	29.3	7.5	42.9
Cohort 2	4,965	0.9988	5.22%	28.6	7.7	45.6
Cohort 3	2,825	0.9987	4.75%	27.8	7.2	47.2

*Generated from the NBD/Pareto estimates of Reinartz and Kumar (2000) and those of the current study, respectively.

**The P(Alive) of Reinartz and Kumar (2000) and P(Alive) of the current study.

between lowest and highest lifetime estimate, the standard deviation of the lifetime estimate, and the relatively small value of s in the NBD/Pareto model. Thus, we expect considerable scope for exploring the factors that affect lifetime duration. Note that the lifetime duration estimates that incorporate projected profits are different from the one that doesn't incorporate profits.

12.4.5   ANALYSIS

In the proportional hazard model, the hazard rate $h_i(t)$ for individual i is assumed to take this form:

$$h_i(t) = h_0(t)e^{x_{it}\beta} \tag{3}$$

where $h_0(t)$ is the baseline hazard rate and $(x_{it}\beta)$ is the impact of the independent variables. We can estimate the hazard model with the semi-parametric partial likelihood method.[22]

Variable Operationalization

The criterion variable is the household specific estimate of profitable lifetime duration. The time varying variable *Purchase amount*$_{it}$ enters the model as the monthly spending level (\$). The time varying variable *Cross buying*$_{it}$ is operationalized as the number of different departments shopped in, in a given six-month period. There are a total of 90 different merchandise departments. The *Focus-of-buying* variable is operationalized as a dummy variable. The percentages of customers coded as 1 (buying consistently in one department) are 0.04, 0.05, and 0.04 across the three cohorts. The time varying variable *Average interpurchase time*$_{it}$ is measured in number of days between purchases. AIT_{it}^2 is the square of the AIT_{it} variable. The *Return*$_{it}$ variable is the ratio of returned goods (\$ value) to purchased goods (\$ value). The *Loyalty instrument* variable is operationalized as a dummy variable, indicating ownership of the corporate charge card. The proportion of customers holding a charge card is 0.39, 0.52, and 0.59 across the three cohorts. The effect of *Mailings*$_{it}$ will be operationalized as a lagged finite exponential decay of past marketing efforts, similar to procedures in advertising–sales relationship literature. Since the merchandise changes on a continuous basis, the use of a finite decay period seems more realistic than an infinite period. The variable is measured in terms of the number of efforts/mail pieces sent to the customer. The dummy variable *Product category*$_i$ describes whether a buyer predominantly shops in hard goods or in soft goods. The proportion of customers buying predominantly hard goods is 0.50, 0.49, and 0.45 across the three cohorts. The variable *Population density* enters the model as the absolute population number in a given two-digit ZIP code into the model. These numbers were derived from the 2000 U.S. census. The variable *Income* comes from the firm's database and is coded on a scale from 1 to 7, where 1 is a yearly income of lesser than \$10.000 and 7 is a yearly income of more than \$150,000. The mean rating is 5.19, 4.88, and 5.01 across the three cohorts. Finally, the *Age* variable is measured as the age of the individual in years, calculated from birthdate information from the database. The mean rating is 34.4, 34.8, and 35.2 years across the three cohorts. A summary of all variables is given in Table 12-5.

The complete model specification is given in equation (4). The hazard of a lifetime event of a household i at time t is given as follows:

$$h_i(t) = h_0(t) \, \text{EXP} \, (\beta 1 \, \text{Purchase amount}_{it} + \beta 2 \, \text{Cross buying}_{it} +$$
$$\beta 3 \, \text{Focus of buying}_i + \beta 4 \, \text{Average Interpurchase Time}_{it} +$$
$$\beta 5 \, (\text{Average Interpurchase Time}_{it})^2 + \gamma 1 \, \text{Returns}_{it} +$$
$$\gamma 2 \, \text{Loyalty instrument}_i + \gamma 3 \, \text{Mailings}_{it} + \gamma 4 \, \text{Product category}_i +$$
$$\delta 1 \, \text{Population density}_i + \delta 2 \, \text{Income}_i + \delta 3 \, \text{Age}_i) \tag{4}$$

| TABLE 12-5 | VARIABLES FOR PROFITABLE LIFETIME MODEL |

Dependent Variable	Measured As
Profitable Lifetime$_i$*	Months

Independent Variables	Measured As	Hypothesized Directional Impact on Profitable Lifetime
Purchase amount$_{it}$**	Monthly spending level ($), moving average over a six-month period	+
Cross buying$_{it}$	Number of departments shopped in	(+)
Focus of buying$_i$	Dummy: 1 = buys consistently in single dept. only; 0 = all other	Nondirectional hypothesis
Average interpurchase time$_{it}$	Number of days	(+) Inverse U-shaped relationship for AIT and AIT^2
(Average interpurchase time$_{it}$)^2	(Number of days)^2	(−) Inverse U-shaped relationship for AIT and AIT^2
Returns$_{it}$	Proportion of returns (of sales)	(−)
Loyalty instrument$_i$	Ownership of charge card. Dummy variable, 1 = owns card, 0 = no card	(+)
Mailings$_{it}$	Number of mailings sent in last six months (= 1 season) since current t, exponential decay, one month lag	(+)
Product category$_i$	1 = more than 50 percent of purchases in softgoods, 0 = more than 50 percent of purchases in hard goods	No directional hypothesis
Population density	Number of people in two-digit ZIP code	(−)
Income$_i$	Scale from 1 to 9 where 1 is < $10,000 and 9 is > $150,000	(+)
Age$_i$	Age of individual in years	No directional hypothesis

*Subscript$_i$ = variable value does not change over time; subscript$_{it}$ = time-varying variable.

**Time-varying variables are updated each month.

12.4.6 RESULTS

The results of the profitable lifetime duration model for the three cohorts are reported in Table 12-6. The table contains the final model parameters, including an interaction term (Returns × Purchase amount).

Effects of Exchange Variables

Purchase Amount We hypothesized the level of spending for merchandise (β_1) is positively related to profitable lifetime duration. We find support for this hypothesis across all three cohorts and across all three models ($p < .01$). Thus, H_1 is supported. Due to the strong association between these two measures, it is important to take information on amount of purchases into account when managing profitable lifetime duration.

To better understand the relative impact of this variable on the hazard of relationship termination we analyze the risk ratio. From a managerial standpoint, the risk ratio helps in gauging the impact of the drivers of profitable lifetime duration. The risk ratio can be interpreted as the percent change in the hazard for each one-unit increase in the independent variable—controlling for all other independent variables. The risk ratio is

TABLE 12-6 COEFFICIENTS (STANDARD ERRORS) FOR PROFITABLE LIFETIME DURATION MODEL

Independent Variables	Parameter	Cohort 1			Cohort 2			Cohort 3		
		Model 1†	Model 2	Model 3	Model 1	Model 2	Model 3	Model 1	Model 2	Model 3
1. Purchase amount$_{it}$	$\beta 1$	.0497* (.00209)	.0360* (.00212)	.0354* (.00213)	.0486* (.00186)	.0373* (.00192)	.0364* (.00192)	.0433* (.00228)	.0341* (.00240)	.0324* (.00239)
2. Cross buying$_{it}$	$\beta 2$	1.389* (.0407)	1.293* (.0417)	1.276* (.0419)	1.226* (.0327)	1.172* (.0338)	1.154* (.0340)	.970* (.0346)	.908* (.0356)	.912* (.0360)
3. Focus of buying$_i$	$\beta 3$	−.315* (.0647)	−.257* (.0660)	−.270* (.0662)	−.297* (.0624)	−.306* (.0630)	−.269* (.0632)	−.289* (.0841)	−.213** (.0862)	−.177** (.0865)
4. Average interpurchase time$_{it}$	$\beta 4$	.0121* (.000521)	.0133* (.000521)	.0127* (.000521)	.0146* (.000515)	.0153* (.000517)	.0147* (.000519)	.0171* (.000718)	.0178* (.000724)	.0171* (.000726)
5. (Average interpurchase time$_{it}$)^2	$\beta 5$	−8.994 E−6* (6.276 E−7)	−9.880 E−6* (5.900 E−7)	−9.487 E−6* (5.892 E−7)	−.0000121* (6.243 E−7)	−.0000123* (6.013 E−7)	−.0000119* (6.046 E−7)	−.0000151* (8.912 E−7)	−.0000154* (8.660 E−7)	−.0000147* (8.747 E−7)
6. Returns$_{it}$	$\gamma 1$		−2.214* (.222)	−2.050* (.226)		−1.690* (.214)	−1.557* (.215)		−1.323* (.320)	−1.323* (.320)
7. Loyalty instrument$_i$	$\gamma 2$		.666* (.0577)	.685* (.0577)		.745* (.0482)	.753* (.0484)		.598* (.0618)	.614* (.0622)
8. Mailings$_{it}$	$\gamma 3$		.00552* (.00153)	.00686* (.00154)		.00628* (.00148)	.00712* (.00148)		.00610* (.00224)	.00898* (.00229)
9. Product category$_i$	$\gamma 4$		−.0278 (.0437)	−.0554 (.0438)		−.0360 (.0414)	−.0476 (.0414)		−.0422 (.0556)	−.0740 (.0558)
10. Returns × Purchase Amount$_{it}$	$\gamma 5$		.221* (.0188)	.208* (.0189)		.148* (.0155)	.134* (.0155)		.105* (.0186)	.0985* (.0183)
11. Population density$_i$	$\delta 1$			−3.475 E−8* (1.252 E−8)			2.23 E−8** (1.196 E−8)			5.305 E−9 (1.584 E−8)
12. Income$_i$	$\delta 2$			.124* (.00863)			.111* (.00805)			.133* (.0104)
13. Age$_i$	$\delta 3$			4.032 E−7 (4.668 E−6)			3.628 E−6 (4.123 E−6)			4.684 E−6 (5.446 E−6)
−2 Log Likelihood		13728.6	13337.7	13126.8	15.678.0	15200.7	15004.6	9089.4	8807.7	8639.2
R^2		0.697	0.727	0.743	0.684	0.719	0.730	0.652	.672	.693

†Signs of coefficients have been reversed to reflect effect on lifetime.

*Significant at 0.01.

**Significant at 0.05.

calculated as $((\exp(-\beta) - 1) \times 100)$. Applied to the purchase amount variable, a change of only $10 in the monthly spending results in a decrease in the hazard of termination of between 31 and 35 percent, depending on cohort.

Cross Buying The degree of buying across departments (β_2) was argued to be positively related to profitable lifetime duration because a broader scope of interaction constitutes a stronger relationship. This contention is supported for all models and for all cohorts in our model ($p < .01$). Apparently, a long customer life is sustained by a higher degree of purchasing *across* departments. Given a certain income, people need longer time to fill their needs if they purchase across the board rather than in a focused manner. When calculating the risk ratio for this variable, we find that purchases in an additional department are associated with a decreasing hazard of between 59.6 percent and 72.8 percent, depending on cohort. Thus, it seems to be extremely desirable for the firm to induce customers to engage in cross-departmental shopping. Hence, H_2 is supported. This is an important finding because the effect of cross-buying on lifetime duration has not yet been documented.

Focus of Buying We did not advance a directional hypothesis with respect to focus of buying (β_3) because of conflicting arguments. The empirical test resulted in a negative relationship between focused buying behavior and lifetime duration. Thus, the result is in line with the results of the cross-buying construct—broader buying is generally associated positively with an increase in lifetime duration.

Average Interpurchase Time AIT (β_4) was hypothesized to be related to profitable customer lifetime duration in an inverse U-shaped fashion. That is, the longest profitable lifetime should be associated with intermediate interpurchase times. We tested for this relationship by introducing a nonlinear term AIT^2 (β_5). We do find support for our hypothesis with both terms being significant at ($p < .01$) and having the hypothesized sign (β_4 positive and β_5 negative). That is, lifetime tends to be shorter when interpurchase times are either very short or very long and lifetime is longest with an intermediate value of AIT. Hence, H_3 is supported. Together, the impact of the core exchange variables on profitable lifetime duration is substantial. Between 65.2 and 69.7 percent of the variance is explained by this group of variables. This once again demonstrates that the exchange variables dominate even in a noncontractual situation.

Returns Regarding the proportion of returned goods (γ_1), our reasoning assumed a negative association of returns and profitable lifetime. That is, the higher the proportion of returned goods, the lower the associated profitable lifetime duration. Our original results (not shown in Table 12-7) showed the effect was significant at ($p < .01$), but had a *positive* sign for all three cohorts. Thus, the hypothesis that higher returns were a sign of greater dissatisfaction and therefore would lead to shorter lifetimes was not supported (H_4). A possible explanation for this outcome could be that customers who returned merchandise had a positive encounter with the firm's service representatives, which then might affect their future purchase behavior.[23] It is interesting to mention that managers told us (upon further inquiry) of their experience, that heavy buyers tend to return proportionately more. A possible reason for this might be that these buyers are accustomed to the procedures of returning merchandise and are able to do it efficiently. Thus, it might be that these customers see the return process as part of the mail-order buying process. If this effect dominates, then one would expect a positive relationship. Likewise, this would probably mean that as customers spent more with the firm, the effect should become stronger. To pursue this line of thought, we added, post-hoc, an interaction between amount of purchases and the proportion of returns to the model. The final results including the interaction are included in Table 12-7. The interaction turns out to be significant for all three cohorts ($p < .01$). Thus, we find evidence for the conjecture that the degree of returns depends on the degree of spending. Thus, the positive impact on lifetime duration is greatest when the level of dollar purchases and the level of returns are high. Figure 12-8 depicts this situation graphically. Evidence[24] has been shown of the impact of positively disconfirming complainants' expectations to achieve (restore) satisfaction. Moreover, the impact of this response seems to be maintained over time. Therefore, we believe, proportionally higher returns might be an indication of this positive disconfirmation. If, for example, the firm has a no-hassle return policy and the customers have come to accept the technical return procedures, greater satisfaction with the exchange can result and therefore greater profitable lifetime duration. Clearly, it would be desirable to have stated satisfaction measures at hand to add additional validity to our results. Similar empirical support for our finding comes from another study[25] in which Omaha Steaks, a mail-order supplier of high-quality meat, found higher profitability for those customers for which it had quickly resolved complaints.

Loyalty Instrument Interestingly, the loyalty instrument (γ_2) is significantly related to profitable lifetime duration ($p < .01$). According to our hypothesis, the use of the charge card as a loyalty instrument should lead to a higher lifetime. Thus, in our sample, issuing a charge card appears to be successful as a loyalty instrument because it does seem to be associated with longer customer lifetime. Thus, H_5 is supported. Remember, the findings in literature thus far are not very favorable in terms of loyalty instrument efficiency. However,

TABLE 12-7	**SUMMARY OF RESULTS**		
Hypothesis	**Description**	**B-to-C Setting**	**B-to-B Setting**
H_1	Profitable customer lifetime duration is positively related to the customer's spending level.	Supported	Supported
H_{2a}	Profitable customer lifetime duration is positively related to the degree of cross-buying behavior exhibited by the customers.	Supported	Supported
H_{2b}	Profitable customer lifetime duration is related to the focused buying behavior exhibited by customers.	Supported However, the relationship is negative, indicating that buying in only a single department results in shorter lifetime duration.	Supported However, the relationship is negative, indicating that buying in only a single department results in shorter lifetime duration.
H_3	Profitable customer lifetime duration is related to average interpurchase time in an inverse U-shaped manner, whereby intermediate AIT is associated with the longest profitable lifetime.	Supported	Partial Support Only the linear term is significant.
H_4	Profitable customer lifetime duration is inversely related to the proportion of merchandise returned by the customers.	Not Supported However, the interaction of returns with purchase amount variable is significant.	Not Supported However, the interaction of returns with purchase amount variable is significant.
H_5	Profitable customer lifetime duration is positively related to the customer's ownership of the company's loyalty instrument (B-to-C) or the availability of line of credit (B-to-B).	Supported	Supported
H_6	Profitable customer lifetime duration is positively related to the number of mailing efforts of the company (B-to-C) or the number of contacts (B-to-B).	Supported	Supported
H_7	Profitable customer lifetime duration is higher for customers living in areas with lower population density (B-to-C) or businesses existing in lower population density (B-to-B).	Supported	Not Supported
H_8	Profitable customer lifetime duration is positively related to the income of the customer (B-to-C) or income of the firm (B-to-B).	Supported	Supported

in this case, it seems at least successful with respect to profitable lifetime duration. Nevertheless, we cannot make a statement about the cost effectiveness of the program. In terms of magnitude of effect, the risk ratio analysis indicates adopting the loyalty instrument is associated with a 45 to 52 percent decrease in hazard of relationship termination—a substantive amount.

FIGURE   12-8   **INTERACTION BETWEEN PROPORTION OF RETURNS AND PURCHASE AMOUNT**

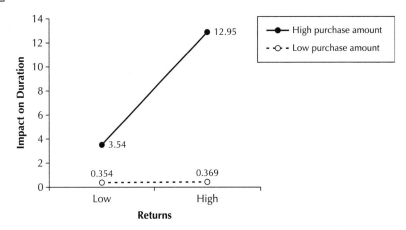

Mailings   The mailing variable (γ_3) was introduced as an important control variable specified as a lagged effect. Recall that mailings and sales are typically not independent in a direct marketing context. The hypothesized effect on lifetime duration was positive. We find a positive significant effect ($p < .01$) for all three cohorts—thus, our decision to control for the variable is correct. Hence, H_6 is supported in that the mailing effort is significantly related to profitable customer lifetime duration.

Product Category   A concern in our modeling effort was that the choice of product category (γ_4) could have a systematic effect on a customer's lifetime. For example, it could be that durable goods (i.e., hard goods) have a potentially long lifetime and thus there is little need for replacement, leading to a potentially shorter customer lifetime. This concern, however, is not substantiated since the parameter γ_4 for the dummy variable is not significant ($p > .1$) for any cohort.

Effects of Observed Heterogeneity

Spatial Location of Customer   It was argued that the spatial location is linked to a customer's tenure with a direct marketer (δ_1) such that the population density is inversely associated with customer lifetime duration. Our results confirm this hypothesis (H_7) for two out of the three cohorts ($p < .05$), thus underlining the need (1) to account for observed heterogeneity in duration modeling, and (2) to demonstrate support for the transaction cost minimization argument.

Income and Age   In terms of the two demographic variables representing income (δ_2) and age (δ_3), we find that while age does not seem to be related to profitable lifetime duration ($p > .05$), income does ($p < .01$). Our model indicates higher income is associated with longer lifetime. Thus H_8 is supported.

Overall, the information on observed customer heterogeneity adds explanatory power to the duration model, above and beyond the exchange variables. The results are validated in a B-to-B setting. The summary of results is available in Table 12-7.

12.4.7 TECHNICAL APPENDIX: ESTIMATION OF P(ALIVE)

The likelihood of a customer being alive can be computed either through the *method-of-moments* or through *maximum-likelihood* approaches. Due to the computational constraints imposed by the maximum likelihood estimation (MLE), method-of-moment estimates have been the method of choice. It has also been shown for the NBD model that the method-of-moments approach and MLE yield approximately the same results.[26] Thus, there seems to be support in favor of the more manageable method-of-moments routine.

Using the likelihood as given in A1, we estimate the four parameters of the NBD/Pareto model (r, α, s, β) with a Fortran routine. The likelihood is:

$$L(r, \alpha, s, \beta) = \prod_{i=1}^{M} P[X_i = x_i, t_i, T_i | r, \alpha, s, \beta] \tag{A1}$$

with M being a random sample of customers, and customer i made $X_i = x_i$ purchases in $(0, T_i)$ with the last transaction time at t_i. The resulting MLE parameters are $r = 3.01$, $\alpha = 9.65$, $s = 0.82$ and $\beta = 11.91$ (estimation horizon 30 months). The parameters are quite consistent with the estimates derived by Reinartz and Kumar, who used estimates of $r = 4.24$, $\alpha = 14.95$, $s = 0.93$ and $\beta = 13.85$.[27] In particular, the critical parameters $r/\alpha = 0.312$ and $s/\beta = 0.069$ are similar to Reinartz and Kumar ($r/\alpha = 0.281$ and $s/\beta = 0.069$), resulting in little bias in the P(Alive) estimates (see Table 12-8). Since the results are robust and the computational resources required for MLE are substantially larger, the method-of-moment estimation is preferred.

The model parameters can be explained as follows. The variation across customers in their long-run purchase rate is reflected in the estimate of r only and is independent of α. The larger the value of the shape parameter r, the more homogeneous the population of customers in terms of purchase rate. Thus, r can be viewed as an overall inverse measure of the concentration in purchase rates across households. The larger the value of the shape parameter s, the more homogeneous the population of customers in terms of dropout rate. The concentration in dropout rates, β, depends on the parameter s only. Overall, the model estimates seem reasonable and show a high degree of face validity and internal consistency. Having calculated the distribution parameters, the characteristic of interest is the probability that a customer with a particular observed transaction history is still alive at time T since trial. Schmittlein, Morrison, and Colombo show this probability depends on the customer's past purchase history (through the number of purchases x) and the time t (since trial) at which the most recent transaction occurred.[28] The desired probability for $\alpha > \beta$ is given in equation (A2) as follows:

$$P[\text{Alive} | r, \alpha, s, \beta, x, t, T] =$$

$$\left\{ 1 + \frac{s}{r + x + s} \left[\left(\frac{\alpha + T}{\alpha + t} \right)^{r+x} \left(\frac{\beta + T}{\alpha + t} \right)^{s} F(a_1, b_1; c_1; z_1(t)) - \left(\frac{\beta + T}{\alpha + t} \right)^{s} F(a_1, b_1; c_1; z_1(T)) \right] \right\}^{-1} \tag{A2}$$

where $a_1 = r + x + s$, $b_1 = s + 1$, $c_1 = r + x + s + 1$, $z_1(y) = (\alpha - \beta) / (\alpha + y)$, $F(a_1, b_1; c_1; z_1)$ is the Gauss hypergeometric function, r, α, s, β = model parameters, x = number of purchases, t = time since trial at which the most recent transaction occurred, and T = time since trial.

It is important to mention that this methodology requires cohorts of customers. Only the cohort analysis yields insight into the dynamic pattern of defection over time, whereas a simple cross-section of customers would not give such insight (because customers are at different stages in their lifecycle).

TABLE 12-8	**ACTUAL REVENUES AND PROFITS FOR THE SELECTED GROUP OF CUSTOMERS BASED ON NBD/PARETO, RFM, AND PAST CUSTOMER VALUE SELECTION (COHORT 1)**		
Customer Selection Based on	**Percentage of Cohort (Selected from Top)**	**Evaluation at 18 Months ($)**	**Evaluation at 30 Months ($)**
NBD/Pareto with ECM	30 (n = 1,260)	590,452 (123,076)	318,831 (62,991)
	50 (n = 2,101)	756,321 (148,922)	361,125 (61,636)
	70 (n = 2,941)	864,114 (165,735)	380,855 (60,305)
Advanced RFM	30 (n = 1,260)	442,534 (78,555)	140,781 (27,582)
	50 (n = 2,101)	599,100 (99,831)	186,267 (36,380)
	70 (n = 2,941)	687,163 (110,244)	216,798 (42,839)
Past Customer Value	30 (n = 1,260)	508,997 (86,820)	179,665 (35,916)
	50 (n = 2,101)	648,772 (112,723)	210,860 (41,729)
	70 (n = 2,941)	789,526 (138,124)	225,910 (44,738)

Notes: Profits are in parentheses. Results are similar for Cohorts 2 and 3.

12.5 STUDY 3: A MODEL FOR IDENTIFYING THE TRUE VALUE OF A LOST CUSTOMER[29]

12.5.1 CONCEPTUAL BACKGROUND

The authors of this study, John E. Hogan, Katherine N. Lemon, and Barak Libai, argue the traditional customer profitability models evaluate customers in isolation from one another and that the effects of social interactions are not accounted for. Customers are involved in social interactions and they may advocate positive or negative word of mouth about the products and the firm. This, in turn, could influence future prospects to become customers and existing customers to cease transactions. The exclusion of these indirect social effects could lead to misallocation of scarce marketing resources during the critical early stages of a new product market. The value of a lost customer depends on whether the customer defects to a competing firm or disadopts the product category. Customer defection refers to a situation where a customer leaves one firm and starts transacting with a competing firm. As a consequence, the firm loses direct sales from that customer. Disadoption by contrast, is when a customer stops purchasing from that product category altogether. This affects the long-term profitability in two ways—one is the loss of direct sales and the other is in terms of indirect effects of word of mouth, imitation, and other social effects.

12.5.2 MODELING THE EFFECTS OF DISADOPTION ON THE VALUE OF A LOST CUSTOMER

If $\propto$ is the proportion of disadopters in a firm's lost customers, then the value of an average lost customer (VLC) is calculated in equation (A3):

$$VLC = \propto VLC_{\text{disadopter}} + (1 - \propto) \, VLC_{\text{defectors}} \tag{A3}$$

The value of $\propto$ may vary across firms and markets. The sales effect of slower customer acquisitions caused by the social effects and reduced level of word of mouth is then estimated using the Bass new product growth model. The profit impact of a lost customer is estimated by calculating the difference in the expected profitability of the firm before and after the customer has disadopted. In other words, profit impact of a lost customer = sales estimate from new product growth model without disadoption – the sales estimate when the customer disadopts after certain time. This takes into account both the direct and indirect effects of disadoption.

12.5.3 THE KEY DETERMINANTS OF THE VALUE OF A LOST CUSTOMER

To study the phenomenon of the lost customer, a Monte Carlo simulation was used in which the key parameters such as external influence (p), internal influence (q), discount rate (r), and disadoption time (t_1) were variable based. The results indicated: (1) the time when customer disadopts has the largest impact on the value of the lost customer, (2) the external influence, p has a negative impact, (3) the internal influence, q has a positive impact on penetration because higher q signifies stronger word of mouth, and (4) discount rate has positive impact on the value of lost customer. The study shows that the earlier a customer disadopts, the more money the company loses. This is because at the early stages of a product life cycle, there are only a few adopters to influence the future adoption through word of mouth. Hence, a single disadoption can have larger impact. The effects of various variables on the value of a lost customer are given in Table 12-9.

It is also important to note the value of a lost customer is affected by stages in the product life cycle, the firm's market share, and the rate at which competitors' customers disadopt. This has important managerial implications in terms of spending on customer retention, allocation of retention, and acquisition spending over time, extended return on investment analysis, and managing competitive environment.

12.6 SUMMARY

A study of the lifetime-profitability relationship in a noncontractual setting highlights a concern with the widespread assumption of a clear-cut positive lifetime-profitability relationship and underlines the importance of a differentiated analysis. In the conceptual model, individual customer lifetime profits are modeled as a function of a customer's lifetime duration, revenue flows over the course of a customer's lifetime, and firm cost is associated with the marketing exchange. In a noncontractual scenario such as the direct marketing context, promotional costs are typically the largest nonproduct cost factor in a

TABLE	12-9	**EFFECT OF FIRM AND MARKET VARIABLES ON THE VALUE OF A LOST CUSTOMER**

Parameter		Standardized Coefficient	P Value
p	External influence	−0.432	< 0.0001
q	Internal influence	0.147	0.0103
r	Discount rate	0.213	0.0003
t_1	Disadoption time	−0.594	< 0.0001

Source: John E. Hogan, Katherine N. Lemon, and Barak Libai, "What Is the True Value of a Lost Customer?" *Journal of Service Research* 5 (2003): 196–208.

customer firm relationship. A possible reason for higher value consciousness of long-term customers might be that customers learn over time to trust lower-priced items or brands as much as established-name brand products.

The empirical evidence showed that (1) a strong linear positive association between lifetime and profits does not necessarily exist, (2) profits do not necessarily increase with increasing customer tenure, (3) the cost of serving long-life customers is not lower, and (4) long-life customers do not pay higher prices. However, these factors may have differential impacts in different industries.

The objectives of the second study were (1) to empirically measure lifetime duration for *noncontractual* customer-firm relationships, (2) to incorporate projected profits to the structure of profitable relationships and to identify the antecedents of customer's profitable lifetime duration, and (3) to develop managerial implications for building and managing profitable relationship exchanges. The model first estimated the probability of a customer being alive and then integrated this with the individual lifetime duration. The main drivers of customer's profitable lifetime duration are classified as exchange characteristics and customer heterogeneity. The customer's spending level, cross-buying, focus of buying, average interpurchase time, amount of returns, customer's ownership of loyalty instrument, and the mailing efforts of the company are identified as important exchange characteristics. Spatial location of consumer and his age and income are the important customer heterogeneity factors influencing the profitable lifetime duration.

In the third study, a model is developed for determining the effects of disadoption on the value of a lost customer. This takes into account not only the direct effects of lost sales but also the indirect effects of social effects such as word of mouth. The key determinants of the value of a lost customer are identified as disadoption time, external and internal influence, and the discount rate. The disadoption time is found to have the maximum negative impact on the value—that is, the earlier a customer disadopts, the higher the value of the lost customer.

12.7 EXERCISE QUESTIONS

1. Discuss the differences in the analysis of customer loyalty between contractual and non contractual settings.

2. In the credit card industry, what drivers of profitable lifetime duration would you expect?

3. Discuss the effect of a lost customer on a firm. How would you capture and quantify this effect?

ENDNOTES

1. Adapted from V. Kumar and G. Ramani, "Taking CLV Analysis to the Next Level: A Multistep Approach to Better Understanding Customer Value," *Journal of Integrated Communications* (2003–2004).

2. R. Venkatesan and V. Kumar, "A Customer Life Time Value Framework for Customer Selection and Optimal Resource Allocation Strategy," *Journal of Marketing* (2004).

3. V. Kumar, Girish Ramani, and Timothy Bohling, "Customer Lifetime Value Approaches and Best Practice Applications," *Journal of Interactive Marketing* 18, no. 3 (2004): 60–72.

4. W. Reinartz and V. Kumar, "On the Profitability of Long-life Customers in a Non-Contractual Setting: An Empirical Investigation and Implications for Marketing," *Journal of Marketing* 64 (October 2000): 17–32.

5. Jagdish N. Sheth and Atul Parvatiyar, "Relationship in Consumer Markets: Antecedents and Consequences," *Journal of the Academy of Marketing Science* 23, no. 4 (1995): 255–71.

6. Neeli Bendapudi and Leonard L. Berry, "Customers' Motivations for Maintaining Relationships with Service Providers," *Journal of Retailing* 73 (1997): 15–37.

7. Frederick Reichheld and Sasser, "Zero Defections: Quality Comes To Services," *Harvard Business Review* (September–October 1990): 105.

8. Frederick Reichheld and Thomas Teal, *The Loyalty Effect* (Boston: Harvard Business School Press, 1996).

9. Grahame R. Dowling and Mark Uncles, "Do Customer Loyalty Programs Really Work?" *Sloan Management Review* (Summer 1997): 78.

10. Ruth N. Bolton, , "A Dynamic Model of the Duration of the Customer's Relationship with a Continuous Service Provider: the Role of Satisfaction," *Marketing Science* 17, no. 1 (1998): 45–65; Shaomin Li, "Survival Analysis," *Marketing Research* 7 (Fall 1995): 17–23.

11. Robert F. Dwyer, "Customer Lifetime Valuation to Support Marketing Decision Making," *Journal of Direct Marketing* 11 (Fall 1997): 6–13.

12. "Catalog Sales Growth Continues to Outpace Overall Retail Growth" http://retailindustry .about/library/bl/q2/bl_dma060401a.htm, accessed on January 4, 2005.

13. Gordon A. Wyner, "Customer Relationship Measurement," *Marketing Research: A Magazine of Management and Applications* 11, no. 2 (1999): 39–41.

14. Leonard Berry, "Relationship Marketing of Services—Growing Interest, Emerging Perspectives," *Journal of the Academy of Marketing Sciences* 23 (Fall 1995): 236–45.

15. W. Reinartz and V. Kumar, "The Mismanagement of Customer Loyalty," *Harvard Business Review* (July 2002).

16. At this point, we are concerned with the sign and strength of the relationship—a one-shot, ex post assessment. In addition, in P_2 we examine the dynamics of the relationship over time.

17. Frederick Reichheld and Thomas Teal, *The Loyalty Effect* (Boston: Harvard Business School Press, 1996).

18. David C. Schmittlein and Robert A. Peterson, "Customer Base Analysis: An Industrial Purchase Process Application," *Marketing Science* 13 (1994): 41–67.

19. The analysis of the test of propositions does not include the acquisitions costs for each customer, as the data are not available. If acquisitions costs were available, they can be easily integrated into the proposed framework. If acquisition costs are somewhat similar across all customers, the findings of the study hold good. For example, the acquisition costs for catalog companies to acquire a customer on the Web is $11, compared to $82 for Internet-only retailers. If acquisition costs are so low for catalog companies, then the variation in acquisition costs across customers should not affect the results of this study. See: Rebecca Quick, "New Study Finds Hope For Internet Retailers," *Wall Street Journal* (April 18,2000): A2.

20. W. Reinartz and V. Kumar, "The Impact of Customer Relationship Characteristics on Profitable Lifetime Duration," *Journal of Marketing* 67 (January 2003).

21. V. Kumar and K. Charade, "The Effect of Retail Store Environment on Retailer Performance," *Journal of Business Research* 49 (August 2000): 167–181.

22. Kristiaan Helsen and David C. Schmittlein, "Analyzing Duration Times in Marketing: Evidence for the Effectiveness of Hazard Rate Models," *Marketing Science* 11 (Fall 1993): 395–414.

23. A. O. Hirschman, *Exit Loyalty and Voice* (Cambridge, Mass.: Harvard University Press, 1970).

24. Gary L. Clark, Peter F. Kaminski, and David R. Rink, "Consumer Complaints: Advice on Companies Should Respond Based on an Empirical Study," *Journal of Consumer Marketing* 9 (Summer 1992): 5–14.

25. Lori Kesler, "Steak Company Welcomes Customer Grilling," *Advertising Age* (October 17, 1985): 36–37.

26. David C. Schmittlein, Donald G. Morrison, and Richard Colombo, "Counting Your Customers: Who Are They and What Will They Do Next?" *Management Science* 33 (January 1987): 1–24.

27. W. Reinartz and V. Kumar, "On the Profitability of Long-life Customers in a Non-Contractual Setting: An empirical Investigation and Implications for Marketing," *Journal of Marketing* 64 (October 2000): 17–32.

28. David C. Schmittlein, Donald G. Morrison, and Richard Colombo, "Counting Your Customers: Who Are They and What Will They do Next?" *Management Science* 33 (January 1987): 1–24.

29. John E. Hogan, Katherine N. Lemon, and Barak Libai, "What Is the True Value of a Lost Customer?" *Journal of Service Research* 5, no. 3 (2003): 196–208.

Application of the Customer Value Framework to Marketing Decisions

Contents

13.1 OVERVIEW

The ability to know exactly who is going to buy what product and when, and the resources and communication strategy needed to make it happen, will no doubt be on the top of the wish list for CEOs. This ability will help the firm invest on the most profitable customers at the most appropriate time, and in the most effective way. This will not only avoid overspending or underspending on customers but also increase the revenue and profit from them. However, many companies continue to spend resources on large number of unprofitable customers. They could either be investing on customers who are easy to acquire but are not necessarily profitable or trying to increase the retention rate of all their customers, thereby leading to wastage of limited resources. Allocating resources optimally on an individual customer was not a feasible process before the introduction of the customer value framework. By utilizing the customer value framework, researchers have now devised models to allow customer-level actions. We present these research findings in this chapter in an easily comprehensible way. The first section in the chapter describes the model for arriving at the optimal resource allocation. This model will help a manager know the extent to which he should use various contact channels to communicate to a customer. A model to predict the purchase sequence is described next. The model addresses questions like: (1) What is the sequence in which a customer is likely to buy multiple products or product categories? (2) When is the customer expected to buy each product? The third model addresses issues related to allocating resources between acquisition and retention with the objective of maximizing a customer's long-term profitability. It tries to answer questions like: (1) What should be the total budget for acquisition and retention? (2) How much should be spent on customer acquisition and customer retention? and (3) How should these expenditures be allocated between contact channels?

13.2 Optimal Resource Allocation across Marketing and Communication Strategies

Customer equity is the aggregation of the expected lifetime values of a firm's entire base of existing customers and the expected future value of newly acquired customers.[1] A firm needs to make trade-offs that reserve strategic resources for the areas in which the expenditures will generate the greatest impact on customer equity.[2] The Inter-purchase time for a customer is influenced by marketing initiatives taken by a firm. A mathematical model for interpurchase time as discussed in Level 3 in previous chapter includes the frequency and nature of marketing and communication efforts. A model to predict the cash flows from each customer can be simultaneously developed. The NPV objective function required to maximize the customer equity of a firm is related to the cash flow from each customer, the expected interpurchase time, and the cost and frequency of the marketing/communication strategies employed. A manager can determine the frequency of each of the available marketing and communication strategies such that the NPV objective function is maximized. An optimization technique can be utilized to accurately arrive at the differential allocation of strategic resources to individual customers across a variety of integrated marketing strategies.[3] The objective function is thus based on three elements:

1. A *probability-based model that predicts the interpurchase time* of each customer, as a function of marketing communication inputs and the customers' past purchase behavior observed over time.

2. A *panel data model that predicts the cash flows* from each individual customer, also as a function of marketing communication inputs and the customers' past purchase behavior observed over time.

3. An *optimization algorithm that maximizes the profits* from each individual customer by examining the impact of various levels of marketing communication inputs.

By applying an optimization model, a manager can know the extent to which he should use various contact channels. For example, for individual customers, should there be a decrease in face-to-face meetings and an increase in the frequency of direct mailers, or vice versa? Or, for segments of customers, how can total profitability over these segments be maximized? To illustrate the application of the optimal resource allocation procedure, it is useful to look at the results of a real-world situation.

First, it was necessary to establish that the model would do a good job of predicting whether a particular customer would buy in the next twelve months. Based on an analysis of a sample of 324 customers, out of 246 customers the model predicted would buy a product, 225 of them actually bought. Similarly, out of the 78 customers the model predicted would not buy the product, 66 of them did not buy. This suggests the model had a total accuracy, or hit rate, of 90 percent (See Table 13-1.)

Hit Rate = 225 + 66 ÷ 324 = 90%

Given this reassurance, we needed to examine if the customer value approach could eventually lead to an improvement in profits relative to the duration of association

TABLE 13-1	**PREDICTIVE ACCURACY OF THE MODEL**		
	Actually Bought in the Next 12 Months	**Actually Did Not Buy in the Next 12 Months**	**Total**
Expected to buy in the next 12 months as per the model	$N = 225$	$n = 21$	246
Not expected to buy in the next 12 months as per the model	$N = 12$	$n = 66$	78
Total			324

approach currently being employed by the firm to select customers and prioritize its marketing action.[4]

Table 13-2 shows the results of a duration of association approach in terms of the classification of customers and their average profits.

The firm studied would break its customer base into two groups—short-duration customers and long-duration customers. Short-duration customers were those customers who had been transacting with the firm for less than a predetermined cut-off value of years. Consequently, the long-duration customers were the customers who had been transacting with the firm for longer than the cut-off value. From Table 13-2 it seemed as if they were doing the right thing, because the average profits from the short-duration group were much lower than the average profits from the long-duration group.

However, a cross analysis of duration of relationship and customer value, obtained on the basis of the NPV maximization objective function, indicates not all short-duration customers deliver lower profits, and not all long-duration customers deliver higher profits. A superior approach could be thus adopted by identifying and targeting responsive and profitable customers and by deemphasizing efforts on some customers who were not profitable, irrespective of whether they are classified as long-duration or short-duration customers. Some of the profitable customers had escaped the firm's attention when only the duration of association approach was being followed. Also, the firm was allocating disproportionately higher resources to some long-duration customers in the mistaken belief that the duration of their association with the firm was indicative of their profitability (See Table 13-3.)

TABLE 13-2	**COMPARISON OF AVERAGE PROFITS IN A DURATION OF ASSOCIATION APPROACH**	
	Duration of Customer-Firm Association	
	Short	**Long**
Average Profit per Customer	$29,235 ($n = 170$)	$141,655 ($n = 154$)

TABLE 13-3	**CUSTOMER VALUE VERSUS DURATION OF CUSTOMER-FIRM RELATIONSHIP**	
	Shorter Duration	**Longer Duration**
Low Customer Value	$N = 78$ *Cell I* Average profit = $1,387	$N = 82$ *Cell III* Average profit = $1,245
High Customer Value	$N = 92$ *Cell II* Average profit = $52,976	$N = 82$ *Cell IV* Average profit = $302,542

The observations in *Cell III* indicate more than 50 percent of the customers that the firm was chasing in the long-duration segment were actually low-value customers. The observations in *Cell II* indicate the firm was ignoring a sizable set of customers by classifying them as short-duration customers, when indeed they were contributing significantly to profits. Thus, the customer value–based approach demonstrated its superiority to the duration of association approach in terms of profitable segmentation of customers.

By using the optimal resource allocation model, we can improve profitability in each of the cells as shown in Figure 13-1. The analysis recommends changing the frequency of face-to-face meetings, direct mail, and telesales in each cell to an optimal level, thereby enhancing the effectiveness of the marketing/communication initiatives. By changing over to the optimal frequencies, recommended by the model for face-to-face meetings and direct mail/telesales, in each of the four cells, a 10 percent decrease in overall costs and a 6 percent increase in overall profits were observed.

13.3 PURCHASE SEQUENCE ANALYSIS: DELIVERING THE RIGHT MESSAGE TO THE RIGHT CUSTOMER AT THE RIGHT TIME

In the case of a multiproduct firm, it is important to understand which product in the portfolio is likely to be needed next by a customer. An ideal contact strategy is one where the firm is able to deliver a sales message relevant to the product likely to be purchased in

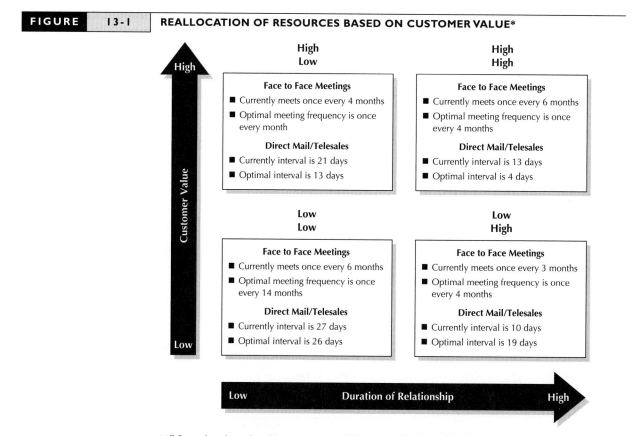

| FIGURE | 13-1 | **REALLOCATION OF RESOURCES BASED ON CUSTOMER VALUE*** |

High / Low

Face to Face Meetings
- Currently meets once every 4 months
- Optimal meeting frequency is once every month

Direct Mail/Telesales
- Currently interval is 21 days
- Optimal interval is 13 days

High / High

Face to Face Meetings
- Currently meets once every 6 months
- Optimal meeting frequency is once every 4 months

Direct Mail/Telesales
- Currently interval is 13 days
- Optimal interval is 4 days

Low / Low

Face to Face Meetings
- Currently meets once every 6 months
- Optimal meeting frequency is once every 14 months

Direct Mail/Telesales
- Currently interval is 27 days
- Optimal interval is 26 days

Low / High

Face to Face Meetings
- Currently meets once every 3 months
- Optimal meeting frequency is once every 4 months

Direct Mail/Telesales
- Currently interval is 10 days
- Optimal interval is 19 days

Customer Value (High → Low)

Duration of Relationship (Low → High)

*All figures have been altered by a constant multiplier for confidentiality reasons.

the near future by a customer. The next level is therefore the development of a *purchase sequence model.*

A purchase sequence model[5] addresses three questions:

1. What is the sequence in which a customer is likely to buy multiple products or product categories?
2. When is the customer expected to buy each product?
3. What is the expected revenue from that customer?

This model captures the differences in the durations between purchases for different product categories. The interdependence in purchase propensities across products is modeled by incorporating cross-product category variables. An individual customer level profit function is developed to predict customer value. To demonstrate such a model delivers superior results in the field, an experiment was set up in the sales department of a high-technology B2B vendor, which markets multiple categories of products.

The model was developed for the hardware products of the firm. The model is able to prioritize customers by indicating the propensity to purchase different hardware products for each of its customers. It also predicts the expected profits. Empirical evidence from this experiment suggests profits predicted on the basis of a purchase sequence model are accurate and that using the model results in a greater return on marketing investments. Table 13-4 is an illustration of the improvement for the hardware category, over the previous year, in profits generated by the test group of salespersons who adopted strategies based on the outcome of the purchase sequence model versus the control group of salespersons not provided the predictions given by the model.

As Table 13-4 shows, there is a significant decrease in the cost of communication resulting in a saving of $750 on last year's base of $3,625. In comparison, the control group saw an increase in its cost of communication by $75 on an already high last-year base of $4,580. The test group was able to reduce the average number of attempts before purchase by four, whereas for the test group this number increased by one, compared to the respective figures for last year. Similarly, for the test group, profits were higher and so was ROI.

Table 13-5 provides the difference in performance between the test group and the control group.

We see again during the experiment period, the test group revenue is higher, cost of communication is lower, number of attempts before a purchase is made is lower, profits are higher, and ROI is higher, when compared to the control group. The success of the

TABLE 13-4	**CHANGE BETWEEN CURRENT YEAR AND PREVIOUS YEAR**	
	Test Group	**Control Group**
Revenue ($)*	1,050	1,033
	(18,130)	(17,610)
Cost of communication ($)	−750	75
	(3,625)	(4,580)
Number of attempts before purchase	−4	1
	(15)	(18)
Profits ($)	3,000	637
	(9,080)	(6,275)
Return on Investment (%)	5.4	2.2
	(3.7)	(2.0)

Note: Number indicates change from base level (previous year). Base level is in parentheses.

*The reported values are unit values per customer.

TABLE 13-5	DIFFERENCE IN PERFORMANCE BETWEEN TEST AND CONTROL GROUP

	Difference between Test and Control Group
Revenue ($)*	537
Cost of communication ($)	−1,780
Number of attempts before purchase	−8
Profits ($)	5,168
Return on investment	4.9

*Number indicates change from base level the previous year. Base level is in parentheses. The reported values are unit values per customer.

experiment indicates the scope that the customer value approach offers in improving the quality of marketing decisions.

13.4 THE LINK BETWEEN ACQUISITION, RETENTION, AND PROFITABILITY: BALANCING ACQUISITION AND RETENTION RESOURCES TO MAXIMIZE CUSTOMER PROFITABILITY

Measuring, managing, and maximizing customer profitability is not an easy task. From a marketing resource allocation perspective, it requires a manager to (1) set a budget, (2) balance how much to spend on customer acquisition and customer retention, and (3) determine how the expenditures are allocated between contact channels. The objective is, of course, to maximize a customer's long-term profitability. For example, a manager of a paper company distributes sales force efforts and directs marketing efforts among its set of 350 business customers. The manager also has to constantly juggle how many new prospects should be targeted at a given point in time vis-à-vis the portion of time and effort to be directed to existing customers. In this section, we summarize the findings of a study that examines these questions.[6]

In contrast to most other studies, the acquisition process is an integral component of the research model. The conceptual link between the acquisition and the retention process is important for two reasons. First, only by linking the two, one can see a complete and unbiased picture of the drivers behind customer selection/acquisition, relationship duration, and customer profitability (See Figure 13-2.)[7] Prior research has specifically shown that a failure to link acquisition and retention can lead to biased results and incorrect inferences.[8] This is due to the selection bias resulting from the omission of information on nonacquired prospects. Second, offensive processes and defensive processes compete for the same resources. Making the necessary trade-off requires a full specification of the key dimensions of the customer–firm relationship. Thus, a more complete model specification allows us to address a key managerial question: "Does the maximization of the respective objective functions (a.k.a. acquisition likelihood, lifetime duration, and customer value) lead to convergent or divergent resource allocation recommendations?"

It is important to note this model applies mainly to situations where managers mostly rely on direct customer communication, such as via sales force, direct mail, or Internet. This is the case for most B-to-B environments, as well as for many direct marketing contexts.

FIGURE   13-2
LINKING CUSTOMER ACQUISITION, RELATIONSHIP DURATION, AND CUSTOMER PROFITABILITY

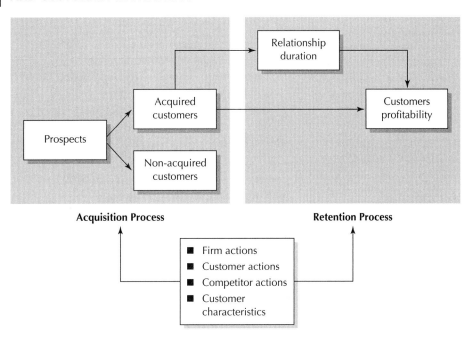

The interest of this study lies mainly in the impact of (1) amount of spending and (2) contact channel type on three dependent variables: acquisition rate, retention rate, and customer profitability.

As firms increase their acquisition budget, the associated acquisition rate and customer profitability will be less and less responsive (concavity). Even if, for all practical purposes, there were no limits on acquisition expenditure, firms are able to capture only a certain share of the potential targets. We can expect that acquisition expenditures will have diminishing marginal associations with the likelihood of customer acquisition. Also, acquisition expenditures will have diminishing marginal associations with customer profitability. Similarly we can see that increasing retention expenditures will cease to be profitable beyond a certain level. Thus, we can expect retention expenditures will have diminishing marginal associations with relationship duration and with customer profitability.

We would also like to see if the nature of the contact channel affects acquisition and relationship duration. We can expect highly interpersonal contact channels have a greater association with the likelihood of customer acquisition than less interpersonal contact channels. Also, highly interpersonal contact channels have a greater association with relationship duration than less interpersonal contact channels.

At the most simple level, different contact channels may be seen as having independent effects on the respective dependent variables, acquisition, duration, and customer profitability. However a potential interaction effect between channels is likely to exist. For example, one could argue that contacting a prospect via telesales and via direct mail at the same time may have a stronger effect than the sum of the separate effects administered at different points in time. This is due to the mutual reinforcement of the message delivered through the different contact channels at the same time.

The empirical context for this research is the same B-to-B firm as in the previous two examples. The following substantive conclusions emerge from this empirical context:

1. The *amount of investment* in a customer as well as *how it is invested* has an impact on acquisition, retention, and customer profitability.

2. Investments into customer acquisition and retention have diminishing marginal returns.

3. How much is invested in a customer–firm relationship has a larger impact on long-term customer profitability than how the expenditures are invested across communication channels. Thus, optimizing the amount of relationship investment is of prime importance.

4. The relative effectiveness of highly personalized communication channels is much greater than the less personalized communication channels. However, the relative cost also needs to be taken into account when deciding the communication strategy as it affects the overall profitability.

5. Underspending in acquisition and retention is more detrimental and results in smaller ROIs than overspending.

6. When trading off between allocating expenditures to acquisition versus retention, a suboptimal allocation of retention expenditures will have a larger detrimental impact on long-term customer profitability than suboptimal acquisition expenditures.

7. The customer communication strategy that maximizes long-term customer profitability maximizes neither the acquisition rate nor the relationship duration. Instead, developing a communication strategy to manage long-term customer profitability generally requires a long-term and holistic perspective of the relationship. This perspective tends to give more emphasis to more interpersonal and interactive communications than a limited focus on acquisition.

Although the results are specific to the empirical context, the model can be applied to any environment where acquisition and retention efforts can be separated. Managers can use the proposed integrated framework not only to better understand the drivers of profitability, but also to know how to maximize profitability through optimal allocation of resources.

13.5 SUMMARY

Customer equity is the aggregation of the expected lifetime values of a firm's entire base of existing customers and the expected future value of newly acquired customers. The NPV objective function required to maximize the customer equity of a firm is related to the cash flow from each customer, the expected interpurchase time, and the cost and frequency of the marketing/communication strategies employed. The objective function is based on a probability model which predicts the interpurchase time of each customer, a panel data model which predicts the cash flows from each customer, and an optimization algorithm which maximizes the profits. By applying an optimization model, a manager can know the extent to which he should use various contact channels. Cross analysis of duration of relationship and customer value obtained on the basis of the NPV maximization objective function indicates not all short-duration customers deliver lower profits, and not all long-duration customers deliver higher profits. Identifying and targeting responsive and profitable customers and deemphasizing efforts on some customers who were not profitable—irrespective of whether they are classified as long-duration or short-duration customers—would be a better approach. Customer value–based approach demonstrated its superiority to the duration of association approach in terms of profitable segmentation of customers.

Purchase sequence model captures the differences in the durations between purchases for different product categories. An individual customer-level profit function is developed to predict customer value. The success of the experiment based on the model demonstrated by higher revenue, lower cost of communication, lower number of attempts before a purchase is made, higher profits, and higher ROI for the test group, when compared to the control group, indicates the scope to which the customer value approach offers in improving the quality of marketing decisions.

The acquisition process is an integral component of the research model. By linking acquisition and the retention process, it is possible to see a complete and unbiased picture of the drivers behind customer selection/acquisition, relationship duration, and customer profitability.[9] Also, making the necessary trade-off between offensive processes and defensive processes requires a full specification of the key dimensions of the customer–firm relationship. A more complete model specification addresses the key managerial question of whether the maximization of the respective objective functions as acquisition likelihood, lifetime duration, and customer value would lead to convergent or divergent resource allocation recommendations. This model applies mainly to situations where managers rely mostly on direct customer communication. Acquisition expenditures will have diminishing marginal associations with customer profitability. Retention expenditures will have diminishing marginal associations with relationship duration and with customer profitability. Highly interpersonal contact channels have a greater association with the likelihood of customer acquisition and relationship duration than less interpersonal contact channels. Though the results are specific to the empirical context, the model can be applied to any environment where acquisition and retention efforts can be separated. Managers can use the proposed integrated framework not only to better understand the drivers of profitability, but also to know how to maximize profitability through optimal allocation of resources.

13.6 EXERCISE QUESTIONS

1. Consider a multiproduct company and discuss the likely sequence in which the average customer would buy these products. Why do you think an average customer may not be the best way to consider this problem?

2. Discuss the relative importance of the customer acquisition and retention processes from the perspective of customer lifetime value.

ENDNOTES

1. John E. Hogan, Donald Lehmann, Maria Merino, Rajendra K. Srivastava, Jacquelyn S. Thomas, and Peter C. Verhoef, "Linking Customer Assets to Financial Performance," *Journal of Service Research* 5, no. 1 (2002): 26–38.

2. Roland T. Rust, Valarie A. Zeithaml, and Katherine N. Lemon, *Driving Customer Equity: How Customer Lifetime Value Is Reshaping Corporate Strategy* (New York: The Free Press, 2000).

3. Rajkumar Venkatesan and V. Kumar, "A Customer Lifetime Value Framework for Customer Selection and Optimal Resource Allocation Strategy," *Journal of Marketing* 68, no. 4 (October 2004): 106.

4. Duration of association (one of the traditional measures of loyalty) indicates how long a customer has been transacting with the firm.

5. V. Kumar, Rajkumar Venkatesan, and Werner Reinartz, "A Purchase Sequence Analysis Framework for Targeting Products, Customers and Time Period," forthcoming, *Journal of Marketing*.

6. Werner Reinartz, Jacquelyn S. Thomas, and V. Kumar, "Balancing Acquisition and Retention Resources to Maximize Customer Profitability," forthcoming, *Journal of Marketing* 69, no. 1 (January 2005): 63.

7. Heckman, "Sample Selection Bias as a Specification Error," *Econometrica* 47 (January 1979): 153–61.

8. Jacquelyn S. Thomas, "A Methodology for Linking Customer Acquisition to Customer Retention," *Journal of Marketing Research* 38 (May 2001): 262–268.

PART IV

Channels and CRM

14 Impact of CRM on Marketing Channels

CHAPTER 14

Impact of CRM on Marketing Channels

Contents

14.1 OVERVIEW

Channels perform the task of moving goods and services from firms to consumers and other businesses. From a customer relationship point of view, firms also use channels to interact in many ways with their customers. Each customer has varied preferences for distribution or contact channels. To meet the needs of various customers, businesses must provide the right blend of direct (Web sites, e-commerce stores, call centers, and enterprise sales representatives) and indirect (distributors, retailers, solution providers, and online resellers) channels. In other words companies should adopt a multichannel strategy. From the consumer's perspective, multiple channels represent greater choice. From the retailer's perspective, multichannel poses new challenges, ranging from delivering consistent experience across all channels to fully utilizing the strengths of each channel.

Enterprises are rapidly moving toward establishing more collaborative partnership with traditional sales and distribution channels. For manufacturers operating in this interactive era, channel members provide the critical customer relationship link because in most of the cases, channel partners are in control of the relationship with customers.[1] Hence, we see enterprises compete with each other for distribution partners. Establishing a partnership with the channel members has direct benefits for both the manufacturer and the retailer. The manufacturer can build a strong relationship with the channel member and the channel member, in turn, can develop a strong relationship with customers, thus bridging the gap between the manufacturer and the end-user customers. At the same time, the manufacturer can better learn about channel partner needs and can meet those needs, which is beneficial for the channel members.

However, multichannel marketing poses certain challenges for customer value management. Since focal firms interact with the end user through channel intermediaries, it is difficult for the firm to build and nurture an effective customer relationship program directed at the end customer. The firm should ensure its messages and offerings of the relationship program reach the target consumer without dilution or digression. This is especially difficult when the channel intermediaries have conflicting customer relationship programs. This indicates the focal firm has only indirect control over CRM implementation. Also, multichannel marketing poses the challenge of eliciting customer information from multiple channels for central processing.

This chapter deals with the challenging issues related to channel management in the context of CRM implementation. We also look at the emerging channel trends and the recent opportunities and challenges associated with distribution channels. The final section of the chapter describes the results of a study on the factors associated with the usage of multiple channels by customers in the context of a business-to-business (B-to-B) situation. Based on the insights from the study, we discuss the drivers of multichannel buying behavior and characteristics of multi-channel buying.

14.2 How Does the Traditional Distribution Channel Structure Support Customer Relationships?

14.2.1 IMPORTANCE OF CHANNELS FOR CRM

The effectiveness of CRM depends to a considerable extent on the channel strategies of the firm. Since marketing interactions with customers occur primarily through channels, conventionally customer relationships are created and sustained through marketing channels. Thus, marketing channels are the primary vehicles of relationship building.

What Are Channels?

The word *channel* is used mainly in two ways. The first use refers to the *flow* of the organization's offerings (e.g., physical goods or information) to the ultimate end users (end customer), as well as that of sales proceeds or realizations from the customer back to the marketing firm. The term *marketing or distribution channels* stands for all entities (e.g., distributors, wholesalers, retailers, broker, agents, etc.) who perform certain functions for the marketing firm. These functions include stocking inventory, conducting sales transactions, conducting payments, providing point of purchase information, and sometimes providing upfront liquidity to the manufacturing plants.

The second use of the term *channel* refers to the mode of communication between a firm and its customers. These so-called *communication or contact channels* convey information to the customers to raise their awareness about the firm's products and services and persuade them to make purchases.

Whereas the term *distribution channel* often refers to several organizations (in the channel), the term *contact channel* typically only refers to two parties. For example, the distribution channel of Adidas includes several entities such as wholesalers and retailers.

FIGURE 14-1 **FIRM INTERACTION WITH CUSTOMERS THROUGH CHANNELS**

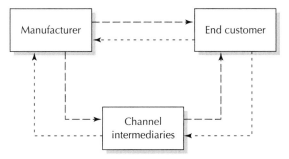

The contact channels between Adidas and its end customers refer to the modes of communication comprising Internet, direct mail, and SMS or wireless text messaging.

Although distribution channels and contact channels are not always cleanly separated (remember—information exchange is a core task of distribution channels), we will differentiate these terms here because the management of contact channels is a very important topic in CRM. In addition, the term *channel management* is often used to refer to contact channels even though this may not be technically precise.

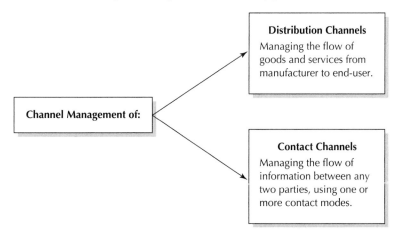

Conventionally, for a given geographical market, firms have a single distribution channel setup which performs all aforementioned channel functions except advertising. For example, BMW uses its network of licensed dealers to sell cars to the market. In addition, BMW engages in direct-to-consumer communication (on top of the dealer communication) via its mass and direct advertising.

Before the advent of the Internet, a direct sales channel between the marketing firm and the customer was often very costly and/or arduous to implement. Direct interaction was, therefore, often limited to trade fairs and test marketing. Third-party agencies typically performed the various channel functions. Thus, the customers interacted with the marketing firm indirectly through the channels, which acted as intermediaries. Only in the case of B-to-B marketing did manufacturers typically get to know the end users and also deal directly with them.

14.2.2 THE ROLE OF TRADITIONAL CHANNELS IN CUSTOMER RELATIONSHIPS

Indirect Customer Relationship

The process of managing customer relationships involves the gathering and processing of customer and sales-transaction information, which can be done by both the channel member as well as the marketing firm. The entire focus of customer relationship management in the traditional channel structures has been on (1) building a good working relationship with the channel member (referred to as an *upstream relationship* in Figure 14-1) and on (2) providing the channel member incentives to build a strong customer relationship (referred to as a *downstream relationship* in Figure 14-1). These incentives encourage the channel member to gather and process sales and customer information and share this information with the marketing firm. Big consumer nondurable marketing firms, such as Henkel and Procter & Gamble, traditionally had significant power over their distribution channels and were thus able to control the channel's activities to such an extent that the channels conform fully to the customer relationship agenda of the marketing firm. However, this ability to control changes as the level of power changes (e.g., due to the arrival of private-label goods on supermarket shelves). Now, this results in much less control over the retailer's CRM activities.

Direct Customer Relationship

Traditionally, a direct channel between the firm and the consumer took the form of a communication or contact channel. The firm communicates product information to the consumer through contact channels, such as TV or print, to persuade the consumer to reach out to the sales or distribution channel most accessible to him or her. Point-of-purchase advertising and promotions at the channel outlet (e.g., retail point) further persuades the consumer to make this purchase. Consumer information, however, usually flows indirectly to the firm (except in case of marketing research programs) through the channel's sales data.

Another traditional form of direct customer relationship is achieved through brand equity. The value of the brand embeds in itself an expected relationship in the future. By building brand equity, firms often try to build a *pseudo-relationship* with all prospective consumers (by assuring them consistent quality, differentiation, and risk insurance).[2] The term *pseudo-relationship* implies that even before an individual consumer has made a purchase or has interacted with a channel of a marketing firm, the brand equity acts as though there was a prior relationship between the consumer and the firm. Firms known to vigorously pursue brand building will attract consumers who value the expected future relationship. Thus, rather than being a trade-off between customer relationship building and brand equity, there is the creation of brand equity as a specific form of building customer relationships.

14.2.3 KEY FACTORS AFFECTING CRM THROUGH TRADITIONAL CHANNELS

For a successful CRM strategy directed at the final customer, a conventional channel structure should consider the ingredients listed in this section.

Incentives for Coordinating Information Exchange

The focal firm should provide adequate incentives to the channels members to gather and process sales and customer information, and share the information with the firm. For example, Procter & Gamble and its powerful retailer Wal-Mart shed their adversarial association and invested in an EDI (Electronic Data Interchange) technology which allowed Procter & Gamble access to real-time customer data to forge customer relationships, as well as reduce the cost of operations involving distribution. By making investments specific to their relationship with Wal-Mart, P&G secured the trust and commitment of a powerful retailer—not only to improve its own relationship with the end customers but also to reduce the cost of operations for Wal-Mart.[3] In another case, Unilever Bestfoods Germany, with a brand portfolio that includes Knorr, Bertolli, Becel, and Lipton, implemented a consumer goods customer information system to generate a single, comprehensive view of each and every account and retail outlet in support of its sales and merchandising operations throughout Germany. In particular, they aim to streamline and enhance account management and trade promotion management by anticipating and responding to changing and local consumer preferences.

Protecting the Interests of the Channels

The focal firm needs to further safeguard the proper interests of channel members while executing its own CRM strategy directed at the end customer. To this end, the firm needs to nurture its relationship with the channel members to induce them to build and maintain relationships with the customers in accordance with the CRM strategy of the firm. The most successful CRM strategies have always integrated their downstream channel partners' interests. Note that channels are also de facto customers of the firm, and end customers are the customers also of the channels. This implies that both the upstream and the downstream relationships in Figure 14-1 are important factors leading to the success of CRM.

When Toyota Motor Corporation's Lexus division established itself in the United States in the 1980s, it asked its dealers to invest in facilities, systems, and personnel required to deliver extraordinary customer service. In return, Lexus enabled its dealers to make several thousand dollars on the sale of each new car—considerably above the industry average.[4] In addition, it made sure to explain to the dealers the purpose and functioning of its own market intelligence operations. The goal was not to circumvent dealers (e.g., via direct sales) but, rather, to help dealers sell the cars.

14.2.4 MAJOR CHALLENGES FACING CRM THROUGH TRADITIONAL CHANNELS

Prevent Dilution of CRM Strategies

The challenge for most firms that interact with their final customers through channel intermediaries is that the traditional intermediary entities make a continual and direct interaction with the end customer very difficult—if not impossible—to accomplish. Thus, it is no trivial task for the firm to build and nurture an effective customer relationship program directed at the end customer. The firm should ensure its messages and offerings of the relationship program reach the target consumer without dilution or digression.

For example, most European retailers such as Carrefour, Dia, and J. Sainsbury sell high-quality private-label brands which directly compete with the established brands of renowned manufacturers. This creates a conflict of interest with the manufacturers, since the private-label promotions often go diametrically against the customer relationship programs of the national brands.

Indirect Control of CRM through Channels

The primary methods of implementation of CRM includes direct control and monitoring of the CRM program (directed at the end-customer) at the channel by manipulating the upstream relationship with the channels (as shown in Figure 14-1) such that the channel has incentives to manage the downstream relationship in alignment with the firm's overall CRM. However, the objectives of the firm and the channels might be more aligned than expected. Although there may be multiple sources through which an end customer receives marketing information such as advertising, he would still use the same distribution channel to purchase. Thus, the focus should be on the implementation of CRM at the customer's preferred channel, albeit in sync with the overall marketing mix strategy of the firm. Firms often resort to vertical integration and strategic alliances to control or align interests of their channels with their customer relationship strategy. The P&G Wal-Mart strategic alliance is a notable example.

Eliciting Customer Information from all Channels for Central Processing

The lack of precise information about individual customers does complicate the implementation of CRM in the traditional channels. Firms often obtain from their distribution channel partners only an approximation of customer preferences. The customers remain, for the most part, anonymous to the firm. Thus, the firm would supply to each channel according to their estimation of the customer tastes and preferences. Customer identification associated with CRM demands the physical distribution be responsive to variations in customer mobility and contact channel preferences in terms of shopping habits, for example. CRM therefore demands that customer information from different contact channels be centrally processed by the firm and forms a critical input to the planning and execution of the physical distribution of the goods. Given that retailers often compete against one another, it is difficult for many firms to convince them to part with critical sales information that will be centrally processed.

Central customer data processing across different contact channels is essential even among the traditional channel agents. Sophisticated information systems are therefore the key to implementation of any CRM program although new distribution channels and customer mobility across contact channels place additional demands on the system.

14.3 EMERGING CHANNEL TRENDS THAT IMPACT CRM

14.3.1 PROLIFERATION OF DIRECT CHANNELS

The ubiquitous presence of the Internet and electronic channels in business and daily life has tremendous impact on the firm's channel options. Whether through a Web site, a self-service kiosk, or sophisticated voice response systems, consumers are taking advantage of this great variety of direct channels to seek information as well as to transact business directly with the firm. Computers, travel, books, music—the list of products customers are familiar with purchasing electronically is getting longer. Under this scenario, firms suddenly have not only direct access to the end-customers but they can also recognize at every instance of interaction a prior customer, and since the interaction occurs through a technology-enabled channel, the option exists to record and store all the relevant information about the customer; all this without the trouble of negotiating with, providing incentives to, and training a third-party channel member, such as a retailer.

14.3.2 CHANNEL PROLIFERATION AND EMERGENCE OF MULTICHANNEL SHOPPERS

Recent times have witnessed a virtual explosion of the number of media channels which seek the individual consumer's attention: Internet, e-mail, kiosks, mobile phones, cable TV,

SMS, MMS—the list goes on. Each of these new channels is vying for different individuals, and each is obtaining only limited attention of the overall customer base of the firm. In response to the emergence of these new channels, people change their channel habits and consumers derive differing benefits from different channels. Depending on the product (e.g., books), some customers may switch completely from their original transaction channels to the new outlets like the Internet (e.g., Amazon.com) while others may be influenced by different channels at different stages of their buying process, driven by hierarchy of effects.[5] For example, one may search the Web for the best price quotes to be better informed of prices and to be able to better negotiate the deal. But for various reasons (misgivings about the security and privacy of the Web to transact, uncertainty about the quality of the Web-based offer, etc.) one might still plan to eventually purchase from the local retailer. For the firm, this situation means it cannot neglect its traditional channels, but needs to provide enough information on the Web and yet have a dealer next door to secure the deal.

Furthermore, these new channels allow agents other than the firm and its dedicated marketing channels to transmit or even broadcast information related to the firm's merchandise. These include not only competing firms and products, but also other interest groups such as the environmentalists or consumer interest forums. Thus, different people obtain different information through different channels. This proliferation of channels and its effect on customer behavior and information offers new opportunities to the firm, but it also creates new difficulties in managing the marketing flow.

14.4 Recent Opportunities and Challenges for CRM with Respect to Distribution Channels

The proliferation of channels opens up a whole range of opportunities for CRM activities. At the same time, it poses new challenges to marketers. We discuss these in the following two sections.

14.4.1 OPPORTUNITIES FOR INCREASING RETURNS FOR CRM

Widening Coverage of the Consumer Population

The most immediate impact of distribution channel and contact channel proliferation is the increase in coverage of the population of potential consumers by the channel networks of the firms. If individuals have more choice among different communication and transaction channels, they will choose those channels which best fit their preferences and habits. Potential customers, who did not shop a firm's products earlier because the firm's channels did not have access to him, now have the possibility to consider buying the products. This increases the firm's potential customer base. For example, working executives who are hard pressed for time and thus travel to the nearest outlet to shop, might use the opportunity to access Internet offers. However, it takes time for people to get accustomed to the emerging channels and gain confidence shopping from them.

Improved Customer Information for the Firm

Multiple channels open the floodgates of multiple sources of consumer and demand information. The firms now have unimaginable access to multiple sources of the same information, which allows them to verify and cross validate the veracity and reliability of the longitudinal information available through multiple channels. More importantly, firms increasingly have the additional option of a direct channel to the customer. Through direct channels, the firm is now able to acquire unfiltered information about individual customers' preferences and needs, independent of the dealer. The need for interchange of customer information across channels makes it imperative to have central customer databases at the firm level, thereby allowing the firm additional leverage to directly interact with the end customers.

Smart firms leverage this information into detailed customer information databases across channels over multiple shopping instances, which, in turn, enable the marketer with better forecasting ability and understanding of behavior and needs of individual customers. Customer identification at each channel makes it possible not only to individualize the marketing mix offering (including products and services) more precisely to each customer, but also opens up opportunities to sell complementary products competing firms may not be aware of or may be able to offer. The firm may be even able to tailor its CRM strategy for each channel, inducing certain types of customers to self-select and lock in to certain channels for information and/or purchasing. Sophisticated customer databases may also allow firms to conceive and test-market new products to meet other unsatisfied needs of the customers, of which the customers themselves might not yet be aware.

Lower Dependency on Specific Channel Partners

The channel proliferation also increases the firm's power vis-à-vis its channel partners. Not only does channel exclusivity no longer exist, but channel partners are also more dependent on the firm to help in the cross-channel coordination of the flow of customer information, marketing communications, and physical distribution. While different channels owned by different agencies may compete for sales volume and margins, they need to coordinate to deal with customers who keep switching between them. Therefore the firms' CRM strategy cannot be too channel-specific to ensure uniform customer satisfaction across shopping instances and channels. Thus, an essential ingredient of a multichannel strategy is channel coordination.

Customer Self-Selection across Channels and Individualization

Channel proliferation also allows consumers to select channels of their choice. For example, the recent rise of different subscription television networks not only brought variety of choice to the viewers, it also provided marketing firms the chance to tap into micro-segments of customers. Marketers of Indian food and grocery items in Europe for example, used the telecast channels of World Cup Cricket 2003 to advertise their products to a very targeted, but small segment, of potential consumers hailing from the cricket-crazy Indian subcontinent.

14.4.2 NEW CHALLENGES FOR THE FIRM TO BENEFIT FROM CRM

While several recent technological developments promise a more effective CRM strategy, they at the same time add to the complexity of the task of customer relationship management as explained next.

Media Planning Becoming Increasingly Difficult

As pointed out earlier, the proliferation of channels not only changes customer behavior; it also changes how customers obtain information. The spurt in the number of channels leads to a strong competition among these for the consumers' attention, thereby making a communications strategy focusing only on a few channels rather limiting. Furthermore, in the face of competing information from firm independent CRM sources, implementing a coherent communication plan can turn out to be a veritable nightmare. Companies face the challenge of integrating their approach to the customer, whether inbound or outbound. This becomes all the more difficult in the face of shrinking budgets, and an explosion of new technologies, which enable new ways to interact with customers.

In their media planning, the firm should consider different contact channels are proficient at performing different channel functions. Selection of the channel to perform a certain marketing function should recognize not only the customers' contact channel preference i.e., the amount of exposure to the customer the channel gets, but also the ability of the channel to deliver the service output required for the marketing purpose. For example, although marketers of tennis rackets can get a very high exposure through TV ads to tennis fans during the French Roland Garros Tournament, transacting sales may be very difficult through the same channel. However, temporary kiosks at the gates of the stadium can be very effective in actually transacting the sales, although they can hardly match the coverage of TV ads.

Consistency in Service Level and the Need for IT Systems

The proliferation of channels (e-mail, Web, wireless) over the past few years has the additional effect of making it increasingly difficult for companies to deliver a consistent level of service and marketing flows across different channels, old and new. If a firm wants to offer differentiated service to different customers, it will now have to ensure, the same customer obtains the same level of service if he switches between different channels. For example, customers are increasingly fed up with purchasing an item online and not being able to return it in the bricks and mortar store.

The need for consistency increases the importance and the challenge of building an IT system capable of customer identification across all channels. The IT system, as well as the marketing decisions of the firm need to be flexible enough to extend the customer information database whenever a new channel of interaction with customers is introduced. This is a major consideration for managers when introducing a new contact or distribution channel.

Channel Conflict and Channel Differentiation

Proliferation of contact channels in recent years (e.g., e-mail, Web, wireless, sales force, contact centers, enterprise portals) has made it possible not only to communicate but also to transact business with more and more consumers. Consumers, too, have started deriving different benefits from different channels. Emergence of multiple channels does not only add to the complexity and difficulty of effective CRM due to the multichannel shopping behavior, but also leads to conflict of interest among different members of the distribution channel that then invariably attenuates the marketing efforts of the principal firm. Interchannel competition for the share of wallet of the same customer makes it a bigger challenge for the firm to ensure seamless interchange of information between channels without hurting a channel member's interests. The firm therefore needs to do a tightrope walk between conflicting interests of different channel entities and its own objective to fulfill customer's needs, maintaining equity at each instance.

However, channel competition might not become as fierce as this sounds. One study states that[6] channels are becoming more specialized, and thus, the implementation of CRM has become less vulnerable to issues of channel conflict. For example, the Internet seems to be more proficient in prospecting/attracting new customers rather than actually transacting. Although people may learn about the firm's offers through the Internet and make their purchase decision based on this information, most people prefer going to their local departmental store or show room for the final transaction. By actively managing a portfolio of specialized channels (e.g., a Web site for prospecting and the show room for harvesting), the firm will not only be better able to nurture the relationship with the customer; it might also render issues such as channel conflict[7] less contentious than what they would be without channel specialization. In the current business environment, however, most channel setups perform both functions—information and transaction—simultaneously. Given the importance of this issue, we will discuss the impact of channel differentiation and specialization in greater detail in the next section.

Table 14-1 summarizes the opportunities and challenges to CRM due to the evolving channel environment.

14.5 IMPLICATIONS FOR CRM

The key issues pertaining to channel management in the context of CRM are:

14.5.1 ELECTRONIC CHANNELS AND AVAILABILITY OF PRECISE CUSTOMER INFORMATION

Detailed customer information databases across channels over multiple shopping instances arm the marketers with the ability to more accurately forecast shopping behavior and needs of individual customers. Customer identification at each channel makes it possible not only to individualize the marketing mix offering, including products and services more precisely to each customer, but also opens up opportunities to sell complementary products competing firms may not be aware of or able to offer. Further, the need for interchange of customer information across channels makes it imperative to have central customer databases at the firm level, thereby allowing the firm additional leverage to directly interact with the end customers. Thus, CRM systems assist in deciding which channel mix is most appropriate for a particular customer. Sophisticated customer databases may also allow firms to conceive and test market new products to meet needs of the customers, of which the customers themselves might not yet be aware.

TABLE 14-1	IMPACT OF EMERGING CHANNEL ENVIRONMENT ON CRM
Opportunities	**Challenges**
Access to a larger number of consumers.	IT systems and physical logistics must be reengineered each time a new channel emerges and captures the customer's imagination.
Multichannel habits of consumers. Increasing number of consumers derive different benefits over different channels.	Media dilution and message dissonance occurs across different channels.
Direct and customized interaction with customers over different channels. This nurtures differentiated customer relationships.	Multichannel conversation with the consumers— Interchannel coordination problems: problems in managing integrated marketing communications (i.e., maintaining context and continuity with a particular consumer through multiple channels) can put the relationship at risk.
Customers self-select into channels— individualization and segmentation.	Channel conflict—multichannel interaction with consumers can lead to conflict of interest among the competing channels for the same share of customer contact or service.
Channel specialization each performing a different channel function can mitigate channel conflict.	Possible rise in consumer expectation of product or service quality.

14.5.2 SEAMLESS CUSTOMER INFORMATION SYSTEMS

There is a need to make available seamlessly customer specific information across all channels where a particular customer is identified as shopping, so that the marketing proposition and initiatives remain consistent to a particular end customer across channels. Firms need to gear up to enhance customer information processing needs for effective CRM across a number of channels.

14.5.3 COOPETITION AMONG CHANNELS

There is a need for cooperation in terms of exchange and availability of customer information across channels. Although the different channels will continue to compete for their share of wallet, the cooperation will help to increase the overall customer base across different channels. In other words a system of *coopetition* is emerging. The principal firm as a result has an enhanced role to play coordinating between channels flows of customer information, as well physical logistics of products and services to meet differential needs and functions of the channels.

Figure 14-2 shows an example of how differentiated channels may support the purchase decision process of the same consumer. Here, for example, mass media and the Internet can perform efficiently as Channel 1, whereas a well-trained sales force can be more effective as Channels 2 and 3. Word of mouth plays a greater role as Channel 4, although the marketer can use experts' opinions and consumer reports to augment favorable customer evaluation. Thus, specialized channels need to cooperate and coordinate with one another to persuade the consumer to make a purchase. At the same time, they may even compete when the consumer has an option to choose one of them to finally make the purchase.

Distribution and contact channel decisions of the firm have critical bearings on the firm's CRM strategy. Although the dramatic increase in the number of channels and the reduced reliance of consumers on any single channel pose severe challenges to the channel management process of firms, it also presents an unprecedented opportunity in terms of greater channel coverage, greater channel specialization, auto-segmentation due to customer self-selection into channels, and improved customer information.

FIGURE 14-2 CUSTOMER RELATIONSHIPS THROUGH DIFFERENTIATED CHANNELS

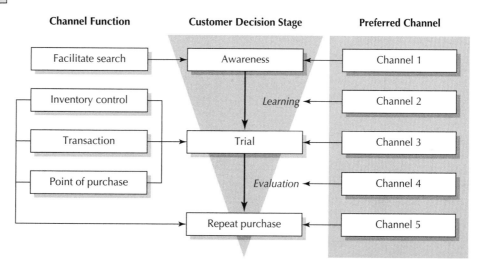

CRM AT WORK 14.1

CRM THROUGH A DIRECT CHANNEL—THE INTERNET

Communication and Sales

The Internet is a channel capable of delivering broadcasted and customized marketing communication. The outreach and the number of different tasks that can be performed through the Internet are enormous. It is also a low-cost (direct) channel for transacting business. The firms, however, need to sometimes coordinate the logistics with specialized consolidators,[8] who often have advantages confined to geographical areas. Thus customer relationship using the net as an effective channel may also entail a relationship with the suppliers of logistics services.[9]

On the one hand, this allows the marketer opportunity to obtain information about the prospective consumers' preferences, prior purchases, and concerns while they are browsing the Web to gain awareness and other product information. This information is useful to build and sustain customer relationship in future. On the other hand, for the consumers, every new channel comes with its own risks, such as reliability of transactions, security, and privacy. The latter two are still important issues with Internet shopping. One way for consumers to deal with this risk is to gain awareness and price information online but finally purchase the product from the traditional retail outlets.

Auto-Segmentation

A large number of individuals connected to the Internet can be assumed to have self-selected themselves in terms of their demographics. They tend to be younger, more educated, with a higher than average income, and probably with a lower base-rate loyalty. Thus, the Web is not only a new channel, but also a channel which automatically targets a certain segment of consumers. Conversely, it puts the onus on the marketer to manage the Web offering to cater to the need of the prevailing customer profile.

Channel Specialization and Differentiation on the Internet

On the Internet alone there are numerous channels which specialize in very distinct functions. There are some channels that merely function as *advertisers*. For example, a large number of Web portals such as Yahoo, Excite, and AOL target volumes—that is, the number of prospective customer eyeballs. Another form of online channels captures customer attention by offering them some *incentive*. CyberGold and NetCentives, among others, pay customers for viewing content and filling in forms. Yet another kind of online channels operates as *bargain discounters*. For example, Buy.com sells at cost to attract shoppers. By contrast, FreeMerchant and BlueMountain are *free offerers* (i.e., they offer shoppers something free to increase volumes). Online *Infomediaries* supply consumer information. EMachines and NetZero sell consumer information to merchants and offer consumers freebies. Other channels *supply information* to customers about products and services offered by online vendors. Gomez offers Web site information to consumers. Deja.com and ePinions are *recommendation systems* which monitor user habits and provide feedback to online vendors. NYTimes.com uses its online subscribers registration information to *track user navigation and habits* for targeted advertising. Finally, there are the most ubiquitous Web-based direct marketers such as Amazon, OnSale; catalog merchants, and *click-and-mortar* marketers such as Gap and Wal-Mart (online and via stores).

14.6 MULTICHANNEL BUYING BEHAVIOR: DRIVERS AND BEHAVIORAL CHARACTERISTICS

This section describes the results of a study by Kumar and Venkatesan[10] on the factors associated with the usage of multiple channels by customers. Their study is in the context of a B-to-B company where the organization deals directly with its customers (no intermediaries). In this study, multichannel shoppers are defined as customers who have made a purchase in more than one channel in the observed time period. The rationale associated with the increase in multichannel buying is due to the customer and to the vendor. Thus, the drivers of multichannel buying can be classified into *customer characteristics* and *supplier factors.* Customer characteristics can be explained using the following measures—degree of cross-buying, number of customer-initiated contacts, purchase frequency, number of returns, number of Web-based contacts, and length of customer tenure. Supplier factors can be assessed from the following—communication across multiple channels, type of contact channel, and contact mix. Figure 14-3 depicts the multichannel buying phenomenon.

We discuss each of the elements in the multichannel buying framework and the hypothesized effects they are likely to have on multichannel buying behavior.

14.6.1   CUSTOMER CHARACTERISTICS

Cross Buying

Cross buying is defined as the number of different product categories a customer has bought from the firm. We can reasonably expect customers who exhibit a high degree of cross buying to be familiar with the firm. Also, familiarity with a brand or firm is expected to reduce the perceived risk in customer purchases leading to the customer indulging in a higher degree of multichannel buying.

FIGURE   **14-3**   **DRIVERS OF MULTICHANNEL BUYING AND CHARACTERISTICS OF MULTICHANNEL BUYING**

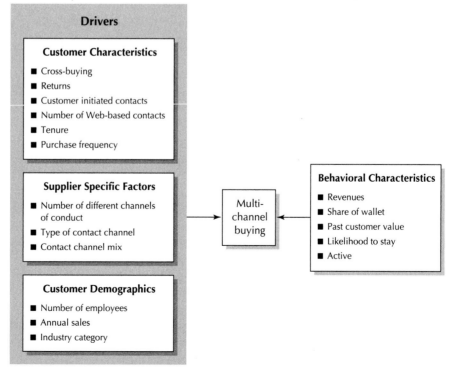

Customer-Initiated Contacts

Customers who initiate a larger number of contacts with a firm can be expected to have a higher degree of familiarity with the firm and the various channels of communication with the firm.[11] Hence, we can expect a higher degree of customer-initiated contacts to be associated with multichannel buying.

Purchase Frequency

Customers with a higher frequency of purchases would be willing to improve the efficiency of their transactions. Also, the frequency of interactions might lead to greater trust and willingness to explore multiple channels. Hence, we can expect that the higher the purchase frequency of a customer, the higher the likelihood of multichannel buying.

Returns: Product returns can have a positive association with multichannel buying. However, the influence of returns on customer purchase behavior is also found to be nonlinear. Specifically, customers who exhibit high levels of return behavior (in other words if the number of returns exceed a certain threshold) tend to purchase less frequently. As a consequence, a high level of returns (or beyond a certain level) could decrease motivation to purchasing products from multiple channels of a firm.[12] Hence, we expect returns to be positively associated with multichannel buying until a certain threshold, beyond which an increase in the number of returns can lead to a decrease in the motivation to shop across multiple channels. We therefore expect an inverted U-shaped relationship between returns and multichannel buying.

Frequency of Web-Based Contacts

Awareness of a supplier's Web site indicates customer willingness to utilize new technology. Hence, we can expect that the higher the frequency of Web-based contacts, the higher the likelihood of multichannel buying.

Customer Tenure

Customers who have been purchasing from a firm for a long time are familiar with the brand and the firm. Also, these customers can be expected to be aware of the multiple channel options available for purchasing products. Thus, the longer the tenure of a customer with a firm, the higher the likelihood of their buying from multiple channels.

14.6.2   SUPPLIER FACTORS

Number of Channels Used for Contact

Suppliers can initiate contacts with customers through multiple channels such as direct mail, telesales, e-mails, salesperson, and retail stores. Supplier contacts through multiple channels can inform a customer regarding the multitude of options available for purchasing products. In addition, suppliers can use their contact strategy in one channel to migrate customers to other channels. Hence, we could expect that the higher the number of different communication channels a supplier uses to contact a customer, the higher the likelihood of multichannel buying.

Type of Contact Channel

Contact channels such as salesperson, telesales, and direct mail can be classified as being more or less interpersonal. Salesperson contacts, which is at one extreme of the communication continuum, is dyadic in nature, offers the ability for message customization, enables rich interaction, and allows for personal relationship building. Another notable aspect of salesperson contacts, which relates to its high level of interpersonal interaction, is the explicit physical nature of the communication. This is in contrast to a telephone interaction, which can be very interpersonal like the sales call but it lacks the face-to-face interaction. On the other extreme of the communication continuum, instruments such as direct mail are unidirectional, limited in content, and nonpersonal. Firms can gain greater understanding of customer needs and/or preferences, educate customers on the various channels available for making transactions, and respond to customer predilections if the communications are two-way. It follows that more interpersonal contact channels are likely to be more effective than less interpersonal contact channels. Based on the relative effectiveness of the different contact channels, we can expect contacts via more interpersonal channels have a greater positive impact on multichannel buying.

Contact Mix Interactions

Contacting a prospect via telesales and via direct mail at the same time may have a stronger effect than the sum of the separate effects administered at different points in time. This is due to the mutual reinforcement of the message delivered through the different contact channels at the same time. We could thus expect a positive synergistic effect by contacting through more than one channel on multichannel buying.

14.6.3   DRIVERS OF MULTICHANNEL BUYERS

The study proceeds to empirically test the influence of these customer-specific and supplier-specific factors associated with multichannel buying. In the model, the number of channels a customer used for making purchases is the dependent variable. Four channels were considered:

1. Salesperson
2. Direct mail
3. Telesales
4. Online

Customer Characteristics

Customers who exhibited a higher degree of cross buying seemed to be using more number of channels to place their orders. There seems to be an inverted U-shaped relationship between returns and multichannel buying, since up to a certain level, higher returns are associated with greater use of multiple channels, and after that level, higher returns are associated with decreasing use of multiple channels. Customers who initiate contact with a firm exhibit a greater degree of multiple-channel shopping than customers who are proactively contacted by the firm. A higher level of Web-based contacts also plays a role in getting customers to transact through multiple channels. Customer tenure is also found to be positively associated with multichannel buying, which means customers who have been transacting with the firm for a longer duration had over a period of time used multiple channels. Also, customers who buy more frequently tended to migrate toward multichannel shopping.

Supplier Specific Factors

With respect to supplier-specific factors, the analyses show the number of different channels the supplier chooses to contact the customer is positively associated with multichannel buying. In other words, firm-induced exposure to multiple channels does get customers to try multiple-channel options. We also see salesperson contacts have the highest association with multichannel buying, followed by telesales and direct mail. We further notice a positive synergy between supplier contacts through multiple channels and multichannel buying. Hence, exposure to multiple channels seems to have a multiplicative effect on the probability of a customer exhibiting multiple channel shopping.

14.6.4 BEHAVIORAL CHARACTERISTICS OF MULTICHANNEL BUYERS

In addition to the drivers of multichannel buying, managers are also interested in knowing if customers who shop across multiple channels are different from single-channel buyers in terms of revenues, share of wallet, past customer value, and likelihood of being active. To evaluate the characteristics of multichannel buyers, the researchers divided the sample into two segments—customers who have shopped in more than one channel (Segment A) and customers who have shopped in only one channel (Segment B). Then they calculated the mean revenue, share of wallet, past customer value, and likelihood to stay active in each segment.

The study finds the difference between the two segments in likelihood to stay active is significantly different and higher for the multichannel buyer. The mean revenue of multichannel buyers is significantly higher than the mean revenue of customers who shop in a single channel. Finally, the mean share of wallet for multichannel customers is also higher than the single channel customer.

14.6.5 SYNOPSIS OF EMPIRICAL FINDINGS

Customers who buy across multiple product categories, initiate more contacts with the firm, have past experience with the supplier through the online channel, have longer tenure, purchase more frequently, are larger, and have been communicated to by the supplier through multiple communication channels, especially through highly interpersonal channels, are also more likely to shop in multiple channels. There is also evidence for a nonlinear relationship between returns and multichannel buying. There is a positive synergy from multichannel buying when customers are contacted through various channels. Multichannel buyers are likely to provide higher revenues, higher share of wallet, have higher past customer value, and have a higher likelihood of being active than single channel shoppers.

The study and its findings lend support to the investments made by several firms to integrate information across multiple channels for better management of customers. It identifies for business-to-business context the factors associated with multichannel buying. Also, these findings lend credibility to the channel strategies of many firms, including IBM, Merrill Lynch, and Citibank, who have recognized the benefits of providing products across multiple channels.

14.7 SUMMARY

Customer relationships are created and sustained through marketing channels. *Marketing or distribution channels* stands for all entities that perform certain functions for the marketing firm, as well as act as the mode of communication between a firm and its customers. *Distribution channel* is an intermediary through which a seller markets the products, and it often refers to several organizations (in the channel). The term *contact channel* or communication channel typically refers to two parties only. Traditional form of direct customer relationship is achieved through these communication or distribution channels and through brand equity. For a successful CRM strategy directed at the final customer, conventional channels structure should provide incentives for coordinating information exchange, in addition to integrating their downstream channel partners' interests. Firms often resort to vertical integration and strategic alliances to control or align interests of their channels to their customer-relationship strategy. CRM demands customer information from different contact channels be centrally processed by the firm and forms a critical input to the planning and execution of the physical distribution of the goods.

In response to the emergence of new channels such as Internet, e-mail, and cable TV, people change their channel habits and different consumers derive differing benefits from different channels. The most immediate impact of distribution and contact channel proliferation is the increase in coverage of the population of potential consumers by the channel networks of the firms. It increases the firm's potential customer base. The need for interchange of customer information across channels makes it imperative to have central customer databases at the firm level, thereby allowing the firm additional leverage to directly interact with the end customers. Channel partners are also more dependent on the firm to help in the cross-channel coordination of the flow of customer information, marketing communications, and physical distribution. Specialized channels need to cooperate and coordinate with one another to persuade the consumer to make a purchase. At the same time, they may even compete if the consumer has an option to choose one of them to finally make the purchase—a process termed as *coopetition.*

Multichannel options are advantageous in terms of greater channel coverage, greater channel specialization, auto-segmentation due to customer self-selection into channels, and improved customer information. A study by Kumar and Venkatesan[13] on the factors associated with the usage of multiple channels by customers classified the drivers of multichannel buying into customer characteristics and supplier factors and identified their attributes. An inverted U-shaped relationship was found to exist between returns and multichannel buying, since up to a certain level, higher returns are associated with greater use of multiple channels, and after that level, higher returns are associated with decreasing use of multiple channels. Multichannel buyers are likely to provide higher revenues, higher share of wallet, have higher past customer value, and have a higher likelihood of being active than single channel shoppers, and justifies investments made by several firms to integrate information across multiple channels for better customer management.

14.8 EXERCISE QUESTIONS

1. What are the challenges of managing the traditional channel partners when engaging in a CRM process directed at the end customer?

2. Manufacturers such as Henkel or P&G are very detached from the final customer. Given the increasing power of retailers, how can they reestablish closer contacts with the final customer?

3. Describe some of the recent challenges firms face in their channel environment.

MINI CASE 14.1

MANAGING A MULTICHANNEL
ENVIRONMENT IN DIRECT MARKETING

Otto Versand in Hamburg, Germany, runs the world's largest mail-order business, with subsidiaries in all continents. The mail-order and specialty mail-order divisions form the core area of the Otto Group. In this business, the company has a strong presence in Europe, through the French company, 3 Suisses France S.C.S., the market leader in France, Belgium, and Spain. Otto owns a majority stake in Crate and Barrel, a chain of home furnishing stores. This company is a major supplier of houseware, furniture, and accessories. A well-defined customer orientation has helped the company build a continually expanding product range and a reputation for quality. Of the entire group, the Otto company alone issues 62 catalogs per season, amounting to 109 million copies.

While originally a pure mail order operation, the Otto Group in Germany has been increasingly adding communication and delivery channels. This is due to customers' demanding more customized access to the company and technological developments such as in the case for e-commerce. Today, the company operates in the following channels of distribution and communication: catalog, call center, TV shopping, mass advertising, Internet, and store pick-up. Multiple challenges arise in this multichannel environment. First, the company needs to create a single view of the customer. Although this might sound easy for a company without intermediaries, it is a challenging feat in practice. Given that the operational and IT systems behind each channel are very specific, it is not straightforward to create from all of these contacts a meta-database with all customer contacts in a standardized and scalable fashion. A second key challenge is, given that one can integrate information seamlessly across several channels, how can you leverage that information for marketing decisions? For example, a customer is being sent a catalog but then goes on to buy via the Internet. Did the catalog really create the purchase impulse in the first place, or would the customer have bought in any case via the Internet? Stated differently, customers may not react to catalogs because they do not want or need them. Or, customer may not react to catalogs (seemingly), but the catalog has an important trigger function. Teasing out these types of channel interactions is important for Otto in its quest for economizing on acquisition cost, while at the same time maximizing acquisition results. Thus, the reality in a multichannel environment, like the one at Otto, is understanding the interactions of contact channels and contact channel allocations to customers in order to maximize their lifetime value.

Questions:

1. Can you think of experiments which would allow Otto to make some inferences on whether one channel functions as a lead to another channel?

2. Would you expect a customer who entered the company through different channels would have differential value to the company? Why?

ENDNOTES

1. Don Peppers and Martha Rogers, *Managing Customer Relationships—A Strategic Framework* (Hoboken, NJ: John Wiley & Sons, Inc., 2004).

2. Barbara Gutek, "Service Relationships, Pseudo-Relationships and Encounters," *Handbook of Services Marketing and Management* (Thousand Oaks, CA: Sage Publications Inc., 2000).

3. Nirmalya Kumar "The Power of Trust in Manufacturer-Retailer Relationships," *Harvard Business Review* 74, no. 6 (1996): 92, 15p.

4. *Ibid.,* 99.

5. Ming Zeng and Werner Reinartz, "Beyond Online Search: The Road to Profitability," *Management Review* 45 (Winter 2003): 107–130.

6. Challagalla Kohli, Jaworski and Lurie, Marketing Science Institute (MSI) note (2002).

7. Coughlan, Anderson, Stern and El-Ansary, *Marketing Channels,* sixth edition (Upper Saddle River, NJ: Prentice-Hall, 2001): Chapter 9.

8. Coughlan, Anderson, Stern and El-Ansary, *Marketing Channels,* sixth edition (Upper Saddle River, NJ: Prentice-Hall, 2001): 117.

9. Hence the link with Supply Chain Management. Add the Tupperware (p. 135) example from the Coughlan, Anderson et al (2001).

10. V. Kumar and R. Venkatesan, "Who Are the Multichannel Shoppers and How Do They Perform? Correlates of Multichannel Shopping Behavior," *Journal of Interactive Marketing* (2004).

11. D. Schoenbachler and G. L. Gordon, "Multichannel Shopping: Understanding What Drives Channel Choice," *Journal of Consumer Marketing* 19 (2002): 42–53.

Glossary

A

Active marketing database: An active marketing database is a database in which the results of marketing programs are used to update the database, so that the updated database can be used to help marketers adjust or redesign the strategic marketing plan.

Activity-based-costing: ABC is a costing model which identifies the cost pools, or activity centers, in an organization and assigns costs to products and services (cost drivers) based on the number of events or transactions involved in the process of providing a product or service.

Aggregate share of wallet (ASW): ASW is defined as the proportion of category value accounted for by a focal brand or a focal firm within its base of buyers. It indicates the degree to which the customers of a focal firm satisfy their needs on average, in a category with a focal firm.

Analytical data mart: Analytical data marts focus on capturing, monitoring, and storing key metrics that link strategy with tactics instead of storing all the detailed information required to compute the metrics.

Attitudinal loyalty: Attitudinal loyalty refers to the perceptions and attitudes a customer has towards a particular product or service.

Attrition rate: Attrition rate is the rate at which customers defect.

B

Behavioral loyalty: Behavioral loyalty refers to the observed action that customers have demonstrated towards a particular product or service.

Breakeven value (BE): Breakeven value is the point where the net profit from a marketing promotion equals the cost associated with conducting the promotion.

B-to-B: Business to business marketing.

B-to-C: Business to consumer marketing.

C

Campaign: A campaign is a series of interconnected promotional efforts designed to attract the customers' interest and thereby achieve precise marketing goals.

Channel: A Channel refers to the "flow" of the organization's offerings, e.g. physical goods or information to the ultimate end users (end customer), as well as that of sales proceeds or realizations from the customer back to the marketing firm.

Cluster database: Cluster databases consist of clusters of people having common or similar interests, attitudes, purchasing habits, and preferences.

Competitive advantage: Competitive advantage is the ability of a firm to create and sustain superior performance over time.

Communication or contact channels: Communication or contact channels convey information to the customers to create awareness about the firm's products and services and to persuade them to make a purchase.

Coopetition: Coopetition is the phenomenon where different channels compete for customers' share of wallet while cooperating with each other to increase the overall customer base across different channels.

Customer relationship management (CRM): CRM is the strategic process of selecting the customers a firm can most profitably serve and of shaping the interactions between a company and these customers. The goal is to optimize the current and future value of the customers for the company.

Cross buying: Cross buying is defined as the number of different product categories a customer has bought from the firm.

Cross merchandising: Cross merchandising refers to offering different brands from different categories to the same customer.

Cross selling: Cross selling refers to selling additional products to existing customers.

Customer acquisition rate: Customer acquisition rate is the proportion of prospects converted to customers, calculated by dividing the fraction of prospects acquired by the total number of prospects targeted. It is normally reported in percentages.

Customer acquisition cost: Customer acquisition cost is defined as the acquisition campaign spending divided by the number of acquired prospects.

Customer dormancy: Customer dormancy refers to the period of time between purchases when customers are inactive (or do not buy).

Customer defection: Customer defection refers to a situation where a customer leaves one firm and starts transacting with a competing firm.

Customer equity: Customer equity is the aggregation of the expected lifetime values of a firm's entire base of existing customers and the expected future value of newly acquired customers. It is an indicator of how much the firm is worth at a particular point in time as a result of the firm's customer management efforts.

Customer equity share (CES): CES is the relative share of the sum of the lifetime value of a brand across all its customers to the sum of the lifetime values of the customers for all the competing brands that exist in a market.

Customer value: Customer value is the economic value ($-metric) of the customer relationship to the firm, expressed on the basis of contribution margin or net profit.

D

Data analytics: Data analytics is the process of combining data driven marketing and technology to increase the company's knowledge and understanding of customers, products and transactional data to improve strategic decision making and tactical market activity.

Database marketing: Database marketing comprises of activities that involve data collected on existing customers and prospective customers that help identify groups of customers who are similar in identifiable ways.

Data mining: The data-mining process consists of extracting predictive information from data by using automated statistical procedures.

Defection rate: The defection rate is defined as the average likelihood that a customer defects from the focal firm in a period (t), given that the customer was purchasing up to the previous period ($t-1$).

Disadoption: Disadoption is when a customer stops purchasing from a product category altogether.

Down-stream relationship: A down-stream relationship is one that is developed between the channel member and the end customer.

Duration of association approach: A duration of association approach is a customer prioritization approach based on how long a customer has been transacting with a firm.

E

Effectiveness profits: Effectiveness profits are long-term profit consequences realized through better learning about customer preferences over time.

Efficiency profits: Efficiency profits are immediate profit consequences, as compared to profit consequences without loyalty programs, net of the LP cost.

Enhancement database: An enhancement database is one used to transfer additional information on customers and prospects to an existing database.

Enterprise resource planning (ERP): ERP is the software which integrates various departments and functions across a company onto a single computer system in order to serve their specific needs.

F

Frequency: Frequency is a measure of how often a customer orders from the company in a certain defined period.

Front-end analysis: Front-end analysis is the use of expert opinion and common sense to highlight issues required to be addressed during a project and to identify opportunities to resolve them.

H

Hard rewards: Hard rewards refer to financial or tangible rewards.

Hedonic products: Hedonic products are those whose consumption is associated with pleasure and fun.

Hierarchical database: A hierarchical database is one where all information pertaining to a customer is located in a master record.

I

Individual share of wallet (ISW): ISW is defined as the proportion of category *value* accounted for by a focal brand or a focal firm for a buyer from all brands that the buyer purchases in that category.

Integrated marketing communications (IMC): IMC is a process which involves the management and organization of all the marketing communication tools (media, messages, promotions and channels) in a way that delivers a clear and consistent message about the company and about the product.

Inverted database: Inverted databases are databases which are column oriented rather than row oriented.

K

Key performance indicators (KPI): Key performance indicators are snapshots of a business or organization based on quantifiable measures that reflect the success of the business.

L

Legacy system: A legacy system is a computer system or application program that continues to be used because of the high cost of replacing or redesigning it, often despite its poor competitiveness and poor compatibility with modern equivalents.

Lifetime segmentation: Lifetime segmentation refers to dividing customer groups according to the length of the period of association with the firm.

Lifetime value (LTV): LTV is a multi-period evaluation of a customer's value to the firm.

Loyalty instrument: Loyalty instrument refers to a card or any other form of identification issued to a customer which allows the customer to participate in a loyalty program.

Loyalty program (LP): A loyalty program can be defined as a marketing process that generates rewards to customers based on their repeat purchasing.

M

Marcom: Marcom is a short form for marketing communications; targeted interactions between the company and its customers and prospects, using one or more media.

Marketing or distribution channels: Stands for all entities (e.g. distributors, wholesalers, retailers, broker, agents, etc.) that perform certain functions for the marketing firm.

Market share (MS): Market share is the share of a firm's sales relative to the sales of all firms—across all customers in the given market expressed as a percentage.

Mass marketing: Mass marketing refers to developing a common product and a common marketing mix expected to appeal uniformly to a large group of people.

Maximum likelihood estimation (MLE): Maximum likelihood estimation is the process of maximizing the probability of obtaining the observed set of data, given the chosen probability distribution model by representing the probability in an expression containing the unknown model parameters.

Method of moment estimates: The method of moments principle is to choose, as estimators of the parameters the values that render the population moments equal to the sample moments.

Monetary value: Monetary value is the amount a customer spends on an average transaction.

Multichannel shoppers: Multichannel shoppers are defined as customers who have made a purchase in more than one channel in the observed time period.

N

Net present value (NPV): NPV is the present value of an investment's future net cash flows minus the initial investment. In other words, it expresses how much value an investment will result in.

O

Optimal resource allocation model: The optimal resource allocation model captures the response of each individual customer to variations in the marketing activities directed at the customer and allows the user to vary the mix to maximize each customer's lifetime value.

P

P(Active): P(Active) refers to the probability that a customer will be active (or will buy) in a particular time period.

P(Alive): same as P(Active).

Passive marketing database: A passive marketing database is a mailing list which passively stores information about acquired customers, and has no active influence on the company's strategic marketing decisions.

Past customer value (PCV): The PCV of a customer is determined based on the total contribution (towards profits) provided by the customer in the past by adjusting the contributions made at different points in time using the time value of money.

Predictive modeling: Predictive modeling uses statistical computing techniques to predict future customer behavior by anticipating the effect of changes in a set of independent variables.

Profitable lifetime duration: Profitable lifetime duration is the duration after which a customer ceases to be profitable for a firm.

Prospects: Prospects are non-customers with profiles similar to the profiles of existing customers.

Purchase sequence model: A purchase sequence model allows a firm to select the appropriate product category that would interest any given customer at a given point in time in the relationship.

R

Rate of rewards: The rate of rewards refers to the ratio of reward value (in monetary terms) over transaction volume (in monetary terms). In other words, it tells you how much a consumer is getting in return for concentrating his or her purchases.

Recency: Recency is a measure of how long it has been since a customer last placed an order with the company.

Relational database: Relational databases are comprised of many simple tables. Users can create queries to extract information from these tables and recombine it.

Relationship marketing: Relationship marketing refers to all marketing activities directed toward establishing, developing, and maintaining successful relational exchanges between customers, partners, and the firm.

Retention rate: Retention rate is defined as the average likelihood a customer who purchases from the focal firm in a period (t), given that this customer has purchased in the previous period ($t - 1$).

Return on investment (ROI): ROI refers to the quotient of revenue minus cost divided by the cost, normally expressed as a percentage.

RFM: RFM analysis refers to the technique of using the recency, frequency, and monetary value variables to sort and prioritize customers.

S

Share of category requirement (SCR): SCR is defined as the proportion of category volume accounted for by a brand or focal firm within its base of buyers.

Share of wallet (SOW): Share of wallet is defined as the ratio of the total customer spending with the firm to the total category spending (the firm plus its competitors) for that customer.

Size of wallet: Size of wallet is the amount of a buyer's total spending in a category for, the category sales of all firms to that customer.

Soft rewards: Rewards in the form of psychological or emotional benefits are called soft rewards.

Survival rate: The survival rate indicates the proportion of customers who have "survived" (or in other words continued to remain a customer) until a period t from the time we began observing these customers.

T

Touch points: Touch points are various modes of contacts between a customer and a firm which help carry out relational exchanges.

U

Up-selling: Up-selling refers to selling a superior product (with more features or additional services) to customers who already use similar products.

Up-stream relationship: Up-stream relationship is the relationship developed by a firm with the channel member.

V

Value alignment: Value alignment refers to aligning the cost to serve a particular customer with the value he/she brings to the firm.

W

Win-back rate: Win-back rate is the proportion of the lost customers acquired in a later period. It is used as an indicator of how successful the firm's turn-around efforts are.

Index